Keep Out

Keep Out

The Struggle for
Land Use Control

Sidney Plotkin

University of California Press
Berkeley / Los Angeles / London

University of California Press
Berkeley and Los Angeles, California

University of California Press, Ltd.
London, England

© 1987 by
The Regents of the University of California

Library of Congress Cataloging-in-Publication Data

Plotkin, Sidney.
  Keep out.
  Bibliography: p.
  Includes index.
  1. Land use—Government policy—United States.
2. Right of property—United States. 3. Capitalism
—United States. I. Title.
HD205.P56 1987   333.3'0973   86-30807
ISBN 0–520–05806–2 (alk. paper)
ISBN 0–520–06127–6 (ppb.)

Printed in the United States of America

1 2 3 4 5 6 7 8 9

*To the memory of Edith Sarch Plotkin
and to the love of my friends who
helped me to find my way*

Unscrew the locks from the doors!
Unscrew the doors themselves from their jambs!
Walt Whitman, *Leaves of Grass*

Contents

Acknowledgments

Domination and resistance form the central themes of this book, which is an examination of some of the high-level controls of capitalist society and of the ability of human beings to say no to power. These concerns have been nurtured in me by a succession of magnificent teachers.

My education for the book started in James Farganis's class on Congress and the presidency at Brooklyn College in 1968. His lectures on the meanings of human freedom and the terrors of technological rationality were searing; they made me see the world in a new way. Carey McWilliams blended my learning with a sensibility about the uniqueness of the American experience. He first showed me the fragile roots of fraternity that remain embedded in the culture. But my greatest intellectual debts are owed to Robert Engler and Martin Fleisher, my dissertation mentors at the City University of New York. Bob Engler, a teacher with masterful control of the innocent question—and a man of much patience with his sometimes all-too-deliberate students—gave me the courage and the model to take a different road in the writing of social science. It was also his suggestion that something might be learned by exploring the fight over national land use policy. Martin Fleisher, a brilliant and inspiring teacher of political theory, whose insights into this material I was much too slow in appreciating, never let me settle for the easy answer. His challenge was constant, and his standards were impeccable. Neither of these men will be satisfied with this study—each would have written it very differently—but I hope they see some of their intellectual spirit in it, for that is what drove the project forward.

Whatever value this book has is derived from more than the formal training of the classroom, however. I have also been educated by excellent colleagues.

Bill Scheuerman has not stopped asking the tough questions since our first meeting at CUNY, and he has read and commented on more versions of this text than I'm sure he'd care to remember. Tom Baylis, John Booth, R. Michael Stevens, and Rick Gambitta, the core of an extraordinary little group of political scientists at the University of Texas at San Antonio, each gave me important lessons in how to think about power, government, and law. Rudolfo Rosales, whom I met late in my San Antonio career, brought Gramsci to my attention; he also became my brother. And when I moved to Vassar, I not only rediscovered Jim Farganis but also found a new host of colleagues—Bruce Smith, Peter Stillman, Adelaide Villmoare, Fred Bunnell, Obika Grey, Iva Deutchman, and Sondra Silverman—all of whom either talked with me about power, land use, property rights, and writing, or graciously read drafts, or both. I am thankful that none ever said "Keep Out!"

I benefited too from an able and illuminating rejection of an early article, by the editors of the journal *Politics and Society*. An exceptionally detailed analysis by Michael Heiman for the University of California Press also helped me to clarify my thoughts on the contradictions of consumption and production property. My confidence in the basic analysis was abetted by warmly supportive readings from Chester Hartman and Neal Smith. Moreover, like other teachers, I also gained from the lessons of some very special students at the University of Texas at San Antonio and at Vassar. John Johnson, Sulema Trevino, Miriam Gordon, Carol Gardner, Charles Roberts, Frank Fink, David Behrstock, Scott London, David Rosenbaum, Dan Halston, and the students in my Land Use Policy Seminar during the fall of 1981 at Vassar were especially articulate influences and critics.

Thanks must also go to a talented quartet of research assistants and typists: Linda Hull, Joan Hanlon, Julia Rose, and Ann Holden. Mrs. Mildred Tubby typed the final drafts with speed and competence. Vassar College helped with small but timely research grants. And my editor at the University of California Press, Naomi Schneider, was consistently loyal to the project. Her backing helped me to deal with the hard issues raised by my referees. The journals *Politics and Society* and *Polity* kindly allowed me to use material first published in their pages, as did the University of Nebraska Press.

My wife, Marjorie Gluck, greatly enriched my life as this work entered its final stages; her love and her patience with my anxieties were important conditions of my ability to get the job done. She also put up with my cats, who pawed over the manuscript at various stages of production, and whose purrs indicated occasional approval.

All of these people share the credit for whatever is valuable in the study, though, of course, none is responsible for its deficiencies. Attribute those to my own limitations, not the least of which is stubbornness.

Like other first books, this one began as a doctoral dissertation. Just as typically, it has undergone drastic revision since its original design. The circumstances under which those changes were made, however, were horribly atypical. In the spring of 1979, my wife, Edith Sarch Plotkin, died suddenly and tragically. Her love, intelligence, unpaid labor, and spirit were mixed into every page of the original work, just as they were in every aspect of my life. When she died, I was not certain that I could go on without her courage, good sense, and laughter. I survived this terrible and difficult time and ultimately managed to complete this book, but only because I had the privilege of drawing deeply and often from the strength of a giving circle of friends: Ray Boryczka, Bill Scheuerman, Jeff Stein, Bernadette Brusco, Marty Rosen, Michael Stevens, Mary Schwendeman, Joan and Mike Kearl, Tom Baylis, Rob Patch, John Booth, Robert Milne, and most of all, Terre Fleener, who taught me how to believe and care again. Without such friends and their abundant spirit of inclusion, I could never have found the way again. It is to Edith's memory and their love that this book is dedicated.

Introduction

This book is a study of resistance to capitalist development and political centralization. It does not center on the usual suspects: the unruly peasants and displaced factory workers who are typically seen as the enemies of change. The focus here is on an opposition deeply loyal to private property and to its most fundamental right, the right to keep others out. The subject is American landowners and their enduring fight to use the control of land and land use policy to hold corporations and government at bay. This is, in short, a study of private property and land use control and of their combined power to check corporate expansion and government centralization in the United States.

In today's political economy landownership and land use policy are regularly used to deflect the advance of industry and its trail of physical and human wastes. The means of resistance are wielded vigorously and with effect. Numerous projects suffer expensive delays or cancellation; toxic wastes mount into higher piles of deadly garbage; the homeless trek in larger numbers; even the MX missile lacks shelter. "Communities raise their hands not to volunteer," cries New York's mayor, Edward Koch, "but to point somewhere else"; he deplores a national outbreak of "community selfishness." Investment banker Felix Rohatyn agrees: our system "has become all checks and no balances. . . . Today we could not build our road system, the TVA, or the Manhattan project." Instead, complains George Gilder, "faithless and shortsighted men attempt to halt the increase of knowledge and the advance of technology." America, the vanguard society of global technological change, seems besieged by the obstreperous. As Harvard policy planner Robert Reich concludes, "We all are at the mercy of recalcitrant minorities." [1]

1

Well before the Union Carbide disaster in Bhopal and the Chernobyl nu-clear meltdown in the Soviet Union finally exploded the myth of a benign in-dustrial science, Americans were reluctant to make room for the dangerous and undesirable functions of industrial capitalism. In the more exclusive neighborhoods and communities, such issues rarely arose: it was simply un-thinkable to locate factories next to suburban split-levels. So corporations and government builders followed the paths of least resistance to rural backwaters and urban industrial districts, where people did not have the power to pull in the welcome mat. But lately, at least since the 1960s, the less well off have begun to close doors, too, successfully repelling highways, waste dumps, drug rehabilitation centers, lower-income housing, shopping malls, and an as-sortment of lethal technologies, in the interest of community protection and preservation. And today, in a fascinating switch on the suburban fight against public housing, poorer neighborhoods battle to keep out the rich in struggles against gentrification. Even the "goods" of the system are no longer wel-comed everywhere.

Corporate and government elites, the leaders in charge of the big institu-tions of private production and public order, grow restless with the rising squeamishness about community change. Although those at the top are well acquainted with the pleasures of quiet affluence, stable neighborhoods, and open space—and stoutly defend them—they insist that room must be made for progress; the essential facilities of a growing industrial society must go somewhere. Even President Ronald Reagan, well known as a friend of local control, declares that private groups and political jurisdictions must not "thwart projects" of national significance. If communities won't budge, others warn, then the political machinery of space making will have to be cen-tralized, for the effects of land use controls often reverberate outward into wider regions, the nation, and even across national borders. When they do, as in the cases of toxic- and nuclear-waste disposal, power-plant siting, low-income housing construction, or weapons deployment, elites insist that local decision makers must be policed by higher authorities. Communities have pa-triotic obligations to make way. Toxins, surplus humans, and the means of nuclear defense must be sited with efficiency in mind.

The questions involved here slice deep into society's core. Nothing is more intimate in the life of a community, or more reflective of its most sacred com-mitments and prerogatives, than its treatment of land. Fundamental matters are at stake: rights of exclusionary private property and community self-defense, public obligations to the wider nation-state, the corporate control of technological and economic directions, the expansionist logic of capitalism itself, the substance and procedures of democracy. These are "key issues"; they touch on what Peter Bachrach and Morton Baratz call "predominant val-ues" and "the 'established rules of the game.'" [2]

The Challenges of Method

The question, though, is how to go about the study of such issues.[3] One way to approach them would be to plunge immediately into the thick of the fights. We could launch our analysis by studying some of the key battles to centralize decision making—the conflicts over national land use policy in the Johnson-Nixon years, for example, or President Jimmy Carter's proposal to establish a federal board to override the land use and environmental rules blocking a national energy buildup in the late 1970s. Or we could start closer to home and investigate the difficulties encountered in an individual community's effort to protect itself against potentially ruinous development.

Such cases will in fact be explored. But before we can understand why these specific examples were chosen for study, much less what the political structure and dynamics of these conflicts are, we need to consider something else. We need to look more generally at the relationship between political conflict, social structure, and organized power.

Individual case studies can afford useful insights into the centralizing pressure at work within land use policy. But it would be ingenuous to suggest that such pressures have not been noted by others. The literature of land use policy and reform is vast, and although not much has been written on the national fights, thoughtful and curious readers could draw informed conclusions from careful study of the extensive bibliographies of local and regional activity. Why then another work in a field already loaded with footnotes?

The main reason is that most land use studies tend to take the issues, interests, and values of land use conflict for granted, rarely subjecting them to the untutored question of why the political organization of interests has developed in just this way. Put a little differently, most scholars of land use policy and politics have assumed that what's needed are descriptive and tactical accounts of the group forces. Although occasionally a writer such as Robert Nelson has come along to suggest that a good close look at the tensions of property rights would help to explain the organization of the field, the majority of analysts tend to accept the disarray of local activity as a given, usually going on to suggest why consolidation would help to reconcile the differences between local and more regional and national interests. A few, such as Nelson and Frank Popper, have their doubts; many lawyers, for example, show increasing interest in market-oriented or compensatory solutions. In other words, they want to pay individuals and communities to accept the unacceptable. But the main drift of the literature is that political centralization of at least some land use controls is a necessary step for an ever more complex technological order.[4]

In this study, however, the working assumption is that the empirical patterns of land use conflict, the patterns that show up on the outer layers of political reality, do not necessarily reveal all that is at stake in land use politics.

To understand the big and small wars over land use control, it is necessary to do more than tell legislative tales, calibrate group power, and identify institutional strain. We need to understand something of how the politics of land use came to take the forms it has taken and why these forms are no longer seen as desirable by the top-level managers of American development. In other words, the suggestion here is that the methods of conventional policy analysis, methods rooted in the conceptual outlook of pluralist political science, do not take us far enough for an understanding of the historical development and social structuring of land use politics. And this is a critical omission because it is only in the context of such an understanding that we can appreciate the larger implications of land use politics.

Neo-Pluralist Reflections

Methodological doubts about pluralism are nothing new, of course. Critics such as E. E. Schattschneider, Peter Bachrach, and Morton Baratz carefully exposed the limitations of the mainstream pluralist method twenty years ago.[5] They have shown why it is extremely unwise to take interests and conflicts for granted in politics, for the very definition of issues and conflicts is itself a supremely political matter. The neo-pluralists taught us that every political system mobilizes itself—its rules, procedures, institutions, and ideology—to defend the interests and values of leading social and economic groups. "There is in any given society a pattern in what it is 'for' and 'against,'" said sociologist Robert S. Lynd, a "mobilization of bias," to use Schattschneider's phrase, that favors the grip of certain groups and interests over others and over the political system itself.[6] Political arrangements, it is now widely understood, are profoundly ideological. They are inconspicuously but effectively organized to take what Bachrach and Baratz call "non-decisions," actions that inhibit people from even thinking about alternatives to the status quo, that squelch demands for a different allocation of social values well before they can be raised.[7]

A critical methodological implication follows: political scientists who wish to understand the relevance of bias to the struggles of public policy must study not just any group conflicts; they need to focus on battles over the biases themselves, issues that involve serious efforts to change the mechanisms of value allocation in society. Thus the truly serious power struggles are signaled by efforts to switch the existing patterns of private or public control over values, or the level of government that usually oversees value allocations. Such conflicts test the long-established biases and linkages of groups and government, the persistent forms of social control that constitute organized power. In these cases, as John Dewey pointed out years ago, the proponents of change have "to break existing political forms . . . because these forms are themselves the regular means of instituting [and thus limiting] change."[8] As

Schattschneider would argue, therefore, the most illuminating cases are to be found in disputes over the legitimacy of political conflict itself and over the procedures for resolving it. Battles over the nature, definition, and appropriate sites for the consideration of political issues furnish the best clues to deeper shifts and strains in the relative weighting of power.

Because of its strategic and indispensable role in production, land and the local controls designed to assure its reliable protection and supply are necessarily crucial factors of power in the society. Thus serious moves to change the locus of decision making in the land control system furnish useful testing grounds for theories of power in the United States. Indeed, in the original version of this study, written as a doctoral dissertation, the conceptual framework was largely inspired by the neo-pluralist critique.[9] Although that work was placed in a historical framework, the analysis did not penetrate much beneath the political whirl of interest-group activity that forms the core of pluralist and neo-pluralist thought. To see why and how the present analysis advances upon the old base, it would be useful to sketch out the intellectual migration that led away from neo-pluralism to more radical perspectives.

Toward a Structural Perspective

As revision of the original work went forward, it became increasingly clear that the neo-pluralist approach suffered from limitations of its own. In their attempt to enlarge the perspective of conventional pluralist political science— by pointing out needs to grasp the dominant social and ideological biases as the context for individual conflicts—neo-pluralists, such as Schattschneider, did not explicitly show how to study the relationship between political power and the broader context or structure of society. Nor did the neo-pluralists explain why and how changes in society might occasion struggles over political change. In other words, by maintaining their disciplinary allegiance to the boundary lines of political science, the neo-pluralists could take the vital step of insisting on the critical relevance of society and economy to politics, but not the more radical one of actually attempting to follow problems through by making an independent inquiry into the roots of significant conflicts. But this sort of inquiry is inescapable if we are to understand why and how such conflicts arise socially and historically, and what they might mean for changes in the broad landscape of social power.

To understand the emergence, contours, and limits of struggles to centralize land use controls in the United States, I had to probe beneath the outer layer of political institutions and biases. I had to explore what Lynd called the "over-all structure of power," its roots in "the basic social relations" of the society, and the ways in which these relations repeated themselves "in the values and institutions by means of which the society lives and maintains itself."[10] Because capitalist America "lives and maintains itself" through the "social relations" of class-based production, it became necessary to study how the social production of land use issues influenced political conflict over the distribution of access to land.

To do this work, I had to delve into basic features of capitalist production, especially the intersection of private landed property, economic class, the dynamics of accumulation, and the ideology of consumption.[11] Next, it became crucial to link the understandings drawn from a critical appreciation of capitalism to an analysis of the group struggle over land use control in the United States, to show how this struggle is embedded in the paradoxes of private property, capitalist development, and class conflict. But the more such connections became clear, the more evident it became that each of these phenomena itself reflected the presence of political institutions in its very formation. That is, the work took shape as a study of the reciprocal or dialectical relations of capitalist production, group politics, and government organization and policy. In essence, it became necessary to show how the themes and organization of pluralist patterns of land use conflict are stamped by the social relations and forces of capitalist production; how capitalist accumulation is itself limited by the interest-group process; and how each of these elements is, in turn, both structured by and working to mold the state and its policies. As there are few models for this kind of integrated analysis, the main methodological challenge became the need to invent a way to weave radical and conventional modes of analysis into a single coherent whole.

This task was exceptionally formidable. My reading suggested that the richest theoretical insights into the politics of capitalism are to be found in the varieties of neo-Marxist state theory, a discourse often expressed in forms so dense as to be forbidding even to scholars reasonably well versed in basic Marxist texts,[12] and all but impenetrable to general readers and non-Marxist specialists alike. This reality imposed important choices in connection with the presentation of the material. Kenneth M. Dolbeare has expressed the problem sharply: Radical social scientists "have a real dilemma," he writes. "If they talk the language of dominant beliefs, they end up playing somebody else's game and give up their unique perspective and the goals that go with it. But if they frame their appeals in their own perspective, most people just do not understand them."[13]

The choice made here was to be as straightforward and clear as I know how to be in explaining the capitalist roots of land use politics. Moreover, in keeping with the original design of the dissertation, I have used history as the connective tissue linking structural themes and categories with the forms of land use politics.[14] Thus chapter 3, which is a study of the shifts in American land use and property policies in the nineteenth and early twentieth centuries, is an especially crucial chapter because it ties the theory and concept of the first two chapters to an account of the conflicts over land use policy surveyed in Part Two.

I have tried to do all this without wearying the reader with unnecessarily detailed and abstract theoretical analysis. The working principle has been to use some very powerful theory to explain what is really at stake in the struggles of land use policy centralization. Judgments of theoretical necessity are, of course, open to debate. But it should be understood at the outset that I did not view theory construction as an end in itself. Put somewhat differently, although the next section does outline the main theoretical issues of the study, in general I have tried to present theory as it was needed in the course of the analysis, letting it emerge organically, as a way of showing why the empirical material fails to reveal its own significance.

Although some theorists will object to this as a yielding to empiricism, and some general readers may object to occasionally difficult and abstract language, I hope that this approach will be taken as an effort to interconnect conflicting methods in sensible ways, ways that expose more of the subtlety and multidimensionality of politics than either Marxism or pluralism alone can. At the very least, perhaps, the relatively open form of expression may indicate where the deepest problems lie in connecting explanations of social structure and political process and may help to stimulate further development of our ability to express the difficult relations of political and social reality. In the final analysis, of course, readers may judge the study in any way they please. Authors must accept the fact that their products become public things separate from their private will. Writing is inevitably an act of alienation, just as it is an act of freedom. With the caveats duly noted, we can take our first steps into the conceptual minefield of land use conflict.

The Factors Behind the Facts

If the current rules and rights of land use control no longer seem adequate to business as usual, if the collisions of corporation and community are louder and more jarring than in the past, this is not because we are more "selfish" than our parents, or because today's corporations are more grasping; it is because the license of free enterprise to press economic change has been at least partially revoked. Rights of resistance and control have been carved into law. Friction has been built into the system as power shifted "from those groups in society responsible for initiating economic change to those who bore the brunt of the social costs in the past." [15] More and more, owners and citizens act on the belief that change must be conditioned by the consent of the governed, especially when the consequences of innovation threaten to hit dangerously close to home. As a recent report in the *New York Times* put it, citizen-landowners "have propelled 'not in my back yard' politics into the political foreground." [16]

But the scope and intensity of much of the recent outpouring of land use protest in the United States and other capitalist societies is a product of more than hard-won rights to resist. It also reflects opposition to a massive wave of urban and industrial restructuring that has washed over the "free world" since the end of World War II. Thus it is a protest against the reconfiguration of metropolitan areas for corporate activity, culture, and convenience; against housing shortages, evictions, and homelessness; against deepening environmental degradation and the severe dangers unleashed by the hyperlethal technologies that energize advanced capitalism; and against the superhighways, airports, and power lines used to wire the system over ever greater swaths of territory.

In counterpoint to this resistance, political and economic leaders and many intellectuals plead for the unchaining of the forces of production. "Do not struggle against the tide," citizens are told, "for many negative things are going to happen regardless of what government tries to do about them." [17] Speed and quickness, the race horse virtues, are proclaimed as the best guides to economic and resource policy. "The answer is not to slow down the movement of capital," argues Reich; "we must speed up the movement of capital." Pollution and land use regulations must be tailored to allow the restructuring of American cities and industry; impediments and barriers to growth must fall. [18]

For Samuel Bowles and Herbert Gintis, this painful debate reflects the collision between fundamental values in the culture, a deep-seated opposition between what they see as two expansionist logics competing for control of American society: the logic of capitalist production and the logic of personal rights. The capitalist logic centers on business's "ongoing search for profits," whereas the logic of personal rights aims at "bringing ever-wider spheres of society," such as the economy and family, "under at least the formal if not the substantive rubric of liberal democracy." [19]

My studies of land use battles, however, do not indicate that the people fighting to save their communities want to manage the economy or alter the social relations of the family. Rather, it seems as though, in fighting to keep out the unwanted—the production system and its facilities—many Americans are desperately trying to *preserve* their personal rights and existing community and family relationships. Thus, the fights seem to center not on the collision of two expansionist logics at all, but rather on the clash between capitalist growth and a powerful counterlogic of exclusion.

Exclusion and Expansion

In land use politics, exclusion and expansion seem always to emerge as the dominant alternatives and the pressing interests. Despite frequent calls for an evening-out of the costs and benefits of development, such a balance has never been achieved, certainly not on a regional or a national basis. The forging of an inclusionary type of balanced development is like a dream beyond the society's grasp, frozen out of reality by the more strenuous competition of interests bent on exclusion and expansion. But why? What is the source of this exclusionary counterlogic?

To understand how and why exclusion and expansion establish the limits and framework of land use politics, and to begin to progress beyond those limits, we need to uncover the real roots of the conflict, what Herbert Marcuse once so aptly described as "the factors which made the facts." [20] The political and social relations of land use control must be placed in the context of their long-term encounter with the production system. This view sees private property and capitalism not as one side in the conflict, but in fact as the main constituent factors of the battles for land use control. For the struggles of land use policy, no matter how much they may influence the general interests of society as a whole, have been governed by the themes and interests of landed property and industrial capital, not merely because these forces happen to be well organized but also because they happen to be the organizing framework of our relationship with the land and with other people.

The strains of land use have historically been the strains of expanding capital banging up against exclusionary property rights. The history of land use conflict is a long-running reflection of general capitalist forces in painful opposition. The whole organization of capitalism rests on the twin forces of exclusion and expansion. In Marxian terms, capitalists as a class are defined by their legal power to exclude workers from direct access to the means of production. Because of exclusion, workers can be compelled to labor for the owners of capital, to produce ever more wealth for the latter's reinvestment and accumulation. As Bowles and Gintis themselves note, "private property is nothing if not the right to exclude." [21] Expansion is the be-all and end-all of the system, but class exclusion is its primary social condition.[22] Without exclusion, the perpetual growth of production for profit would be impossible, at least in the capitalist terms most of us have come to accept as facts of everyday life.

Exclusion and expansion are much more than forces in land use conflict: they are system-wide pressures that emanate from deep inside the social relations of capitalist production. They are not the property of particular groups or classes; they are the general interests of capitalist property itself. Every major property group that seeks to benefit from the wider circulation of wealth has simultaneous interests in both exclusion and expansion—even the millions of working-class homeowners who count on rising property values as their stake in the system. This means that no homeowner can take a rigorously consistent no-growth position on issues of development. It also means that popular tendencies to see land use politics in terms of divisions between pro- and anti-growth interests are deceptive and one-sided. Property cannot be kept unless incomes and revenues flow to keep owners going economically. Within the free enterprise system, even the most fervent environmentalists and exclusionary suburbanites need jobs and paychecks, which depend on economic growth. Ultimately, someone's property and community have to be used for the dirtier work of production. But, by the same token, not even the biggest corporation can risk the destruction of exclusionary property rights, which would explode the incentives and securities of the very institution that business desperately needs to protect its wealth and channel its investments.

In capitalism the logic is inescapable: expansion is the condition of exclusion just as exclusion is the condition of expansion. But the fact remains that when it comes to land use, exclusion and expansion are also the conditions of intractable conflict. Here property owners turn hostile to investment, while investors grow impatient with the exclusionary rights of property. When these forces collide, people come to be against what they have been for, and for what they have been against.[23] Thus conflicts over the meanings, rights, and freedom of property have been the stuff of land use dispute in America since the eighteenth century. Economic forces driving toward centralized capitalist production have always had their troubles in getting access to space when those living off the land business, in the more marginal arenas of competitive real estate, small-scale agriculture, and home ownership, have refused to yield. Other land interests, notably those of environmental protection and low-income housing, have lately helped to expand the scope of conflict and to enlarge the range of values served by policy, though nearly always by hitching themselves to the causes and interests of the main economic rivals. A land policy independent of the property system has been inconceivable in America. Public interests in land have been squeezed between the poles of contradictory property rights.

Another way of seeing this point is to note that land use conflict offers a unique angle of vision on the challenge of capitalist development to basic American values: individual property, community, grass-roots democracy, and political freedom. Obviously, the development of capitalism is not ordinarily seen as a force working against the grain of important elements of the culture, just as private property is not usually linked with anticapitalist interests. But the study of land conflict suggests a different face of capitalism than the one celebrated in real estate pages or Chamber of Commerce handouts, a capitalism more indifferent to the long-established boundaries, well-rooted sense of place, and expectations of security that are supposed to come with landownership and private property. In the nineteenth century, in a dramatic passage near the end of his brilliant work "The Eighteenth Brumaire of Louis Bonaparte," Karl Marx tried with all his passion to make this point so that French peasants would never forget that they lacked for friends in high places: "The bourgeois order," he wrote, "which at the beginning of the century set the state to stand guard over the newly arisen small holding and manured it with laurels, has become a vampire that sucks out its blood and marrow and throws them into the alchemistic cauldron of capital."[24]

The resistance of small landholders to the centralization of land use controls suggests that owners in the United States are not without garlic and crucifix. As C. Wright Mills once observed, the hallmark of modern elites is that they "may smash one structure and set up another." [25] But this is precisely what American elites have failed to do in relation to the political control of land, though not necessarily for want of trying.

Capital and the State

To pose the issues of land use in these terms is to set them in the context of the political economy as a whole and the theory of the capitalist state. "Capitalism," Sheldon Wolin writes, "is America's way of organizing power." [26] But it has always needed a government strong enough to clear pathways blocked by the groups whose lives and communities are threatened with being overrun by economic change. Capitalist expansion has required political rationalization, uniform laws, and rules that enclose a boundless economic space for investment. Business craves both the freedom, as Marx once put it, to "nestle everywhere, settle everywhere, establish connections everywhere" and the knowledge that every situation and site can be turned to profitable account. [27] The history of modern democracy, by contrast, has been preoccupied with checking unlimited expansion and the pure rule of markets. In Alan Wolfe's words, "For the past 200 years at least, the maturity and cohesion of a society has been advanced only by protecting certain areas of human conduct from the dictates of profit and loss." [28] Much of the legitimacy of capitalist politics has rested on its sensitivity to human needs for protections against capitalism, including the preservation of what geographer John Friedmann calls "life spaces . . . bounded territorial spaces," places with identities, histories, and loyalties: political communities. [29]

The capitalist state, then, is constantly pushed and pulled in opposite directions. The twists of expansion are inextricably connected with and opposed by the turns of exclusion. Nothing is more important to legitimacy than growth, yet nothing would be more illegitimate than a wholesale attack on the exclusionary rights of property and community self-protection. Exclusion is the most rational social condition of class-driven expansion, but nothing would be more irrational from a corporate standpoint than to permit small landowners and communities to dictate the paths of development.

Naturally, political theorists who have speculated about how capitalist governments respond to such contradictions have been extremely pessimistic about the ability of officials to keep the contending forces in line and out of each other's way. Nicos Poulantzas nicely summarized the prevailing sense of exasperation when he wrote that the contradictions of capitalism tend to stick officials into a rut, where they "can go neither backwards nor forwards." [30]

But the fact is, of course, that capital does move and communities do resist; and they do so because governments in capitalist society are not only immobilized by contradictions but also driven by them. In the crunch of land use conflict, choices are made; political and legal weight is thrown behind and against the contending interests; public policy gets capital moving and also stops it from moving. Inevitably, the gearing of law to the needs of expansion has never been complete, but the power of property and community to exclude has never been truly secure. That is, the government cannot take sides for long without switching partners. This paradox is very much part of what theorists like to call the "relative autonomy" of the capitalist state: the freedom of officials to do things that are necessary and even unpalatable if the system is to survive.[31] Thus, although it is true, as Alan Wolfe writes, "that the late capitalist state is incapable of working its way out of the contradictions" between "the conditions of production and the expectations of political life," it may still, with its relative autonomy, work its way over, around, and even through its difficulties, often with extremely painful consequences for people in the way; sometimes even the biggest businesses get stopped.[32]

The questions, then, are, How are the government's momentum and direction determined? How free are the various levels of the government to move for and against property rights? What factors govern the lean and slant of government power in the struggles of exclusion and expansion? The best way to tackle such questions is to trace the dialectic of exclusion and expansion historically, to explore the challenges it raises for the U.S. government, and to examine the ways in which these have been met. More questions arise: What problems has the expansion-exclusion dialectic posed for the law of property, and how have these problems been manifest? How have the tensions and responses changed with the development of the system? What are the various capitalist and noncapitalist interests in expansion and exclusion? How are they organized, represented, absorbed, and deflected? What patterns are revealed in the battles for land use control, and what do these revelations suggest about the nature of political power in capitalist society?

These are very big questions. Together they add up to a sizable test: an exploration of the relationship between capitalist contradiction, government's ability to manage the system, and the implications for democracy. Obviously, case studies cannot provide definitive answers to problems of such magnitude. Yet it is equally true that theory alone will not do the job. Empirical evidence needs to be piled up, and it needs to feed the ongoing labor of theory. That is the intention here.

The Plan of the Book

This work is divided into two sections. Part One explores the general political and legal themes of land use policy and their roots in private property. Chapter 1 begins with a sampler of the exclusion-expansion theme in American culture, noting how Americans like to celebrate the society as an open,

fenceless land of opportunity even while they busy themselves with the post-
ing of "Keep Out" signs and the erection of private walls. The larger cultural
ambivalence is traced in the politics of land use; we note some of the more
recent fights for control, with their patterning in the political sociology of
class and community in American life. The chapter ends by considering land
conflicts within the business system and by assessing the space hunger of capital as the dominant factor behind moves to suppress local controls.

Chapter 2 offers an overview of how the social position of landed property
in capitalist society has changed. It summarizes the historical antagonism of
land and capital in Europe and America, focusing especially on the changes
this antagonism has experienced as capital has taken over much of the productive land. A major theme here concerns the shift that occurred at the end of
the nineteenth and the beginning of the twentieth centuries in the popular conception of property, a shift from productive property to consumption property
as the chief popular symbol of economic interest and social status. This
change had crucial consequences for big business, inasmuch as it helped
greatly to legitimate the social system in the eyes of workers; it also, however,
expanded the ranks of potential excluders in society. The chapter concludes by
examining how the social tensions of conflicting property rights are held
within the bounds of law. I argue that this is accomplished through the skilled,
if not always logically consistent, use of alternative theories of property
rights. On the one hand, individualistic conceptions are trotted out to celebrate the rights of property, but on the other hand, social theories of property
are used—more frequently—to support political intervention on behalf of
particular exclusion or expansion interests.

Chapter 3 concludes our attempt to lay out a theoretical, historical, and
legal framework for understanding land use conflict in the United States, examining in detail the historical challenge posed for American land policy by
the exclusion-expansion dialectic, particularly in the context of rapid industrialization and urbanization in the nineteenth century. The chapter focuses
initially on the judiciary and its dismantling of eighteenth-century legal biases
favoring exclusionary over expansionist rights. The discussion suggests how
capital was able to shift huge costs of progress from its own ledgers to those
of landowners and society at large through the benefit of seemingly slight
changes in the rules of property. Then the details of the gradual recovery of
landowner rights are explored—how urban planners, local merchants, real estate capitalists, and middle-class homeowners learned to employ the scientific
rationales of conservation, planning, and zoning as legitimations for new
forms of municipally imposed exclusion. In essence, then, chapter 3 exam-
ines some of the more intimate legal struggles aimed at fitting exclusion and
expansion into the contradictory system of capitalist property rights, and it
attempts to show how the battles for land use control today are part of an old
tradition of growth and resistance in the development of capitalism.

In Part Two, the focus shifts from framework to concrete struggles. Three case studies form the crux of the empirical analysis. The first is a local example, a close-up look at the San Antonio, Texas, battle over construction of a regional shopping mall on land situated above Edwards aquifer, the city's only source of drinking water. San Antonio's experience was selected for several reasons. First, because it involves a classic land use debate, the Edwards aquifer controversy furnishes a setting in microcosm for viewing the forces and interests, the claims and counterclaims, that, because they were so unmanageable at the local level, stimulated lawyers and planners to call for statewide and even national land use policy solutions. The frustrations the city encountered in mounting successful defenses against unwanted public and private-sector investment also help to expose other key issues of community protection, especially the difficulty of safeguarding regional resources within a system of fragmented federalism and the institutionalized power of expansion interests within government agencies and public law. More, the controversy reveals the promise of multiclass and multiracial coalitions as the basis of increasingly democratic community politics.

Perhaps most important, I chose to focus on the San Antonio experience in order to debunk a myth. Although San Antonio is the nation's eleventh largest city and a fast-growing urban area,[33] nevertheless it, like many other Sunbelt cities, has gone largely unnoticed by urban scholars. For too many students of urban politics, southern and southwestern cities continue to be seen as places where politics is dormant because business goes unchallenged. According to one analyst, "the business community" in Sunbelt cities "has a virtual monopoly in deliberation on solutions to civic problems," while another advises that "the lack of political conflict" is a main feature of southwestern urbanism.[34] Such generalizations may once have been accurate; they no longer are. As a recent news report noted, "Most of the new concern over excessive growth is occurring in and near fast-growing cities in the West, like Phoenix, and Austin, Texas, as well as in California."[35] As the Edwards aquifer controversy makes clear, skepticism about expansion flowered in San Antonio, too.

Chapter 5 takes the issues of land use politics to the national stage with an explanation of how legal, corporate, and political elites tried to streamline the land development system by centralizing the government's power to manage the contending interests. The spotlight here is on the movement for a national land use policy. The national land use proposal requires a hard look because, except for the frustrated and half-hearted planning attempts of the New Deal, it represents the first time that the federal government tried to create an explicit framework for the planning and regulation of large-scale private development. Washington, of course, already exercised a profound influence on land use patterns through its many policies dealing with highways, housing, mass transportation, sewer systems, defense installations, and so forth. But, for reasons that need to be carefully investigated, in the 1960s and 1970s the process of land use decision making itself became the object of federal attention. Land use control was recognized as a pivotal function in the national scheme of economic development, a function important enough to warrant the establishment of a federally arranged framework for resolving the land battles of grass-roots democracy.

In chapter 6 the political fate of national land use policy is examined. We begin with the efforts of the Nixon administration and the Congressional Interior Committees to produce an approach effective enough to rationalize the process but innocuous enough to leave the major beneficiaries of local control feeling unchallenged. Senate passage of land use bills in 1972 and 1973 suggested that a workable solution had been found. The early success was deceptive, however. Petty urban and rural capitalists, economically dependent on close and effective access to local politicians, feared centralization as a major threat to their economic survival—and these fears were vigorously and successfully fanned by the U.S. Chamber of Commerce. With the Chamber's astutely orchestrated leadership, the legislation was stopped in the House of Representatives in 1974 and 1975, helped not at all by the political crisis of Watergate and the economic crisis of exploding energy prices.

In chapter 7 we will see that the defeat of land use policy reform did not end the pressures to centralize. In 1979, the energy industry, enjoying the commercial benefits of escalating petroleum prices, found itself embroiled in nasty land fights nationwide. Its drilling rigs, power plants, pipelines, and utility lines seemed to be blocked at every turn. Emboldened by the fuel crisis, and pulled along by a Carter administration that wanted to validate its competence, the industry urged Congress to create a national Energy Mobilization Board (EMB), a special, executive-branch agency to speed construction of large-scale projects by overriding restrictive local, state, and national rules. The bid for the EMB was an unusually blunt effort by a major business and the White House to centralize administrative power in order to minimize local resistance.

The EMB case allows us to examine the relevance of patterns found in the earlier case studies to this concentrated and narrowly focused instance of land use centralization. Were the forces and problems of the energy corporations related to those that generated the earlier national land use fight? Did the patterns of resistance to energy bear any resemblance to the localized patterns of resistance in San Antonio? Or, by contrast, was the energy instance qualitatively different from the earlier patterns of land use conflict and institutional strain? Does the EMB issue in fact illustrate how land use conflicts are best seen as isolated matters, unrelated to larger, systemic issues? Is it, in other words, an exception to the hypothesis that land use conflicts represent the contradictory interests of capitalist property? Or does it represent an example of those more basic forces contributing to the general rule of unruliness in land use politics? Such questions make the EMB case an intriguing testing ground for studies of the politics of land use centralization.

Finally, chapter 8 will review the unifying themes of the book and try to relate them to the earlier theoretical questions about power in the capitalist state. More specifically, the conclusion takes a last critical look at the tendency to see land use issues as isolated, technical matters, offering instead an approach to the politics of land use that defines the issues of location and exclusion in relation to the goal of democratic control of the U.S. production system. The concluding argument is that no society can develop a responsible, democratic approach to conflicts over land use unless it is first in a position to decide publicly its priorities for the investment of its wealth. Democracy, in short, needs freedom to select the human values it wants the economy to serve. And it needs the time to engage in thoughtful deliberations. But as long as the production question is off the national agenda, this freedom is beyond our reach, and capital brooks no delays in the race for wealth.

Without the democratization of investment, it is inevitable that the already tense location questions of land use will only become more vicious, as the hazards of lethal technology mount and millions of people prove unwilling to roll over and play dead when elites make surprise demands on their neighborhoods' space. It is perfectly natural, after all, that citizens use the exclusionary rights and powers of property to check capital—unless of course those rights are removed from local hands. The main contention here is that this removal is a real possibility, if not immediately, then in the decades ahead. Whether it happens depends on how people define the questions and how they mobilize to provide their own answers. This book is offered in the hope that it may contribute in some small way to a democratic victory in the struggle for land use control.

Part One

Land Use, Property, and Power

A Fenceless America 1

To beat an animal of the same species on his home turf, the invader must be twice as strong as the defender.

Lester Thurow

On a recent trip to West Berlin, President Ronald Reagan peered anxiously across the Wall. The well-publicized stare dramatized American contempt for bondage. Winston Churchill's earlier image of the "Iron Curtain" evoked the same sense of revulsion. And public passions were enraged by the Soviet shooting of a Korean jet wandering through its sensitive air space. Foreign Minister Andrei Gromyko charged the craft with "plane trespassing," but American leaders saw the shooting as the bloody defense of barbarous walls. The Cold War has been an ideological war against walls.

At home, Americans are eager to scale the walls or at least to cloak them. We cheer batters who slam baseballs over outfield fences; mask the walls of our rooms with pictures; drape our best college walls with ivy; keep our jails downtown, where we are advised not to go after dark, or in distant hinterlands away from the suburban mainstream; and we splash graffiti across the walls of our public institutions, concealing them behind a blaze of paint. "Something there is that doesn't love a wall," wrote Robert Frost.[1] It is perhaps an abiding affection for liberty, or as D. H. Lawrence once suggested about Americans, the freedom to flee: "They came largely to get *away*—that most simple of motives. To get away. Away from what? In the long run, away from themselves. Away from everything. That's why most people have come to America, and still do come. To get away from everything they are and have been."[2] They ran, said Lawrence, to be "masterless" in a land without fences. Thus the American Revolution, like the Cold War, was a battle against walls. Listing the colonies' grievances against Britain, an angry Jefferson complained in the Declaration of Independence that King George wanted to contain America, keep it bottled up between the Alleghenies and the Atlantic by "raising the conditions of new appropriations of lands." American escapists would not have it. No barrier could stop American expansion west; it was our "manifest destiny" to knock down walls.[3]

As a people we share many suggestive symbols formed of a deep cultural pride in the image of an America without walls, a fenceless America. The Statue of Liberty celebrates this theme, as does the "Western": we long for the "wide, open spaces," sing "don't fence me in," and dream of the "virgin land." Frederick Jackson Turner articulated the image of a fenceless America as the key to our whole past: "The existence of an area of free land," he said, "its continued recession, and the advance of American settlement westward explain American development." Some of Turner's sharpest critics stressed that "mobility" more than "free land" was the master clue to development in the United States—but this idea too implied the fenceless image. And Tocqueville's concept of democracy in America had, at its core, the idea of a land stripped of social fences, where men stood "side by side" though "unconnected by any common tie." But Woody Guthrie saw a "common tie"—in joint ownership of the fenceless country. "This land is your land," he sang, fully intending the proprietary implications to be taken seriously. Guthrie equated trespassing with freedom.[4]

"Keep Out!"

Yet, as Frost reminds us, we also firmly hold to the idea that "good fences make good neighbors." If Americans see restriction as "imprisonment," they see exclusion as "security." Thus we demand rights to roam free, but we reserve rights to set our land apart and keep others at bay. The recent calls for a "tortilla curtain" along the Mexican border, the detention of Haitian immigrants, the banning of AIDS victims, and the denial of visas to notables such as Nobel Prize winner Gabriel García Marquez all come on top of an existing U.S. immigration policy that excludes "prostitutes, polygamists, drug addicts, beggars, lepers, homosexuals" and those "foreigners whose activities would be contrary to the public interest."[5] Foreign products are kept out, too, as corporations and trade unions use their political power to win the exclusion of foreign-made steel, motorcycles, automobiles, textiles, even clothespins. And Ronald Reagan wants to keep out Soviet missiles with a space shield of killer satellites. But these restraints on foreign entry only mirror the forms of exclusion that exist inside America, where the national affinity for walls reaches its apotheosis in the private-property sector, which could not exist without a vast legal wall against the public.

If a man's home is his castle, the fence is his moat. Americans ran to a fenceless America and made it a land of private fences and "keep out" signs. When individual fences couldn't stand the pressures of development, collective ones were added. Zoning laws were built to lend whole neighborhoods and communities the right to exclude. "Hundreds of small-scale governments," write Danielson and Doig, used "zoning codes and other regulatory devices to pursue parochial development goals." Scores of reports documented the exclusionary bias of land use controls in the sixties. Zoning was accused of playing a critical role in splitting the country into "two societies, one black, one white—separate and unequal." [6]

Economic stagnation in the 1970s and 1980s only increased pressures to tighten the locks—for now the homeless were coming. According to one report, "officials in the resort town of Fort Lauderdale" considered "spraying beachfront trashcans with kerosene or chemicals to keep transients" from sleeping in neighborhood streets and "living off the garbage." Lumping the homeless with vermin, the mayor proclaimed: "If I find anybody crawling in my garbage, I would spray them." Meanwhile in New York, where an estimated 60,000 people wander the streets, "the rapidly growing number of homeless people seeking shelter has forced the city to seek new housing space quietly and move people in quickly before community opposition has a chance to develop," for neighborhood resentment runs deep. As one Brooklyn resident cried, "We worked all our lives for this and we're going to keep it for us." Back in Florida, another resort community, Golden Beach, elected to protect itself by closing "six of the seven streets heading into town," placing "a guard at the seventh." [7]

Fiscal crisis can be an even stronger inducement to exclusion. Walls tend to rise in rough proportion with taxes. Even the rich are stunned at the removal of once carefully laid welcome mats. According to Michelle White, "Suburbanites seem to be closing the gates behind them. Communities that once permitted the construction of only large, expensive, single-family houses are now signalling that they would prefer no new housing at all or as little as possible. In other words, the rich used to be welcome in suburbia; now even they are not welcome anymore." Half of those questioned in a recent poll of New York City suburbanites said they "want a halt to local growth." Towns with names like Petaluma, Ramapo, and Boca Raton have become landmarks in the "keep out" tradition for imposing strict controls on municipal growth rates. [8]

But big-city dwellers can be exclusionary, too. Both former President Richard M. Nixon and Madonna, rock's "material girl," know what it means to be unwanted: each has been refused the right to buy a condominium at choice Manhattan addresses. The city's mayor, Edward Koch, has dealt with its street peddlers in equally unkind fashion. After heavy pressure from local merchants, he vowed to sign a new ordinance intended to reduce "the crush of pushcarts selling hot dogs, ice cream, knishes, pretzels, and other foods during daylight hours on some of the world's busiest sidewalks and street corners." Young people are also learning the lesson, as ever more apartment complexes post signs opposing the residence of children and pets. The list of the zoned-out grows more distinguished and petty all at once.[9]

But there is nothing petty about the social logic of exclusion. There are important reminders here of every black who woke up to discover the ashes of a burned cross on the lawn, or each Jew who had to face a swastika painted on the garage door. Yet exclusion transcends racism. Some black neighbors in a working-class section of Philadelphia recently complained about the unwholesome living habits of a nearby radical group. Property and neighborly values were endangered by the group's bullhorns and threats, as well as by its rejection of modern sanitation. When peaceful efforts at eviction failed, police tried a new strategy: urban bombing. The resulting fire destroyed sixty-one nearby houses and left ten dead. The logic of urban exclusion can be murderous.[10]

Property, Land, and Exclusion

Obviously, the currents of exclusion cut through all strata of the society. Zoning is one of the most important means by which they are allowed to run their course. As Peter Wolfe notes, "Zoning ordinances are the most pervasive and powerful part of the lexicon of land law in America." That they are embedded in the institution and sentiments of private property is no accident. Zoning, writes the English planner John Delafons, "won such remarkable acceptance in American communities" because it was quickly seen "as a means of strengthening the institution of private property."[11] It represents the collective extension of traditional landowner rights to keep out the unwanted. The Latin root of "fence," after all, is the same as that for "defense": *defendere*—to ward off, repel, exclude. Zoning is best understood as the protective public armor of landed property in a nation that holds trespassers in contempt. Driven to possess the wealth, power, and honor that are socially attached to property, the American, in Tocqueville's words, severs "himself from the mass of his fellows . . . to draw apart with his family and friends" into "a circle of his own."[12] Thorstein Veblen called this a "race for reputability."[13] Philip Slater, however, sees it as "the pursuit of loneliness," the repression of enduring communal aspirations by a hyperactive drive for insulation: "We seek a private house, a private means of transportation, a private garden, a private laundry, self-service stores, and do-it-yourself skills of every kind. An enormous technology seems to have set itself the task of making it unnecessary for one human being ever to ask anything of another in the course of going about his daily business."[14] This, adds Robert Lynd, has resulted in "the disproportionate structuring" of private property in American culture, the erection of walls far stronger than the dangers from without.[15]

James Madison long ago urged otherwise, however. For him, the fences around property could not be built too high, for the mass pressures to scale them were great and growing. "An increase of population will of necessity increase the proportion of those who will labour under all the hardships of life, & secretly sigh for a more equal distribution of its blessings. . . . Symptoms of a levelling spirit . . . give notice of the future danger." Walls had to be built against majority rule, "walls around democracy." [16]

Yet, as Madison himself admitted, "no agrarian attempts have yet been made in this Country." The statement applies with equal force today. Land reform has never been taken seriously on the national agenda.[17] Although land ownership is now highly concentrated—one estimate has 3 percent of the population owning 55 percent of all American land and 95 percent of private land—the "land question" has been omitted from the agenda of twentieth-century American politics.[18] "Curiously," writes Peter Meyer, "in the United States the link—between control of the land and . . . political and economic power—has rarely been seen as an organizing theme" in modern public policy.[19] It does not follow, however, that the public walling of private property is fueled by exaggerated or irrational fears. The protections of landed property have not escaped threats to their integrity. Landowners have encountered serious assaults on their self-defense rights; typically, however, invasion has come from above, not from below.

"Something there is that doesn't love a wall"

Business expansion has periodically threatened substantial inroads on landowner rights. In the early nineteenth century, for example, owners discovered that traditional powers to resist injury or expropriation at the hands of government and corporate builders were cut back by judges eager to promote development. Rights to sue for damages resulting from industrial pollution were, as we shall see in chapter 3, greatly reduced. But at the same time, government powers to expropriate private property for "public advantage" were liberally dispensed to private outfits. Capital made headway when government acted against the owners of private property.

The fast spread of zoning laws in the 1920s was a response to a century's worth of attacks on protectionist rights in land. It was a form of anti-business resistance within the business system itself. But zoning, too, has become the recent target of corporate and state challenge; it is indicted not only for fostering racism but also for inflating costs in the economy as a whole. Suburban excluders, it is argued, raise charges by limiting housing supplies, encouraging land speculation, monopolizing public services, and leapfrogging away from preexisting utilities, thus forcing the construction of expensive new facilities and wasting land. Danielson and Doig summarize the critics' case: zoning, it is said, produces "a recurring pattern of inefficient development and disorderly growth, characterized by monotonous housing tracts, highly limited residential options for the lower and middle classes, vanishing open spaces, misplaced industry, overcrowded schools, congested highways, polluted air and water, overburdened utility systems, and spiraling taxes."[20] Market-oriented attorneys insist that towns must compensate owners for such "inefficient" restrictions on land use.[21] The Supreme Court may be ready to agree. In a stinging dissent to its decision in the case of *San Diego Gas & Electric Co.* v. *City of San Diego* (1981), one that missed winning a majority by a single uncertain vote, Justice William Brennan urged not only that abusive land controls should be overturned, as they always have been, but also that cities should be punished by being forced to pay landowners for values lost during the period of the law's effect.[22]

The 1982 report of President Ronald Reagan's Commission on Housing lauds Brennan's dissent. After years in which "the pendulum has swung too far away from the right to enjoy the ownership of real property and the important societal interests of increasing mobility and access to housing opportunities," Brennan's language was welcomed as "possibly signaling increasing judicial concern for protection of private property rights." Modern zoning, after all, "is used not only to separate land uses"—its legitimate role in society—"but also to exclude people from the community." For President Reagan's housing experts, "exclusion is clearly not an acceptable governmental interest."[23]

To combat this trend, the commission recommends tactics more radical than Brennan's. Preferring to strike at the heart of the zoning power itself, the panel argues that the courts and state legislatures should adopt far stricter tests for the legitimacy of local land policies. Instead of the present judicial tendency to permit local regulators substantial discretion, by holding them to an "arbitrary and capricious" standard, land use controls should be held to the yardstick of the "vital and pressing" needs of government: the protection of crucial local values—such as health, natural resources, historic buildings, and public works—from imminent harm. This yardstick would not, presumably, include what Justice William O. Douglas once described as the community's right to "be beautiful as well as healthy, spacious as well as clean, well-balanced as well as carefully patrolled." These are values, in the commission's view, best left to the court of real estate competition. If municipalities want them, they should have to pay the going price. In a position not entirely consistent with the president's affection for local control, though quite in line with his faith in markets, the Commission on Housing wants the courts not to leave local legislators alone in the practice of land policy. Here the commission and Justice Brennan meet.[24]

Centralizing the Control of Land

Zoning advocates are confused and worried. Where are the walls that fail to exclude? How, they wonder, can land use be limited without limiting the users? Robert R. Wright, reflecting a more sympathetic and a sociologically candid assessment of land policy, argues that "all zoning provisions as well as other forms of land use control are exclusionary in one way or another, and . . . limit the rights of certain individuals to move into a particular area." The issue for Wright is not the distinction between nonexclusionary and exclusionary approaches to land use control, but "what forms of exclusion are legitimate and what forms are not?"[25]

From this vantage point, issues of exclusion are seen less as legal matters and more as planning and regulatory issues, questions involving political ideas about the nature of community life and economic needs generated by an expanding industrial system. An appropriate blend of people, resources, and activities can be achieved within the existing order, but only through the use of carefully planned controls, balancing the preferences of local citizens and the spatial needs of wider constituencies. Sagacious administration is seen, in the long run, as a more reliable route to improved land use policy than expanded judicial review.

For liberal critics of land use planning, walls have a place in the good society, but their value can only be appraised by aerial inspection. What counts is the overall patterning of walls and fences; what needs to be judged are the broader lines of division and exclusion they establish, and the impact of these on the mix and flow of people and resources. From this perspective, the problem is not the existence of walls, but the absence of comprehensive efforts to evaluate exclusion in relation to greater system needs. The best course, then, would be to widen the scope of regulation, to add some land use watchposts at higher levels of government while leaving plenty of room for the expression of local opinion and the upkeep of local walls. Liberal reformers have looked to the states as an "optimal structure of decision-making authority."[26]

The push to make communities pay for protection follows a larger drift in the legal and political systems to check local decisions with regional, state, and in some cases even national oversight. Numerous calls have been made to centralize the rights to land use control, especially at the state level. Indeed, in the 1960s an odd group of lawyers, builders, planners, energy companies, public officials, and conservationists insisted that basic reform of the system to regulate development was essential if America was to achieve balanced growth and a healthy environment. Expansion and exclusion were too important, they argued, to be left to narrow decisions at the grass roots. Frank J. Popper calls this loose grouping "the land-use reform movement."[27]

Several states, notably Florida and Vermont, took hesitant steps in this direction; in many others, less comprehensive regional-planning and facility-siting programs were adopted. In New York, Pennsylvania, Massachusetts, New Jersey, and, more recently, California, "fair share" housing policies were introduced by courts and legislatures, requiring affluent communities to plan ahead for low-income neighbors. Maryland established a statewide program for power-plant siting that included a land bank for private utilities. Other states were less aggressive in their aid to power companies, but added centralized regulatory mechanisms to oversee the inevitable siting battles. Meanwhile, regional controls were developed to "balance" expansionist and exclusion interests in sensitive environments. Examples include the Hackensack Meadowlands Development Commission in New Jersey, the San Francisco Bay Conservation and Development Commission, and the North Carolina Coastal Resources Commission. Such organizations loomed over traditionally local controllers, striving to link their policies with the needs of regional corporate and governmental planners.[28]

In other states, however, such as Texas, efforts to protect regional resources were thwarted by conservative regimes that saw little need for planning. The unevenness and unpredictability of local control and state centralization inspired Congress to consider the formulation of national approaches. A National Land Use Policy bill was promoted in 1970 to establish uniform guidelines for state action. Frustrated at the seemingly endless delays encountered by corporate and government builders, as well as by the indifference to ecology often exhibited by pro-growth zoners, Senator Henry M. Jackson (D-Washington) sponsored the bill out of a belief that "the climactic land-use conflicts we have faced in recent years should not have become public 'causes célèbres.'" Even President Richard M. Nixon publicly opposed the monopoly of land use control by local landowners, arguing that "the time has come when we must accept the idea that society as a whole has a legitimate interest in proper land-use. There is a national interest in effective land-use planning all across the nation." Corporate voices also added their imprimatur. Testifying before Jackson's Senate Interior Committee, John L. Loftis, Jr., vice president of Exxon Company, U.S.A., explained:

> The federal government has a non-delegable role to act in matters of truly national concern. . . . In some instances, the activities of State or interstate land use agencies may impinge on or be at variance with the welfare of the nation as a whole. In such instances, federal policy must dominate and thereby affect State and local government decisions and private initiatives.[29]

In 1975, after the National Land Use Policy bill failed for the second time to pass the House of Representatives, the issue seemed to fade from view. However, during the 1976 presidential campaign it poked briefly and controversially into the public domain when candidate Jimmy Carter proclaimed his belief in "ethnic purity" and the principle that "it's good to maintain the homogeneity of neighborhoods if they've been established that way."[30] Some observers thought the statement hurt Carter's chances among black voters; it was probably welcome news, though, in exclusively white precincts.

For all the clamor about "ethnic purity," however, what went less noticed by the press was the Ford administration's 1975 counterproposal to the National Land Use Policy bill. In its Energy Facility Planning and Development

Act the White House proposed that unless states met the Federal Energy Agency's plant-siting requirements, the FEA should be empowered to suspend "any statute, rules, or regulations" that local protectionists used to block fuel projects. Lost in the debates over gasoline prices and taxes, the siting measure answered corporate demands for quicker and more affirmative settlements of their fights with local landowners and environmentalists.

The proposal languished for several years, but continuing struggles over Alaskan lands, oil pipelines, terminals, refineries, utility plants, and other energy projects kept it close to the energy industry's heart. Corporate resentment, hidden by TV appeals for public trust, burst through in 1979 during the spring oil crisis. Responding to intense public pressures to "do something" about lengthening gasoline lines, President Carter scuttled his earlier preference for "the homogeneity of neighborhoods" by declaring that "when this Nation critically needs a refinery or a pipeline we will build it." Moving on the earlier Ford administration's precedent, Carter proposed the creation of an Energy Mobilization Board (EMB), which, in its most extreme version, would have been authorized to waive any existing procedural or substantive impediment to plant construction, as well as to prohibit communities from adding new regulations once work on a project was begun. In effect, the EMB would have constituted a national zoning-appeals board for the energy giants.

The proposal for an EMB was defeated when a coalition of local officials, westerners, environmentalists, and conservative Republicans joined forces in 1980 to block the measure. It should be noted, however, that Congress rejected the Conference Committee version only after each house separately voted in favor of the concept. It seems fairly clear now that the demise of EMB was crucially related to President Carter's unpopularity following the taking of hostages in Iran.

Land Use Conflict in the Reagan Years

The enduring pressures to ease the way for corporate expansion have hardly abated in the Reagan years, though the strategies of the executive branch have shifted. With burning faith in the "magic of the marketplace," and eager to work on the "supply side," the Reagan administration placed top priority on the opening of doors to public lands. Of course, the activities of the former secretary of the interior, James Watt, attracted the greatest attention in this drive. His proposals to lease a billion acres of offshore lands, sell $2 billion worth of "surplus federal property," and open National Wilderness areas to petroleum drilling and mining stimulated massive opposition as well as business interest. The Sierra Club alone gathered one million signatures on a petition demanding his resignation. His attacks on liberals as not being "real Americans," and his blunt warnings to Jews that U.S. sympathies for Israel depended on their support for the administration's energy policy, also kept the focus on the Department of the Interior. It deserves to be there: the federal government is, after all, landlord to one-third of the national estate, and the drive by business for a fenceless public domain offers important clues to its wider anti-landowner interests. But the public domain, for all its publicity, does not exhaust President Reagan's land use plans.

Though a fervent believer in the prerogatives of energy capital and the military, Reagan was forced by protectionist resistance to waffle on two of their chief priorities: the MX missile and coal-slurry pipelines. A combination of western agricultural, environmental, and local government groups mobilized intense opposition to the Air Force's plan to transport two hundred mobile missiles along underground tracks strung between 4,600 sites across millions of frontier acres. Although the administration denied that "political" factors played a role in its decision to drop the mobile "basing-mode," one analyst concluded that the Mormon Church's participation in the anti-MX coalition "had a profound impact" on the president as well as on the Utah public. After its public declaration condemning the proposal, polls showed public sentiment rising from 50 percent to 76 percent against the MX.[31]

A similar coalition of political, economic, and environmental excluders, this time aided not by the Mormon Church but by the equally impressive voice of the railroad industry, convinced the administration to oppose long-pending legislation granting coal-slurry-pipeline companies eminent domain authority across western lands. The lines were meant to increase competitiveness in the coal-hauling business, thus presumably lowering fuel costs. But environmentalists saw them as spurs to strip-mining and worried over their effects on scarce water supplies in the West. Farm and ranching groups feared expropriations of land and water rights. Railroads fought to protect their monopoly profits. After months of hesitation, President Reagan announced his reluctant refusal to back the bill, though in doing so he warned that it is "clearly contrary to the national interest for private parties or for individual states to thwart projects" of national significance in order to protect their own "parochial purposes." Recently, however, the president changed his mind, throwing his support behind the federal grant of eminent domain powers because slurry pipelines are "in the national interest."[32] Even the magical marketplace sometimes needs helping hands and strong arms.

Nuclear energy issues have also befuddled the Reaganites. Efforts to expedite placement of high-level nuclear-waste dumps foundered in Congress, strongly resisted by state and local officials. A bill finally passed only after states won the right to veto national site proposals.[33] Similarly, the Federal Aviation Administration began a "drive against what it considers unreasonable curfews and other limitations" on airport use. This effort included proposed new legislation giving the agency authority "to review and veto" local noise-abatement plans.[34] Many states and localities were also hostile to White

House plans "to open a network of 181,000 miles of highways to large double-trailer trucking rigs." The 80,000-pound vehicles would have access to city streets as well as to ten-foot-wide country roads. Connecticut answered by banning the rigs altogether; Georgia, Vermont, and Pennsylvania obtained court orders to block parts of the plan.[35]

But by far the administration's greatest land use headache is the issue of land pollution by hazardous chemicals such as dioxin. Not only did its careless, if not criminal, governance of toxic-waste regulations lead to the resignations of the top echelons of the Environmental Protection Agency (EPA), including the agency's chief administrator, Anne Gorsuch Burford, but it also confirmed the public's worst fears about the dangers of placing new sites near residential areas. Most Americans do not want to live anywhere near a chemical waste disposal site. No wonder the chemical industry is increasingly restive with the buildup of lethal garbage. Though twenty states have set up toxic-siting programs, few dumps have actually been permitted. According to a recent report, companies "are meeting strident local opposition despite . . . laws that take decisions out of local hands." As another study, in the *Harvard Environmental Law Review*, concludes, "Finding sites for new hazardous waste treatment and disposal facilities is one of the most challenging problems facing society today," though, as it hastens to add, finding sites "is largely a problem of managing local opposition."[36]

Too Much Democracy?

The proliferation of local land use battles, the inability of centralized institutions to win land clearance, the persistent influence of politicized landowners coupled with broader strains of resistance to imperial technologies—all are important factors behind a surge of antidemocratic complaints by elites. The higher managers of governmental and corporate power are losing patience with provincial demands to "keep out." Intellectual voices, responsive to systemic needs for a redesign of authority, supplement the separate policy initiatives with considered laments about the unruliness of decision making. *Business Week* trumpets the need for a massive "re-industrialization" program for the U.S. economy, but wonders out loud whether there are "too many interest groups" and "too much pluralism" for a "consensus" to be achieved. Similarly, M.I.T. economist Lester Thurow complains in *The Zero-Sum Society* that while "our economic problems are solvable . . . everyone wants someone else to suffer the necessary economic losses, and as a consequence none of the possible solutions can be adopted." Analysts for the Trilateral Commission wonder whether "political democracy as it exists today is a viable form of government for the industrialized countries." Harvard analyst Robert Reich warns that America must leave "inefficient special interest policies" and "institutional paralysis" behind and get "organized for economic change." But James R. Schlesinger, former secretary of both the Department of Energy and the Department of Defense, offered the clearest summation of elite frustration when he observed that "we have reached the stage of participatory democracy where almost everyone in the society can say 'no,' but no one can say 'yes.'"[37]

The Political Sociology of Resistance

Considered together, the illustrations of policy and the samples of elitist criticism suggest evidence supporting the view that prime dangers to landed property, environmental protection, and local control stem not from the poor but from the highest levels of national political and economic power. Ordinarily the "land use issue" is not portrayed in this way. Students of the subject typically stress that landowners are enemies of the environment or that environmentalists are opponents of the poor. Frank Popper writes, for example, that "ownership interests—whether large developers or industry or small homeowners, or local governments serving their landowning constituency—always resist the introduction of measures that even vaguely infringe on ownership or its economic rewards." Peter Wolfe agrees, and notes that "through the forces of zoning the landowner loses mastery of his property. Neither the double-gauge shotgun nor the picket fence protects his borders any longer."[38] Danielson and Doig, however, see homeowners as rather more impressed with the protectionist powers of zoning. Tight land use controls, they argue, are crucial to "maintaining property values, preserving the residential character of the community, stabilizing local taxes, and providing adequate public education." For Bernard Frieden, these are euphemisms; suburban environmentalists are really selfish owners in disguise: "their opposition to homebuilding," which grows directly out of the all too considerable ability of zoning to protect private property, "is usually opposition to someone else's opportunity to buy a moderately priced house." Richard Babcock, Anthony Downs, Edward Banfield, and others have asserted similar arguments; this idea is now accepted wisdom in pro-construction circles.[39]

Such views are superficially plausible, but one-sided. They overlook the facts that exclusion and expansion are the double-sided interests of property; that corporations are eager to use eminent domain powers, when they can get them, to expedite land clearance; and that local landowners are equally happy to embrace zoning where it keeps their property values up and undesirables out. Property owners are anything but hostile to "infringements on ownership" when it serves their interest to control other owners. Indeed, in a society committed to the view of land as a commodity, protections of private-property interests are likely to be the strongest checks against untrammeled abuse of the earth.[40] That the poor are left out when ambition counteracts ambition over land use is attributable less to the greed of homeowners than to the biases of a social order built on platforms of property. Thus construction interests protest too much when they presume to be surrogates of the downtrodden. Can it be true that low-income shelter, in the era before zoning, was truly superior to that available today? Anthony Downs comes closer to reality when he observes—without mentioning the capitalist framework—that "a certain amount of neighborhood deterioration is an essential part of urban development."[41]

The Divisions of Land Use Politics

A much more complicated and subtle alignment of interests dominates the politics of protection. Undoubtedly, conservationist snobs and middle-class racists add their fire to many causes of local resistance.[42] But less sleazy factors weigh in, too—that is why the philosophical attack centers on local democracy itself. For example, on questions of big, dangerous, or intrusive technologies, broadly based regional defense coalitions are frequent. Centralized efforts to site poisonous waste dumps, weapons systems, airports, energy plants, highways, and shopping malls are likely to bring all sorts of different people together: progressives, nature-lovers, and trained environmentalists; middle- and working-class homeowners as well as upper-class landowners; small-business people, including ranchers, fishermen, and farmers; whites, blacks, Hispanics, and Indians; and an army of local officials.[43]

On urban housing and other neighborhood-based issues, however, the popular forces of land use resistance show much more internal fragmentation. When it comes to potential changes in the class composition and economic value of neighborhoods, residents turn sharply against public and private developers who want to bring in people of a higher or lower social rank or, often as not, people of different color and background. Thus white worker-owners and tenants strongly oppose the interests of poor people and nonwhites who, it is feared, will lower property values and threaten safety. Indeed, middle-class blacks still meet resistance in white neighborhoods, despite their ability to pass the income tests of more affluent neighborhoods. Similar patterns of opposition show up against urban government programs to house drug users, mental patients, the homeless, and juvenile offenders in working-class areas. In well-worn city districts, wealthier arrivals who threaten to "upgrade the neighborhood," driving land values, house prices, and rents beyond the reach of existing residents, are opposed just as strongly. Neighborhood people will hotly defend their right to keep out anyone whose presence they fear and distrust. The motivations in such battles stretch from understandable wishes to stabilize housing situations to concerns for physical safety and, finally, to racism.[44]

The Unities of Resistance

It is important, however, not to let the diversity of clash and coalition in land use protests obscure the more fundamental point: U.S. neighborhoods are geared for self-defense. In 1979, the National Commission on Neighborhoods counted no fewer than eight thousand community organizations in the United States, each a potential obstructor of corporate and state construction plans. ACORN—the Association of Community Organizations for Reform Now—claims 25,000 member families in nineteen states, including veterans of many a pitched battle to save cherished homes and towns. As a *Christian Science Monitor* poll discovered, in cities with populations over 50,000, one-third of the residents said they had participated in local defense actions, and a majority proclaimed a willingness to fight for their neighborhood's future if it were threatened. Clearly, millions of Americans believe they have a right to declare their towns off-limits to undesired economic and social change, or, in Ralph Nader's words, "to quarantine themselves from corporate depredations." [45]

This resistance defies reduction to the usual categories reserved for "snob zoning." Suburban exclusionism persists, and it is a serious problem, but it should be seen for what it is: manipulation of the poor and nonwhites in conflicts between competing property interests in land. Protectionism stretches well beyond the divisions of suburban property, however. Encompassing small-scale agrarian business interests and working-class homeowners as well as middle-class environmentalists, it has given rise to a rich and variegated politics of resistance, one whose target is not just the poor, but a host of large-scale economic projects sponsored by absentee private owners and central development agencies in the public sector.

A Politics of Consumption

Many social scientists have sought common threads in these battles in order to aid our understanding of the underlying unities of opposition politics. A major explanation is that the growth of community resistance reflects the fact that in advanced industrial societies, the key class divisions center not on the Marxian contrast between workers and capitalists but on a new basic cleavage between consumers and producers. In this approach, the intellectual roots of which can be found in the work of Max Weber and Thorstein Veblen, it is the defense of private consumption interests, especially the single-family house, and of collective consumption goods, such as the natural environment, that drives the protests—not the pursuit of production-based class interests. [46]

J. David Greenstone offers a clear example of this perspective. Writing on the evolution of American labor politics, Greenstone observes that "since World War II class conflict between American workers and employers has . . . given way to a new class cleavage between producers and consumers. Producers seek greater economic efficiency, profitability, and growth through the rationalization of production. Consumers . . . insist on protecting the quality of life—as expressed by individual and collective patterns of consumption—against the dislocations that this rationalization can impose." [47] Harry Boyte argues along similar lines that citizen action grows "mainly out of those places in modern society which have not been destroyed by the forces of contemporary life—families, religious groups, civic traditions, ethnic origins, neighborhoods, and so forth." [48] Conspicuously missing from Boyte's list, the consumption theorists would suggest, is the workplace, the one area of life most often found at the cutting edge of economic modernization.

In sharp contrast to the absence of shop-floor militance, the prominence of neighborhood as a springboard of the new citizen activism is exemplified by the dramatic role of women as organizers and leaders of local opposition politics.[49] As feminist scholars argue, females have been structurally positioned by their domestic roles to have permanent watch over neighborhood changes and outside threats. They tend to be the ones, writes Martha Ackelsberg, "who negotiate with landlords, markets, welfare officials, health-care providers, and the like." [50] Women also tend to articulate and represent the household interest to local zoning boards, city officials, and developers; they marshal the forces of resistance, forming the picket lines of angry mothers, trailed by toddlers and waving exclusionary banners.

All these observations strongly suggest that land use protest does not just happen; it is patterned and unified by a particular form of social consciousness, an ideology that identifies interests in terms of where people live and what they own. Community and consumption are its organizing interests, place and property its controlling themes. These factors lay the basis for the spread of what Max Weber called "communal action," action inspired by the "feeling of the actors that they belong together." [51] Ira Katznelson argues that the sources of this community consciousness lie in traditions forged in nineteenth-century American politics. He has shown how the open and decentralized nature of the American political system encouraged workers in the United States to develop a split consciousness on matters of community and work—the idea that labor-related matters should be fought through the agency of trade unions in the factory, whereas community issues are best promoted by civic groups and political parties in the neighborhood. Such distinctions underlie what Katznelson calls the "city trenches" of local political division, trenches that divide worker neighborhoods from one another and that separate the politics of consumption from the politics of production.[52]

Land Conflict as Class Conflict

The division of workplace and community politics does afford an ideological unity to the themes and interests of land use politics. At least most people tend to *think* of these facets of their lives as distinct and separate spheres. But does this mean that class in Marx's sense is largely irrelevant to the politics of land use protest? Some important urban sociologists think so. Peter Saunders, for example, insists that "urban politics have their own specificity with no necessary relation to class politics," at least not where class is defined in terms of relation to the means of production, as here.[53] For Saunders, and others of the urban consumption school, if urban politics can be said to have a class basis at all, it stems from the ownership of consumption property, especially housing. Working from Weber's idea that class relations can be derived not only from positions in the production process but also from power to dispose of significant goods or skills in markets of various types, these theorists contend that homeowners of differentially valued property can be said to have different class interests, interests especially different from those of tenants, who own no property at all. The major conclusion of this perspective is that housing classes unalterably divide the working class, leaving radical hopes for the unity of urban workers permanently frustrated.[54] There are good reasons, however, for doubting the housing class theory.

For one thing, while the divisions within the working class over housing issues are real enough, those divisions are formed by capitalist processes: by the economic boundaries of exclusionary capitalist property rights and by the businesslike desire of workers to use socially produced scarcities of space to gain increased land values.[55] And just as real is the fact that the emergence of housing issues is determined by the capitalist production (and nonproduction) of housing itself. Unquestionably, the dominant factor in housing politics in the United States is the shortage of decent, affordable housing.[56] Lacking profit incentives—including those derived from federal subsidies—to construct homes and apartments for lower-income markets, private builders meet upscale demands instead, fueling the animosities and pressures that lead workers to fight it out for the scarce shelter opportunities that remain. Intra-class housing disputes are promoted by the inter-class reality that housing is a commodity produced by capital for profit. In urban land fights, the organizing formula is: No profit, no housing, plenty of conflict.

This situation suggests an even more basic point about the production-class foundations of land use politics. Although urban protest should certainly be analyzed in the terms supplied by the workers themselves, it must also be analyzed in more than subjective terms. Land use protest is not only a matter of the conscious understandings of the participants; it is also very much a matter of the objective material situation of people and communities. Capitalists, not communities, command the dominant means of land development, the investment resources to determine what gets built, the kinds of technologies that prevail, the economic patterns that give land use its main forms. Because this power is used to ensure that capital accumulation is the chief concern of land use, local resistance to corporate expansion represents, in effect, a challenge to the prerogatives of business. In other words, the political economy itself infuses land use politics with its class character, systematically creating the land use demands that threaten communities, the demands that move working people to resist the outcomes of capitalist processes as well as government decisions that are geared to the logic of accumulation. As Joe Feagin writes, "The conflict over land use and development is a barely hidden class conflict," a battle between those who control the means of development and those who need the tools and products of development to sustain their private and community lives.[57]

We should also note that the very neighborhood feelings of community that inspire land use protest are themselves tied to class forces. Local affections are everywhere imbued with tacit understandings that individuals share not only social backgrounds but also similar incomes and occupations. Their collective situation in the workplace buttresses what Robert and Helen Lynd defined so well as "the long arm of the job." It sets people on an economic par, allowing them to enjoy roughly similar styles of life at home.[58] As their patterns of consumption coincide, along with other deeply felt forces of identity such as race, nationality, religion, language, and regional background, people come to share commitments to the defense of their overlapping social ties, even against other members of their own economic class. The framework of such connections and divisions is not the independence of community relations from the economy, but the way the economy pushes and pulls people of similar class positions into more or less common patterns of living, patterns deeply vulnerable to the giant tides of market forces. Nothing shows this vulnerability more clearly than the corporate demand to use community space for unwanted activities or the corporate decision to abandon a community as an unprofitable site. In Enzo Mingione's words, when it comes to land use conflicts, people oppose "general capitalist reproduction processes to use land in an alternative way."[59]

Even if we set all these reasons aside, there is one more that leaves the consumption theory suspect as an adequate account of the unities of land use politics: not only do battles over land use divide consumers from producers, but they also divide producers themselves along definite economic lines. As a result, some of the most potent political support for local land use control resides in the precincts of small-scale capital.

Small Business and Local Control

In the hierarchy of modern capitalism, small- and medium-scale firms have interests that conflict sharply with those of the largest corporations. In the competitive struggles over markets, labor, raw materials, and profits, the smaller firms of urban and rural capital are desperate to achieve the kind of economic control that comes with bigness. Typically, they find it in politics and public policy. Power in local and state government gives smaller capitalists, in industries such as construction, real estate, and agriculture, the ability to shape critical policies such as zoning, highway construction, and taxation in line with their private plans. Indeed, the very first city to adopt a comprehensive zoning ordinance—New York City in 1916—did so largely at the behest of local merchants agitated over the prospect of having to share valued selling space with dirty textile factories and grubby workers.[60]

For local and regional business interests, influence over key policies and officials comes close to being a force of production itself. "Typically," as James O'Connor points out, "there is a one-to-one relationship between local capital in competitive industries and local power elites."[61] Indeed, this fact has been at the root of hundreds of bitter municipal land use battles between homeowners (who want to increase the value of their houses by making land scarce) and developers (who want to increase the value of their firms by selling ever more houses on ever more land), each side struggling to convert local officials and agencies to adopt their preferred patterns of exclusionary expansion as public policy. But the press of real estate capitalists to control local government is aimed just as much against the interests of other businesses as it is against consumers. The urban land market is a snakepit of rival business groupings.

As Kevin Cox has argued, in many cities the key economic interests are sharply divided between what he calls downtown boosters and suburban property capitalists. Central-city "booster lobbies" typically embrace the main real estate and development companies as well as financial and retailing interests, corporate service businesses such as law and advertising firms, and local elected officials—especially activist big-city mayors, who often play the decisive role in organizing such coalitions, as John Mollenkopf has shown.[62] To protect and enhance central-city land values and company interests, as well as to expedite land clearance for industrial expansion, the downtown boosters, who often include leaders of the most prestigious corporations in America, frequently strive to control—if not altogether exclude—development in the outer reaches of the metropolis. They do this by fighting publicly subsidized utility extensions in the hinterland, opposing zoning variances that permit large-scale suburban construction, and promoting comprehensive urban planning and the centralization of land use controls as ways of holding suburban development in line with the interests of central-city capital.[63]

Suburban property lobbies, frequently led by aggressive young developers, fight for more radical, pro-expansion policies to push suburban growth as far and as wide as the metropolitan economy will allow, and then some. They characteristically insist on liberal zoning policies and variances to allow for extensive development, urban annexations of rural areas, and publicly financed water and sewer line extensions and highway improvements to serve their far-flung projects. Most important, they also tend to oppose comprehensive urban planning because it threatens to limit outward physical expansion.

Moreover, as Cox points out, when the suburban growth coalitions are confined by central-city interests, the former will fight to secede from big cities, establishing smaller political entities whose policies and taxes they can better control and sometimes forming alliances with rural capital against the city. By favoring municipal incorporation of outlying housing developments and the creation of special utility districts that can be financed outside central-city budgetary controls, suburban property capitalists increase the fragmentation of local authority that frustrates centralized corporate coordination.[64]

The Limits of Exclusion

Our survey of the political sociology of land use conflict suggests that the forces opposed to centralization do not come from the consumption sphere alone. We can also find them in the production system, particularly in the fiercely competitive ranks of small business. The relevant political groupings cut across the political spectrum, from left-wing antinuclear activists to right-wing real estate entrepreneurs, and they represent all segments of the social structure, working-class tenants as well as affluent homeowners. Protection and security are the unifying motives here, though the scope and diversity of coalition in any given case will depend heavily on the scale and nature of the targets. Technological issues, as I have suggested, tend to unify people, housing issues to divide them. But in the end, the decisive, strategic question for resisters has to do not so much with the range of their alliances, but rather with whether a politics based on "communal action" at the local level is enough to counteract the kind of massive industrial and political pressure symbolized by the MX missile or nuclear power. Nineteenth-century landowners fared poorly against the claims of expansionist canal and railroad companies when they sought defense in individual lawsuits. Overly reliant on courts to furnish traditional protection, they discovered instead a new legal order that mobilized its collective power for the active interests of capitalist property. Their awakening came late, only after perhaps hundreds of cases, widely scattered and seemingly unrelated, signaled new biases that cut against the grain of protection.

Some theorists of urban political action, such as Manuel Castells, Francis Fox Piven, and Peter Saunders, would argue that such failure is almost inevitable.[65] Local, home-based opposition movements are unlikely to have long-lasting impacts on the basic structure of organized power, for it is the nature of community protest movements not to target the centers of power. The orientation of communal protest is governed by the individual's daily experience in the community, not by the more abstract controls of the central state or the big corporations. People fight to be left alone in their neighborhoods, not to change the society. From this point of view, it is hardly accidental that the national legislative struggles over land use were, as we shall see, dominated by organized business interests, not by the homeowning protestors typical of urban land use politics.

The assumption of this book, however, is that there are differences between long-lived historical patterns and statements about inevitability. We need to remind ourselves of the big, national questions and the big, national powers because, whether we acknowledge them or not, such issues and powers determine the facts of our lives. And likewise, we need to criticize established perspectives when they obstruct comprehension of the factors behind the facts.

In this spirit, contemporary protectionists are wise to remember Barry Commoner's Second Law of Ecology: "Everything must go somewhere," and its corollary: "There is no such thing as waste." [66] Most practitioners of land use control in the United States try to sidestep these simple rules. Battles to keep out the undesirable are hard-fought, whereas little care is given to understanding or to changing the political and economic processes that spew out the hated poisons or cause the poverty in the first place. And just as little sensitivity is shown for the fate of other communities as rejected siters move on to the next test. Excluders too often act as if they believe that anything undesirable is "waste." Philip Slater pointedly calls this attitude the "Toilet Assumption." His words speak volumes about our notions of "land use" and the "other America":

> Our ideas about institutionalizing the aged, psychotic, retarded, and infirm are based on a pattern of thought that we might call the Toilet Assumption—the notion that unwanted matter, unwanted difficulties, unwanted complexities and obstacles will disappear if they are removed from our immediate field of vision. . . . Our approach to social problems is to decrease their visibility: out of sight, out of mind. [67]

But the demands and pressures do not recede. As Max Weber noted years ago, "a wider range of capitalist activity" has usually been associated with "a legal leveling and destruction of firmly established local structures." [68] Political centralization has accompanied economic centralization throughout the industrial capitalist world, though in the United States localism has managed to retain impressive footholds in what Samuel Huntington calls the American Tudor polity. For him, "political modernization in America has been strangely attenuated and incomplete." But he adds that "the centralization of power varies directly with the resistance to change." [69] The proponents of private property and local democracy face a cruel irony: the very success of their resistance accelerates the pressures to remove their rights to resist. But economic conditions themselves may defeat the resisters long before the triumph of centralized reform. Nothing strengthens business more, after all, than a sustained dose of unemployment.

Cutthroat Deregulation

As economic stagnation continues to plague much of the nation, municipalities feel intense pressure to open their gates to expansion—even of the most dangerous types. When communities confront factory shutdowns, job losses, declining revenues, and corporate evacuations, the restrictionist core of land policy becomes increasingly irrelevant. Impoverishment switches the defensive bias of land policy into the offensive mode. Stagnation thrusts communities, states, and regions into what Robert Goodman describes as "a scrambling, clawing, and shoving . . . process" of economic competition for new business locations. "Public entrepreneuring" is the result, "a process in which the public takes enormous financial risks, while business surveys the willing suitors and moves freely to where the public risk-taking is greatest." [70]

The states sell themselves in business journals as if their public environments were products designed especially for company consumption. Corporate siters learn, for example, that Oklahoma is "the profitable place to be," though "entrepreneurs in Kentucky have an edge on the competition," and that "in South Carolina, we believe that profitable business is the goose that lays the golden egg . . . we help the goose feather her nest."

Certainly the most glaring recent example of public nest-building was Detroit's decision to hand a part of itself over to General Motors Corporation. In 1980, after GM announced intentions to close a plant and cut 6,000 jobs along with it, local officials quickly huddled with corporate leaders. Promises were made to do anything within the city's power to keep GM in town. The company responded with plans for a new Cadillac factory. All it would take was a tax and land package of $800 million, which included 465 acres of the Poletown neighborhood, a living multiethnic enclave for 3,000 Detroiters. Within a year the city's powers of eminent domain were swung against Poletown, leveling the residents' homes, churches, and businesses to make way for a plant whose shiny new doors remained shut until 1985, when its use finally became profitable. [71]

Detroit lived up to its name as the "Motor City," but its eagerness to furnish aid and comfort to an expanding business is hardly unique. In at least eighteen states free land is provided to potential employers; half the states finance speculative building; and practically all states encourage their subdivisions to develop industrial park sites for "hi-tech" firms. As a recent headline proclaims, "Everyone's Trying to Start the New 'Silicon Valley.'" [72]

President Reagan's proposal for an "urban enterprise zone" makes a fetish of such competition. Under the plan, federal tax relief would go to businesses locating in selected urban districts. The secretary of housing and urban development "will evaluate the various applications" from cities "on a competitive basis." According to the president, "A key criterion in this competitive process will be the nature of the state and local incentives and their harmony with the overall enterprise zone theme of creating an open market environment by removing government burdens." [73]

Further undermining protectionism is the increasing cooperation between private corporations and local governments to deliver services. According to a recent *New York Times* overview, "City governments across the nation have become so hard-pressed for resources that they are beginning to share much of their authority for governing and development with business and other private interests." In New York City, for example, a recent measure conferred on local merchants the authority to set up special "business improvement districts" under which local entrepreneurs can "get together and agree to assess themselves additional taxes that the city will collect" and then return "to the merchant group to be used for whatever local improvement it chooses." As Mobil Oil reminds us, "Business, generally, is a good neighbor, and most communities recognize this fact." [74]

Some local governments are doing more than conceding authority to business, however. A handful of wealthier cities, such as Boston, New York, San Francisco, and Washington, D.C., noticing the power advantages that flow from their control of desirable land, have begun to link land use policy directly with the pursuit of other social objectives. In these "linkage" strategies, rich cities use land development rights as bargaining chips with business, trading building permission for "exactions" such as funds for low-income housing, child care centers, job training, and parks. Not surprisingly, business has begun to challenge the exactions in court, seeing them as a kind of municipal "public interest extortion" [75] that violates the companies' rights against illegal taxation. Just as important, exactions can work only in affluent cities, with their highly prized real estate markets, and then only for as long as the local economy is rapidly expanding. So, although linkage represents a more enlightened understanding of the connections between land use and social needs than most American cities have historically demonstrated, it remains an approach highly vulnerable to economic declines. In this sense, the long-run capacity of local governments to use land use controls to keep out bad things or to extend good things remains dubious. As the channels to space and opportunity become more clogged, and as stagnation diminishes the number of successful firms prepared to expand, social inequalities and ecological risks increase. In short, the present situation threatens to undermine the few public rights that exist to control economic change.

Sagging Walls

Elite criticisms of local protectionism are not without merit. It is true that the local structures of land use policy are struggling to bear up under the weight of pressures and imperatives for which they are ill prepared and poorly designed. Constructed in an ad hoc manner, patched into municipal governments that are as often as not accidents of political geography, the zoning laws reflect a period when industrial and social pressures were more easily managed by local elites because they were more readily tolerated by workers. Today this apparatus is an anachronism in contrast to giant technology and centralized power. Our society needs more than local controls if it is to appraise and regulate economic change with a view to general interests. Moreover, local defenders should not expect that the United States Supreme Court's 1926 affirmation of zoning will hold forever. Even at that early date the Court was not insensitive to instances where "the general public interest would so far outweigh the interest of the municipality that the municipality would not be allowed to stand in the way." [76] Commenting on this important reservation, Alfred Bettman, a key figure in the history of zoning, observed: "This passage is noteworthy in that it presents the conflict not as one between the individual and the community, but rather as between different communities, different social groups, or social interests." [77]

Bettman perceived that although land use conflicts might erupt in local arenas, their causes were embedded in the broad fabric of socioeconomic relationships. "Land use," after all, is a basic expression of systemic power; it lies at the crossing point of fundamental social patterns. Capitalist production, government investment, private consumption, and public housekeeping all find their nexus in land use. Land use is, in fact, a cool, technocratic euphemism for the organization and production of our entire existence. [78] In effect, we ask our local zoning systems to address every conceivable type of social conflict and contradiction on the simple presumption that they share the common thread of human needs for space. When observed from this angle, our land use policy seems like an astonishing oversimplification.

Resting on the proposition that every clash over land can be reduced to a locational common denominator, the land use policy nonsystem assumes the inevitability of rising demands on community resources and the right of business to set the agenda of change. Though it is fundamental to the politics of land use, however, few students of the subject have bothered to probe the implications of the role of business behind the steering wheel of investment. Most land use scholars tend to take it for granted that the scales of development and ecological threat are great and growing, the natural results of inexorable technological change and a growing economy. The industrial machine is behind it all. But behind the machine is a specific social structure of business motives, corporate controls, and private powers. These are not neutral but political facts. By accepting them without question, land use analysts sully their claims to scholarly objectivity. Implicitly, their work tends to center around the search for methods to rationalize the control of land and people with business imperatives. Only in the legal literature—where it is expected that sides will be taken—is the pro-investment bias openly proclaimed as the starting point of analysis. A recent overview of zoning law, for example, notes: "One of the most widely acknowledged ends of property law is the maximization of production and efficient management of property resources." Thus private property and, by extension, the land use defense system deserve "that measure of security . . . necessary to promote production." [79]

The battles for land use control cannot be thoroughly appraised unless such assumptions are made explicit and their implications clearly stated. Otherwise we fall into the conventional trap of focusing on the excluders while leaving the forces of expansion unexamined. It is, in short, necessary to understand the offense as well as the defense in the fight for land use powers.

Making Room for Business

So far in this chapter we have considered the power of capital in terms of its control of the means of production and of the forces of development. But this is not enough. To understand how the politics of land use developed through time and why the situation seems to be changing once again now, we must see that capital is not really capital until it moves, until it circulates and recirculates through the systems of production and exchange, until it accumulates profit and expands.

For capitalism, change is imperative. Its whole point is to profit from what Marx termed the "constant revolutionizing of production." Joseph Schumpeter said it even more plainly when he wrote that the "process of Creative Destruction is the essential fact about capitalism." [80] The reason is basic: the worst fear of any entrepreneur or manager is to be economically outgunned by the competition. To lose out in the race for markets and profits is not only to sacrifice status in the commercial prestige system, but it is also to come face to face with the real devaluation or loss of investment property. [81] Competition delivers strong incentives to increase technological innovation as the surest route to growth. The more capitalists recognize and respond to this logic, and the more fervently they answer pressures to accelerate the development of their forces of production, the faster the velocity of capital becomes, and the wider its geographic scope and sweep. For to diminish the circulation time of capital while increasing its spread across the landscape is, as David Harvey writes, "to increase both the sum of values produced and the rate of profit." This is why George Gilder calls capitalism "the kinetic economy." [82]

But keeping up with capital is no easy chore, for change unsettles everything. Industries, communities, products, skills, property values—all rise and fall depending on the collisions of supply and demand. They are, after all, the objects and tools of accumulation, not its end. Their survival is contingent, whereas only capitalism as a system seems necessary. Perpetual change in land use is a regular feature of this process—thus the constant digging and gouging of the earth, the demolition of still-useful buildings, the construction of new and unnecessary ones, the waste of sound structures, the familiar patterns of uneven development, all brought on by the lure of profit and the fear of loss.

For capitalism, no amount of land is ever enough; physical supplies are secondary. What counts is the ability to see the outlines of industrial change ahead and to anticipate its geographic consequences. Everything depends on the social relation between land and economic change, on "location, location, location," and the speed to beat the crowd to the next real estate gusher. "The successful operators in evaluating land," writes Dana Thomas, "can see beyond the use to which it is put at the moment and realize its vast potential. The current worth of land might be meager, but if it can be developed in such a way as to change its employment dramatically, its value can be revolutionized." In the words of land mogul William Zeckendorf, "I make grapefruit out of lemons." [83] In other words, competition in the land of business is directly linked to the powerful forces of creative destruction in industry.

Land speculation and real estate trading clear paths for development: opening new sites, altering old ones, reconfiguring the landscape for accumulation. Thus real estate moguls scratch at the changing land market for the "best diamonds in the city," the sites where new capital can be produced and exchanged most profitably. Inevitably, they overlook acres of bombed-out space a few miles away because "there's no money in it." The tiniest slivers of space in desirable locales get built up, while the homeless wander through valleys carved between the skyscrapers, reassured by economists that "the physical supply of space—of land—is independent of human beings." [84]

But space is not a given; it is made. When people build their environments and mark boundaries, they make space as well as fill it. By constructing and defining claims to space, by specifying who is in and who is out, the producers of space both reflect and distribute power over land and people. Space making, in short, is an altogether human process, a fundamental means of organizing people, power, and places. [85]

The recent battles for land use control need to be seen within the greater context of capitalism's unrelievable hunger for space, its fundamental denial that land has any "intrinsic value" or that it is anything more than the "standing room needed—for the continued operation of machinery, improvements, fertility, laborers, managers, or markets." [86] For despite the conventional understanding of private property as a system of fixed and settled boundaries, the requirements of capitalism are more radical. Capitalism embraces property, not as a permanent barrier frozen into the soil by law, but only as a temporary limit, to be put up or knocked down depending on the needs of expanding production.

Most property shifts, of course, occur painlessly. A vast real estate market is relied on to move rights around. Nearly 10 percent of the national income is wrapped up in land trading. Real estate brokerage is the country's largest single occupation—we have more land traders in America than school-teachers. And as Thorstein Veblen once noted, most of the nation's "municipal affairs . . . coverge upon its real estate values . . . [the] enterprise in 'futures' designed to get something for nothing from the unwary, of whom it is said that 'there is one born every minute.'"[87]

As we have seen, however, land markets do not meet all of the needs of business. Property owners can be ornery people: sometimes they hold out. And ever since the advent of zoning, landowners have developed ever more sophisticated tools to restrict supply. From corporate perspectives, zoning often turns out to be the sabotage of space production. With the recent outpouring of environmental conservation laws, this sabotage threatens to spread outward to include whole regions. As one observer sees it, the development of regional and statewide environmental policies "is a principal element in current feudal tenure trends."[88]

If capital is to keep moving and creatively destroying, such trends must be bucked. Private and public rights to self-protection must be hedged. The market mechanism, after all, is a pushy thing. But when it lacks the strength to budge the obstreperous, government is invited to lend its assistance. That is, government's role in capitalist systems is far from limited to the protection of property rights against assaults from the impoverished. The really ticklish issues involve policing the propertied. How, for example, is the defense of property to be maintained when capitalism is in endless need of Lebensraum? Or, to put the question as it is usually posed in the higher circles, how is the developer to get room for progress if landowners are opposed to progress?

When rights conflict over the same space, and they often do, rights have to be redefined. Judges and legislators must make hard and solemn judgments about the arrangement of furniture inside the shrine of private property. Space must be preserved or remade. Someone must be pushed aside or kept out. Legal claims must be guaranteed and broken. In capitalist systems, governments reserve the ultimate power to settle boundaries or to destroy them; to make, remake, and organize space; and to establish the procedures for resolving such questions. From the policy maker's perspective, as from the business owner's, the system of private borders is expedient, what Nicos Poulantzas calls a series of "limits capable of being moved along a . . . discontinuous loom which everywhere fixes insides and outsides." Without this power to work for and against property, private revolutions in economic activity and technology would be blocked.[89] Thus capitalist governments must have great leeway in reconciling the conflicting forces of exclusion and expansion.

Of course, except for exceptional remakings such as the Poletown case, most of this fixing never gets beyond a local headline. It happens in the matter-of-fact evolution of law, or in the jungle of the zoning system. Only the law journals keep track of the twists and turns inside property. But over time, historical contours are formed, expectations are shaped, and the corporate train moves, sometimes slower, sometimes faster. Today the train seems unable to keep on track. Policy engineers call for the laying of new rails. As the society debates a new "competitiveness" policy it would be useful to get the legal lay of the land, to trace out the broader patterns of land use policy. To see what industry has in store for rights of private property and community protection, it is important to check the record of past accomplishment and ever-present need. The following two chapters explore these themes.

History, Property, and Law 2

It is . . . precisely in the development of landed property that the gradual victory and formation of capital can be studied.

Karl Marx

There needs no insistence or illustration to gain assent to the proposition that the habit of holding private property inviolate is traversed by the other habit of seeking wealth for the good repute to be gained through its conspicuous consumption. Most offenses against property, especially offenses of an appreciable magnitude, come under this head.

Thorstein Veblen

The politics of land are nothing new in American development. The politics of land use control are something else again. Throughout the nation's history issues of ownership and control have divided land interests from the government, banks and big corporations. Today such questions seem archaic; only faint echoes are heard rebounding off the courthouse steps when another small farm is foreclosed or when Indians press to have old scores settled. Even the recent "sagebrush rebellion"—the move of western states to reassume control of the federal lands inside their borders—was short-lived. For us, land politics does not focus very clearly on who owns the land and what this means for economic power; it is concerned with which level of government shall regulate owners and the implications for growth and community-protection rights. Although the issues have shifted a long way, they have moved along a common fault line. The issues of land politics have been routed across the path of American development through the institution and law of private property, pressed and pulled by the forces of exclusion and expansion.

But why did the themes of land politics change? Why were connections between land and private power replaced by debates over the rightful place of public land use regulation? In what ways, perhaps, have the old questions reappeared in new guises? How have the institution and the law of private property narrowed the scope of land use conflict? This chapter will suggest some answers by outlining the ways in which history, property, and law are implicated in the structuring of modern controversies over land use control.

We begin with a brief outline of the historical changes in land conflict. The main focus here is on the ideological and social shifts from the production-based politics of land, which typified nineteenth-century agrarianism, to the consumption focus of modern metropolitan exclusion. Changes in the power implications of landownership were blunted ideologically by the spread of homeownership, the main vehicle for establishing a mass, working-class property interest seemingly outside the production system, breaking the tie between stakes in ownership and power over the means of production. But expansion also led to more restriction, as the spread of worker housing and community-protection interests vastly increased the exclusionary pressures within the political economy. In keeping the working class in line, government and corporate policies in housing gave workers a line to defend. Worker ownership was a fine solution to class tensions from the standpoint of legitimacy; but it contained the makings of a new, land-based barrier to accumulation and expansion. Moreover, it intensified demands on the law to keep the contending interests battling around the line of private interests in exclusion and expansion. This issue opens the other main theme of the chapter—the displacement of property contradictions into contradictions of legal theory.

The modern contradictions of land use conflict are largely contained by the legal system. Despite big changes in the organization, power, and ideology of the main contestants, traditional legal approaches were conserved, even as the government's regulatory powers were enlarged. The key is that strict adherence to the rule of law has always been irrelevant in the adjusting of land use rights; it would never do here, for the demands are much too contradictory and have to be met by letting the law say "stop"in some cases and "go" in others. Double-dealing is mandatory when the rights of property cut two ways at once. This is the hidden story of the land use law. Just as important, the law's technicalities and ambiguities give the legal system much-needed autonomy. It frees the legal experts to work out the tensions in ways that reflect class realities without invoking class interests. The law, in short, is government's first line of defense in meeting the internal crises of capitalist property.

A Troubled Marriage:
Capital Against Land

Contemporary demands to centralize controls over land use, or to refine the means of exclusion, invoke classic themes in new garb. In the words of Charles Abrams, "As our society evolved the contrast between industry and land grew more and more vivid. The cultural and economic gap between them widened and deepened with the passing years." Thus, Abrams concluded in 1939, "land and industry still occupy opposing camps." [1]

The contest between landed property and capital is both a historic truth and a contemporary fact; but it is a theme not much given to serious discussion.

The real estate page covers a multitude of sins. Land merchants promise that ownership is "the poor man's joy and comfort, the rich man's prize, the right hand of capital, the silent partner of many thousands of successful men." Free trade in the soil unites us, for America is a "nation made free and great by men and women who . . . like you . . . believe in the stronghold of enterprise . . . real estate."[2] But the land market never crowds us. Indeed, where else but the real estate page is the national penchant for "absolute privacy" and "total security" so amply supplied? There is no dissonance in the weekly songs to landownership.

But conflicts are pervasive; they commence when new neighbors arrive, when someone or something moves next door whose presence lowers the upward trajectory of land values, or worse, threatens the local health. At this all too familiar juncture, homeowners have second thoughts about "enterprise"; they start building walls. The battles of location begin anew, driven by local rights to exclude and corporate rights to expand. But the sundry struggles of location are really nothing new. They are merely up-to-date examples of a long, troubled marriage between land interests and capitalists.

Landlords, Peasants, and Capitalists

Five centuries ago, at the dawn of capitalism, English nobles began to work up a keen thirst for the profits of wool production. Eager to join an expanding international market for textiles, they wanted to capitalize on their land. The trouble was that their property was not yet their capital. Earlier centuries endowed the soil with a feudal stamp. Peasants shared with their lords many useful rights to common land. But with the appearance of new market opportunities, the old ties and obligations seemed irrational. Peasants were in the way of profits. The question became one of sheep or people, and the people lost. Enclosures—agricultural fence-building on a massive scale— were an early sign that serfs made poor students of avant-garde economics.[3] As Marx explained sometime later, land did not slip easily into the grasp of merchants and entrepreneurs. Those backward enough to claim traditional property rights had to be "dragged," screaming and kicking, into the businesslike "movement of private property." Peasants could not help but ask silly questions: How, they wondered, could land move? Such is "the idiocy of rural life."[4]

Marx's insights into the difficult early relations of landowners and business were anything but startling in the sophisticated world of nineteenth-century political economy. Adam Smith, David Ricardo, and John Stuart Mill—commercial thinkers all—gave Marx high-toned instruction in the frictions of industry and real estate.

Adam Smith pointed the way to the awkward coupling of land and capital when he explained that while landlords and laborers had economic interests in common with the public, manufacturers did not. For, whereas rents and wages tended to grow with increased output, industrial prices declined with abundant supplies. Manufacturers had a natural interest in widening the market and excluding the competition. Indeed, for Smith, their class interest was "to deceive and even oppress the public," including the landlords. Moreover, Smith warned, entrepreneurs were likely to prove highly skilled at this game. Their intimate understanding of production and market conditions gave them "superior knowledge of their own interest." Workers were too busy laboring to keep up with the main economic and political currents. And landlords were indolent rentiers, whose lucky control of a monopoly resource not only allowed them to extract wealth from the landless, but also rendered them "too often, not only ignorant, but incapable of that application of mind which is necessary to foresee and understand" the connections between their class interests and "public regulation." Smith cautioned landlords and laborers to beware of entrepreneurs bearing policy suggestions. "The proposal of any new law or regulation of commerce which comes from this order, ought always to be listened to with great precaution, and ought never to be adopted till after having been long and carefully examined, not only with the most scrupulous, but with the most suspicious attention."[5]

David Ricardo replied that Adam Smith's finger pointed at the wrong villain. The landlords, not capitalists, were the social predators. Having done nothing to create the "original and indestructible powers" of land, they extorted unjust rents from its control. For Ricardo, landlords savaged the prospects of economic progress. They boosted charges on lands of declining fertility and then compounded the punishment by using their political power to exclude imports of foreign corn. Far from being ignorant of political economic realities, the landlords were past masters of the "narrow competition." They stemmed the growth of British capital by forcing workers to demand higher wages in order to pay food prices inflated by agricultural protectionism. The cash-hungry lords had to be put in their place—outside the industrial class struggle. The business class, strongly supported by Ricardo and his colleagues among the mature political economists, fought to break the hold of the "rotten boroughs" and expand suffrage rights in the middle classes. When enough political influence was mustered in 1846, the ports of England were forced open and the landlords were compelled to feel the first flushes of competition.[6]

Although the great landlords remained at the helm of British politics, the engines of the society were reliably in capitalist hands. John Stuart Mill reminded the proprietors to behave well, however, or the pain of the abolition of the corn laws would seem trivial compared with what might befall them if they got in the way again. "No exclusive right should be permitted in any individual, which cannot be shown to be productive of public good," wrote the author of *On Liberty*. "The claim of the landowners to the land is altogether subordinate to the general policy of the state."[7]

Karl Marx glanced over from the German Left and put the battle in context. "Rent of land is conservative," he surmised, whereas "profit is progressive. Rent of land is national, profit is cosmo-political; rent of land believes in the State Church, profit is a dissenter by birth."[8] Later, in volume 3 of *Capital*, Marx took a longer look, but he arrived at the same conclusion: in landownership business "meets an alien force which it can but partially or not at all overcome, and which limits its investment in certain spheres."[9] Marx predicted that the business class would manifest its impatience with exorbitant rents by buying up the land. A shrewd strategy, to be sure, but in a nation as large as the United States not even the Fortune 500 are in a position to purchase the national estate. Besides, landownership can be a drain on profits. Mortgage interest and tax payments are costs best left to those who cannot afford the more lucrative investments in industry. Unless sites are carefully chosen or they harbor precious resources, landownership is a relatively unproductive source of capital. Ultimately, then, the problem of the obstructive landlords would have to be dealt with as a more selective problem of power on the terrain of politics.

Land Versus Capital in American Development

The animus against landholders was not foreign to the United States, although it took somewhat different forms here. In America rent was nothing like the problem it turned out to be in Europe. As David Ricardo observed, in a new country, featuring "an abundance of rich and fertile land . . . there will be no rent."[10] But surplus, too, made villains out of the landholders: it seemed they could do nothing right.

America was labor-short, observed Secretary of the Treasury Richard Rush in 1827. This shortage increased capital costs and blunted America's already dull competitive edge in world markets. Abundant land considerably worsened the problem by encouraging the flight of labor into the country. Workers wanted land to secure their independence, not to enable them to become an idle landlord class, but they were strongly urged not to vote with their feet. Rush pleaded that it was wiser to "increase capital" than to increase the mere "means of subsistence." When workers failed to be persuaded, the Treasury Department, then in control of the sales of public land, suggested that they be denied the choice. The reason, like Jefferson's rights, was self-evident:

> It is a proposition too plain to require elucidation, that the creation of capital is retarded, rather than accelerated by the diffusion of a thin population over a great surface of the soil. Anything that may tend to hold back this tendency to diffusion from running too far, and too long, into an extreme, can scarcely prove otherwise than salutary.[11]

Attempts were made "to hold back" the agrarian tide. Land surveys were delayed and government real estate prices kept disproportionately high. But as President John Quincy Adams was finally forced to admit, the "system of [land] administration . . . failed."[12] Historian Frederick Jackson Turner offered a reason; for him, too, the answer was "plain": "A system of administration was not what the West demanded, it wanted land."[13] Indeed, as every schoolchild knows, the nation's early pioneers were a rebellious bunch: they paid land taxes only with reluctance, and their contempt for authority is legendary. Mortgage bankers, land speculators, and the federal government were perennial targets of agrarian resistance.[14] One statistic is especially telling: despite—or rather because of—the nation's conservative land-disposal policies, percentages ranging upward from "one-half to two-thirds of the settlers in any new region were normally 'squatters'"—illegal "takers" of the public wealth.[15] Anyone who neglects to recall that "free land" did not become national policy until 1862—when Republicans needed something to inflame western patriotism—fails to appreciate the roots of western scorn at public fences.

In the United States, however, the struggles between land and capital have been kept well within limits faithful to free enterprise. From time to time, though, threats of concentrated landownership have ignited temporary bursts of indignation and resistance; numerous agrarian rebellions dot early American history. But even as late as the 1830s an English-born reformer, George Henry Evans, tried to organize workers nationally on the basis of land reform.[16] Evans was keenly sensitive to the main drift of market forces. He knew that over the long haul commerce and industry would tear people off the land unless restrictions were carefully placed on its alienation. When he demanded that small-scale tenures be secured by entails on public-land grants, that is, restrictions on future rights of sale, the House Committee on Public Lands shot back the more popular view:

> The true and liberal policy of the government is to entertain no projects of agrarianism . . . [but] to treat all men as of equal right of acquisition and of alienation, to unshackle the titles and conveyance of land from all ancient feudal embarrassments, and trust to the rivalships of intelligence, industry and enterprise, in a fair field of competition.[17]

As Thorstein Veblen once so aptly commented, American farmers give their "unwavering loyalty to the system." They never stop dreaming of the day when they might "take [their] due place among the absentee owners of the land and so come in for an easy livelihood at the cost of the rest of the community."[18] But the farmer is no lonely champion of real estate; the urbanite too dreams in green. When America's arch foe of land speculation, Henry

George, excoriated the grabbers of unearned increment—he borrowed the phrase from John Stuart Mill—a loyal following rallied to his single-tax cause. George, in fact, almost rode the land reform wave right into New York's city hall.[19] But the city's voters, urged on by Tammany Hall, lusted for land more than for reform. "The Georgian critique," concludes one economist, "has never been quite respectable" in America.[20] But then no society, not even the most sober and businesslike nation, closes all outlets to its passions. Land speculation is the intoxicant of American enterprise.

The Twin Meanings of Property

Contemporary land use battles thus carry a double load of historical freight. Part of it falls on the side of enduring suspicions that divide landowners and capitalists, suspicions that each side is really committed to a kind of property and progress inimical to the goals of the other. The rest of the load drops on the side of a solid consensus that favors the right to profit. Undoubtedly, this is the weightier freight. Only a fool would deny that a long-standing bridge runs between capitalism and populism in America. Allen Tate put it well, back in the 1930s: "If there is a contest between property and non-property—between real private property, as the average American understands it, and collectivism, the small owner will come to the support of the big corporation. And this is what the big corporation is using every means to make the small owner do."[21] The problem, though, is that the meaning of the term "real private property" is not as clear as Tate's comment suggests.

When the English bourgeoisie demanded landed property in the seventeenth and eighteenth centuries, they were standing against feudal exploitation by the landlord class. Their calls for private property rights were linked to revolutionary claims for a new system of liberty in production and politics. And when American farmers fought for land in the nineteenth century, it was for land as productive property, for agrarians understood that with this property came the ability to influence the material and cultural direction of the society. Like the liberal opponents of the English aristocracy, American farmers saw that social power flows from the control of productive property, for the forces and instruments of production are the essential means of creating social life. Jefferson knew this, as did Hobbes and Locke, and so they made property rights the cornerstone of modern liberalism. Karl Marx was dangerous only because he applied the same critical bite to the new monopolizers of industrial capital, extending the liberal theory of productive property on behalf of the working class. Marx made the case for social ownership of the means of production. It was working, industrial property that captivated all these writers, property in the form of raw materials, machinery, and labor that would determine the economic structure of society. To the extent that control of this property was seen by farmers as the fundamental political issue—and land *was* the key factor of production in the early U.S. economy—farmers could at least be said to have taken on a central issue of their time.

Today, though, if landownership is not widely seen as a matter of power, and land issues are not regarded as problems of leverage over the larger drift and direction of social relationships, this is largely because property ownership no longer means to most of us what it once meant to the early rebels of English and American liberalism.

Part of the reason is itself economic; land simply no longer occupies the core economic position it did in early capitalism. As Herbert Marcuse has argued, to the extent that technological development is today's key to economic expansion, "political power" over the direction of society "asserts itself through its power over the machine process," [22] not the control of land. When capitalist accumulation displaced land—first with labor, then with technology—it virtually transformed the ways in which property, especially landed property, could become an object of social dispute. The social meanings of land were changed, as was its place on the public agenda. The growth of modern consumer capitalism, the spread of gigantically productive technologies, and the promotion of government programs designed to industrialize agriculture and spread homeownership—all have helped to turn the United States from a nation of land producers into a society of land consumers. One federal government report celebrated the dominant trend in 1919 when it observed that "true access to land is achieved only through industrial processes. . . . Mere living in the country will not make a living." [23] The long history of removing people from the soil, begun in the sixteenth century, has nearly run its course in the United States. Only a handful of citizens feed 230 million others. For most of us, land has become a matter of the use of space, not the production of life.

The Emergence of Consumption Property

Today, landownership and property ownership are symbols of status, playing fields for consumption, and objects of investment that frame single-family homeownership. They have become instruments of leisure rather than means of industrial power. Although women continue to experience the home as a workplace (for, despite the increasing prominence of women in the work force, most men still look to their wives to keep up the house) and although increasing numbers of people regularly work for pay at home, these realities are not well reflected in popular understandings and advertised images. For most people, property has become an icon of leisure and play. Thorstein Veblen caught this change brilliantly when he observed that the dominant class of early twentieth-century America was beginning to present itself as a "leisure class," a class whose privilege seemed to come from the avoidance of work, not its control.[24]

Following Marx, but within a later American context, Veblen was impressed at the ideological ability of the business system to separate the mass of the population from control of productive property, on the one hand, by reconnecting property with leisure, on the other.[25] Given the classic Jeffersonian traditions of the culture, it was a remarkable achievement: the more that individuals were structurally compelled to work on other people's property as a condition of their survival, the less they thought of property as a matter of survival.

With "the theory of the leisure class" as his clue to the new consumer culture, Veblen mapped a basic split in the American consciousness of property. The old notion of working property would come to be identified with an amorphous abstraction called "industry," a term that loosely and anonymously reflected vague understandings that the good things of life had to be made somewhere, by someone. The new notion of property, by contrast, referred to the goods of the house, goods that were essentially useless from a serious industrial viewpoint, although they were closely and personally owned.[26] "Industry" was not itself "property," not in any meaningful personal sense; and the property that most people wanted was not industrial in the old liberal sense. Through the arts and science of selling, modern capitalist industry turned private property into a distinctively "homely" institution. In the process, the national concept of working property was converted into its opposite.

When Veblen discovered the new order of the "leisure class," he realized that the popular understanding of property had been stripped of its subversive character. Absentee industrial ownership was rendered secure as the property of conspicuous consumption became identified with property in general. Private property was now a matter of individual claims to personal possessions, socially produced to engender feelings of privilege without conferring real power.

The equation of consumption and production property took the radical sting out of property rights issues. But at the same time, workers were not conspiratorially fooled into confusing a true notion of property with a false one. Consumption rights to shelter are not trivial, and wanting a decent place to live is hardly a sign of "false consciousness." Matthew Edel and his colleagues are right to insist that labor's late-nineteenth-century struggle for owner-occupied housing was necessary and reasonable, given the state of squalor within which workers lived and the paucity of alternative housing proposals from the Left.[27] A critical analysis of worker property interests does not necessarily warrant the belief that the working class was simply manipulated on housing issues.[28] But it does require that we attempt to understand how historical changes in the organization of work and the structure of class relations, changes that reflected the direct power of business to establish the conditions of labor and consumption, helped to diffuse nonsubversive property rights, thus solidifying the exclusionary perspective as the popular focal point of land use politics. In this process, the emergence of a new middle class could not have been more important: it broadened the spread of the domestic property interest, gave labor an image of social opportunity in proximity to its own experience, and opened pathways to a qualitatively better life for many workers within the system.

Changes in the Structure of Work and Class

The big ideological change in conceptions of property did not happen spontaneously, nor did it happen purely in the realm of ideology. It was directly linked, at the end of the nineteenth century, to the rationalization and bureaucratization of modern corporate capitalism, to its increasingly planned and systematic character and its rearrangement of internal work relationships. In this period, jobs, formerly controlled by the workers, were now reorganized by capital into hierarchies of finely graded skill, authority, and power. Income differences within the working class multiplied as business pitted workers of different racial and ethnic groups and different skill levels against one another.[29] As rights to organize the work process were confiscated from labor, business added new levels of technical, administrative, and supervisory personnel to design and oversee production. A vast new sales staff was called into being to market the consumer goods of advancing capitalism. These occupations, which required a greater knowledge of business administration and advanced technology, formed the basis of the new middle class, a group that filled an extremely contradictory niche in the emerging social structure of modern capitalism.[30]

On the one hand, the new middle class was akin to labor in that it embraced people who were separated from direct ownership of the means of production; the two groups shared a fundamental lack of power to influence basic investment and production decisions. In this sense, the new middle class was very different from the old independent middle class, whose members owned production property. On the other hand, however, the new middle class included people whose "primary function [was] to sustain the profits of the firm and to exercise social control of, and over, the workforce."[31] This function gave middle-class employees the organizational position to dominate workers and the income to purchase superior housing, more land, and other symbols of higher prestige. Situated between the shop floor and the top ranks of corporate power, the middle class experienced the pull of interests in two social directions at once. With labor, the new class had an interest in increasing the democratization of production and investment; but with capital, the new class enjoyed the perquisites of status and wealth that came from a position higher than that of production-line workers. Property proved a stronger lure than democracy. Ownership of domestic property stabilized and conservatized the middle class politically, settling it into a strongly defensive posture on community development issues. Domestic property gave the middle class a compass with which to chart its political direction and turned it into a major force of exclusion in American life. In the politics of housing and land use, middle-class patterns became a model for working-class aspiration and behavior.

Clearly, the modern relations of capitalist production are anything but simple. For the purposes of this analysis, however, the most important point about the new gradations is not so much where we choose to draw the line between workers and middle-class people, a line the position and rationale of which theorists of class have tirelessly debated;[32] rather, the main point is that the gradations are reproduced and extended within the capitalist system of production itself. They are indivisibly linked with the spread of exclusionary property rights and help to form a growing base of social fragmentation and social alienation. In other words, as the expansion-exclusion thesis suggests, capitalism expanded by dividing, separating, and excluding people from one another, along many social lines, most profoundly those of class. But just as important, by grasping the ideological fusion of domestic and industrial property, we can also see how capital united all the members of the society in common allegiance to the value of undifferentiated private property. Or, to put the same point somewhat differently, we can now see how the ideological separations of workplace and community, noted in chapter 1, are tied to the ideological unities of property, how the erosion of distinctions between consumption and production property helped to turn working- and middle-class people into owners of exclusionary property rights against the industrial projects of capital.

For all these reasons, the old issues of land economics and land-based power resurfaced at the borders of the household. Rents and land reform were replaced by mortgage interest rates and property taxes as the popular themes, just as tax rebels have replaced squatters in the unruly traditions of American land politics. The only issue remaining constant in the landowners' struggles with capital is exclusion itself. To understand this is to see how property, and especially landed property, continues to have implications, albeit muted ones, within the centralized system of corporate and governmental power.

The Enduring Significance of Land

For the production system at large, land remains a vital, if subordinate, ingredient in the work of society. The social industrial workshop cannot expand without space. The drive of capital to "nestle everywhere, settle everywhere, establish connections everywhere" rarely abates. Indeed, the growth of capitalism as an integrated industrial system, elbowing out across huge, interconnected metropolitan centers, places high premiums on well-located sites. Paradoxically, whereas land no longer focuses the politics of production and class, it remains the one industrially relevant resource—aside from labor itself—still in the hands of a population otherwise disconnected from the means to control industry. John Kenneth Galbraith is right: the control of labor or land accords no reciprocal power to command capital. But like labor, which can strike, the controllers of land restrict capital by refusing its cravings for space.[33]

When corporate capitalism produced the house as a target of production and sales, it also reproduced ancient ties between people and land in new commodified forms. Numerous vested interests were created along with the high-consumption economy. The more that goods and values were unloaded into the house, and the more that the house and community became vehicles of expanding production, the more important it became to isolate the sphere of consumption as a separate aspect of life, walled against society and thus against industry itself. But it should never be forgotten that this boundary exists within the very production system itself, for the house, its equipment, and its cultural meanings are all manufactured in more or less direct compliance with business necessity and salesmanship.

Inevitably, though, the human meanings of residence, consumption, and community membership are much more than the manipulated variables of corporate advertisers. People resist reduction to the one-dimensional status of commodity. They continue to take themselves and their places seriously. They can still reflect on and seek to control the wider forces at work in the industrial system, especially where these represent direct incursions on local ground. The motives repeatedly celebrated on the real estate pages are interwoven with prebourgeois and petty bourgeois values, values that stress permanence in people's relations with their community, their family, God, and the land, values that were cherished long before the advent of *House and Garden*. And as these meanings are themselves portrayed in commercial appeals, as corporations bank on the past to sell the future, the economic system paves the way for its own internal resistance; it generates friction along with markets.[34]

Today's battles for land use control illustrate what has always been true: the community itself is an instrument of production precisely because it is the very framework or matrix of production. Insofar as communities say no to corporate-state expansion plans, then, they are disruptive forces within the general scheme of social production. Counter moves to rationalize and centralize land use controls are, in their essence, efforts to de-institutionalize, or de-represent, landed property and community politics as potent means of resistance within the capitalist system. Community land use controls are seen from top-level corporate and intellectual perspectives as outmoded boundaries that must be redesigned to allow for continued economic progress. Robert Reich, for example, looks forward to "completing" a "transformation" in which "business enterprises are rapidly becoming the central mediating structures in American society, replacing geographic communities as the locus of social services and, indeed, social life." Current celebrations of the Japanese model of "cooperative" industrial relations—a model that depends heavily on the weakness or the lack of trade unions—and the recent expansion of home-based contract labor—a tendency that capitalizes on the profit potential of female labor that has been historically exploited in the form of unpaid household work—are suggestive clues to this looming "transformation" of the geography of work and residence.[35] Thus the stakes of modern-day battles for power to control land use should be seen in the widest social context, for they involve nothing less than the meanings of community itself amid larger corporate tendencies to convert work and residence into mutually reinforcing production sites within more efficient business networks.

David Noble states the issue well: "Empowered by the second Industrial Revolution, capital is moving decisively now to enlarge and to consolidate the social dominance it secured in the first." But Noble overstates the case when he laments that "only one side" in this struggle "is armed."[36] Capital does control the direction and momentum of technology, but homeowners, farmers, small businesses, and conservationists are dug in throughout the nation. For these diverse segments of society, land and the power to control it, and private property and the means to protect it, still mean the right of citizens to defend themselves against total incorporation by advanced industrial society. For all the changes in the structure and themes of property, the basic double-sided form of property continues to control the social and political relations of land and capital. Even more, private property remains the master institution for the organization of economic activity in capitalist society: it still frames the pressures of expansion and the limits of exclusion. Thus, in addition to understanding how historical distinctions between consumption and production have complicated the social understanding of property, we also need to understand how their fusion within the general legal institution of private property continues to order and disorder the conflicting interests of land use.

Private Property and Private Power

In America social change is accomplished or resisted largely through the legal machinery of private property. Much more than a set of rights to things people own, private property is a critical social control, a basic source of power in the dynamics of change. Except for the state, no other institution rivals its influence in promoting and limiting national directions. Property gives capitalists the legal power to wage wars of creative destruction in the marketplace, and it supplies landowners with the right to fend off intruders with the aid of the courts. In a fundamental sense, the limits, needs, and rights of property are the organizing themes of battles for land use control. The laws of property tend to define the legitimate interests of land use as those of proprietorship. Thus the whole system of land use adjudication is weighted in favor of private outlooks and exclusive stakes.

Property is the great informal qualifier for participation in land use politics. But then it is also the great informal disqualifier: its immense social prestige stigmatizes the propertyless and demeans the worth of their noncommercial claims. Occupation and use of space are physical conditions of human existence, but the needs to satisfy these minimum daily requirements carry no guarantees where space is divided into private parcels. The propertyless are expected to find their way through a social maze bounded by private walls. And even where public claims are identified and pursued, as in recent efforts to assert environmental and low-income-housing interests, the structure of law and society forces public advocates to show cause why property rights must be restrained. Nonproprietors are rarely given the benefit of the doubt. And where community laws have supplanted individual rights as the main ramparts of private economic power over land, political membership has merely been added to ownership as a way of narrowing the scope of potential conflict. Nonresidents, even where they speak in the name of property interests (power-plant builders and low-income-housing developers are good examples), encounter difficult trials in trying to crack legal biases thrown up against outsiders.[37]

Property, then, is the dominant power in land use policy. Its continued acceptance all but guarantees that debates over land use will answer to the necessities and contradictions of real estate and capital; contradictions between the interests of owners and nonowners remain silent themes and uninvited guests in the politics of land.[38] The omission of power "as an organizing theme" of land policy is much more, then, than Peter Meyer's "curiosity." The question of social power is kept out of the land debates by the acceptance of property as the preferred means of organizing the spatial and social relations of people.

Americans need few lessons in the basic facts of corporate power, but it is easy to overlook the power implications of the institutions that frame the holding of wealth. For inasmuch as the institution of property is the "organizing theme" of capitalist society, its overwhelming presence in everyday life blinds people to its role in shaping consciousness. Property is such a basic ingredient in the fixtures of our existence, it so profoundly arranges the patterns of our experience, that we are unable to see it in any terms other than those of eternal facts and transcendent realities. Institutions as fundamental and pervasive as property, as thoroughly ingrained in the culture as real estate, as central to the social structure as capital—these *are* the material framework of power.

They set the stage for the power plays of politics. But their profoundest influence consists precisely of their unquestioned acceptance. As Lukács once pointedly remarked, the concealments of dominant powers and relations are "not a sign of the imperfect understanding of society; on the contrary, they belong to *the nature of reality itself and to the nature of capitalism,*" especially to its fetishistic tendencies to assign prominence to the social relations of things, that is, land *uses*, at the expense of the social relations of human beings, that is, the relations of proprietors, capitalists, and the propertyless.[39]

The Rule of Law and the "Accidents" of Competition

The requirements of capital expansion, mystified by the fetishisms of property, tend to make the law of land use into an ongoing debate over the rights of property to exclude private enterprise. The marketplace, after all, is a scene of repeated sideswipes and collisions between the right to exclude and the right to expand. Left to themselves, the forces of capitalist expansion would shatter the expectations of landed property; but given its way, landed property could cripple the economically rational distribution of investment. Thus, as we have seen, private property is both the condition and the limit of capital accumulation. This is the essence of the exclusion-expansion dialectic, a twilight zone where, in Claus Offe's words, "the necessary becomes impossible, and the impossible becomes necessary." [40]

Liberal capitalist governments have no ready answers for this dilemma. They promise to deliver the rule of law, decisions reached on the basis of clear, obeyable standards. But in the face of the internal paradoxes of property, predictability becomes impossible. Clear standards are precisely what cannot be provided, for consistency in the law of property would preempt at least one side of the expansion-exclusion couplet. Any general rule would destroy half the rights to property.

The rapidly changing dynamics of capitalism are stabilized by steadiness and uniformity in the law. Where "everything solid melts into air," the law is heavily relied on to furnish lasting expectations. As one legal scholar put it, "The human motivations which result in production are such that they will not operate in the absence of secure expectations about future enjoyment of product." [41] When one fails to be astonished at the reluctance of American corporations to invest in Lebanon or El Salvador, one understands the point.

Business thrives on calculability, on the knowledge that legal power will be exercised in predictable ways. Without this the economic edifice built on contracts would collapse.[42] Economist Friedrich A. Hayek explains the implications for a liberal theory of law: "The state should confine itself to establishing rules applying to general types of situations and should allow the individuals freedom in everything which depends on the circumstances of time and place, because only the individuals concerned in each instance can fully know these circumstances and adapt their actions to them." [43] Hayek's analysis states the liberal ideal well. But how is this ideal to be applied in the land law? It is, after all, in the very nature of site-specific contacts between expansion and exclusion rights that government must perforce "direct the use of the means of production to particular ends," either by upholding property restrictions or puncturing them in the interests of property. Thus do contradictions make the necessary impossible and the impossible necessary. [44]

Legal observers of the land use scene are quick to acknowledge the messy results of trying to keep the contending interests out of each other's way. Of zoning law one attorney writes: "I doubt that the most intransigent disciple of anarchy ever wished for or intended the litter that prevails in the area of local land use regulation." Of eminent domain another complains: "Under the law as it presently is interpreted, it is impossible to determine the limits, if any, of the exercise of the power." [45]

The confusions of the land use law are created by the contradictions of private property. The law should, perhaps, be forgiven for its failure to keep straight what capitalism muddles. Clear signals are out of the question when forces are moving forward and in reverse all at once. But contradictions notwithstanding, roadways must be cleared and retaining walls upheld. Such cumbersome matters are deposited by the American system at the doorstep of the judicial branch. "Where competing land interests vie to dominate," writes Charles Haar, "the court is the traditional forum for decision." The judiciary "may be seen as pricking out the scope of and extent of interests in land: delimiting at the same time both the owner's power of free use and his neighbor's power to veto such use." [46] Judges become tinkers of private property, the fixers of its insides and outsides; they repair the collisions between exclusion and expansion rights. More profoundly, in taking this role the judiciary structures the space of private property. More than anywhere else, it is in the courts that private property emerges, in the words of Poulantzas, as "but a space which the modern State constructs in the very process of traversing it." [47]

To do their highly sensitive spadework, the courts need plenty of freedom from the pressures of the conflicting interests, perhaps more than any other segment of capitalist government. In the endless process of institutional upkeep, democratic scrutiny must be minimized. Casualties are shielded from a public kept innocent; citizens are excluded from the inner judicial world where property rights are carved up and sometimes cave in. These are deemed technical matters involving persons of "nice judgment," well trained in the arts of small distinction. Such people are unmoved by the sight of paradox and worldly enough not to shout fire in a crowded market. It is a fair assumption that as far as the legal community is concerned, the public would rather not know. A study of land use policy published for the Council on Environmental Quality offers this observation to those it fears might be put off by "technical and detailed" presentations: complexity is necessary, argue the authors, for the book is "designed to assist government officials and attorneys who seek to fashion solutions," not merely "catchy clichés." [48]

The technocratic complexities are ingrained in the potentially explosive nature of the issues. They are necessary if legal experts are to patch up the inevitable dents in the property system without fear of political reprisal from excluders and expansionists. This is very difficult because each side wants to have the louder voice. In any given battle, excluders and expanders both want government to be their tool, whereas, to deal with the vast range of battles, professional land adjudicators want maximum political autonomy.

How, then, do attorneys and judges manage the paradoxes of property? They apply contradictory views of property to the resolution of site-specific conflicts. Thus the tensions of expansion and exclusion resurface as legal debates between proponents of individualistic and social theories of property. Although such debates contribute little to legal consistency, they do help to keep the system in working order.

Absolute Individual Property Rights

From an individual perspective, individual property rights stand nearly as far apart as separate nations. Borders are carefully patrolled; hedges are neatly trimmed; "Do Not Enter" signs are plainly posted. Units are enclosed, independent, and powerful. Society is kept out, except that the state's enforcer role is recognized, though carefully disciplined. These properties are the pistols of creative destruction—their rights to expand are fully loaded. But they are also the "ultimate means of exclusion," with walls that are solidly bricked.[49] Holding these rights, owners are free, strong, and resistant, happy in a world where they can invest without fear of restraint.

This popular song of property certainly extolls the familiar right to do with one's land exactly what one pleases; it is expansion's anthem and exclusion's rhapsody. But it is more than cant; prestigious voices sing this tune. Sir William Blackstone, for example, the eminent eighteenth-century British jurist, opined that "there is nothing which so generally strikes the imagination, as the right of property; or that sole and despotic dominion which one man claims and exercises over external things of the world in total exclusion of the right of any other individual in the universe." [50]

So lofty is the reverence for this right, Blackstone noted, that the law "will not authorize the least violation of it; no, not even for the general good of the whole community." [51] Adolf Berle and Gardiner Means, in their historic work *The Modern Corporation and Private Property,* invoked the same idea. For them, "the atom of property" was "the very foundation on which the economic order of the past three centuries has rested." [52] A contemporary review of American law surveys the nucleus of rights that belong to individualist property:

> It is generally recognized that property includes the right of acquisition, the right of dominion, the right of possession, the right of use, and enjoyment, the right of exclusion, and the right of disposition. There are frequent statements [in the law] that these rights may be exercised to the exclusion of all others, freely, and without restriction, and without control or diminution save only by the laws of the land. [53]

This is the land right that speeds through the market system, is held for speculation, used for production, counted on for leisure, traded for profit, subdivided into parcels, passed on to children, taxed for public revenue, and, on occasion, taken for public use. Obligation has little place in this conception. This property right knows only advance, never retreat. And still, for all its power, it is an idea and an institution with deep internal imperfections, not the least of which is an inability to secure itself against the danger of equally pushy neighbors. The individualist right is perfect until someone else picks it up next door.

When the market produces disturbing neighbors, the rights in which owners take such stock and pride are easily found wanting. If, for example, the neighbor turns out to be a pornographer, a toxic-waste hauler, a mortician, or simply a person who happens to enjoy loud rock music, our original owner seeks in vain for an intrinsic right to say, "No—not here!" Sudden exposure to what David Harvey calls "the costs of proximity"—the result of an unfortunate location in society—can dim the brightest hopes of an eager proprietor. [54] At this moment, Blackstone's individual owner is like Tocqueville's democratic citizen, "at once independent and powerless," severed from "the support of his connections." [55]

The Social Conception of Property

Proprietors of that "sole and despotic dominion" often make altogether naive assumptions about the behavior of others. Private expectations of stability are nourished by false hopes that neighbors will behave well or show a willingness to sell out at a fair price. Such views are overly optimistic and leave landowners vulnerable to commercial attacks. Capitalist property needs more: a plan for mutual obligation, a defense for dangers more subtle than physical trespass. Security for the rights of landownership requires a headier theory of its environment than the childlike innocence embodied in individualism. This it extracts from the social view of property.

It should probably be said at the outset that the social theory of property is neither derived from socialism nor is purely theoretical: its orientation is unabashedly private; it merely counsels the acceptance of help from those offering to build "connections" in defense of property. Similarly, the idea represents a good deal more than speculation about what ought to be; it gives a good description of what is. The assembly of modern land use controls rests solidly on tacit assumptions about the social basis of private property. Of course, the assumptions remain tacit because in American democracy the prevailing view holds that cooperation in defense of private-property interests is not a political matter, but rather an expression of neighborliness and mutual aid in defense of private and local freedom. As Grant McConnell asserts, "Massive endorsement of the private association as an essential of democracy is one of the most striking features of American political thought." [56] Collective action is regularly endorsed and practiced as a means of guaranteeing private values and interests.

The social theory of property as applied in the American case is built on ancient foundations. Roman law, which anticipated American notions of absolute ownership by two millennia, offered a simple, straightforward rule: *sic utere tuo ut alienum non laedas,* or in the more useful vernacular: use your property so as not to injure that of another. In English common law, which served as a kind of historical conveyor belt to bring Roman concepts into American practice, the same principle is expressed in the idea that "no plot of land is 'intire of itself.'" As law professor Charles Haar explains, "The value of land depends on its physical location with respect to other land; and upon the line drawn by society between the privilege of use and the interest of surrounding owners in the untrammeled use of their land." [57] In the social perspective, then, use is seen no longer as an intrisic right but as a "privilege" conferred by society and based on collective judgments of what's good for the landowners taken as a group. In effect, the land powers of government are employed as a kind of collective landowner authority that introduces those controls necessary to avoid the sorts of collisions that rational proprietors would avoid if they could see the whole picture.

Land use law has never really embraced the fundamental Madisonian injunction that "ambition must be made to counteract ambition," though it pervasively reflects the idea that "the regulation of these various and interfering interests forms the principal task of modern legislation and involves the spirit of party and faction in the necessary and ordinary operations of government." In this domain conflict has been seen not as the principal mechanism of political control but rather as the main target of legal regulation. Abrasion is viewed as something best avoided. Thus the *sic utere* rule is designed to prevent nuisances and preempt fights. William H. Rodgers, Jr., argues, for example, that "nuisance law . . . yields a working illustration of friction minimization—the use of best efforts to avoid interference with other parties." [58] The goal here is no greater good to the community than the promise of smoother proprietary relations. Cutthroat competition is abated and ownership protected. Responsibility in the use of private property and thus private power is measured against the collective good of the individual owners. Rodgers adds, "The object . . . is not community betterment but individual security and freedom." [59] The theme, of course, is central to the liberal idea of the state, in which people join, said Locke, "for their comfortable, safe and peaceful living one amongst another, in a secure Enjoyment of their Properties." [60]

Modern land use law presumes that property cannot safely be enjoyed unless neighbors arrange social defenses. A collective landowner is indispensable. In this theory walls become a complex matter. Private boundaries exist, of course; but owners have the right to shout over the wall and to call the neighborly nuisance to a halt. In law, suggests one attorney, the right to shout "Stop!" is equivalent "to an implied easement restricting nearby uses." [61] In this theory, naive assumptions of "sole and despotic dominion" are rejected in deference to pragmatic acknowledgments that owners sink or swim together. They are in truth classmates whose connections, abetted by government, embody security, condition freedom, and organize power. [62]

Again, the social theory as understood in the U.S. tradition has little to do with morals and much to do with interest. It answers the material needs people have for others, needs that even the most individualistic, ambitious, aggressive, and acquisitive people have, to be in possession of "the support of their connections." In the case of landownership, that need comes from the earth's refusal to budge, from the proprietor's inability to pick up the land and leave when threatened from without. If land could really "be dragged into the movement of private property" land use policy would not be necessary. But because land is stuck, so oftentimes is the owner; the land's connection to the earth compels the owner's connection to neighbors. Joseph Sax provides one of the clearer descriptions of this view in American legal scholarship:

> Property does not exist in isolation. Particular parcels are tied to one another in complex ways, and property is more accurately described as being inextricably part of a network of relationships that is neither limited to, nor usefully defined by, the property boundaries with which the legal system is accustomed to dealing. [63]

However, and this point is critical, the social theory of property need not be read from a landowner perspective at all. It is possible to insist, with John Stuart Mill and the judges in *Poletown* v. *City of Detroit*, that owners must make room for the social forces of production. That is, owners may be said to have obligations not only to other owners but to capitalist society as well.

Here the working rule may be said to be this: Use your property so as to create maximum output for the market, or stand aside. From this perspective, which will be explored in fuller detail in chapter 3, the government is engaged not as a collective landowner but as a collective capitalist, the assembler of space for innovative and creative destroyers.

The Contradiction and Legal Powers

The individual and social theories play equally important roles in justifying the use and restriction of landed property, though only the former is publicly celebrated. But like the expansion and exclusion rights they embody, the theories are caught up in contradictions. Landed property requires social controls for both its protection and its development. Any workable controls must defeat significant rights. Land use policy is hounded by the barking dogs of expansion and exclusion—Get out! Keep out!—the demands never stop. How far may the controls go to limit investment or knock down walls? These are the nagging questions of land use policy—not environmental protection, housing for the poor, or community planning. The substantive issues of land use spin around the axis of property, imprisoned in a closing circle of contradictory rights, as is the law itself. But landowners and entrepreneurs have little patience for evasive judges. Answers are demanded here and now. Expectations must be stabilized, fences locked, land cleared, rights carved out. The insides and outsides of property must be fixed so things can move and values can rise. The state, of course, owns the hammers and chisels. Powers of police and eminent domain are used to nail down answers; predictably, however, they are uncertain answers.

Police Powers

The police powers consist of government's authority to protect the health, lives, morals, and properties of the population. In the U.S. political system their repository is state government. They are prominent among "the powers . . . reserved to the States" by the Tenth Amendment to the Constitution. As a result, municipal land use controls may be enacted only where state legislatures expressly delegate the authority to do so.[64] Moreover, police regulations are held by the courts to tests based on their reasonableness as well as their relation to the general interest of the community as a whole, though as property law amply illustrates, the general interest is frequently identified with the needs of an ideal community of proprietors. Nonetheless, ordinances that appear to be arbitrary or capricious, or those explicitly aimed at benefits to privileged groups, are, generally speaking, poor candidates for judicial support.[65] According to one legal compendium, the police power "embraces everything to promote the general welfare; everything essential to the great public needs, including security for the enjoyment of property." [66]

The police powers share a crucial intersection between the economic mode of production and the political system of protection. They are the basis of community rights to control change. A glimmer of their strength is reflected in the authority to regulate land use. Because the declared objective of nuisance and zoning laws, for example, is the protection of essential public interests, it is argued by the courts that owners must expect to suffer regulation without "just compensation." Police regulations are thus seen as a legal category separate and distinct from the Fifth Amendment "takings" clause of the U.S. Constitution, which provides that citizens shall not lose their estates for "public use, without just compensation." Property, the courts have held, does not carry entitlements "to injure or endanger the public." Owners have no right to benefit from the sacrifice of powers to harm others. Indeed, uses in opposition to the public interest "are not property" at all.[67] The U.S. Supreme Court confirmed the principle in a well-known late-nineteenth-century decision *Mugler* v. *Kansas,* upholding the state's right to forbid the use of property to produce and distribute liquors:

> Such legislation does not disturb the owner in the control or use of his property for lawful purposes, nor restrict his rights to dispose of it, but is only a declaration by the state that its use by anyone, for certain forbidden purposes, is prejudicial to the public interests.[68]

If, as *Mugler* v. *Kansas* suggests, the police power is akin to capitalist society's superego, the legal basis of the state's relative autonomy, then land use policy is the special conscience of proprietors; the controlling channel for what James Madison would call their "permanent and aggregate interests"; the means by which exclusion is conferred with the legitimacy of the public interest. Clearly, police regulations presuppose a social conception of individual rights and, in practice, give life to the principle that land use rights can be exercised profitably only where landowners join to limit use by renegade neighbors. But what are the limits of the police power? According to the prevailing judicial precedent, the answer is highly ambiguous.

In the crucial 1954 case *Berman* v. *Parker,* Justice William O. Douglas declared for the majority:

> Any attempt to define its reach or trace its outer limits is fruitless, for each case must turn on its own facts. The definition is essentially the product of legislative determinations [of] purposes neither abstractly nor historically capable of complete definition. Subject to specific constitutional limitations, when the legislature has spoken, the public interest has been declared in terms well-nigh conclusive.[69]

Before excluders rally in celebration, however, they should scrutinize Douglas's opinion. A close look reveals that the decision upheld a broad reading of police powers to justify confiscation of private property for public use; it stressed that "public use" is determined by the "public purpose" and that the powers of police are not limited "merely because . . . eminent domain is involved." [70] As long as legislatures state clearly the public ends to be served by land clearance, whether for military bases, parks, schools, or private urban-renewal projects, the courts should retire from second guesses. Naturally, Berman's language helped General Motors get the land it wanted in the Poletown case, just as it has helped so many other corporations in their land grabs. [71] More important, it suggests that in general the police power is as contradictory in its implications as are the ends and dynamics of private property itself. The strength that is employed for property can be aimed against it. But can the regulation of property itself ever constitute a taking? That is, it is one thing for police purposes to justify condemnation of private property for the public use. Are there circumstances, however, where the control of use, short of condemnation and seizure, ranges so far across the board of development rights that owners may reasonably expect to be treated as involuntary sellers? To get at this question requires a brief look at the power of seizure, the power of eminent domain.

Eminent Domain

Eminent domain, the state's power to condemn and seize private property for the public use, is a formidable power indeed, especially when considered in the light of Douglas's broad reading of the police authority and the historical willingness of U.S. governments to delegate confiscation rights to private interests. Paradoxically, though, its strength probably is best confirmed by the silence of the Constitution on the right of the state to take. Nowhere does the basic text explicitly state that government has superior claims to any site in the national territory. Yet from the beginning of the Republic the legitimacy of eminent domain has never been questioned. The Founders were above all careful men; they were hardly guilty of an oversight. Rather, just because they were eighteenth-century progressives, they tended to assume, with other up-to-date people of the time, that the authority to expropriate land for public use was, in the words of a later judicial opinion, an "inherent and necessary attribute of sovereignty, existing independently of constitutional provisions and superior to all property rights." [72]

The state is, after all, in Max Weber's famous definition, "a human community that [successfully] claims the monopoly of the legitimate use of physical force within a given territory." And, as Weber was quick to add, "'territory' is one of the characteristics of the state." [73] The governmental monopoly of arms and law fully embraces the power to control the land and, with it, the power to organize internal space and govern private boundary claims. All sites, like all citizens, are equal under the law and thus equally susceptible to conscription. The land, like the citizen, can be drafted for the public good. Underlying all this is the physical fact of conquest. However it may be draped in legitimacy, "conquest . . . precedes government," writes Theodore Lowi, "and government is inconceivable without it." And what is conquest if not the bringing of a "territory and its population under control"?[74] Only with the domination of borders, populations, and spaces does the state, as Poulantzas said, tend to monopolize the procedures for the reorganization of space, bringing them into line with the changing demands of production and demography.[75]

The power to take is itself taken for granted, a power which, in Lowi's words, is "almost completely beyond the boundaries of the Constitution."[76] The qualification is necessary and appropriate, however; government may not take just as it pleases. The Fifth Amendment to the Constitution places three important restrictions on would-be government land grabbers. Real estate and other forms of property may not be seized without the application of due process of law, a showing of public use or necessity, and, in the event of confiscation, the payment of just compensation. Of course, it is the government itself—or more precisely, its judicial branch—that specifies the boundaries of these terms. The limits on eminent domain are in this sense self-imposed. The larger commitment to private-property rights ensures that such limits receive scrupulous attention. Still, however independent from the "political branches" judges may be, they remain part of the officialdom of the state, with close understandings of public necessities as well as of private rights. They are themselves caught within the paradoxes of property and its opposing requirements of expansion and exclusion.

From the standpoint of battles for land use control the most pressing aspect of the eminent domain law concerns the question of whether police regulations can ever be understood to pass the line into the compensatory world of the Fifth Amendment. Is payment necessary, not only where property is taken in the physical sense, but also in situations where public regulations substantially downgrade commercial value by limiting the rights of use? In effect, can expansion be cut off without "just compensation"? Does the Fifth Amendment protect exchange value as well as ownership per se?

As we shall see in chapter 3, positive answers to these questions began to issue from the courts after about 1870, though not with any consistency. Certainly, enough affirmation has been given to encourage landowners and their attorneys to make "takings" claims the most popular private defense against community land use policies. Bosselman, Callies, and Banta found in their review of many local land use fights that, frequently, communities are so intimidated by the "takings" charge that they prefer to forego "strict regulations" where "problems are severe" in order to avoid long and potentially expensive legal entanglements with expansionist owners. The authors conclude that, in contrast to the actual run of legal decisions, "the fear of the taking issue is stronger than the taking clause itself." [77]

Predictably, construction interests have been urged by their lawyers to turn to the "takings" clause as a device to open up the nation's towns. When municipalities are forced to choose between the proximity costs of location near an undesirable facility and the financial costs of paying to keep it out, fewer communities, it is argued, will show the will to resist. As one attorney explained, "When a municipal enactment has prohibited a landowner from carrying out a land-use activity that cannot be characterized as a nuisance [e.g., the building of low-income housing], his prima facie case for a taking should be much less onerous: merely proof that the restriction has caused a substantial drop in the market value of his land." [78] Justice William Brennan's dissent in the *San Diego Gas & Electric* case gives backing to such views, insisting that communities *should* be compelled to weigh the financial implications of land use regulation for restricted-property owners.

In the San Diego case, the city had recently changed its zoning ordinance to conform to California's requirement that localities adopt "long-range preservation and conservation" plans providing for open spaces inside city and county limits. At one such site, SDG&E had proposed to construct a nuclear power plant. With the new ordinance in place and the land designated as an open space, the city council urged passage of a bond issue to defray the costs of purchasing the land, thus paying the company for its loss. However, the voters rejected the bond issue, leaving the land use restrictions in place and the corporation without its compensation. The gas company sued, charging an unconstitutional seizure of its property rights. After the Supreme Court of California denied the company's plea—holding that remedies for police power abuses are limited merely to invalidations of offending law—the U.S. Supreme Court dismissed the utility's case on procedural grounds. However, Justice Brennan, speaking for a minority of four that but for the procedural issues would have included Justice William Rehnquist, both reaffirmed the court's long-held view that "takings" questions are matters of degree and added the new principle that

> once a court establishes there was a regulatory "taking," the Constitution demands that the government entity pay just compensation for the period commencing on the date the regulation first effected the "taking," and ending on the date the government entity chooses to rescind or otherwise amend the regulation. [79]

Brennan not only reaffirms the contention that regulation can pass the line into the costly realm of eminent domain, but he also insists that where communities evade the constitutional protections of individual ownership they should expect to be punished by the need to make damage payments calculable from the moment the offending statute goes into effect. Brennan's sympathies with the claims of individual ownership, a reflection of his broader concerns for individual liberties, threaten to raise considerably the stakes and costs of community land-use-control efforts and thus to vastly complicate the calculations of local governments.[80] Were his approach to become the law of the land, it might be fair to say that the social theory of property embodied in Douglas's *Berman* decision finds its outer limit in the Brennan doctrine, except for the fact that Brennan in no way challenges Douglas's principal thesis: that the state police power confers on government officials a wide-ranging authority to control private property in the public interest. The dissent makes it clear, after all, that regulations become "takings" only when they "destroy the use and enjoyment of property," when "the effect . . . is to deprive [the owner] of *all* beneficial use."[81] As much of the recent land use law suggests, great encroachments on individual property can legitimately be undertaken, that is, without compensation, even in cases where most or perhaps all "beneficial use" is "destroyed."

Many suburbs have been accorded impressive powers to regulate and exclude without having to suffer the pains of compensation payments. This is especially true where localities and states have come to see control of undeveloped land as the key to handling the social and environmental pressures of economic change. Tough controls on land use, some amounting to outright bans on commercial action, have been sustained as legitimate police regulations because their purpose is to avoid "public harm." Coastal and floodplain properties have been subjected to especially tight restrictions, for example, without compensation to their owners, despite the near-total suppression of industrial rights. In a 1972 decision, for instance, the Wisconsin Supreme Court made it clear to the state's landowners that development is anything but an unconditional right of property. On the contrary, it argued, as "the people become more sophisticated" in their understanding of the connection between ecological processes and social health, they are entitled to make development a socially responsible process, without fear of billing by aggrieved proprietors. As the court explained, "An owner of land has no absolute right to change the essential natural character of his land so as to use it for a purpose for which it was unsuited in its natural state and which injures the rights of others."[82] Indeed, in the view of the Task Force on Land Use and Urban Growth, a private study group financed by the Rockefeller Brothers Fund, it was deemed imperative that such decisions become part of a broader national policy to "treat development rights as created and allocated to the land by society," one in which "landowners may be fairly required to bear . . . tough restrictions . . . without payment by the government."[83] According to a review of the case law published several years after the Rockefeller Report, the panel's recommendations seem close to fulfillment. Sondra Berchin found a "recent trend in the law which suggests that land ownership has been re-defined so that it no longer entails a constitutional right to develop." [84]

City residents of working-class districts, whose homes and shops have been demolished to make way for urban renewal, would doubtless be sur-prised to learn that the courts are faithful defenders of the land use status quo. For in urban eminent domain cases, judicial backing for the most radical land use changes has been quickly supplied. Indeed, it is difficult to find either in the case law or in law journal discussions many instances where major urban renewal projects have been halted as the result of Fifth Amendment defenses. Most local judges seem altogether willing to follow the counsel of Lawrence Berger, who urges that "it would be better to err here on the side of public experimentation to cure urban ills" than to halt progress in the name of indi-vidual or neighborhood rights. [85]

Indeed, where eminent domain powers are applied, the collective land-owner and its protections do seem to vanish. Private property reverts to its individual status; local government becomes the collective capitalist. Even where whole urban sections or neighborhoods are threatened with razing, pro-prietors are treated as independent units. In these contexts it is supposed that property right is attached to nothing but the earth and its owner. No queries are made concerning the proprietors' relations to the community or to the so-cial networks into which they may have fitted their lives. As Laura Mansnerus explains, in eminent domain cases the human intangibles of property—asso-ciations with "community, social and family ties"—are almost always ig-nored by judges. [86] Otherwise respected property connections fall victim to a kind of judicial amnesia. All that can be remembered is the marketplace logic: all property rights are interchangeable, all property rights are reducible to money. It is enough, presumably, that the owner can up and buy a place else-where. Something ventured, nothing lost—this is the rule of thumb in urban land clearance.

Conclusion

Justice Douglas's opinion in *Berman* v. *Parker* cut a wide swath through which the police powers can drive eminent domain as well as noncompensable regulations of individual property. Today, it seems, progress and the public good have double meanings in the land use law. In the suburban and rural open-space cases, the law is increasingly linked with suspicions of economic change, with a strong sense of social obligation to regulate and exclude in the public interest. In the field of urban eminent domain, however, proprietors are expected to yield to those very same forces of expansion and creative destruc-tion. Secondhand urban land seems to count for less in the estimation of the law than virginal country land, especially where cities are desperate for investment. It is difficult not to conclude that the rights to private property and community protection have come to have meanings that vary with political setting and income attributes closely related to class position. The law, in other words, tends to deal with deep tensions inside the property system by splitting its preferences according to the status, value, and location of residential property. In this way, the extent of consumption property rights becomes the effective test for determining whether capital mobility will be opposed. The more land one owns, especially of the unused suburban variety, the greater the likelihood that exclusionary rights will prevail. This principle seems to furnish what consistency there is in the paradoxical law of land use.

To suppose, however, that the legal theories and powers sketched out here represent comprehensive answers to the expansion-exclusion contradictions of private property would be an oversimplification. Predictability in the application of these rules is extremely low. In cases where regulations have taken more than 75 percent of existing land values, compensation has been denied. But at the same time, community efforts to regulate or halt economic change of extraordinary harm have been deflected by the "taking" and public-use clauses of the Fifth Amendment. Frank Michelman summarizes the law thus: "It is no insult to the judicial performance . . . to remark that it has sometimes yielded answers surprising to the uninitiated." [87]

The police and eminent domain powers are broad enabling powers, not carefully crafted legal tools. Their uses are determined less by judges than by what lawyers like to call the "political branches" and the larger power system of society itself. In a fundamental sense, the legal powers have little meaning apart from the social relationships in which courts and legislatures are themselves embedded. Police and seizure powers are, in this respect, crude weapons in the enduring struggles between expansion and exclusion interests.

None of this means that the land law is simply reducible to class conflict or to class power. The legal system, with its panoply of roles, processes, institutions, and ideologies, is both formally and in the view of its participants something "distinct and separate from the system of social relations which it regulates." It does tend "to take on a life of its own." [88] Not only does this require that the rivals agree to narrow the range of conflict to legally acceptable forms, but those forms themselves also shape the course of development of social and political relationships. Hence it is necessary to study the development of these legal forms in order to see how they have patterned the rights to private property and community protection in the face of often massive forces of economic change. To this subject we turn in the following chapter.

The Bumpy Road to Zoning 3

*There are two modes of invading private property:
the first, by which the poor plunder the rich, is sudden and violent; the second, by which the rich plunder the poor, slow and legal.*

John Taylor

Land and capital have played at tug-of-war for the better part of four centuries. The struggle has been tense. Occasionally, tempers have even flared to
the point of open gun battles. Cattle ranchers and sheepherders—landowners
all—once wrote rules for the conduct of blood feuds. Today farmers gather in
front of western banks to block the foreclosures of neighboring farms; others
opposed to the expansion plans of the electric utilities pick up hunting rifles to
chase linemen off their land. But even in the more plentiful and prosaic cases
of passive resistance through the courts, threats of legal coercion are frequently necessary to keep the combatants agreeable.

The problem, however, is much deeper than the mere absence of order, for
much more than order is needed. The property system, and thus the law, must
show a high degree of tolerance in the face of extraordinary appetites for
space. This is imperative if capitalist revolutions are to unfold apace. Entrepreneurs cannot afford too much time for doubt and second guesses, for the
clock of economic advance runs ever faster. In the Alice in Wonderland world
of business, stability is necessary so that the earth can be turned upside down.
Landowners, naturally, like to have their feet on the ground; for them, resistance is necessary just to stay right side up. But then capitalism makes for a
topsy-turvy world. This chapter traces the legal bumps on the path to zoning
and modern land use policy. It is a two-part story of the fall and rise of rights
to insure landed property against the costs of change.

The first section—"The Attack on Exclusion"—explores how protectionist
law was redesigned to accommodate and even accelerate capitalist expansion
in the early nineteenth century. It is a case study in David Harvey's thesis that

"the agency of the state is vital" to the spatial expansion of capital.[1] The second half of the chapter—"Rebuilding the Walls"—traces how landowners achieved their revenge: the redeployment of exclusionary rights through the creation of government land use controls, especially the zoning laws. This section is a case study in George Gilder's idea that "government . . . is almost always an obstacle to change."[2] In short, this is a chapter laden with contradictions, but contradictions that cohere within the singular institutional arrangement of capitalist property.

More than conflicting biases separate the two halves of the story, however. The shifts in the property law also illuminate some of the different ways that political change happens in capitalist society. The most striking quality of government's early "move out ahead" of expansion is that it occurred so quietly that it rarely, if ever, aroused sustained or organized opposition. It unfolded, as it were, behind the backs of the landed interest, through a slow, gradual accretion of isolated precedents. Only by looking at the cumulative effect is it possible to see how close it came to revolutionizing the social relationships of landownership and industrial capital. This was creative destruction through legal subtlety; its premise—the immature political consciousness of landowners—could not be counted on to last.

Indeed, as we shall see in the second half of the chapter, the muted pattern was not duplicated in the giant factory cities and growing suburbs of the early twentieth century. For the more affluent—property owners of the new middle class, the scattered segments of the independent petty bourgeoisie, and the rising entrepreneurial capitalists and corporate managers—consumption-based property rights came to be vocally identified with the exclusionary power of land use policy. And this area of policy itself came to be seen as a field of government especially wide open to the public participation of land- and homeowners. Compared with the blind shifts of the previous century, this involvement was a big advance for local democracy and the conscious creation of political change to temper the explosiveness of capitalist growth.

But the growth of landowner consciousness did not happen by itself. It was spurred not only by the obstreperousness of industrial capital; the new planning profession played a key role, too, by showing local homeowners, government officials, and capitalists alike the rationality of land use classification and separation. Like lawyers, the traditional land-conflict adjudicators, the emerging professional planners were akin to what the Italian political theorist Antonio Gramsci would call "organic intellectuals"; they were thinkers and policy experts who help in "organizing the general system of relationships external to the [production system] itself."[3] Unlike attorneys, however, planners were much less directly tied to the individual parties at law. Their unstated allegiance was to the assumption that the existing patterns of production and property could thrive only if the physical and spatial relationships of the main property classes were more carefully divided. Thus for all the aid they gave in making better neighbors out of the main landowning and urban capitalist groups, their solutions invariably left the poorest residents of cities out in the cold.

And for all the importance that needs to be attached to the role of the planners, they did not have the power necessary to change the law of property. Their efforts were essentially limited to the realm of thought, until the traditional forces of law and business came to see the light of zoning as a reasonable solution to the exclusion-expansion conflict. Once this happened, a new local administrative system was grafted onto the traditional police-power format, and the basic form of modern land use control was established, the one that continues to this day.

The Attack on Exclusion

The Old Walls

Early American ideas of landed property favored private ownership, of course, but in a legal context that reflected social needs and private obligations. Personal independence was a social goal struggled for in relations with others. Even the first squatters formed claims associations to protect their rights against speculators.

Owners knew better than to go it alone. Long before the Constitution protected property rights with the hallowed Fifth Amendment, the common law of the colonies was relied on to provide mutual aid against overly active or harmful neighbors. For example, after the great fire in Boston in the late seventeenth century, the city placed legal restrictions on careless homebuilders. Walls had to be constructed of brick or stone and roofs made of slate or tile. Penalties were stiff—fines for noncompliance could equal twice the value of a building. Philadelphia issued similar ordinances to regulate the construction of party walls, shared by adjoining structures. For these early cities, private walls were no private matter.[4]

Early policy aimed at more than ensuring the sound construction of walls. It also targeted public nuisances for exclusion from the main byways of life. In 1692 Boston required that slaughterhouses and other unpleasant buildings be placed where they "may least be offensive." Some years earlier the city of New Amsterdam ordered such undesirables as hog-pens and privies off the public roads. Philadelphia went further and used controls not merely to avoid harm, but also to achieve the public good. It required landowners to plant leafy trees in front of their houses "to the end that the . . . town may be well shaded from the violence of the sun in the heat of summer and thereby be rendered more healthy."[5]

Such controls did not stop at the city line. The ancient principle that owners must use their property so as not to injure that of another was widely embraced by farmers, too. Rural proprietors expected one another to abide by tacit agreements to keep their land in agriculture. When enterprising neighbors tested such local commitments, the typical reply was "Stop!" Private owners were held by the courts to limits of "natural uses." A slightly modified version of this test was an inclination to protect first users against latecomers: "first in time is first in right" was the preferred rule. A review of the relevant cases led historian Morton Horwitz to conclude that "the frequency with which eighteenth-century courts solemnly invoked the maxim *sic utere* is a significant measure of their willingness to impose liability for injury caused by any but the most traditional activities." Even the eminent Blackstone believed that otherwise lawful activities could legitimately be enjoined if they harmed one's neighbors.[6]

The collective landowner was a welcome presence in colonial America. Given the prevailing mercantilist outlook among eighteenth-century Americans, few doubts were expressed about community rights to regulate the tempo and scope of change. How else could stability be achieved? What was property without restrictions, except an open invitation to assault? Eighteenth-century landowners looked rather matter-of-factly to the law to afford "the support of their connections." There was little question but that "property was . . . legally limited and subordinated to the public good."[7]

British imperial preferences, of course, strengthened the local conservatism. As Louis Hacker notes, "Stern checks [were] imposed by the [British] Board of Trade on attempts by the colonial assemblies to encourage native manufacturing."[8] Bounties to private entrepreneurs, extensions of public credit to stimulate investment, tax exemptions for industrial innovators, access to western lands, and encouragement for new urban developments in the West were all regularly opposed by the mother country, especially after 1763. Creative destruction was forbidden, except in the rural and "natural" industries that fed British enterprise: farming, fishing, logging, and mining. A notable exception was shipbuilding, but this was permitted largely to expedite whaling. American artisans reluctantly subsidized English capital by subduing their ingenuity. Such policies kept strains on the land use system to a minimum.

Capital on the Move

The first decades of the nineteenth century found business getting busy. Commercial and industrial activity rose sharply. Domestic manufacturing was especially helped by the War of 1812. The production of textiles, arms, iron, machinery, and paper experienced impressive expansion. But even in 1810 the U.S. Treasury reported the existence of fourteen woolen and eighty-seven cotton mills. Later, between 1830 and 1850, the cotton industry would double in capacity, turning its threads on more than 22 million spindles. Domestic trade multiplied as the division of labor expanded and intensified. In 1820 the value of commercial traffic that moved between Pittsburgh and Philadelphia, for example, equaled $18 million, and receipts in New Orleans doubled from $5 million in 1807 to $10 million in 1816, more than doubling again to $22 million in 1830.[9]

As industry and commerce thrived, demand built for new systems of energy and transport to underpin the expanding economy. Water mills, canals, turnpikes, and bridges were needed to expedite the movement of goods. Dozens of public enterprises were promoted. The well-known Erie Canal project and the earlier Cumberland Road symbolized wider public commitments to the expansion of production and trade.[10] The federal government got into the act early by supplying free land for internal improvements, what today we call "infrastructure." In its Enabling Act for the State of Ohio, passed in 1802, 5 percent of the proceeds from the sale of public land within the state were set aside for road building. Similar grants were made to other western states. In 1824 Congress passed legislation granting Indiana a right-of-way ninety feet wide to locate a canal connecting the Wabash River and Lake Erie. Later, seven more canal grants were made to spur the river trade, including a half-million-acre donation to Ohio for "canals generally." All together the states received over 3 million acres for wagon roads, 13.9 million acres for canals and other internal improvements, and 37 million acres to assist railroad construction. Private rail corporations alone received directly over 94 million acres to spur construction of a mechanized transport system.[11]

Legal Rumblings

As capital took flight, the law slowly awakened to the buzz of new needs. Judges gradually assumed more progressive, expansionist outlooks, a disposition more eager to aid what James Willard Hurst aptly called "the release of energy."[12] Landowners were greeted with new frames of reference in a series of local battles with public and private enterprise. Judges delivered lectures on private obligations to flow with the tide of economic development. As one early nineteenth-century judge suggested, the role of law is not to protect stick-in-the-muds but to "enlarge the resources, increase the industrial energies, and promote the productive power of the community."[13] The weight of society must shift to the legal accelerator; progress must be spurred. In Hurst's words, "We were a people going places in a hurry. Men in that frame of mind are not likely to be thinking only of the condition of their brakes." By the 1830s Alexis de Tocqueville was sufficiently impressed to proclaim that in America "nothing checks the spirit of enterprise."[14] But, in fact, the shift was not so radical or so quick, and society did not entirely lose the feel of its "brakes"; Tocqueville somewhat overstated the case. Land use and property controls continued to honor some of the older and more conservative social obligations. Indeed, some legal scholars inspected the land laws and found them inattentive to needs for the fast turnover. As late as 1832 James Kent was annoyed enough to write in his *Commentaries on American Law* that the rules of real property form

> a technical and very artificial system; and though it has felt the influence of the free and commercial spirit of modern ages, it is still very much under the control of principles derived from the feudal policy. . . . The deep traces of that policy are still visible in every part of the doctrine of real estate.[15]

For Kent, too many rules suppressed the use of land for productive purposes. He reflected an increasingly fashionable opinion, for it was widely held that land rights needed to be set into faster motion. As one New York legislator put it, "property was improved" less by hard work than "by passing from hand to hand."[16] As commodity exchange and industry took hold as the new delights of social policy, settled enjoyment was devalued; Jefferson's celebration of farmers for being "tied to their country . . . by the most lasting bands" was perhaps a song still sung in the fields, but in the fast-growing towns it was a tired old standard. Proprietors who stood pat were warned to beware. A later nineteenth-century commentator looked back on the new perspective and found a simple lesson: the "quiet citizen must keep out of the way of the exuberantly active one."[17] In this age, railroad ties began to replace communal ties as symbols of national approbation.

Breaching Walls

With the great early rush of U.S. business, passive ownership rights continued to provide strongholds—as long as they did not impede progress. But if expansion came, the settled were increasingly expected to yield. The vested interests of property suffered a number of ideological and legal attacks. The rights of use were redefined to accord with expansionist objectives; and where private landowners were themselves oriented to market relationships, use came to be replaced by utility as the appropriate economic measure of comparative rights. Gradually, productivity replaced possession as the prevailing "nine tenths of the law" in economic conflicts. Moreover, in cases where the issues involved not damages but the direct control of space itself, powers of eminent domain were widely and loosely applied to clear out the obstreperous. And here too the legal rules were adjusted to minimize liability to the injured. Regretful denials were the typical answers as farmers and others chased expansionists into the courts in search of their rights.

Changes in landed property rights occurred wherever growth and protection rights collided, in the public as well as the private sector, and perhaps most graphically on the frontier, where native claims could not be traced through careful record. The taking of public and Indian lands by American expansionists is widely known. What deserves special emphasis, however, is the policy change in property rights advocated by developers. The new wisdom tended to hold that exclusion rights were justified only where active, that is, capital, expansion was vigorously pursued. Anything less venturesome disqualified the first holder. Economic invasion was not only acceptable but also essential to "the national interest." Such shifts were reflected within the ideology of creative destruction, too. Arguments that carried weight on the frontier were not as effective in dismantling private rights. Thus, exclusion was hit with two clubs: traditional arguments based on religion and morals, which asserted industry as the only legitimate basis for ownership, were supplemented in the private-sector battles with newer philosophical arguments based on social utility. The differences that emerged are basic to the later ideological and legal development of land use policy—so basic, in fact, that it is fair to say that the very category of modern "land use" policy is really a misnomer, for it has come to be governed less by the rights, conditions, and interests of simple use than by the commercial test of utility in a system of expanding marketplace relationships. In short, the key to land use policy became exchange value.

Honest Industry

Takers of public and Indian lands had ready-made arguments to justify their private seizures. Biblical commands to "be fruitful and multiply" were entwined with the old labor theory of property to warrant imperial as well as individual land grabs.[18] Nineteenth-century conquests of Indian lands and massive private depredations of federal lands were widely accepted as legitimate steps toward the nation's "manifest destiny," for as John Winthrop of Massachusetts had observed long before, "Why should we stand here striveing for places of habitation . . . and in ye mean time suffer a whole Continent . . . to lie waste without any improvement."[19] Move, take, and build—these were the calls of God and natural law. Indians, by contrast, could have no serious claims, for they failed to work up a "better use of the land." The West rightly belonged, as one congressman intoned, "to the race" that "is most progressive."[20]

Identical themes were advanced by settlers to justify squatting on the public lands. These lands were worthless, announced one congressional backer of frontier causes, until value was "imparted to them by the industry, enterprise and sufferings of that hardy population who preceded the comforts and conveniences of a more advanced condition."[21] As land historian Benjamin Hibbard explained, "The settler rarely hesitated to take possession of government land. He did this apparently with a clear conscience."[22] Nor did the central government act boldly to fend off the private takers. In 1885 the finest of the early U.S. land commissioners, William A. J. Sparks, well described Washington's indifference to the public's exclusionary rights: "It seems that the prevailing idea running through this office and those subordinate to it was that the government had no distinctive rights to be considered and no special rights to protect." [23] There is perhaps no clearer statement of the nineteenth-century belief that exclusionary rights were admissible only as the shield of expansion. Against the more dynamic producers, settled property claims were tissue-paper thin. "The true object of government," writes Rush Welter of the prevailing view, "was to secure the enjoyment of property to those who would put it to use," the most profitable use. [24]

On the basis of these rationales, Indian and public lands were expropriated and privately enclosed. [25] The confiscations were charged as losses of no account; to exact titles from a fenceless America required minimal investments. Thus farmers demanded and won dozens of relief laws cutting short their obligations to pay the federal government for lands entered under the credit and preemption programs. [26] "Sweat equity" was built from "squatters' rights." Together, these claims were invoked to immunize settlers from liability to pay for private takings of public property. Treaties, meanwhile, gave Indians token or, more often, mythical compensations; broken promises abounded.

Utility: The Philosophy of More

But the problem of forced seizures threatened the private takers themselves, for the vast preponderance of industrial and commercial expansion occurred in the private sector. But as befits the society's respect for white owners, the process assumed a more highly sophisticated, refined and technical form in the private sector, what Thorstein Veblen called "a reasoned plan of legalized seizure." [27] Farmers taught government how to take land with a gun; government would show farmers how to take it with a pen.

In the United States, of course, space was abundant. But as we have seen, free enterprise does not need space in the abstract vastness of the frontier; that was for pioneers. Free enterprise requires land in that special social condition that makes "location, location, location" the vital source of real estate values. Builders, therefore, often need land occupied by others, or land so close to that of others that the costs of new production easily spill over adjacent boundaries. But rapid and economically efficient development implies the power to get land cheaply and the right to avoid responsibility when its use harms others. This was especially true for early entrepreneurs and public-sector developers in the United States who were capital poor and heavily dependent on windfalls as their supply line for primitive accumulation. [28]

When the inevitable collisions occurred, proprietors turned to judges for defense and relief. "Where competing land interests vie to dominate, the court is the traditional forum for decision." [29] And "the traditional forum" was expected to give traditional justice. Established doctrine protected natural and prior users against late-coming activists. Landowners fully expected judges to provide the age-old remedies of exclusion and compensation, for use and obligation were inseparable in the legal heritage of *sic utere*. Owners could not make the yards of others their personal dumping grounds. But the farmers, who were avid followers of Locke, failed to go on and read Jeremy Bentham and James and John Stuart Mill. These turned out to be costly omissions, for the utilitarians inspired subtle but influential distinctions that were foreign to the workaday world of seventeenth-century liberalism. Locke defended use, though he certainly esteemed the benefits of exchange and accumulation. Bentham and James Mill, by contrast, defended utility, a social definition of the value of exchange and accumulation that functionally tied it to the claims of democracy itself. When capitalist society shifted from the stage of simple industry and the more complex forms of mercantile trade to the phase of heavy manufacturing capital, when it shifted from Locke to Bentham and the Mills, landowners felt the tremors; some even lost the earth beneath their feet.

Lockean ideology stressed "honest industry" as the basis of property right. Its linguistic root was the old Latin term *industria,* meaning work or working.[30] Owners possessed economic rights because they infused their labor into natural things. As Veblen put it, "by this 'natural' right of creative workmanship the masterless man [was] vested with full discretionary control."[31] Use referred in this context to little more than an individual's skill with tools or a farmer's cultivation of fields, for example. Settlers had this in mind when they justified the taking of soil from the Indians. For industrial expansionists to overcome this traditional argument from use, which was a powerful statement of individual natural rights, they needed a different conception of economic action, a new category of social production.

Some leaders, such as John Quincy Adams's secretary of the treasury, Richard Rush, tried to explain that capitalism was really an economy based on the existence of a large propertyless working class.[32] But this sounded like fantasy, given the tremendous opportunities still available for individual ownership. Besides, the law was hardly prepared to make formal distinctions in the law of property based on structural differences between modes of production. No matter how fast judges raced to keep up with the changing economic relationships of modern capitalist enterprise, they tended to persist in the view that private property was an ahistorical system of abstract rights. The law was limited in its response by its pretension that property was reducible to a single formula of claims and counterclaims. Faced with a contradictory social reality, and equipped only with an abstract legal category, judges tended to look to the prevailing economic controls of competitive markets to evaluate the workability of ancient rights. Society was invited to push the law along. Thus legal answers were to be found, not in distinctions between rival forms of production, but in the relative capacities of different types of property to achieve social benefits within the market economy. Expansionists won largely because the market was embraced by property owners themselves as the preferred channel of economic action. In the process, both individual and corporate property were reduced to the single common denominator of marginal productivity. In effect, two quite different forms of social possession were locked in combat, but as far as their formal status was concerned, they occupied the same category of legal rights. The law stood by in strict neutrality, an umpire committed only to the greatest good for the greatest number, or as Marx would put it, "the mutual interdependence of the individuals among whom the labour is divided." [33]

Early capitalist ideology had stressed equations between individual ownership and individual liberty. Organized power was feared and distrusted. Progress was identified with persons, not associations. Private profits, private power, and private freedom were inextricably linked together inside the institution of absolute, individual property. Feudal and monarchical oppression, those invidious forms of social power, were pushed aside by rebellious individualists seeking free footholds in landed property. In England, however, the old titles to the land were all too often converted from the hold of reactionary nobles to the possession of an anti-industrial landlord class. As we saw in chapter 2, early-nineteenth-century British entrepreneurs scorned the landowners as exploiters of a hostage society. Central to their ideological resistance, and to the increasing split between production and consumption property, was the embrace of a new political ideology called utilitarianism.

Utilitarians such as Jeremy Bentham and James Mill assailed as archaic and exploitative the rule of the rent-gouging landlords, whose selfish stand diminished the social happiness and hampered industrial progress. For utilitarians, no group was entitled to control society at the expense of the happiness of the individual citizens who composed the majority. Collective power could be justified, they insisted, only by its contributions to the pleasure of individuals. This was the appropriate test of public policy and social power, not raw economic interest. [34] In the face of a group whose wealth and power, said James Mill, were "not the result of natural acquisition, but of a sort of force, or compulsion, put upon other people," the utilitarian critique was joined with calls for democracy and majority rule. [35] Democracy allowed that each person was individually capable of judging what was worth doing, being, feeling, or consuming; reasonable social policies could be expected to result from the consultation of individuals. "I have not," Bentham proclaimed, "that horror of the people. I do not see in them that savage monster which their detractors dream of." [36] Bentham and Mill laid a theoretical base for regulating conflicts over the use of property in terms of democratic aspirations for increased happiness through increased production.

Utilitarians stressed that feelings were the basis of judgments, and feelings were not, at least for them, subtle things. In a very real sense, utilitarians reduced human sensibility to the single dimension of superficial aversions to injury and simple attractions to comfort. Utility's human being was a mechanical responder to external stimuli, not Locke's worker, busily laboring in the world, changing it according to individual plans and skills. Locke's natural human being was a producer. Bentham's human being was a consumer, the receiver of unreflected impressions of pleasure and pain.[37] It was entirely logical in this theory, then, to want to maximize the sum total of external pleasures and to suppress the level of social pains. Whatever added to the former was good public policy. And capitalism promised nothing if not to add much pleasure to the everyday life of consumers.

Utility offered new yardsticks for judgments of economic value and public policy. Indeed, the term itself referred to work only indirectly. Its origin was in the Latin root *usus,* which denoted the feelings of satisfaction and pleasure derived from using things, as opposed to the immediate physical work necessary to produce such things. As John R. Commons has pointed out, the distinction was subtle, but very influential. Use, Commons reminds us, means action; utility is a state of mind. Use is self-limiting; it reaches to the boundary of human energies and the tolerances of nature. Utility, by contrast, seems limitless. Its field is controlled by imagination, not the dirty world of raw materials and personal tools. Human feeling has no bounds: it was utility that Jefferson had in mind when he wrote that men pursue happiness. Utility is the carrot always dangled just a little bit ahead of the horse.[38]

When nineteenth-century philosophers insisted that utility should guide choices between conflicting interests, they conferred giant ideological advantages on capitalist entrepreneurs. Individual artisans were weak links in the industrial chain. Constrained by the limits of their bodies and the primitiveness of their equipment, they could manufacture goods, but not abundance. They answered needs; they did not stimulate the definition of new ones. But capitalists mobilized armies of labor and harnessed giant machines; they enlisted the discoveries of science and unleashed technology. By increasing the society's power to produce goods, they were compelled to extend society's ideas about its material wants and needs; utility came into focus as the basis of the market system; production was soon oriented to pleasure and leisure—indeed, farmers were among the first to relish the pleasures of "store-bought goods." As Marx once wistfully observed, anticipating Veblen's concept of the "instinct of workmanship," the ownership and personal mastery of tools gave people the opportunity to discover and to nurture their "true individuality." But this petty industry was "compatible with a system of production, and a society, moving within narrow and more or less primitive bounds."[39] Capitalism, by contrast, opened the door to endless accumulation, and not only of producer goods, but also of what Senator Daniel Webster called "articles of general consumption." As Webster pointed out in a speech in 1836, before, appropriately enough, the Society for the Diffusion of Useful

Knowledge, this distinction was fundamental to the general interests of capitalist society: utility became a synonym for "more."

> There are modes of applying wealth, useful principally to the owner, and not otherwise beneficial to the community than as they employ labor. . . . Not so with aggregate wealth employed in producing articles of consumption. This mode of employment is peculiarly and in an emphatic sense, an application of capital to the benefit of all.[40]

The Tests of Utility

As the studies of Morton Horwitz have carefully shown, early-nineteenth-century American judges gradually learned to equate use with utility in deciding conflicts between landowners.[41] The natural-use doctrine, with its anti-expansionist implications, was gradually forgotten, and the prior-use test began to be evaluated against new bench marks. Judges proceeded to date it from the onset of "new technology," not agriculture. Owners were soon compared on the basis of their efficiency at increasing wealth and social utility.

At first, the changes cropped up in riparian rights cases. The flooding of farmlands by mill owners incited typical contests. In these battles judges maintained rhetorical commitments to the mutual obligations of landowners; but in practice they treated rights in highly individualistic terms. When judgments of comparative utility were made, the relevant image was not a fabric of interwoven claims. Rather, judges thought in terms of separate blocks, each productively used in distinct activities. Social utility called for the splitting of property ties and "the release of energy" by competitive units, each of whose output could be rated against quantitative criteria of growth and abundance.

In the first water-mill cases, for example, active entrepreneurs were often excused from liability on the ground that common-law restrictions against interference with neighbors must themselves "be restrained within reasonable bounds so as not to deprive a man of the enjoyment of his property." Even more, the public should be afforded the "advantage . . . which always attends competition and rivalry."[42] Hence, the principle of *sic utere* "must be taken and construed with an eye to the natural rights of all." For if land "becomes less useful to one, in consequence of the enjoyment by another, it is by accident, and because it is dependent on the exercise of equal rights of others."[43]

The new outlook indicated that the more productive owners would be given a healthy leeway in generating social costs, whereas less efficient owners were expected to absorb them. "Accidents will happen" became the preferred cliché. Market forces assured that in the long run—when we are all dead, as Keynes once observed—society would come out the winner. Thus the not-so-automatic adjustments produced by judges were in accord with the greater logic of self-regulating markets and invisible hands. Losers could take heart that they were being moved not by other persons but by the forces of natural law. Gradually, then, assessments of the future, driven by a powerful new technological optimism, came to determine public policy toward the treatment of social relationships in the present. As David Noble has forcefully argued, this "resulted . . . in the loss of the present as the realm for assessments, decisions, and actions. And this intellectual blindspot, the inability to comprehend technology in the present tense, much less act upon it, inhibited the opposition [to economic change] and lent legitimacy to its inaction." In essence, changing concepts of time lent support to radical changes in the organization and control of space.[44]

Nowhere were these changes more directly and painfully evident than in the law of eminent domain. Takings multiplied as public construction increased. And, what was worse, owners were often commanded to yield their estates to private companies acting under the delegated authority of the state. Once again water mills set the pace. A host of state Mill Acts conferred upon entrepreneurs the right to flood their neighbors' land as well as to take land for private road construction. The mills were deemed a "public use" because they were "open to the public for grinding of corn."[45] In time, however, the "public use" doctrine was expanded to include many less socially accessible operations. Textile manufacturers, railroads, mining companies, and timber corporations were among the industries frequently endowed with rights to take.[46]

An even greater threat to landowners than the expanding category of takers, however, was the strict construction of "taking." By 1820 every state except South Carolina had enacted statutory requirements for "just compensation" in cases of seizure. These were applied to private expropriations as well. Hence the pains of confiscation were at least partially remedied by returns of exchange value, at least where compensation was admissible. But this was not the case where private owners suffered indirect injury, or "inverse condemnation," resulting from public development. Careful steps were taken to limit state and corporate liability in cases of peripheral injury to nearby owners. In effect, these principles were legal vessels from which enterprises could pour proximity costs onto other people's land.

Until about 1870, state courts applied the doctrine that compensation was required only in cases where individual property was physically seized by government. If owners suffered injuries "consequent to taking," or limitations on the beneficial use of their land because of state actions, these normally had to be accepted as the costs of progress. Thus owners whose houses were broken by the regrading of city streets, or whose farms were flooded by mills, could expect no relief. The theme "accidents will happen" was the popular rationale. In one of its more forthright and sympathetic statements, a Pennsylvania judge remarked that "these losses, like casualties in the prosecution of every public work, are accidental, but unavoidable; they are but samples of a multitude of others; so that the plaintiffs have at least the miserable good luck to know that they have companions in misfortune; would that it were in our power to afford them more solid consideration."[47]

This line of thought produced severely anti-protectionist conclusions. If owners were required to suffer direct injury from physical invasion of their property in order to sue for damages, then, logically, they had no rights to seek liability payments for public injuries, for damages collectively suffered along with everyone else. If construction of roads or water-improvement projects, for example, scattered proximity costs across whole neighborhoods, individual owners lacked the right to sue for relief for their share of the harm, for community protection could not be pursued through the legal claims of private property. In Blackstone's words, "The law gives no private remedy for anything but a private wrong."[48]

Even more restrictions were placed on the exclusionary powers of resistance. The early Mill Acts also prohibited owners from taking actions in self-defense, such as "creative destruction" of the offending dams, and lawsuits for punitive damages and permanent injunctions were often forbidden. Traditional common-law approaches to accidents, which required a mere showing of injury, were modified by the new negligence law to include tests requiring a showing of carelessness. Rights to determine compensation awards were widely removed from juries, which often proved overly sensitive to the dispossessed. Expert panels were appointed to give more professional and predictable appraisals. The expert panels often lowered their awards by computing "offsetting benefits" to the owner's leftover land. These were said to result from locations next to the very projects that led to the confiscations in the first place. Underlying all such steps was the firm conviction of state legislators and judges that property was an individual right of physical possession subject to the expansionist imperative of a commercial society. The ties that counted now were the economic relationships of industry and trade, not the protectionist alliances of conservative landowners. To a considerable degree, mid-nineteenth-century landed property could expect defense only against the attacks of lower-class thieves. From the depredations of honest industry, it could anticipate little relief.

Rebuilding the Walls

For all their impressive inroads, expansionists never succeeded in completely overturning society's regulatory power. Capitalism increasingly prevailed, to be sure, but the state's power to police society and to cut down at least some of the worst abuses still stood; authority to sequester flagrant dangers or to restrict private activity of imminent harm to the community continued to be exercised. New York City, for example, citing health reasons, successfully prohibited the use of certain private land for burial of the dead, despite the fact that the owners had a long-standing city lease to operate a cemetery. Massachusetts and other state courts upheld similar exercises of the police power for reasons of community protection.[49]

What vigor remained in the exercise of police powers, however, hardly brightened the hopes of those landowners whose activities were subject to regulation. As far as they were concerned, community-protection controls were nearly as painful as forced seizures. Property owners must often have found themselves wishing that they were not part of society at all, for when their rights collided with public claims to expand or regulate, most judges used strict, physical definitions of "takings" to excuse government from financial liability. After 1870, though, state action began to face new limitations, as the rights of property were gradually expanded to include intangibles such as market value and the potential for unearned increments. Indeed, property now came to be understood less in terms of physical titles than as a commercial institution whose market value could rise independently of advances in real production. The growth of corporations, most notably the railroads, and the passage of the Fourteenth Amendment in 1868 set the stage for a shift back toward a more positive view of exclusionary rights, toward a view of property as an island with legally defensible boundaries. With the states now constitutionally barred from actions that "deprive any person of life, liberty, or property, without due process of law," the U.S. Supreme Court was, more certainly than ever before, entitled to oversee local interventions into the world of private property.

New Defenses Against Taking

An early, though somewhat belatedly influential, clue to the new perspective was an 1871 case, *Pumpelly* v. *Green Bay Company.* Mr. Pumpelly's land was flooded by a Wisconsin dam-builder acting under the authority of the state legislature. Although his estate was not directly taken, the company's action effectively ruined any possibility of further productive use. Cutting against the grain of numerous state precedents, the U.S. Supreme Court awarded Pumpelly his compensation despite the fact that his land was not actually seized. The justices thought it "a very curious and unsatisfactory result" that owners should fail to receive payments when public action destroyed the use of their property, merely because government conveniently refrained "from the absolute conversion of title." [50]

Pumpelly's victory marked a notable judicial retreat from the main line of attack against the landed interest. Traditionally, eminent domain had been applied as if its target were "the land itself," as if real property were a kind of monolithic right that defied separation into discrete claims. The crux of the seizure power had always been the sovereign right to detach a unified, physical claim to the earth, whereas compensation was triggered only by expropriations of solid blocks of property.[51] In *Pumpelly*, though, the Court seemed to be saying that policy operated, not against the land itself, but against the more abstract commercial interests of its owner in market society. Property was, in this sense, not a thing but a legal "bundle of rights" to engage in commercial relationships, any one of which could be severely enough impaired by the state to warrant compensation. In a world where property was held for its value on the market, the right to property could not be reduced to objective physical possessions. Property included a cluster of rights whose value had to be measured in relation to surrounding locational and commercial factors. Property was best seen as a structure of abstract legal claims, each with its own determinate value, which could and should be treated separately when judges calculate the costs of public action to aggrieved owners. Value must be given for value taken.

Revisionists in legal scholarship supported these contentions with the argument that the "just compensation" clause of the Fifth Amendment was designed less to limit arbitrary expropriations than to distribute the burden of confiscation from the landowner to society at large. Public force must not, according to this view, be permitted to suspend the rules of an economic system based on assumptions of free and fair trade. As Joseph Cormack later observed, in eminent domain proceedings "the ideal to be arrived at is that the compensation awarded shall put the injured party in as good a condition as he would have been if the condemnation proceedings had not occurred. Nothing short of this is adequate compensation." [52]

Of course, the *Pumpelly* decision did not overturn a land use regulation. The case hinged on a substantial loosening of the old physical-invasion test for eminent domain, and Pumpelly's land *was* invaded, if indirectly. Still, it is clear in retrospect that a first important step had been taken toward the principle that if exchange-value rights suffered as a result of creative destruction, owners might enjoy compensation despite the fact that title remained in their hands. How far, though, was this position from one that endorsed the safeguarding of market values and market situations *with* public regulation? If property values deserved protection against public impairments, did they also deserve guarantees against destruction by the forces of the market itself? From this standpoint, *Pumpelly* took the Court up to the edge of the basic contradiction between expansion and exclusion rights. For the same logic of commercial value that justified limits on the uses of eminent domain might also be read to warrant police-power protection against the destabilizing forces of expansive capitalism, especially where owners were coming to learn the arts of extracting exchange values by withholding land from urban real estate markets. Did government have obligations to protect "unearned increment" as well as wealth earned "the old fashioned way"? *Pumpelly* had no answers to such questions; indeed, it failed to raise them explicitly. Too much, then, must not be read into the Supreme Court's first excursion into the field of eminent domain. But *Pumpelly* did give new meaning to the multiple rights of landed property, and so it also gave to the states problems in reconciling contradictions that a half-century of pro-expansion policy had tended to suppress.

In fact, the Court was extremely deliberate about pursuing the tentative lead offered by *Pumpelly*. Over the next decade it decided a series of crucial police-power cases that forcefully articulated the right of states to regulate private industry without paying compensation to offending owners. *Pumpelly* seemed to get lost quickly in a blaze of legal fire released by the "slaughterhouse" cases, *Munn* v. *Illinois* and *Mugler* v. *Kansas*.[53]

Judges and legislators in the lower federal ranks, however, were more sensitive to the need to vouchsafe exchange values. A sprinkling of precedents garnished the local law books with pro-landowner decisions even before *Pumpelly*. But only after 1870, when the Supreme Court flashed its yellow signal, did judges come to a broader acceptance of the view that " 'land' is not 'property' but the subject of property," that is, the "subject" of rights to its use and exchange in real estate markets.[54] State legislatures began to get the message, too. Illinois led a trail of other states in amending its constitution to insure that "damages" to property were as eligible for compensation as the traditional forms of physical seizure.[55] With increased legal respect for exchange values, buttressed by increased political power for real estate interests in city politics, some courts even began to overturn municipal street-layout plans for violating the "takings" clause.[56] But exclusion's most important victory before the turn of the century was undoubtedly the Supreme Court's rejection of Minnesota's system of rail-freight regulation in 1890. In the case of *Chicago, Minneapolis and St. Paul Railway Co.* v. *Minnesota*, Justice Samuel Blatchford led a majority in favor of what had hitherto been the dissenting view that "property is everything which has exchangeable value." States may not, even in the interest of the public, regulate this value away. The police power does not immunize government from constitutional limitations: the "power to regulate is not a power to destroy." If states seek to protect public values, and if this requires the destruction of private commercial interests, such action must be switched onto the "takings" track. Careful scrutiny of actions by other states could be anticipated, Blatchford warned. Exclusion had new friends in high places.[57]

Ernst Freund, a distinguished and influential legal scholar at the University of Chicago, followed up on and refined the implications of Blatchford's argument. For Freund, legal theory had failed to give due notice to the difficulties of laying neat boundary lines between police power and that of eminent domain. These were hardly as distinct as nineteenth-century judges tended to assume. Regulation, he insisted, was a hardy and formidable responsibility; its punch could be felt a long way. Indeed, it could go too far, sometimes even packing the wallop of confiscation itself. And in such extreme cases, government must be confronted with the fact that its strength has reached beyond its authority. But the precise measurement of the police power offered strenuous challenges: it was a judicial responsibility to mediate the conflicts between legitimate public aspirations and equally legitimate private rights by balancing the claims of value against authority. "The constitutional right of private property," Freund urged, "must be weighed against the demands of the public welfare, and it is obvious that a public interest which is strong enough to justify regulation may not be strong enough to justify destruction or confiscation without compensation."[58] Takings, in short, were questions not of kind but of degree.

Pennsylvania Coal v. Mahon

The climax of this trend came in 1922, just a few years before the Court upheld the constitutionality of zoning. The case, *Pennsylvania Coal Company v. Mahon,* deserves a close look.[59] Not only were its facts a stark exposure of the contending issues between expansionist rights, community protection powers, and the liberty of property to exclude, but it also emerged as the leading precedent for "takings" claims in modern land use cases.

For decades, coal corporations had eagerly mined the eastern Pennsylvania hills and closely controlled the towns and cities that grew up to serve the young industry.[60] Most of the land in the region was owned by the companies, although many firms had made a practice of selling their surface rights to homeowners. In these transactions the companies were careful to reserve complete control of the mineral rights. Typical deeds included waivers of corporate responsibility for injuries to life or property suffered as a result of mining operations, especially subsidence, the cave-ins that result when so much soil is dug out of the earth that the surface collapses.

During and after World War I, coal production in eastern Pennsylvania soared, and so did the dangers of subsidence. Throughout the hills, the earth began to crumble. The city solicitor in Scranton described the result in his city in graphic terms:

> Scranton bids fair to become a second Verdun. . . . Our once level streets are in humps, our gas mains have broken . . . our sewers spread their pestilential contents into the soil, our buildings have collapsed . . . our people have been swallowed up in suddenly yawning chasms, blown up by gas explosions or asphyxiated in their sleep, our cemeteries have opened and bodies of our dead have been torn from their caskets.[61]

To contain an impending disaster, the Pennsylvania state legislature in 1921 passed a law prohibiting coal mining where the resulting subsidence could undermine the foundation of urban buildings. In that same year, a Scranton homeowner, H. J. Mahon, received a letter from the Pennsylvania Coal Company notifying him that mining currently under way beneath his property would soon "cause subsidence and disturbance" on his lot; he was advised to leave.[62] Mahon, an attorney, sued the company, charging that the imminent destruction of his house violated Pennsylvania law. Pennsylvania Coal replied that the law was unconstitutional: not only did it impair the obligation of a contract guaranteeing the company mineral rights to the soil, but it also effectively took the value of company property without affording due process of law or just compensation.

The lower courts were divided in the case, with the state supreme court upholding Pennsylvania's power to regulate and Mahon's to exclude. The U.S. Supreme Court, however, disagreed. Justice Oliver Wendell Holmes, long an advocate of Ernst Freund's view that police regulations must not be allowed to take, saw the line passed in the Pennsylvania subsidence law. Setting aside the vast social implications of mining in the eastern Pennsylvania region, Holmes insisted that the case involved "a single private house." A cave-in was not per se "a public nuisance even if similar damage is inflicted on others in different places."[63] For Holmes, the issue involved a contest over the ownership of a single parcel of land and constitutional rights to devour its innards: Pennsylvania had flatly denied the company's rights to a legitimate, socially desirable land use. These facts pushed Holmes to declare his now-famous "takings" test, a ruling that has effectively shaped the Court's outlook, if not all its decisions, until today: "The general rule at least is, that while property may be regulated to a certain extent, if regulation goes too far it will be recognized as a taking."[64]

Holmes's dismissal of the social and environmental facts of the case prevented Pennsylvania from applying the brakes to change even where change threatened to split the state into pieces, unless, of course, the state elected to pay the price of protection by purchasing the company's mineral rights at their market value. Just as important, however, the decision's emphasis on "the degree test" dramatized the Court's sensitivity to the inner conflict within the structure of private-property rights. Contradictions between expansion and exclusion could not be treated as matters subject to adjudication on the basis of clear legal principles. Site-specific conflicts involving landed property, capital, and government were best handled by a judicial system pragmatically attuned to the splitting of hairs in particular cases. Moreover, from the standpoint of property theory itself, Holmes neatly tied the "bundle of rights" theory, which nineteenth-century owners worked so hard to invoke against public takings, with implicit support for the logic of creative destruction and capitalist expansion. Indeed, Pennsylvania Coal's case seemed to perfectly symbolize the prevailing motives of capitalist property: a strong exclusionary interest in the expansionist pursuit of private production and profit.

But where did all this leave public rights to community self-protection, or the defense of private exchange values resulting from the restriction of market forces? Superficially, it seemed that such interests were sorely damaged by Holmes's "degree" test. In fact, though, Holmes nowhere precluded a recoupling of police powers and private-property rights on behalf of rising exchange values. On the contrary, his embrace of Pennsylvania Coal's "mineral rights," as well as its corollary rights to market the product, suggests a judicial policy strongly disposed toward a growing trade in land and resources. If land use restrictions were themselves linked to an argument for rising exchange values, then the constitutionality of collective landowner controls might be just around the corner.

Urban Resistance

Holmes's defense of property backed the demands of absentee ownership and exchange value: real estate on the move. But there were limits to the security of urban landowners in a law operating on assumptions of movable wealth. *Pennsylvania Coal* painted an unforgettable picture of what it really meant to send land into motion. The earthy fixture and mutual interdependence of landed-property rights were facts the courts could ignore only temporarily. Local homeowners knew better; one sign was the increasing tendency of urban proprietors to band together in separate residential districts. A fortress mentality took hold, for property owners found themselves in the new environment of the industrial capitalist city, where the conditions of production and life accentuated with unmistakable force the enduring structural fact that property rights are intermixed with the production system and vulnerable to the capitalist advance. Giant factories; big transportation systems; spiraling new energy, distribution, and communication networks; and massive stocks of working-class housing were built swiftly, and often shoddily, from the ground up. Thrown together not according to plan or some secret logic of technical inevitability, they burst forth on the land in rough and barely ready response to the interests and dreams of capitalists and speculators. Exclusionary resistance rose exponentially.

City neighborhoods took on special flavorings and colorings as ethnic, racial, and class counterparts drew close in quest of mutual aid and comfort. Market forces, guided by what Seymour Toll calls the forces of "unplanned attraction," cloistered landowners and renters within high-density urban neighborhoods, whose premiums on space became themselves means of insulation.[65] Of course, the attraction was not altogether "unplanned." The culture favored ethnic separation, racial discrimination, and class stratification. Market mechanisms were excellently suited to the reproduction of social and class differences in spatial form. Hence "unplanned attraction" was everywhere matched by planned repulsion. Sophisticated middle-class Americans had a keen spatial consciousness, one deeply informed by Victorian traditions that celebrated the neat and clean, one that reached a heightened compulsiveness when the lower orders moved next door. Historian Burton J. Bledstein writes that people of the middle ranks believed that "everyone naturally belonged in a specific space, especially the poor." In the 1860s, he adds, "environmental reformers began designing tenement houses for immigrants." The tenements were not mixed randomly among the houses of the affluent. The classes separated. "Entirely new segregated working-class housing districts emerged," writes David Gordon. "Located near factories so that workers could walk to work, the housing was crammed densely together in isolation from the middle and upper classes." [66] Market forces split the nucleus of the congested old mercantile cities, projecting the working and emerging middle classes into distinct cultural and spatial orbits.

But "the middle and upper classes" lacked faith in the repulsive powers of the market; they commenced the great urban pullout. Already a noticeable tendency by 1850, when Chicago was surrounded by at least sixty fringe settlements, nearly half of Philadelphia's citizens lived outside its municipal boundary lines, and Brooklyn supplied Manhattan with much of its bedroom space, suburbanization accelerated with the extension of commuter railways, streetcars, and later, of course, the automobile. According to Robert Wood, the population surrounding America's sixty-two largest cities rose by 33 percent between 1910 and 1920, "for the first time exceeding the growth of the cities themselves," reaching ten million by 1920. At that point, 15 percent of the nation's population were suburbanites. [67] The movement was formally certified by the United States Census Bureau, which began officially to chart the growth of wholly new entities called "suburb" and "metropolitan district." Thus, by 1910 the census revealed the contrary pulls of social attraction and repulsion in its finding that the nation included twenty-five principal metropolitan districts, ranging from New York with almost six and a half million people, to Portland, Oregon, inhabited by a quarter of a million. More than 10 percent of the population in sixteen of the districts lived outside the big-city limits. [68]

The suburb, of course, was only America's latest effort "to get away from it all." Built on tax resistance, fears of the working class, and nativism, as well as on pastoral dreams of life in the wide open spaces, the middle-class suburb, writes Lewis Mumford, represented a "class effort to find a private solution for the depression and disorder of the befouled metropolis." [69] This "private solution" was expressed by more than the single-family detached house, however. It was also reflected in efforts to guard suburbia itself with the armor of public government. Middle-class homeowners made eager allies of rural land-owners in struggles to halt central-city annexations. State legislatures were sharply pressed to liberalize municipal incorporation laws as defensive maneuvers against expansionist cities. [70] Political coalition was vividly understood as the prerequisite to effective class and ethnic segregation. But white, middle-class suburbanites, like their forebears the squatters, ran ahead of the law. They assumed rights to what was not yet a legal fact. Public fencing did not include authority to control overall community land use patterns. Imminent dangers might be avoided, but powers to plan for or against change had not yet won acceptance. And Holmes's finding in *Pennsylvania Coal* hardly augured well.

The weakness of the law in providing authority for town planning was serious. In the older cities, affluent sections were usually sufficiently compact and densely populated to block out low-rent tenants. But with the exception of early company towns, most of the newer suburbs attracted affluent buyers with the lure of peace and quiet through provision of abundant open space. Nevertheless, to the extent that openness was one of the main lures of suburbia, it was an openness that was supposed to remain closed, as most buyers expected or at least hoped that adjacent areas would stay undeveloped. Open space was a utility for the affluent because it was not used by the poor.

But the trouble with exclusion in market systems is that it always attracts a crowd. Thus the process of low-density suburbanization fueled the forces of its own subversion. For the more that outer-city land was selectively used for low-density housing, the more profits could be made from building high-density, lower-income apartment units there, to take advantage of existing utilities and amenities, the available economies of scale. As Robert Nelson explains: "The likelihood that housing for people with low income could be built in high-income neighborhoods represented a much greater threat to these neighborhoods when they were built at low-suburban densities." [71] Suburban exclusion offered opportunities all too ready for expansion, by leaving plenty of room for more of everything that the big city already had.

Strongly adding to the threat was the fact that poorer workers were frequently very eager to move to the suburbs themselves, for many of the same reasons as those of the middle class. Indeed, given the horrendous condition of most worker housing at the turn of the century, labor's incentives for flight were, if anything, even greater than those that pushed middle-income renters out of the better city neighborhoods. Moreover, large-scale industrial capital was itself, in many cases, on the move toward the suburbs. Eager to leave the larger cities, where machine-run governments mobilized working-class power, raised taxes, and provided second-rate services, many corporations took to the urban hinterland not only their factories but also pressing needs for large stocks of easily affordable housing to shelter their work forces. As David Gordon has pointed out, "Between 1899 and 1909, central city manufacturing employment increased by 40.8 percent while [suburban] ring employment rose by 97.7 percent." As Gordon adds, the "new manufacturing towns"— such as Gary, Indiana; Lackawanna, New York; and Chester and Norristown, around Philadelphia—"were being built in open space like movie sets." [72]

The expansionist interests of significant segments of both labor and capital squeezed against the suburban property interest in exclusion. By opening new metropolitan frontiers for residential construction, the pull of the real estate developers, builders, banks, merchants, and industrial capital, increasingly driven by the push of labor's housing demands, was like a locomotive unbreakably connected to its stock cars as well as its upscale sleepers. If class separation was to be maintained, a way had to be found to unhitch the lead cars from the stock trailers; otherwise the real estate market would tend to re-fuse the classes into mixed living and work patterns in the suburbs and continue to undermine the social relations of exclusionary property in land.

Suburban developers took the first steps toward collective exclusion by requiring homebuyers to sign private covenants—deed restrictions that enjoined future sales to "blacks, Jews, and other minorities." Such restrictions became extremely popular and, though later frowned on by the courts, are still used.[73] As President Ronald Reagan and Chief Justice William Rehnquist both observed when asked to explain their earlier signatures on deed restrictions, exclusionary covenants were among those tedious and unremarkable obligations left to the lawyers, not unlike title searches. Private covenants were, of course, much more than technical rules; they were powerful and widely used devices of social exclusion. But over the long haul, private exclusion was battered by the expanding market. Middle-income Jews and blacks might be kept out by private prohibitions, but enterprising builders needed only to purchase land adjacent to exclusive subdivisions, and working-class Christians—East European Catholics, for example—might soon be next door. For the most discriminating excluders, these were distinctions without a difference. Their walls were too easily breached. In order to limit the market, individual agreements needed collective fortification: barriers had to be built at the governmental perimeter of private communities.

Short of comprehensive land use regulations, existing police-power controls against nuisance were the handiest devices available to set the preferred social patterns into place. Early efforts to tap their potential were built on nineteenth-century precedents that allowed for curbs against noxious facilities. Small capital was one of the first social groups to suffer the effects of politically organized, exclusionary land use controls, for the dirtier forms of petty capitalist enterprise—slaughterhouses, livery stables, billboards, and laundries—made easy targets. Whereas giant industrial mills were rarely questioned in cities such as Pittsburgh, fumes, noise, dirt, and traffic could clearly be shown to threaten suburban health, as well as the appreciation of land values, especially when they emanated from the smaller plants of individual manufacturers. In these cases, police-power tests of general interest and reasonableness were relatively easily satisfied.[74] A few cities also successfully experimented with controls dividing the landscape into building-height zones to secure sunlight against the threat of looming skyscrapers.[75] Such measures, which tampered with the freedom of some of the more powerful urban construction interests, were upheld by the Supreme Court as acceptable uses of the police power. Excluders took heart from a judiciary well versed in the logic of real estate values and increasingly sympathetic to community protection. But, as a look at one of the landmark nuisance cases will reveal, banking on exchange value as the groundwork for community protection was a shaky proposition.

Hadacheck's Defeat and
the Frailties of Nuisance Law

In the 1915 case of *Hadacheck* v. *Sebastian,* the Court was asked to rule on the constitutionality of a 1909 Los Angeles "block ordinance" that divided the city into seven industrial districts and a single residential zone.[76] Some existing businesses had been permitted to continue their operations within the now legally codified residential neighborhoods, but a number of small industrial enterprises had been forced to shut down. None was granted compensation, as the regulations were implemented under the city's police authority. Located on a site that it had occupied since 1902, several years before Los Angeles annexed the area, Hadacheck's brickyard was one of the unfortunates to wind up on the neighborhood blacklist. Predictably, the owner sued, insisting that in America the legitimate commercial use of one's land cannot be enjoined without fair compensation. Indeed, since his brickyard preceded the advance of suburban residents into the area, as well as the ordinance itself, there was good reason to believe that both the eighteenth-century "prior use" and the nineteenth-century "release of energy" theory could effectively be cited to back Hadacheck's claim. He was a first-comer who used his property for productive, albeit somewhat odoriferous, purposes. By contrast, the city-suburban booster alliance wanted Hadacheck out, but not at the price of "just," or any other, compensation. For Los Angeles, Hadacheck's loss was a cost of progress, rightfully absorbed by himself alone as one of the social obligations of ownership in a changing society.

Compared with the devastating physical facts of *Pennsylvania Coal,* soon to reach the Court's agenda, Hadacheck's facts were nearly trivial. But the legal questions were identical: Did communities have rights to protect themselves from injurious land uses without fear of having to enter into real estate deals with offenders? Was the "takings" clause of the Fifth Amendment, reinforced by the obligations of the Fourteenth, a check on overzealous uses of the police power? Seven years before it decided *Pennsylvania Coal,* the Supreme Court ruled in favor of cities: utility was defined in terms of rising property values and expanding land markets; noncompensable regulation was in bounds.

Ruling for the right of Los Angeles to segregate a noxious use, the Court said: "A vested interest cannot be asserted against it because of conditions once obtaining."[77] Public policy was supreme over a vested interest, even where that right was actively used to create wealth. Admitting that brickyards were not a "nuisance per se," the Court nonetheless held, as it had in an earlier test involving an Arkansas livery stable, that governments may define as nuisance "in particular circumstances and in particular localities" what were otherwise perfectly acceptable activities.[78]

At the same time, however—and this is more important—the Court did not endorse public rights to exclude as a means of controlling social change. Indeed, the Court refused to identify the Los Angeles ordinance with a settled, residential interest at all. The block ordinance was upheld because it contributed to urban expansion, not because it guarded the status quo. The Court thought it wrong to lessen the promise of municipal growth by confusing the real estate market with garbled signals. This would

> preclude development and fix a city forever in its primitive conditions. There must be progress, and if in its march private interests are in the way they must yield to the good of the community. The logical result of petitioner's contention would seem to be that a city could not be formed or enlarged against the resistance of an occupant of the ground and that if it grows at all it can only grow as the environment of the occupations that are usually banished to the purlieus.[79]

Of course, Hadacheck had originally banished himself to the "purlieus"—his problems began when the Los Angeles land market caught up with him, and the "purlieus" became a "nice neighborhood." Once this happened, the Court was forced to balance the relative productivity of brickyards and subdivisions as factors of expanding urban utility. This test was classic, nineteenth-century vintage; its criteria were expansionist. That the successful defenders in the case turned out to be residential real estate interests was less a reflection of the Court's sensitivity to the need for planned exclusion in urban development than a fortuitous result of the facts at hand. Its standards were derived from the logic of rising exchange values, not the values of neighborhood stability. Thus Los Angeles, like the Pennsylvania Coal Co., represented the leading edge of growth; Hadacheck, like the state of Pennsylvania, overextended the right of exclusion, unconstitutionally barring the benefits of economic progress. Although the rulings were strikingly different in their grounds—Holmes defended individual rights against society, whereas Hadacheck lost his to society—the rulings were identical in their spirit of commitment to the notion that the good of society is to be found in the interests of progressive, dynamic investment, not in the defense of static wealth. That the common expansionist theme should triumph out of such mutually inconsistent logics is testimony to the power of the prevailing expansionist bias and to the distance that community protectors had to travel to reach a solution to the problem of legitimating the rights of community self-defense *against* expansion. Judges still applied growth-oriented tests. Doubters had only to follow the legal trail to Mahon's house or to Hadacheck's brickyard.

Rural Precedents for Exclusion

For excluders to gain the authority necessary to regulate land use prospectively, it was crucial to persuade the courts that an "accidents will happen" perspective was inappropriate to modern urban conditions. Collisions between expansion and exclusion rights had to be seen as something more than just chance occurrences. They stemmed from the massive density and complexity of modern industrial society and, more basically, from the contradictions of capitalist property itself. Ironically, rural land policy came to reflect an appreciation of these facts years before they registered in urban land use circles.

The history of the public lands, of course, was a story of "rip and run." Not until the 1890s were serious efforts made to withdraw public resources from free-swinging expropriation and destruction.[80] Although, with some exceptions, ranchers, timber companies, water-power outfits, miners, and oil interests fought conservation at first, patterns of public-land administration were gradually settled that finally won the support of business.[81] Both the mammoth raw-materials corporations—notably in petroleum, mining, and timber—and the smaller, more competitive agricultural interests discovered lucrative niches in the new systems of regulated access. But whereas the incorporation of private developers took from two to three decades to complete, the early proponents of public-land management never actually challenged the desirability of capitalist development. The early conservationists wanted to discipline, not dismantle, the market. For them, not private use but unregulated private takeovers led to a gorging on resources that threatened the long-term availability of supplies; public policy needed to put business on a diet, leaving capital leaner and more efficient, and thus, in the long run, more profitable.

Conservation policy rested on scientific, not political, theory. But implicit in the claim to neutrality was tacit acceptance of the capitalist institutions of resource development. Scientists emphasized that development must, above all, respect the finite limits of nature. Raw materials were not randomly stockpiled in nature but were locked instead into complex, multidimensional, physical relationships. Climate, soil, vegetation, water, minerals, and animal life were inextricably entwined in ecological systems. Materials could not be ripped out of the land without leaving ruptures whose consequences would return to haunt the population in the forms of drought, flood, erosion, pestilence, or depletion. Human beings had no choice but to adjust themselves to the complexities of nature, utilizing modern techniques of scientific foresight and care. Production could and must be carried on, but only with dutiful planning and supervision by experts in land management.[82] "In the nature of things," wrote a former head of the U.S. Bureau of Land Management, "the use of the federal land is available to some citizens and not others."[83] Experts were needed to resolve difficult questions of access according to seemingly objective criteria. Samuel P. Hays's studies, for example, describe the conservationists' strong conviction that "conflicts between competing resource users . . . should not be dealt with through the normal processes of politics." [84] Thus, the dominant theory and ideology of public-land management emerged as the doctrine of "multiple use," the principle that land could be devoted to many different functions all at once so long as experts controlled the terms of access. Forest land, for example, could be employed simultaneously for wood-cutting, hydroelectric-power production, cattle grazing, and recreation—all under the watchful guidance of the U.S. Forest Service.

In practice, multiple use became a highly sophisticated means for controlling use of the national lands by industrial and agricultural capital. The public lands became in effect a wholesale warehouse that stocked resources for private enterprise. A careful account of this development requires separate treatment; what is important to the story of private land use is that the intellectual founders of conservation, people such as George Perkins Marsh, John Wesley Powell, Gifford Pinchot, and others, provided a powerful analysis of the inevitability of resource destruction, waste, and conflict unless land use was supervised and managed by government. For the scientists, land use collisions were not accidental; they were evidence of human ignorance and indifference in the face of changed industrial and physical conditions. Regulation and exclusion were needed to protect the public's interest in continued supply and development of raw materials. The role of the state as collective landowner was both inscribed in its obligation to serve national development and dictated by nature itself.

Toward the Socialization of Urban Land Rights

Soon, students of the private land use scene learned to make similar observations. Among the most prescient and influential was Frederick Law Olmsted, probably the nation's greatest landscape architect and urban planner. In his battles over the planning and construction of New York City's Central Park and other projects, he was well tutored in the inevitabilities of urban land use collisions. He passed his wisdom on by asking citizens to reflect for a moment about what was required of them just to walk down a bustling city street: "Whenever we walk through the denser part of town, to merely avoid collision with those we meet and pass upon the sidewalks we have constantly to watch, to foresee, and to guard against their movements." Naturally, as cities expanded, "obstructions were more frequent, movements were slower and often arrested . . . the liability of collision . . . greater." [85] Without adequate foresight and control, urban growth produced the very same kinds of conflicts and destruction that ravaged the public domain. For Justice Holmes, too, such struggles were "inevitable, unless the fundamental axioms of society and even the fundamental conditions of life are to be changed." [86]

The insight that land use conflicts were endemic to private property systems was hardly novel. Nuisance law, as William Rodgers, Jr., points out, had always aimed at minimizing friction between users.[87] Olmsted and Holmes, however, implied that under the changed industrial conditions, nuisance law no longer made adequate adjustments to the rate and scale of economic activity. The legal relations between landed property and capitalist enterprise lagged behind the state of the primary economic forces. Joseph Sax suggests that, for Oliver Wendell Holmes, "established economic interests were engaged in a battle for survival against the forces of social change," but the frameworks of law assured neither fairness nor equity in resolving the issues.[88] The law, as always, was preoccupied with individual rights, but the agents clashing in the cities represented highly structured "social interests," not merely legal persons. As Sax notes, the issues were not merely "conceptual or formal"; rather, as Holmes began to understand, they were "manifestations of social conflict." [89] Appropriate answers were now to be found less in law than in new administrative designs for smoothing out relationships between organized groups of interests, that is, through administration rather than jurisprudence.

Obviously, the theory of multiple use was in itself of little help in the private sphere. Homeowners were in no mood to share their space with industrial capital or its army of labor. But the framework of public-land administration did offer clues to possible private-sector strategies. Most important, the public-land system illustrated the chance for stability in land use relationships if only care were taken to adjust access patterns to the needs of key property groups. Land planning had to address not all the public needs, but only the principal property-based demands; these were, after all, the only articulate demands ever made on the land system. The propertyless were mute, divorced from the conflicts by a class disqualification. They would, as always, follow the crowds into the slums, directed silently by invisible hands. The political problem was to keep productive and residential property interests from interfering with each other's market opportunities. To be successful, therefore—that is, to provide for class order—public policy needed only to channel industrial and commercial expansion away from choice residential sites. The result, based on public planning of future need, would be a rational equilibrium of supply and demand among landed-property interests, sensitively guided by the gentle hand of local government. Expansion and exclusion would be rendered compatible by separating "honest industry" from "unearned increment," production from consumption, workplace from home.

Obviously, attempts to make a case for land use policy on explicit class terms would fail the police-power test of equitability. But carefully laid class strategies, much less conspiracies, were hardly necessary. Indeed, they were beside the point, for middle-class property owners had reformers and planners on their side whose implicit assumptions kept policy firmly in line with the needs of settled ownership and rising exchange values. The land use reform-ers' social perspective put them on a definite class plateau, whether they were conscious of it or not. By taking it for granted that land should remain in pri-vate hands, that it should continue to be traded and used as a commodity, and that it should cease to be a topic of social conflict, reformers were led, "inde-pendent of their will," to an outcome inherently biased against the landless. This was not a question of conspiracy, but the logical fallout of a system whose members were preoccupied with property rights as the central organiz-ing theme of land use issues.

Zoning and the Collective Landowner

Between 1900 and 1916, then, the emerging responses to private land use conflict gradually took shape. Building codes, block ordinances, city plans, and nuisance regulations abounded. But their most powerful and effective ex-pression was undoubtedly zoning. Zoning lent modern scientific legitimacy to the law's traditional concern with conflict avoidance. The method was simple and appealingly balanced, altogether objective and efficient in appearance. Space for each of the basic economic functions was specially reserved, with particular attention paid to the most likely sources of collision. Prime residen-tial, commercial, and industrial uses were separated, like boxers in a ring, unclinched at the end of a long tough fight, and retired to their corners. Thus, unlike agricultural bias in the eighteenth century or the promotion of industry in the nineteenth, zoning seemed to preempt one-sided solutions in favor of an evenhanded, modern, technocratic balance. Under zoning, no one's fence need be bumped, no one's property rights need be dented. Improved traffic controls would keep everything in its place.

Like any set of walls, though, zoning had its faults. Superficially, it prom-ised neat answers to the land use jumble. Urban space was to be carefully segregated into use, height, and area districts. But the horizontal distribution of space was far from being based on objective criteria; implicit value judg-ments were invariably used to arrange functions in vertical hierarchies. The single-family house obtained sacred status at the apex of zoning theory. Apartments, shops, and workplaces were all banished from the purely resi-dential zone. The house was a virgin use. Nothing better exemplified Veblen's insight into the modern American deprecation of anything tinged with "pro-ductive labor" than did the single-family residential zone. Here alone was consumption purified for conspicuous performance, happiness and utility cleansed of any contact with Locke's "honest industry."[90] That people had lived for centuries in or near their workplaces was a "scientific" fact overlooked by zoners. Objectivity was measured against contemporary middle-class standards; anything less was hokum. These values were unimpeachable facts.

Of course, zoning theory was far from irrational. In precapitalist societies, people were never forced to live near steel plants, bus terminals, industrial-waste pits, or petroleum-fueled factories. Middle-class Americans understandably struggled to keep their distance from creeping industrialism. Zoning, however, closed this option for the propertyless. Because commercial and industrial districts permitted apartments, workers could still be located near the overly productive neighbors that the middle class shunned. And because class segregation was a basic presupposition of the land trade, and zoners were loathe to question it, they drafted the unofficial class map into official law. They formally decoupled the real estate locomotive from the crowded cattle cars. Low-income renters were now forced by government edict to disembark before arriving at the "single-family" station. The market was no longer their ally.

Zoning doubtless met the test of Barry Commoner's Second Law of Ecology, that "everything must go somewhere"—everything and everybody certainly did go *somewhere*. But whether these restrictions were in the "public interest," or guaranteed "the equal protection of the laws," or avoided serious intrusions in private-property rights were more dubious matters. That the originators of zoning had their own doubts is confirmed by Edward Bassett, one of the leaders of the movement in New York, the first city to adopt zoning. He observed that after the system was introduced in 1916, it was thought essential to establish a special committee of experts to "assist in the administration of the new law . . . and to help extend zoning throughout the country. It was feared that if this rather new innovation of the police power was employed in only one city courts would frown on it because of its limited use. The future of zoning was at the time precarious."[91]

Bassett's doubts stemmed, in part at least, from the knowledge that the New York law came about not because of an outpouring of popular residential demand but because heavy pressure was applied for zoning by a significant component of the city's capitalist class: the exclusive retailers and boosters of the midtown, Fifth Avenue shopping district. Agitated and angry over the increasing location of garment factories and sweatshops in lofts overlooking their prestigious corners and by the trail of immigrant laborers who found their way to work past the more exclusive storefronts, the city's bigger merchants saw zoning as a means of securing their status-conscious customers and uplifting the already enviable real estate values of their stores. Important lessons were taught in the New York case about the expansionist benefits of exclusion, but Bassett and his team wondered whether other towns and other interests would recognize them.[92]

The concerns were quite misplaced; Bassett and his colleagues turned out to be an excellent sales force for an idea whose time had come. According to

Seymour Toll, by 1929 "there were nearly 800 zoned municipalities in the United States. Three-fifths of the urban population, some 37 million people, were living under zoning controls." [93] But the demand was hardly contrived by New York City's boosters. Suburban America yearned for stronger fences. Neighborhoods and suburbs rushed to surround their blocks with walls. In 1924 even the federal government threw its support behind the movement when the Department of Commerce, appropriately enough, issued a standard Zoning Enabling Act. This act gave states a blueprint for delegating powers to localities to control land use. Even before the report sold out its first run of 55,000 copies, the secretary of commerce, Herbert Hoover, observed that "the discovery that it is practical by city zoning to carry out reasonably neighborly agreements as to the use of land has made an almost instant appeal to the American people." [94]

Practicality and popularity were sizable advantages weighing in favor of zoning. It seemed to answer middle-class aspirations for greater utility in land policy. But the courts would have to have their say. Holmes's *Pennsylvania Coal* ruling and the class implications of zoning posed unresolved questions. The principal test came in 1926, in the case of *Village of Euclid* v. *Ambler Realty Company.*[95] The facts were predictable and the issues thoroughly familiar: expansion and exclusion were once again at odds.

The Village of Euclid was a Cleveland suburb, in the Supreme Court's description "a politically separate municipality, with powers of its own to govern itself as it sees fit within the limits of the organic law of its creation and the State and Federal Constitutions." [96] In 1911 the Ambler Realty Company had purchased sixty-eight acres of undeveloped land in the town on a lot adjacent to two railway lines. Prospects were good that the area would one day fall into the path of Cleveland's industrial growth. In 1922, however, following the parade of hundreds of other towns, Euclid adopted a comprehensive zoning ordinance. Local investors were expected to march to new tunes. As a result, much of Ambler's land was placed in a residential district, its future industrial value restricted. Ambler complained that the village policy had shrunk the value of its property from $10,000 to $2,500 per acre. It demanded payment in return. Because the *Hadacheck* and *Pennsylvania Coal* precedents were in conflict, the outcome was anything but certain.

The U.S. District Court in Ohio agreed with Ambler. Free enterprise and equal opportunity were being crushed in the name of parochial, class self-interest. The town ordinance was ruled an illegal use of the police power because it unreasonably controlled private property to serve class ends. In the words of Judge David Westenhaver:

> The purpose to be accomplished is really to regulate the mode of living of persons who may hereafter inhabit [the town]. In the last analysis, the result to be accomplished is to classify the population and segregate them according to their income and situation in life.[97]

The police power did not condone unequal protection of the laws; nor did it permit land use controls to be directed at particular groups. For such privileges, middle-class suburbs had to compensate the owners of affected property by purchasing their rights. The line of cases stretching from *Pumpelly* to *Pennsylvania Coal* prohibited zoning. Individual units of property could not be sacrificed in favor of a collective landowner bent on class discrimination.

Euclid appealed to the U.S. Supreme Court, but after Judge Westenhaver's sharply worded rejection, zoning needed an especially able and scholarly defense. This it received in the form of a brilliant brief, submitted to the Supreme Court, *amicus curiae,* in the name of the National Conference on City Planning. The analysis, written by Cincinnati attorney Alfred Bettman, was a thorough and exhaustive explanation of the need for collective controls in a well-functioning market system.[98] Bettman well understood his task: he had to persuade the Court that zoning authority fell snugly under the police power, without touching the border of eminent domain, without passing Holmes's thin line.

Wisely, he began the defense by asserting needs for overall land use regulation as a means of promoting "the public health, the public morals, the public safety, the public convenience, the public order, the public prosperity and the general welfare."[99] Redundancy did not reflect an impoverished vocabulary. It was intended to amplify Bettman's central contention that zoning was not only justified by the police power but also represented an altogether more rational, disciplined, and comprehensive use of that power. Its purpose, therefore, was not class protection. Zoning was introduced to enable communities to achieve significant general values that communities may reasonably pursue as communities. "In the comprehensive ordinance, the locating of the districts and the height, use and area standards are adjusted to a carefully wrought plan for the promotion of the health, safety, convenience, and welfare of the whole community." "Private land-use rights were undoubtedly restricted," but this was justified by the nature and scope of the pressures of modern social change. Bettman cited "the remarkable growth of the zoning movement" as evidence "that zoning is absolutely essential if conditions of living are to remain tolerable and healthful."[100]

He portrayed the general welfare in classic conservationist terms. The prime benefits of zoning derived from its infusion of order and efficiency into the uncertain urban-land trade. The planned allocation of space was a great improvement over the unpredictable encounters between nuisance law and market forces. Zoning promised a "decidedly more just, intelligent, and reasonable" framework of action, guaranteeing investors and users alike a more calculable and predictable field of action.[101] It would reduce the mounting collisions occasioned by the laissez-faire system and thus help to stabilize private enterprise in land. By contrast, the "private land and building development of cities would be self-destructive if the community did not furnish regulation." [102] The avoidance of conflict found its traditional place at the center point of land use control.

This stabilization, moreover, was as much to the advantage of entrepreneurs as it was to the interest of landowners. By furnishing unchallenged space for growing enterprise, municipalities spared business from wasteful and unnecessary confrontations with neighborhood residents and merchants. "In the industrial district industry is legalized, thus freeing it from the injunctions and other complaints of neighboring properties and stabilizing the investments in the industrial plants; all of which is promotive of property." [103]

Finally, though, Bettman admitted that the special virtue of zoning lay in its power to secure exclusionary rights for the nation's long-vulnerable landowners. In making this point he trod very close to an explicit statement of the relation between public authority and private government for class protection. Searching for legal analogies to strengthen his position, he hit "in passing" on an observation that is, in fact, not marginal but central to the political logic of zoning. He noted similar cases of private alliance, such as "the enforced joint guarantee of bank deposits," which apply the "recognized power to enforce cooperation upon members of a group similarly situated, for the direct benefit of all of the group, with indirect benefit to the general public." [104] Anticipating the reluctance of individual proprietors to accept infringements on their liberty, Bettman said that public force was necessary to insure collective private security. Only by socializing the right to exclude could owners regain what Tocqueville called the "support of their connections" and keep capital and labor at bay. As Bettman put it, "In exchange of the restrictions which [zoning] places on each piece of property, it places restrictions for each piece of property." Moreover, these rights already existed. Zoning created nothing new but a connection. "The property rights asserted are simply those which inhere generally in all owners of land." [105]

Bettman left unexplained the "indirect benefit" enjoyed by the propertyless. But by this point the omission was not important. He had masterfully, if unself-consciously, equated the public interest with the class interest of proprietors. Was zoning an instrument of "the modern State for managing the common affairs" of the landowners and entrepreneurs? Bettman's case implicitly suggested that it was.

The U.S. Supreme Court, led by Justice George Sutherland, warmed to this line of analysis. Private property did need more general restriction for its own good. Economic history imposed new calls on policy. "Until recent years, urban life was comparatively simple: but with the great increase and concentration of population, problems have developed, and are constantly developing, which require, and will continue to require, additional restrictions" on private urban land. [106] These problems, moreover, required subtle judgments of interdependency, political evaluations best left to local legislators. After all, a nuisance was not a use but a matter of relative utility, an appraisal of the heart, not the brain. It need not be something so intrinsically bad that its evil was instantly recognized by all. A "nuisance may be merely a right thing in the wrong place—like a pig in the parlor instead of a barnyard." Admitting that such distinctions may be "fairly debatable," the Court nonetheless concluded that legislative judgments "must be allowed to control." [107]

For those still in the dark, an example was offered. Apartment houses, the Court observed, may in one setting "be not only entirely unobjectionable, but highly desirable," although in another they "come very near to being nuisances," that is, pigs in the parlor. The Court declared that when compared with "detached house sections" the "apartment house is a mere parasite, constructed in order to take advantage of open spaces and attractive surroundings created by the residential character of the district." [108] Apparently, however, it was "unobjectionable" to have them located near factories or on commercial streets, where the more congested and smudgy functions of capitalism were performed. Keeping functions and functionaries together seemed efficient, after all. "In the nature of things," presumably, some people were compelled to live near the "barnyard" uses that other people could legitimately exclude. There was nothing wrong with living next to "barns" if one could not afford otherwise. But if this were true, then zoning had much less to do with protecting people from harmful things than with protecting some people from other people. The focus of zoning was the social relationships of people, not things. Caught in the nexus between exclusion and expansion, the propertyless were forced to accept what the main traffic would not bear. Although the Court expressed reservations about some aspects of zoning "restrictions," especially the loss of liberty to property, these were not "arbitrary and unreasonable," nor without "substantial relation to the public health, safety, morals or general welfare." [109] Zoning thus stood up to its sternest legal test by meeting the call of the public good.

But the Court did make one additional observation that cast a shadow over the new power to exclude. It anticipated the possibility of "public interests" greater than those identified with local homeowners, interests perhaps incompatible with local controls. The justices did not intend by their confirmation of zoning "to exclude the possibility of cases where the general public interest would so far outweigh the interest of the municipality that the municipality would not be allowed to stand in the way." [110]

In a later review of the Court's decision, Alfred Bettman remarked on the significance of this point, seeing in it clear indications that prevailing law had shifted from traditional conceptions of individual rights versus public authority to a more sociologically sensitive awareness of institutionalized contradictions. "This passage in the opinion," he wrote, "is noteworthy in that it presents the conflict not as one between the individual and the community, but rather as between different communities, different social groups, or social interests, which is, when profoundly comprehended, true of all public power constitutional issues." [111] Bettman sensed, quite astutely, that zoning was no final answer to the exclusion-expansion problem and that, left to work out its own private logic, zoning would probably produce wider reactions against it.

Conclusion

Viewed in retrospect, the strong pro-expansion bias of nineteenth-century land policy was exceptional. It represented not the norm of American attitudes toward land protectionism but a break from cultural and legal commitments to restraint as the guiding principle of land use. Eighteenth-century conservatism and twentieth-century conservation surround the epoch of expansion with longer eras of control and regulation. But if a century of land-policy development represented a circuit back to protectionist assumptions, it is also true that, with zoning, the courts' role in settling expansion-exclusion conflicts underwent a secular change.

The *Euclid* decision did more than uphold a modernized version of ancient law. It also reflected the fact that, however obliquely, land use policy had become an intensely political concern, perhaps the most vital issue of community politics. After suffering for nearly a century the subtle suppression of their exclusionary rights, landowners were now sensitized to the need for direct governmental control of land use. Local changes in property rights were far less likely to happen behind their backs. The procedures of land use policy were now much more democratic.

But for several crucial reasons, the democratization was limited. First, the power shift occurred along the trenchline that divided consumption and production property, a line that kept the public community out of major production decisions, the very decisions that created the costs people wanted to avoid in the first place. Furthermore, the originators of change, local business interests, also saw clear benefits in zoning. Not only did it increase the chances for social control and stability—and these are always crucial political conditions of accumulation—but it also provided much-needed economic protection for local property values in shaky real estate markets. In this sense, it also increased the power of local capital to regulate its own political and economic environment. Zoning thus became the magnet for all sorts of organized urban power groups: neighborhood associations, land traders, builders, bankers, insurance firms, lawyers, merchants, manufacturers—all the partisans of property in municipal affairs.

Second, with a much wider range of interests actively participating in land use politics, the courts' ability to furnish clear signals in the dialectics of exclusion and expansion was bound to be more heavily constrained than ever before. After all, it was one thing to stand four-square for the status quo when British imperialism opposed American entrepreneurs, or to push landowners aside when an increasingly powerful entrepreneurial class, state legislatures, and public opinion embraced growth as an unquestionable goal of national policy. It was another matter entirely when the forces of expansion and exclusion were represented by equally vocal and well-organized interest groups.

Historically, the courts' prominence in land use policy, their ability to furnish uniformity and direction in law, was closely related to one-sided distributions of class power. That those relations were now more evenly balanced implied that conflicts between exclusion and expansion could well lead to stalemates that were inherently biased in favor of the more conservative, exclusionary forces. Institutionally, the new equilibria of land use politics set into slow motion the forces favoring corrective oversight by more independent managers at higher levels of the system, the re-creation of the kinds of decision mechanisms that the courts once so effectively supplied.

Part Two

Case Studies, Conflict, and Land Use Control

Introduction to Part Two:
The Restructured
Metropolis

*In America a man's home is his castle, but his town is
fair game for anyone.*

A Wyoming rancher

Zoning was a neat compromise for the contending interests of exclusion
and expansion in early-twentieth-century U.S. cities and towns. Every major
property interest found its place on the new land use maps; even the propertyless had their place affixed—in the tenements and shanties of the industrial
core. By supplementing the inner workings of capitalist property with some
new outer limits of social control, public zoning helped everyone stay in line
with the basic patterns of social restrictions and private growth. Attorneys,
who had the field responsibility for figuring out the local variations of zoning
law, complained, of course, about the absence of clear signals. And so did
planners, who worried that decisions were rarely guided by long-range outlooks. Nevertheless, throughout the long period of depression, war, and postwar boom that transformed American society both socially and physically,
zoning remained extremely popular down at the grass roots of American government. It is testimony to the support for zoning and to its comparative success as a policy that the Supreme Court did not hear a single major zoning
challenge until the early 1970s, when, as we shall see in chapters 5 and 6, a
string of new court tests reflected growing strains between contemporary
capitalist development and rising concerns for community protection.[1]

In the 1960s and 1970s the underlying consensus behind zoning broke
down. "Keep out" replaced "live and let live" as the operative cliché of land
use policy. Increasingly, the local landownership and land-development interests that once settled their accounts by agreeing to keep everything and everyone in their places fought pitched battles over what and who was to go where.
Frank J. Popper suggests that the main cause for the contentiousness was the
post–World War II economic boom. In his words, "By the late 1960s and
early 1970s . . . rapid growth in the economy and population had produced

more people, corporations, and governments with more money, technology, and mobility than ever before." Because all these forces needed more room, spatial pressures built to the breaking point. Thus the popular consciousness of land use issues was raised as "competition for land increased," and more and more people were energized to preserve the last vestiges of urban open space.[2]

Although this argument is probably true, it doesn't really explain much beyond the obvious point that resistance increased along with pressures to build. Even more important, Popper tends to take the outlines of the postwar expansion for granted while seeing the new land use resistance as the only phenomenon to be explained. Thus he argues that before the 1960s "land use was an obscure technical field"; it did not arouse the interest of citizens. "Most communities," he writes, "were undemanding, and most regulation was nonexistent, weak, or unenforced." Land use "did not seem to matter."[3]

One problem with such explanations, and Popper's is typical of the literature, is that they overlook the special characteristics of the postwar expansion, which defined the areas of greatest strain in recent land use politics.[4] By emphasizing the gross demand for space as the key, they fail to see what was really new and different about this expansion and its impact on private property and community. At the same time, such explanations also tend to exaggerate the novelty of exclusion. Community restrictiveness is seen as a unique historical product of the late 1960s, rather than as the historical outcome of a much older, structural feature of capitalist landed property. In sum, the prevailing explanations of land use conflict, which we shall see again in the chapters ahead, tend to understate what was really new in the situation of the 1960s and 1970s, while exaggerating the novelty of what was old.

A richer explanation can be developed by reading the many detailed case studies of land use conflict written throughout this period.[5] They suggest that the fight was not just against a massive corporate demand for more room. Certain kinds of issues and battles tended to recur, and the big controversies tended to cluster around a common core of problems. Fights abounded over highways, energy facilities, low-income housing, shopping malls, and the expansion of large, central-city service institutions, such as hospitals, universities, and government buildings. With the exception of energy plants, factories rarely, if ever, figured in the most recent land use battles. This was an era when the land drive of capital was aimed not at heavy industrialization but at new forms of seemingly clean commerce within and around the existing urban and suburban settlements. Moreover, this pattern was by no means restricted to United States enterprise. As Bryan Anson writes, in his study of the battle in London over the Covent Garden neighborhood, the big changes in metropolitan land use were "a phenomenon that swept the urban areas of the Western world in the late 1960s," resulting in heated battles that raged in places as disparate as Berkeley, California, the Les Halles neighborhood of Paris, the

Nieumarket area of Amsterdam, and the suburbs of Tokyo, where some of the fiercest and most violent fights centered on the construction of the city's new jetport.[6] Only recently, however, with the terrible discovery of the dangers of toxic waste, has the industrial underbelly of all this recent development become obvious and thus a major focus of land use contention.

In retrospect, these fights can be seen as the birth pains of the emerging service capitalism of the late twentieth century. They were battles fought over the reshaping and restructuring of metropolitan life to serve the newest forms of capitalist action. The growth of the aerospace, electronics, computer, and information industries; the sprawl of shopping malls, branch banking, and real estate ventures; the slide of heavy industry—all these phenomena represented huge spatial shifts in the investment, production, and circulation of capital. Inevitably, they inspired correspondingly large changes in the social landscape of residence and consumption. Industrial restructuring lent form and impetus to the big movements of residential settlement, to suburbanization, urban renewal, and gentrification, to the rise of the Sunbelt, and to the related processes of urban disinvestment, impoverishment, and fiscal crisis that have affected cities nationwide. A brief sketch of the emerging industrial topography suggests the way in which the scattered battles were joined by a unifying logic.[7]

Below the surface of the new metropolitan service capitalism burned the petrochemical revolution. Although the history of the petroleum base is central to earlier phases of U.S. industrialism as well, it is crucial to recognize how the economy's reliance on petrochemical activities and substances greatly intensified in the postwar era, when oil and chemicals fueled the astonishing boom that reconfigured American metropolitan life. During and after World War II, petroleum powered the increasing profitability of corporate enterprise. It rapidly accelerated the displacement of human power by machine power in production and reduced the circulation time of capital by powering the trucking and communications industries. The oil and chemical giants also contributed thousands of new compounds to the larger industrial arsenal. These were synthetic materials never found in nature, but quickly integrated into the production lines of American factories. "Between 1940 and 1980," notes Nicholas Freudenberg, "the production of synthetic organic chemicals increased from less than 10 billion pounds a year to more than 350 billion. Each year, one thousand new compounds are added to the estimated seventy thousand chemicals already in use by 1980."[8] As Barry Commoner adds, the industry's ability to lower the costs of its products by constantly spawning new ones to multiply its economies of scale made the "energy-chemical complex" the dominant sector of American, if not world, capitalism. By the early 1970s, when the oil and chemical companies reached the zenith of their pre-OPEC power, they owned "$181 billion in assets, or 29 percent of the assets (and sales) of the 500 largest corporations in the U.S. The sales of these companies represented 18 percent of the total gross national product in 1974. All of this wealth is in the hands of some twenty corporations with average assets of $9.1 billion each."[9] Together—and their interlocks, collaborations, and "joint ventures" are legion—they constituted what Robert Engler aptly describes as a private-energy government of global dimensions and vast international power.[10]

The spread of the petrochemical industry was tightly interconnected with complex accumulation processes throughout the economy. It was a main prop of the emerging service industries and their hi-tech development across the urban edge. As Freudenberg suggests, "The growth of the petro-chemical industry has been both a cause and an effect of other industrial development. The burgeoning automobile industry created a steady market for petroleum products. When many families became able to afford cars, developers were able to build new suburbs, new highways, and new industrial parks, all requiring a myriad of the new substances turned out by industry."[11] Industrial expansion and geographic expansion were merely different sides of the same coin.

The energy plants, which so often aroused the wrath of local communities and environmentalists, as chapter 7 shows, were central to the completion of the transportation and power grids that underpinned the modern service metropolis. As the new roads and power lines led outward to the suburbs, they supported massive suburbanization of housing and the increasing separation of races and classes. The hot suburban battles over public housing and shopping malls were, as discussed throughout Part Two, offshoots of government and corporate efforts to integrate the labor supply with the new framework of industry, commerce, and shelter on the metropolitan fringe. Especially important here, as we shall see in chapter 5, were efforts to reduce the potential for turmoil that followed the concentration of black poor in the cities, a development that was itself the product, in no small measure, of the influence of petrochemicals and energy in cutting the need for southern agricultural labor.

Of course, relocation of the poor also helped clear some of the nation's prime urban real estate for "revitalization." Once rid of the slums, the new downtowns could be swept and refurbished, made ready to furnish choice locales for new corporate headquarters and more room for the expanding service complexes in health, government, the arts, and education. It should not be forgotten that "gentrification" followed "urban renewal" by less than a generation and that both involved basic class shifts in land use. It is not an oversimplification to say that the latter cleared the way for the new jobs, the former for the workers to perform them.

Inside the changing cities, the older industrial workers of all strata contested the voracious institutional demand for space, often allying themselves with rebel students to fight for housing, social ties, and neighborhoods. And in the suburbs, homeowners made similar fights to protect their enclaves from incorporation by the new patterns of growth.

Finally, in the past five years, society has learned new lessons about the continuing industrial basis of this new economy and the poverty of old land use assumptions in coping with it. Excluders have long believed that by keeping their distance from industry, its noxious by-products—noise, fumes, traffic, and explosives—could be warded off. But toxic pollutants, especially those created by the burning of modern petrochemical substances such as plastics, are wandering poisons, forced to move by the simple fact that nature doesn't know them and has no place for them. These artificial substances lack natural fixtures; they enter the air and the water as well as the land and move about irrespective of property rights, individual or collective. Although they cannot be zoned out, hazardous wastes and the struggles to exclude them are the hottest issues in land use conflict today, a harsh reminder that the circle of industrial action must close somewhere.

It was against the grain of this larger restructuring of the capitalist metropolis, a process under way throughout the "free world," that development interests ran headlong into local land use resistance. Home builders, industrial construction firms, real estate traders, mortgage bankers, big energy corporations, the lawyers and planners who organized and defended their interests, and, not least, the builders of giant government infrastructures—all faced steadfast community opposition at hundreds of crucial junctures and spaces in the economic network. In the United States, zoning came to be used increasingly as a means not only of opening but also of closing space to growth. The old solution to the exclusion-expansion dialectic had grown to become an annoying barrier to all too many projects, large and small.

For the more distinguished land economists, planners, and lawyers, who developed the blueprints of the regional interconnections of postwar expansion and who worked in the trenches fighting the spatial battles of private- and public-sector developers, the innumerable conflicts were an agonizing frustration, contributing little to large-scale land preservation while blocking the speedy expansion of enterprise. By the 1960s common sense among the national land policy elite—the organic intellectuals of land use, in Gramsci's sense—held that the time had come to switch battlegrounds. Political and economic rationality dictated that it was better to fight a single national struggle for the centralization of land use authority in the states than to remain ensnarled in the petty battles of a thousand and one localities. Thus, the focus of land use politics increasingly shifted from struggles over given parcels of land to a much bigger contest over the proper place in government to decide such issues.

Viewed solely from national perspectives, however, the larger systemic forces of exclusion and expansion can only be seen as crude blotches on the neat outlines of the nation's political map, the lines that divide the American territory into fifty states and well over seventy thousand local political subdivisions. At any given place and time, these forces are entwined and enriched by diverse motives, overlapping as well as conflicting interests, local colorings, and regional variation. No study of the national land policy issue can ever do justice to the vast range of interests that would stand to be affected by national or even statewide approaches to land use conflict, nor could it do any greater justice to an understanding of the motivations pushing specific local interests to take positions for or against such policies. To make a credible stab at grasping at least somewhat more fully the richness and complexity of the issues and forces arrayed in the national battles for land use control, it is best to begin by looking closely at a single, representative, land use fight in just one place.

Land Use Politics, Texas Style 4

Urban politics is above all the politics of land use, and it is easy to see why. Land is the factor of production over which cities exercise the greatest control.
Paul Peterson

I had rather die with a drink of water in my hand than a fistful of dollars.
Helen Dutmer, member of the city council, San Antonio, Texas

In the early 1970s, just as Congress sat down to debate national land use policy, San Antonians rose up to fight over the control of a large stretch of land on the north side of their city. The area blanketed the city's sole water supply with a portion of the recharge zone of the Edwards aquifer; but because it was the preferred site for new middle- and upper-income housing, local developers saw the land as their choicest marketplace. The forces of exclusion and expansion could not have been more clearly arrayed.

Yet the social forces that battled for control of the Edwards land did not split cleanly into capitalist and noncapitalist factions. To the contrary, careful mining of the case reveals the sort of intriguing subtleties that can only be noticed by looking intensely at individual battles. Not that we can easily generalize from San Antonio's test: rather, by looking at this instance, we can gain some appreciation for how political variations occur on structural themes— another way of saying that the events of individual cases are rarely arbitrary. There are always factors behind the facts, usually powerful ones because they carry the individual instances into variations around a common line, what sociologist Kai Erickson calls "an axis of variation."[1] Thus in looking at the specific, we are merely examining how surface issues illuminate underlying forces.

One theme of the San Antonio story is the contradictoriness of business politics. We see not only how important it is for business to control government as a condition of successful accumulation but also that capital may not be of one mind on the issue of what it means to control government.

The fight over aquifer development exposed cracks in the city's business class, dividing the downtown boosters from the suburban property capitalists

119

(as discussed in chapter 1). The issues making for business disunity in San Antonio centered exactly on the relationship between geographic expansion and urban planning. Suburban property groups fought regional approaches to water protection to ensure that the city's zoning rules favored development of the area's most lucrative real estate. And they relied heavily on the political strength of rural capitalists, who also opposed central controls. Downtown interests by no means strongly supported tough land use planning, but they did favor efforts to prevent growth from exploding beyond the bounds of the city's fiscal and environmental limits. In short, the case raised basic questions for business about its appropriate relationship to local government. Could capital trust local government to plan and oversee expansion in the general interest of the local business class as a whole, or would individual firms and sectors have to go it alone and directly conquer local agencies to guarantee that their particular private plans were set in motion? In a pattern that was to repeat itself in the case of a national land use policy, advocates of the conquest perspective—the suburban and rural capitalists—bitterly opposed the pro-planning faction of downtown booster capital.

The exclusionary forces were no less complex. The environmental opposition to aquifer development was led by an upper-class woman and had a wide constituency, though its political appeal was perhaps greatest among middle-class homeowners who lived on or near the aquifer. In these privileged sanctuaries, however, aquifer development was not seen as an affront to status or as a threat to property values—if anything, development in general only promised to raise northside property values. Growth in the aquifer region was seen instead as portending imminent danger to the public health. Excluders believed that shopping malls, housing projects, roads, and parking lots were potentially destructive invitations to poisoning the water. But the sociology of exclusion here was enlivened by the presence of other voices and needs. Not only were strength and legitimacy drawn from the pro-planning forces within the San Antonio business class, but poor and working-class Hispanics were critical, too. And they joined the fight only partially to keep the water clean. Just as important, community leaders in the barrio saw the cutoff of northside development as a way to reignite investment downtown, next to the city's poorest quarters. For working-class Mexican-Americans, exclusion was viewed as a necessary condition for the expansion of their opportunities.

Finally, the San Antonio case shows in painfully clear relief the implications of the tremendous growth in governmental complexity that in part trailed and in part was led by the enormous growth of corporate capital in the last half-century. The Edwards case unfolded on many levels of government simultaneously, with cross-cutting alliances and interjurisdictional conflict the rule of the day. Corporate and legal pressures for the simplification and rationalization of authority for land use control may well be more comprehensible when stacked up against the confusing realities of land use politics, Texas style.

The Alamo City: An Overview

For most of the twentieth century San Antonio, Texas, contented itself with being one of America's smaller big cities.[2] Of course, it made sure to hold its own, but it left expansion to Houston and Dallas: lacking culture, they thirsted for profits. But racing was not San Antonio's style; sophisticated cities, like great wines, do not advertise. San Antonio was satisfied with its municipal walls, which amply cornered the market on leisurely refinement. San Antonio was the most exclusive city in Texas. But its status quo was purchased with enviable advantages: the Alamo, five U.S. military installations, a rich hinterland of cattle, dairy farms, and citrus groves, plus a large population of Mexican-Americans whose labor was all too cheaply converted into the fruits of a handsome surplus. As a recent business report explained, one of the city's greatest industrial attractions is its impressive labor pool of "highly dextrous females" who can work in the mass production plants of high technology.[3]

In the 1970s, though, San Antonio changed its mind about growth. National economic shifts stimulated northern business interest in warmer climates. Hard-driving local merchants became restless with the slow pace; corporate inquiries were encouraged and eagerly answered. The big Texas cities were emulated. In the words of San Antonio's proposed master plan, the city's leadership was well advised to familiarize itself with the regional shifts in corporate investment and "to grasp the opportunities occasioned by these changes"—in other words, to lure northern business firms that were fed up with high labor costs and taxes.[4] Chicanos were prepared to back the grab for more national capital in San Antonio as long as it promised to further their long and frustrating struggle for political power, decent wages, and enhanced respect. In 1980, San Antonio became the first large city in the nation to elect a Mexican-American mayor, Henry Cisneros. For a city whose business community was on the move, Cisneros struck the appropriate campaign theme: "For too long we have basked in the glory of other Texas cities. Now it's up to San Antonio. . . . America is watching San Antonio."[5] Especially corporate America.

Ten turbulent years preceded the election of Cisneros. San Antonio's electoral system was restructured, its physical size more than doubled, and its population fought bitterly over the fate of water and land. The awakening was painful. Much of the strain stemmed from familiar pressures generated by rapid growth, environmental worries, and social change. But the problems were compounded by head-on conflict between real estate development and water quality. Other cities experienced similar strains as separate matters; in San Antonio, the conflicts were closely interlocked.

Though the "Alamo City" had enjoyed zoning since 1938, land use controls were not ordinarily used to leash developers. San Antonio was one of those southern cities where, as a congressional aide once put it, "homebuilders are more a part of the political economic power structure than they are in other, more developed parts of the country."[6] Attempts to find new exclusionary meanings in the police power caused much excitement in this setting. But the struggle cannot be reduced to the economic power of a single group. The question of aquifer development was part of a larger political economic crisis in the city's history, which boiled over in the middle and late 1970s, a crisis of political participation and rule, a crisis of economic direction and power. The fight over land use both reflected and accelerated broader and deeper changes that were remaking the life of the city. To understand this, it is desirable to get the lay of the land around the city, to picture the physical and social factors that gave San Antonio its form and bias.

The Lay of the Land

Cities are, of course, the creatures of their physical, economic, and political surroundings.[7] Suburbs sometimes rebel against this fact, but cities are forced to live with it. Heavy dependence on regional ecologies, private markets, and intergovernmental ties is inescapable. San Antonio's recent history is a rich case for explorations of the impact of outer connections on inner needs. The story best begins with some bird's-eye views.

San Antonio sits at the meeting point of two imposing natural forces. The green and rocky Texas "hill country" stretches southward from around Austin, ninety miles north of San Antonio, rolling into a flat, semiarid plain, which surrounds the city on three sides and merges with the great prairie land to the west. The hill country offers refreshing slopes dotted with miniature cactus and strangely twisted live oak. It is sprinkled with rivers and rich in broad vistas. Cattle and sheep graze the hills, providing a principal source of income. Those hills were once distant from San Antonio, but growth has brought the metropolis next door.

The low grassy plain around most of the city is fertile, but also hot, flat, and undistinguished. Air Force fliers know it well because every recruit takes basic training at Lackland Air Force Base on the south side of the city. Kelly Field, another air base, is also sited nearby, leaving the area exposed to more than its fair share of plane traffic, as well as to the types of commerce usually associated with forts. Most of the city's white working class lives northeast of the bases, and the Mexican-American majority populates the west side. Due east of the central business district lies the city's small black ghetto. The middle and upper classes live mainly north of downtown, where trees are more plentiful and the land starts its gradual rise into the hills.

Whereas in northern cities the suburbs ring the metropolitan fringe, in San Antonio many of the wealthier citizens live in exclusive "enclave" townships near the heart of the city. These are small independent municipalities, with names like Alamo Heights, Olmos Park, and Terrell Hills; they afford little space for new neighbors.

San Antonians aspiring to the conventionally defined "good life" have few geographic choices. Racism, snobbery, and an understandable aversion to low-flying aircraft draw them around and beyond the enclaves to the further northern reaches where space is plentiful for new homes. This northern side is San Antonio's jewel. But it also plays a more mundane role: it is the city's natural water tank. Beneath the ascending hills sits a portion of the Edwards aquifer.

The Edwards is a great reservoir stretching more than 175 miles across south-central Texas from Kinney County in the west, through Uvalde and Medina counties, and then northward through Bexar, Comal, and Hays counties. Its porous limestone is estimated to hold between 15 and 30 million acre-feet of pure water cradled in a complex network of geologic faults and channels. Although scientists admit they have much to learn about the aquifer, it is generally agreed that the water is recharged through absorption of rain and the seepage of surface streams that flow across the outcrop of limestone formations.[8] This happens in an area called the recharge zone. Only about 0.7 percent of this crucial land is situated within the San Antonio city limits, about 6,900 acres. Only 8.5 percent of the total recharge zone is in Bexar County (pronounced "Bear"). Nearly 60 percent of the water for the reservoir enters the ground in the rural western counties, especially Uvalde.

The Local Political Economy

The fate of San Antonio is dictated not only by physical factors and their influence on real estate but also by the city's place in the Texas political economy. Texas is a very conservative state. As V. O. Key observed in his classic study *Southern Politics,* Texas politics is concerned with two things—"money and how to make it." In their recent updating of Key's work, Jack Bass and Walter DeVries noted little change in the prevailing ethos. Texas, they found, is still governed by "the Politics of Economics."[9] The Texas water law has embodied the ruling conservatism. For well over a century, groundwater received no special notice or public guardianship. Although a large portion of the state, including such cities as Houston and El Paso, depends extensively on underground sources, Texas never required conservation practices. A recent study notes:

> The "English Rule of Absolute Ownership" is the primary rule controlling ownership and use of groundwater in Texas. This rule gives each landowner complete freedom to withdraw and use the water beneath his land without restriction. This . . . is tempered slightly by the "American Rule of Reasonable Use," which prohibits the waste of water from groundwater sources.[10]

Groundwater is considered to be just another part of the bundle of rights conveyed by landownership. Under the only effective control, Rule 20 of the

Texas Railroad Commission, property owners could sue for damages "once pollution has occurred," but "no precedent has been set giving a landowner injunctive relief from the threat of potential groundwater pollution." [11] Frontier reflections sparkle in the state's water law.

The conservatism of Texas was rarely challenged in historic San Antonio. During most of the postwar era, for example, the city was controlled by an astonishingly successful political organization called the Good Government League (GGL). Operated by the city's leading downtown capitalists, the nonpartisan GGL has been described by Thomas Baylis as "the political arm of the San Antonio economic elite," uniting the "leading bankers, developers, manufacturers, and other businessmen with a scattering of other community leaders" into a cohesive ruling class. [12] League members easily dominated the at-large electoral system and the city manager's office on behalf of wealthier whites, especially northside whites. No fewer than 78 of 81 possible city council seats were won by the organization between 1954 and 1973. Most of these representatives came from the north side. Many Alamo City neighborhoods lacked public representatives or voices for a generation or more—and they looked it. Westside streets were often unpaved and lacked drainage facilities; parts of the barrio would not look out of place in the Third World. At-large elections under GGL rule held out little promise of changing this state of affairs. [13]

But the GGL wanted more than at-large elections; it wanted a larger San Antonio economy. Capitalist expansion was central to the GGL public-policy program, and government was clearly seen as critical to providing stability, resources, and capital for accumulation. But the GGL was not committed to just any type of growth, and least of all to industrialization. Historic fears that factories would pollute the labor and tourist climates—the former with militancy, the latter with grime—ensured that San Antonio had services on its mind as the smoothest channel for growth. Thus the GGL sponsored what John Booth and David Johnson call a "particular vision of progress, efficiency, and development," one that aimed to achieve "orderly, rational growth." [14]

In essence, the organization's unwritten economic plan involved a delicate balance between the interests of downtown business, resting heavily on finance, retailing, and tourism, and those of the suburban expansionists—the real estate, retail, and construction capitalists—who wanted ever more rapid development of infrastructure, houses, and malls to the north. Linking the two was a common drive to build up the northside service sector, especially in health and education. Local leaders joined in the late 1960s to push construction of the South Texas Medical Center, a huge complex of seven public and private hospitals—with 7,500 employees—and a big new branch of the University of Texas. Each was sited on the far northwest side of the city, on or next to the recharge zone. Booth and Johnson describe how GGL leaders tried to unify the competitive forces of urban capitalist development by supplying a relatively even distribution of public largesse to the different wings of the local business class:

> The tactic of attracting government services and capital investments dominated the boosters' development strategy. The promotion of Hemisfair [world's fair exposition] with state and federal support, greatly enhanced downtown property values, stimulated a construction boom, and revived the city's flagging tourist industry. The extension of utility lines to suburban housing developments at city taxpayers' expense and the promotion of freeways and an urban loop greatly enhanced the attractiveness and profitability of developers' investments.[15]

Geographic expansion, then, constituted more in San Antonio than simply the spatial reflection of accumulation. It was a crucially important political strategy linking the interests of older downtown commercial and finance capital with the needs and pressures of the city's younger suburban land sellers and home builders. Between 1950 and 1970, the physical area of the city grew more than 250 percent as its leaders pursued an energetic annexation policy. Simultaneously, contract construction in San Antonio rose almost 40 percent above the Texas average, as the land grabs and contracts kept the builders hopping northward.[16] Implications for the water supply were innocently ignored, however, until it threatened to run short.

Groundwater and Expansion

A harsh drought hit south-central Texas in the late 1950s, "the worst ever known in the area."[17] Springs ran dry and well levels plummeted to record lows. Yet, plenty of water rested deep under the soil. The problem was that existing pumps had to be lowered to tap the pool, but as one water engineer remembers, "we just [couldn't] reach it with the pumps."[18] Late in 1957 heavy rains eased the situation, but the dry spell frightened the local farmers and ranchers, who were deeply dependent on the Edwards for irrigation. Expansion of the water supply was indispensable to continued growth of their agribusinesses, so they urged creation of a new government agency to plan for and gather additional supplies. Because water was just as crucial to San Antonio's continued development, the real estate industry joined the call for a new public water program and became a fervent advocate of water projects for the greater south Texas region. Increasingly, the promotion of water supplies unified the rural land interest with urban land developers in a common expansionist program. One local businessman answered criticism of the move by taxpayers:

> Why is all this necessary? Because we can't hardly get along without water. And the recent ten year drought, increased industry and irrigation, more people

using more water—have reduced our supply. And San Antonio and the entire area is growing in population and industry.[19]

After several years of pushing by the South Texas Chamber of Commerce, an Edwards Underground Water District (EUWD) was established by the state legislature and approved by the voters in 1959.[20] The district was composed of fifteen elected commissioners, three from each of the counties overlying the aquifer. The geographic basis of representation amplified rural perspectives. Uvalde County, for example, where most of the essential recharge occurred, had a population of sixty thousand, less than a tenth of Bexar's. Like other agrarians, rural Texans have little liking for urban planning, and the district's electoral arrangements were as conducive to exclusionary land use controls as San Antonio's were to equality for Mexicans. Thus, although the EUWD was legally obligated to "conserve, preserve, protect and increase the recharge of and prevent the waste and pollution of the underground water," it did not entertain authority to restrict the "rights . . . in underground water" belonging to "the owner of the land." [21] The district's board, made up of local ranchers and engineers with strong business ties, quickly affirmed its opposition to controls on private property, reminding urbanites that the agency's organic law "specifically provides that the landowner has the right to use water under his land as he sees fit." [22]

In an important way, then, the water issue helped to soften, though it never eliminated, rural suspicions of big-city business. Farmers and ranchers traded and logrolled with urban capitalists for votes in the state legislature to establish the agency, although rural doubts persisted about the encroachment of San Antonio development on the farm- and ranchlands of south-central Texas, doubts that would come to have severe implications later when the issue became a matter of water protection rather than supply. In the meantime, however, the task of implementing district policies was charged to a retired U.S. Army colonel, McDonald D. Weinert, a professional "water man" whose expertise had been earned through decades of service with the U.S. Army Corps of Engineers. Weinert had few doubts about the logic of expansion; he was a scientific conservationist of the classical school. When asked whether the purpose of the district was to secure additional supplies, maintain the aquifer pool, or protect its quality, he replied, "It was established for all three, except for controlling the use."

The district board and staff saw the agency as a support mechanism for economic growth. Reflecting the fragile alliance of rural and urban capital, their task was to further private controls with a planned search for water. Connections were quickly developed with the national water-development agencies. The Corps of Engineers, the Bureau of Reclamation, and the U.S. Geological Survey were invited to aid in research and planning. A series of surface-water projects was soon envisioned to link the aquifer with nearby rivers and lakes in a regional supply system. In 1961, for example, approval was given to a study by the Army Corps of Engineers concerning "the recharge and replenishment" of the aquifer "as part of plans for flood control, water conservation, and other related water uses." [23]

Local merchant and agribusiness interests joined with the water technicians to stress imports as the answer to the resource needs of south Texas. Their partnership focused on construction, not conservation. The preliminary finding of the study, released in January 1965, recommended building "a series of reservoirs above the recharge zone to hold water from wet years to replenish the reserves in times of drought." [24] Similarly, the San Antonio transportation plan of 1966 emphasized that "the ability of the underground sources to meet the demand is approaching its limit." It predicted that soon the voters would have to select one of the "several long-range studies . . . of surface water supplies for the area" as the basis of continued growth. [25]

Public opinion was actively courted to back the planning for surface-water development. Films were shown telling "the Edwards story." Connections were asserted between water supply and progress. As one board member explained, "Solution of the water problem and improvement of higher education institutions" were "the key to attraction of industry to San Antonio." [26]

Local business owners, especially suburban property capitalists, saw more subtle ties as well. By reducing the city's dependence on Edwards, surface-water projects would help to open hill-country land to free enterprise. Surface water made groundwater less precious. Construction could proceed with less fear of pollution, its costs passed along to regional taxpayers in the form of bonded indebtedness to finance the dams. For San Antonio's growth-conscious elite, abundant water and an expanded real estate market were tightly entwined goals. However, area capitalists were not indifferent to water quality. As Weinert once proclaimed, "Hell, no—businessmen are not against water quality." The point, rather, is that business interests saw an investment in balanced supplies as a reasonable cost for the public to pay in order to assure plentiful water with minimal risk of exclusion from the area's most desirable market. More water meant fewer barriers to growth.

In time local conservationists came to doubt such judgments. They pointed out not only that the Edwards water was pure beyond the federal government's best measure, but also that it was extremely cheap to pump. Aquifer water cost the city about two cents per 1,000 gallons to extract as compared with thirty cents per 1,000 gallons in other larger cities. [27] Asking the citizenry to spend tens of millions of dollars for new surface systems when no evidence indicated a serious shortfall—assuming reasonable conservation efforts—was a demand that citizens yield a decisive cost advantage in order to subsidize unregulated expansion. One city council member, with GGL ties and a strong commitment to regional water planning, summarized the debate this way:

> The prime difficulty we have had over the past twenty years . . . has been, quite simply, the lack of a clearly defined, generally accepted concept as to what our

water requirements will be in the next twenty to fifty years. . . . We seem to have written off the Edwards Aquifer . . . and we have not even paid much attention to the ultimate source—recycled water.[28]

Until the mid-1970s, voices in support of pure water were poorly informed and organized. For one thing, San Antonio's handful of conservationists were caught up in a tough fight against Mayor Walter McCallister's proposed North Expressway, which threatened to disrupt the Olmos Basin, adjacent to some of San Antonio's most exclusive enclaves, as well as Brackenridge Park, the city's major public recreation area. Moreover, for all the commercial interest in northside growth, not much actual construction had taken place; the area remained a frontier. Finally, it should be remembered that "the environment" was not a national issue in the mid-1960s. Sensitivities to toxic dangers were yet to be aroused by Earth Day celebrations, national ecology policies, Love Canal, or a troubled Walter Cronkite asking, "Can the world be saved?" Local citizens dutifully placed their trust in the Underground Water District to guard their water.

Bubbles of Environmental Policy

Despite the shapelessness of public opinion, government slowly brought water quality into focus as a policy concern. In 1965 Congress passed the national Water Quality Act requiring states by 1967 "to establish water quality standards for all interstate waters within their boundaries."[29] Although the Edwards aquifer did not fall into the class of "interstate waters," the Texas legislature was forced to establish a water-policy framework in compliance with federal law. As part of its own Water Quality Act, the legislature reorganized its administration by creating a Water Quality Board (WQB). This agency was responsible for coordinating "all water quality control programs of various State agencies and local governments with those of the federal government."[30] This mandate gave it authority to oversee local efforts aimed at preserving groundwater quality, including those undertaken by special-purpose governments such as the EUWD.

The Water Quality Board was nominally run by seven gubernatorial appointees, but day-to-day influence belonged to its executive director, Hugh Yantis. Yantis occupied the strategic high ground in the intergovernmental politics of water protection. As the effective representative of national and state entities, Yantis was the principal "audience" of regional water disputes.[31] He could apply state leverage to force the district to shift its emphasis from production to conservation. Or, by embracing rural suspicions, he could deny protectionists the aid of state and national power. In either case, the Texas Water Quality Board's executive director was decisively positioned to channel the authority of wider governments in the politics of aquifer protection.

Whatever the city of San Antonio chose to do in defense of its water had to be accomplished within limits set not only by an expansionist real estate market but also by a fragmented federalism that lodged significant power in the hands of surrounding governments. The machinery of local government did not kick into gear quickly. In the fall of 1967, a "Task Force Committee for Protection of the Edwards Aquifer" was organized to oversee pollution in the recharge zone. Like the water board at the state level, it was an intergovernmental agency comprising the city of San Antonio, the City Water Board, the San Antonio Metropolitan Health District, the EUWD, and the San Antonio River Authority. Mainly, it patrolled sites for solid waste disposal. In 1969 the task force was renamed the Edwards Aquifer Protection Committee, announcing that it would take a strong stand against pollution of the recharge zone resulting from garbage dumping and sewage disposal. It did not engage in long-term planning for water quality. Nor did it receive much encouragement from the Texas Water Quality Board. In February 1970, Hugh Yantis signaled his position on water conservation by advising the committee that it was probably cheaper to cleanse dirty water than to maintain its quality. The observation disconcerted San Antonians, who were anxious to keep their water pure.[32] A seed of distrust was planted; it grew rapidly in what became a fertile environment of suspicion. Soon after Yantis complained about the costs of water purity, the WQB invoked construction standards for new septic tanks on the recharge zone. But no means of enforcement were introduced. Newly built septic tanks were neither registered nor inspected.

Despite the flimsy state controls, political anxiety began to grow in Bexar County's western neighbor, Uvalde. Farmers and ranchers were apprehensive that the big-city interests wanted to enforce stiff land use controls throughout the recharge zone, even in rural areas where development pressure and the threat of pollution were slight. Uvalde's representatives in the Texas legislature introduced a bill to open an escape hatch. Individual counties should be permitted to secede from the water district, they insisted. Their bill died, but the secessionist strategy remained alive. Yantis continued to support variations on the exit theme as a means of prohibiting urban control of frontier owners. And after Uvalde's wealthiest proprietor, Dolph Briscoe, became governor in 1972, Yantis's alliance with Uvalde was sealed.[33] The local business community's traditional partnership with the Underground Water District was now reproduced at higher, even more potent, levels of government.

The San Antonio Ranch Proposal

By 1970 the Edwards aquifer stored contradictions as well as water. It was, among other things, a water tank, an irrigation faucet, private property, a hodge-podge of overlapping jurisdictions, and, increasingly, a bone of contention. Still, most of the paradoxes remained buried until a big decision was taken in 1971, when as *Business Week* described it, "a group of influential Texans . . . decided to develop a 9,000-acre tract of richly wooded and hilly land 16 miles northwest of San Antonio into a new town using federal loan guarantees to finance it."[34] Among the backers were close friends of John Connally, then secretary of the treasury in the Nixon administration. They included George Christian, press secretary to former President Lyndon B. Johnson, and Hayden Head, a south-Texas lawyer and rancher who owned half the land slated for the project.[35] Coincidentally, Hugh Yantis was a "former business associate of Hayden Head, and was convinced to take an active role in development and promotion" of San Antonio Ranch (SAR). Yantis was untroubled by potential conflict of interest charges "since no TWQB action on SAR was required by law."[36]

The project was massive. Its backers planned to house 88,000 people above the recharge zone, twenty miles from downtown. This was tantamount to moving more than 10 percent of San Antonio's population out of the old city. It represented a gigantic acceleration of the unfolding real estate logic. Like no other event in its recent history, Ranchtown, as local citizens called it, turned the city's attention to the growth question. As a local conservationist put it, "In a matter of months, 'Aquifer' [became] a household word."[37]

First Stirrings of Exclusion

Leading San Antonians opposed Ranchtown, especially at first. Erwin F. Davis, the city's director of planning, was outraged that the project's draft environmental-impact statement hardly noted possible threats to the aquifer. The federal Department of Housing and Urban Development (HUD) should have known better, Davis felt. After all, a report by the U.S. Geological Survey had determined that

> if development on the Recharge Zone of the Aquifer continues at an accelerated rate and if stringent precautions are not taken to prevent the increased waste load from reaching the Aquifer, deterioration of the chemical and bacteriological quality can be expected.[38]

City leaders were alerted to the dangers, but Davis wisely did not stress environmental implications. Sensitive to the pro-expansion bias, he emphasized economic and political losses instead. The chairman of the planning commission, a local builder, was advised to anticipate unfair competition for northside profits if Ranchtown were built. This argument was taken seriously. The mayor, John Gatti, was convinced to see implications for downtown real estate interests. Suspicions were nurtured that a big grant for Ranchtown would disqualify the city from future consideration by Washington, especially for a long-desired "new town-in-town" grant. At the same time, the *San Antonio Express* began to run articles critical of secret maneuvering behind the project, especially the use of Head's contacts in Austin and Washington. But after strenuous and occasionally intimidating pressure from Head and his political representatives, enough local support was gathered to win city council backing for Ranchtown.[39]

Still, some of the city's elite continued to resist, including Mayor Gatti, Bexar County Judge Blair Reeves, Congressman Henry B. Gonzales, and Colonel Weinert of the EUWD. Reeves and Gonzales even called for public purchase of the recharge zone and a halt to all growth in the endangered area. Local environmentalists sought a federal injunction against construction of Ranchtown on the ground that HUD had deliberately overlooked the aquifer in its approval of the project. Ranchtown, however, won a temporary abeyance from the U.S. District Court to rework its draft environmental-impact statement. A bevy of experts was hired to assist in rapid-fire analysis. Their product was reviewed by a special panel composed of federal, state, and local agencies whose representatives were "determined by the SAR developers." As the Wattersons put it in their case study of the project, the examination "was a carefully orchestrated exercise in public relations, under the cover of scientific enlightenment."[40] Hugh Yantis chaired the board. Few searching questions were asked. The Texas Water Quality Board took the developers' revised draft, passed on by the special review panel, and crowned it with state approval. No independent public analysis was ever made.

Ranchtown's developers promised to monitor aquifer impacts and to introduce controls to deal with concerns such as sewage, toxic-waste disposal, and storm-water runoff. Indeed, the sponsors argued that controls from Washington were the strongest ever to be applied in the region. If the "new town" were blocked and the federal presence eliminated, current local growth patterns would continue unabated, bringing one-acre lots, septic tanks, and shoddily constructed subdivisions that could never meet national criteria for sound development. Moreover, they charged, it was hypocritical and unfair for the city to stop a federally sponsored project when local interests were digging into the recharge zone. Recent state decisions to locate a new University of Texas campus and the South Texas Medical Center in the area were cited as strong indicators of an unstoppable trend.[41]

Ranchtown went to trial in the spring of 1973. Despite strong expressions of environmental concern by the trial judge, the court ruled in the developers' favor. HUD's review procedures were perfectly in accord with federal law. But SAR's sponsors were required to take new environmental precautions, and biannual reports were invited from the EUWD and the WQB.[42] Nonetheless, construction did not soon begin; economic forces overruled the courts. A severe national recession devastated the local real estate market, leaving Ranchtown "on hold," and it has remained there ever since. But the larger questions of expansion versus exclusion on the Edwards aquifer were only beginning to be raised.

A Metropolitan Strategy for
Water Protection

With public consciousness of the water quality issue stimulated, the politics of water and land development became increasingly complex and entwined. Just before Ranchtown went to trial, the Alamo Area Council of Governments (AACOG), guided by its executive director, Al Notzen III, tried to forge an areawide policy.[43] Notzen's goal was to win an effective protection order from the Texas Water Quality Board. At a series of public hearings, local officials insisted on the need for stronger action. But lacking coordination, and disagreeing on specifics, the local efforts were disunited and confused. It was easy for Yantis and the board's hearing examiners to redefine local disagreement over means as a lack of consensus on ends. Policy making was stymied.

In May 1973, after a particularly exasperating public hearing, Notzen began to organize the opposition to Yantis. He persuaded the executive committee of AACOG, composed of elected representatives of area governments, to establish a task force "charged with producing uniform development policies and standards" for the Edwards aquifer, "with . . . the legal tools necessary to implement those policies."[44] The point was, in Notzen's words, "to take away [the WQB's] ability to interpret what the public hearing was saying."[45] In its place the task force introduced a unified report calling for one- and two-acre-minimum lots for houses using septic tanks and drinking wells, and for city-licensed water systems in new subdivisions. EUWD was urged to assume direct responsibility for regional pollution controls. AACOG wanted the district to serve as collective landowner for the aquifer. But neither Weinert nor Yantis made a dash for the power to exclude.

Although it joined local environmentalists in appealing the Ranchtown decision, the Underground Water District was reluctant to take charge. It saw its business as finding water, not controlling land; regulation was repulsive. Publicly, Weinert declared that the district was not authorized to control land use. Privately, he told the board that AACOG's invitation would force the district "to perform a function which is extremely unpopular."[46] He later explained, "If we became involved in taking people to court . . . we would lose our effectiveness. . . . Nobody likes a policeman."

Yantis responded predictably, wondering out loud why the district did not want "the job when it is clearly a part of [its] responsibility."[47] But Yantis was no more willing to play "policeman" than Weinert. His suggestions of new septic-tank, sewer, and development controls lacked standards or explicit means of enforcement. A revised aquifer-protection order, issued in the fall of 1973, depended nearly entirely on Yantis's discretion for its implementation.[48]

Over the next few months, and into the early spring of 1974, the Water Quality Board studied various proposals, only to surface once again in March with essentially the same order it wrote the previous year. AACOG's staff saw only "slight improvement." They concluded that the new order continued to place the burden of aquifer protection on the county's taxpayers "rather than [on] the developers who are building on the recharge zone." [49]

Business Divides

Inside San Antonio, meanwhile, Ranchtown had undermined laissez-faire traditions. Many members of the Good Government League, along with an increasingly large number of middle-class homeowners, were troubled by the toxic implications of unchecked expansion. Sentiment rose for more careful approaches to growth. With this prospect, builders grew restless, too. Although many local business owners were not at all displeased at the failure of Ranchtown—it was widely believed that area profits were rightfully the property of local capitalists—the new doubts about expansion produced frowns. Despite the poor economic climate for construction, builders pressed the city to guarantee a legal framework conducive to growth. Zoning changes, utility extensions, and land annexations were demanded from the city council. But for the first time in recent memory, such claims were resisted. Political debate became the unavoidable condition of physical growth.

It was not that the GGL was becoming exclusionary. The organization never adopted an anti-growth posture. The split centered more on questions of the extent to which expansion should be rationally planned and regulated by public administrators whose perspectives might not always conform to the immediate interests of local builders. Ranchtown sensitized leaders and planners in the GGL to the idea that unregulated expansion could produce unintended consequences damaging to the region as a whole, including the long-term interests of the San Antonio political economy. In other words, physical expansion was much too important to the future of the area to use it as a bargaining chip in efforts to unite the different wings of local capital. To the extent that long-term urban interests might suffer grievously if short-term economic freedom for the construction industry was not limited, GGL officials began to insist on notions of planned expansion that directly conflicted with the freewheeling approach of local realtor and homebuilding firms.

As a former GGL councilman notes, the party brass, as well as younger, more reform-minded league members, "didn't like the strong influence of the developers" or their "positive push to laissez-faire." [50] Support grew within the City Water Board and other agencies for a more controlled advance. Planners talked of alternative growth sketches and new master plans. Expansion was seen to have outer limits, not the least of which included the city's ability to finance ever more distant utility hook-ups. San Antonians read of towns such as Ramapo, New York, and their experiments with timed-growth ordinances that linked expansion to capital-budget planning. National discussions of land use controls filtered down to the grass roots and aroused interests in new ideas about growth management.

All this, plus older resentments against GGL cliquishness, angered suburban retail and construction capitalists. For them, San Antonio was set to take off, and some in the city wanted to close the runway. Simmering divisions were heated by talk of planning. In 1973 the city's oligarchy split, and the internal fissures cracked into public view. After a chain of personal and policy disputes, Councilman Charles Becker led San Antonio's land and house merchants in successful revolt against the GGL by winning the mayoralty in 1973. Becker, who inherited a supermarket chain from his father and turned it into a $200 million enterprise, was also a significant force behind construction of San Antonio's first northside mall—Wonderland Plaza— in the early 1960s. A rambunctious entrepreneur, Becker "liked fine clothes, fine wine, 'spunky people' and the idea of being mayor of San Antonio." What annoyed him were GGL snobs who "lollygagged" around the San Antonio Country Club instead of pushing the city north.[51] Now that *he* was mayor, the city would be sure to grow.

Mayor Becker and his suburban booster colleagues on the council quickly took control of key city agencies. The chairman of the city water board, for example, was literally pushed to the wall at one meeting after a developer, recently elected a council member, exploded, "You son of a bitch, you're killing San Antonio!" The chairman was soon fired, replaced by a builder with heavy northside interests.

In 1975 the construction interests attempted to consolidate their power by forming a new political organization, the Independent Team, to replace the GGL as the ruling party in the city. As one builder explained, the new entity grew "out of a fear that the vacuum left by the GGL" would lead to control of San Antonio government "by forces alien to business."[52] Bankrolled almost exclusively by developers, the new party won a majority of six council seats, although it lost the mayoralty to the last GGL candidate, Lila Cockrell.

The developers' effort to dominate the machinery of growth policy continued. Soon after the election the deputy director of the city Planning and Zoning Department was fired after bitter criticism from several Independent Team council members. The planner's sin was his preparation of an "Alternative Growth Study" that included, among other options, the idea that San Antonio's growth over the next quarter-century could be held *within* the confines of Loop 410, the highway whose northern tier builders viewed as the launching pad of expansion. At a public hearing on the plan, one councilman-builder stood up and tossed his copy in the trash, proclaiming, "That's where it belongs."

To reduce the chance of any further delay, the president of the Greater San

Antonio Home Builders Association was appointed chairman of the newly re-organized Planning Commission. He was not asked to leave his private post. Similarly, in October 1975, the council devised a "zoning overlay" policy to regulate land use in the recharge zone. Several weeks after adoption of the ordinance, the city planning director advised his colleagues in the municipal bureaucracy that the council's new regulation was in full accord with current residential and commercial growth patterns. His memo stated:

> Based on the densities permitted under the zoning *now in effect* on the Recharge Zone, a total of 83,360 people could be accommodated in the residential acreage and the equivalent of sixteen shopping centers the size of North Star Mall [a large suburban-style mall on the city's north loop] could be accommo-dated on the 965 commercial acres. As a point of interest, the combined acreage of the seven largest existing shopping centers . . . is only 430 acres. The pos-sible population of 83,360 represents 27.6 percent of the expected population increase through the year 2000. (emphasis added)

The memorandum then took the fatal leap from "is" to "ought":

> Since zoning is the major implementing mechanism for a master plan and since there is an overabundance of commercially zoned land already over the Aquifer, *allowing the free market forces to determine the eventual use of the balance of the land will have little additional negative impact on the Aquifer.* (emphasis added)[53]

To ensure harmony between the environment and "free market forces" the council also established an Aquifer Protection Office; the invitation list to its first meeting of "all agencies involved with the Aquifer" included seven gov-ernmental entities and "a representative from the Greater San Antonio Home Builders Association." No other private "agency" was invited.[54]

The Political Voices of Exclusion

The breakup of San Antonio's oligarchy liberated and energized the city's politics. Dissension at the top cleared public space for new democratic chal-lenges. Despite efforts by the Independent Team to seal the "vacuum left by the GGL," new groups emerged, and the politics of aquifer protection reached new levels of intensity.

Resistance erupted first on the west side. For years the barrio had seethed with political life. Social cliques, kinship and church networks, bars, sports clubs, and business all promoted political ambitions, ties, and conflicts. But the public spirit was contained within the Mexican community; Anglos ran the city's affairs. Early in 1974, however, a new political organization was born on the west side. It took the name Communities Organized for Public Service

(COPS), from the old sense of indignation that whites had "stolen" barrio taxes to fund northward growth: "You know, they're the robbers and we're the cops." Organized through the parish system of the Catholic Church and modeled on the political strategies of Chicago activist Saul Alinsky, COPS used noisy confrontations with the city's elites—even Walter McCallister's bank was picketed—to win long-deferred investments in drainage and street repairs.[55] Aquifer protection was not an early focus of COPS action—its role in water policy emerged two years later—but its presence in city politics was shocking to elites used to ruling "quiet Mexicans." COPS was the primary force "alien to business" that motivated Independent Team council members to grip the city government tightly.

The appearance of COPS was matched by stirrings in the environmental community on the affluent north side and near-north side. A new group, the Aquifer Protection Association (APA), sprang up from the League of Women Voters, for years a vocal pro-conservation force. Traditionally, the league's activities were sheltered by GGL claims to "nonpartisan" city government. When the builders took over, however, growth became a "political" issue. As the league was obligated to avoid political encounters, it encouraged Faye Sinkin, a forceful and articulate advocate of conservation interests, to organize APA as a means of stimulating public action for groundwater protection.

Discouraged by government hostility to water quality, APA revived earlier calls for public ownership. It urged that fifteen to twenty thousand acres be acquired for between $40 and $60 million, financed by pooling contributions from all the affected governments. By November "the fledgling APA collected twenty thousand signatures on a petition calling for the purchase of the land over the Aquifer. . . . Armed with the twenty thousand signatures, APA marched to the County Commissioners where they received a warm welcome and a 5 to 0 endorsement of the purchase idea."[56]

Sinkin also took the petitions to the city council. A less hospitable climate was found there. Sinkin's son, Lanny, reports that "for one full hour, Mayor Becker and Councilman-developer Cliff Morton browbeat my mother."[57] The petition was tossed aside. But APA still accomplished an important political purpose. For four years San Antonio's council members had nurtured reputations as good guardians of city water and as responsible advocates of growth. The dangers abounded from outside, it was said; Washington's backing for Ranchtown was scored, and Hugh Yantis was widely disliked. But local government cared. APA's insistence on exclusion flushed out the conservative council and ruffled its feathers of concern.

Groundwater Politics at a Boil

Increasingly tense divisions within San Antonio were supplemented by new dips into water policy by outsiders. In Washington, Congressman Henry

B. Gonzales added an amendment to the 1974 Safe Drinking Water Act prohibiting federal assistance to any project that would "adversely affect" urban groundwater supplies. It was received as warmly in the San Antonio City Council as Faye Sinkin had been a few weeks before. Although admitting that existing water protection administration "has been derelict," Mayor Becker complained that the congressman's action would mean "a federal intrusion into state and local affairs." [58] Only a few weeks later, even the WQB seemed ready to "intrude."

A revised Edwards Order was published, which included most of the standards requested by AACOG's Task Force. The main weak spot for environmentalists was the absence of standards to control storm-water runoff from large parking lots, but most pro–water-quality interests greeted the rules as a welcome sign of the WQB's increased sensitivity to ecology. The San Antonio City Council, however, maintained its faith in the frontier style.

Two weeks after adopting its "zoning overlay" in October 1975, "laissez-faire" won its most "positive push" since Washington had helped Ranchtown. The city council backed a zoning change allowing construction of a "super-mall" atop 129 acres of the recharge zone. Located about six miles north of the city's outer loop, the new mall was slated to house only the best merchants—Neiman-Marcus, Macys, and the like. Vividly symbolizing the grand commercial aspirations of San Antonio's new entrepreneurs and their unbounded optimism, the project also involved more than a little of what Veblen called the "enterprise in futures." As one anti-mall council member remembers, the builders were proposing a "regional shopping center without a region." [59] The city planning department's data confirmed this: "Of the 6,880 acres of the Aquifer Recharge Zone inside the City limits, only 590 acres were developed in single family units as of January 1975." [60] Indeed, as builder and planning commission chairman G. E. Harrington admitted, the mall's proponents "weren't ready to build" and probably intended to sell out in a few years with a handsome return on their investment, one he estimated at over 100 percent.

The speculative nature of the mall hardly reassured APA. If anything, it confirmed Sinkin's worst fears of a recharge zone set upon by irresponsible land traders and by a city council all too willing to oblige them. APA was incensed; COPS chanted for Harrington's resignation. Just as had Ranchtown, this decision aroused public fears. But at least in the new-town episode absentee owners and a distant federal bureaucracy could be blamed. The mall decision, however, was made by the local city council. Not even "grass-roots" democracy seemed a reliable defense of water.

Nor did the citizenry find reliable allies on the Texas Water Quality Board. Hugh Yantis answered their concerns about the effects of the mall's storm-water runoff with the observation that existing rules—which, it should be remembered, did not control runoff—would be adequate. "The only extra thing that might be required," said Yantis, "is that [the developers] use street sweepers or vacuum sweepers to keep the parking lots' surface clean." [61] APA struck back by demanding a city referendum on the council's decision. Petitions were circulated and forty-nine thousand signatures obtained, well more than enough to place the question on the January 1976 ballot.

The hopes of APA were boosted by the knowledge that exclusion by referendum had solid legal precedent behind it. In 1971 the U.S. Supreme Court upheld a California initiative forbidding construction of low-income housing without majority approval. And in 1976 it did the same for an ordinance in Eastlake, Ohio, that required all zoning variances to be reviewed by public referenda. [62] What APA discounted, however, was the fact that both the California and Ohio constitutions conferred referendum powers, whereas that of Texas did not. Undeterred by this distinction, APA pressed ahead.

To maximize the excluders' punch, Faye Sinkin invited COPS to join the drive. The Hispanic group eagerly agreed, though not only for environmental reasons. San Antonio's west side enjoyed a deeply ironic relation to the aquifer issue. For five years Mexican-Americans had watched skeptically as the city's Anglo middle and upper classes hotly debated the fate of empty space and invisible water on the north side, while the impoverishment and waste of human potential in the barrio went undiscussed. Indeed, as builders debated intellectuals about the geology of aquifers, undrained surface waters periodically flooded the flat plain of San Antonio's southern tier, destroying homes and, all too often, lives. But government did not rush to wall the tide. Thus the bitterness of controversy over the north side's future underscored the political alienation of Chicanos in San Antonio, and the concealment of their needs from public view.

But the Mexican organization expected more than merely to avenge "theft." It was hoped that by restricting access to the richest north-side properties, public policy could force an end to capital flight, thus deflecting investment back toward the inner city. As one COPS leader put it, "When we first became active in the aquifer issue it was clearly a growth issue," a means for rechanneling public and private investment back downtown. [63] For COPS, environmental exclusion came to be seen as a condition of economic expansion as well as a contribution to the public health.

The weeks of December 1975 and January 1976 were an extraordinary exception to the years of political somnambulence under GGL rule. COPS and APA busily canvassed voters in all the city's precincts, but most especially on the west and north sides. Business replied in kind: a series of full-page newspaper ads were run to undermine APA claims to wisdom on the water question. Quoting numerous public and private technicians, the ads stressed the efficacy of existing regulations. Voters were urged not to be fooled by "a small group of self-styled experts." "Don't let hysteria halt our city's development," pleaded the builders. Vote instead for "clean water and growth."

But San Antonians overwhelmingly rejected the mall. The 4 to 1 margin on election day was a convincing rebuff to corporate pleas for confidence. The aroused citizenry looked forward now to a comprehensive resolution of the growth issue with the introduction of a land use plan for the recharge zone and a master plan for the city. But the builders were not without additional weapons of their own. Insisting that Texas did not permit citizens to hold referendums as a means of directing public policy, they immediately filed suit to disqualify the majority's decision. Aquifer politics now moved on two converging tracks. One followed the direction of majoritarian politics and aimed at establishing regulatory controls and plans for land development. The other was directed by legal norms and was concerned with identifying the limits of public power. While citizens experimented with novel policies of exclusion, builders took heart from traditions which provided that "where competing land interests vie to dominate, the court is the traditional forum for decision." [64]

Intergovernmental Tangles

In February 1976 Mayor Lila Cockrell, who voted for the original zoning variance, now argued that the wisest course was to slow down the rate of development until the land's capacity for use was better known. She called for a temporary moratorium on new growth "because citizens . . . are not satisfied that development can safely occur over the recharge zone." [65] Temporary bans were also proposed by a special council subcommittee, APA, and COPS. The council majority, however, refused to accept this course, for the moratorium would violate expansionist property rights. Instead, the city leaders chose to hire an outside consulting firm to perform new geological tests and to determine once and for all the land's tolerance to construction.

As San Antonians settled down to await word from the experts, the actions of two neighboring authorities renewed the confusion. In March, the Northside Independent School District trustees voted to award a contract for construction of a $6.7 million high school in the recharge zone, but beyond the city limits. Pleading environmental ignorance, the district superintendent stated, "I really can't speak with any degree of authority on the recharge zone . . . [but] we feel like we've established a need for the school." [66]

Within weeks of that decision Hugh Yantis stunned local officials by announcing a new administrative framework for WQB policy. The 1975 Edwards Aquifer Protection Order, praised by Notzen and Weinert for its scope, was now to be implemented county by county. Each jurisdiction was free to determine for itself how and whether to apply the existing standards. Furthermore, a new clause was added stating that water quality must be maintained in a manner consistent with the economic development of the region and the private-property rights of landowners. Yantis went on to vigorously attack metropolitan domination of rural interests. He wanted to assure those outside Bexar County that government power was still on the side of private rights:

The metropolitan areas have exerted pressure on outlying counties through domination of regional councils of government. . . . [We should] restore grass-roots governmental control to the Commissioners Court of each county and . . . lessen the influence of metropolitan areas. . . . Rural officials have made it known they don't appreciate land use controls.[67]

Yantis all but gave Uvalde its long-sought right to secede from the regional government of water. Al Notzen angrily promised to fight the plan at public hearings. His concern was profound: if the rural counties were free to develop as they pleased, then metropolitan control efforts were largely in vain.

Yantis's approach was strongly criticized by officials from Bexar, Medina, and Comal counties. Spokesmen for EUWD and the San Antonio City Water Board also assailed it. But the people in Uvalde were pleased. As one explained at a public hearing:

We are getting annoyed at Bexar County people who are spending all their time worrying about people in other areas. . . . They worry about us when they can't take care of their own sewer they call the San Antonio River. . . . When they clean that mess up they can come and tell us what to do.[68]

After the Texas attorney general, John Hill, declared the new order illegal, Yantis shifted his ground slightly.[69] Instead of exemptions, he now called for seven separate county orders, which would meet the brunt of Hill's criticism while still allowing for local discretion in land use policy. A hearing was held in January 1977 to review the proposal. There Yantis countered attacks by proclaiming: "I see nothing wrong in cutting something up in smaller pieces so that it will run better."[70] The administrative surgery was performed in March 1977. Within days, Attorney General Hill, soon to announce his own candidacy for governor in a race against Dolph Briscoe, went to court to block the action of his fellow administrator. The Texas Supreme Court sided with Yantis, however, opining that the attorney general lacked proper standing to sue another state agency.[71] The board's order remained in effect as divided by Yantis.

Political Change and
a Victory for Exclusion

A crucial legal change prefaced the next skirmishes. Once again it involved the national government, this time more profoundly than ever before. After Congress amended the Voting Rights Act in 1975, the election systems of Texas cities were brought under Justice Department review. San Antonio's vast annexations and its system of at-large districts were challenged because they diluted Mexican-American voting power.[72] The city was ordered by the federal government to institute a new electoral framework, based at least in part on geographic districts. Exclusion of the barrio from municipal politics would no longer be permitted.

After the predictable political wrangling, the city's voters ratified a new electoral system based on ten geographic council districts, including six from the south, west, and east sides, plus a mayor chosen at large. In April 1977 the first election was held under this arrangement, producing a radically different city council in place of the Independent Team. Six new members arrived from areas historically overlooked in city politics: three Mexican-Americans, one Chicano-Chinese member, a black, and an Anglo female from the south side.

The Young Turks responded aggressively to the calls of COPS and APA for a moratorium on growth, so favorably in fact that the limits of debate shifted remarkably to the left. After realignment, the issue was no longer whether to introduce a moratorium on expansion, but how extensive the delay should be. Developers and council moderates talked of a partial, interim ordinance, one restricted to future projects. But the new political realities encouraged stronger steps.

For several years local, regional, and state administrators had treated aquifer protection with attitudes ranging from indifference to contempt. Every opportunity to exercise discretionary authority seemed to produce only more freedom for expansionists. Aquifer defenders were sullied, pushed around, scoffed at, their efforts regarded as "rabble-rousing." As McDonald D. Weinert once observed, APA "caused nothing but trouble and conflict." The leaders of COPS were often red-baited. Political activism for noncommercial causes did not have a good name in San Antonio, and years of frustration had soured the public's trust in local government. In Faye Sinkin's view, the only responsible course was to eliminate government's discretionary power in growth management. Backed vigorously by COPS in its drive to bring business back, APA demanded enactment of an eighteen-month total ban on all building inside the recharge zone, a stop to public-utility extensions for subdivisions currently under construction, and the termination of the platting of new subdivisions. Under the moratorium, government powers to allow expansion by variance would be preempted. Growth would cease until its safety could be demonstrated.

Council moderates pleaded for caution. This group, holdovers from the last GGL victory of 1975, included Mayor Lila Cockrell; Glen Hartman, an articulate former Air Force planner; and Henry Cisneros, a young Harvard-trained urbanist from the University of Texas at San Antonio. Limited controls were wise, they urged, but all-out war against the business class was not. The professional growth managers agreed: the planning commission and the city manager urged limited controls that would protect water without giving the city "a bad image which might hurt economic development."[73] Equally important, warned the city attorney, moratoriums against subdivision platting and utility extensions already under contract were probably illegal, because these powers were controlled by state and county authority.

Business owners too urged caution, but their counsel was backed up by what Charles Lindblom calls the "automatic punishing recoil" that comes into play whenever business interests face changes they do not like.[74] Job losses, plant closings, and economic stagnation were threatened if the city attempted to contain growth within its traditional boundaries. The *San Antonio Express* tried to take a balanced view, but implicit in its advice was a deep commitment to markets: "Investment does not go where there is a lot of controversy. . . . Neither does it go where there is a significant problem with water. . . . So the prudent course is to have [neither]."[75] Sound judgment urged a wedding of growth and environmental control—expansion and regulation. But APA and COPS failed to see a responsible authority willing to exercise responsible controls; they remained adamant for exclusion.

On June 10, 1977, the historic vote was held. Mayor Cockrell was expected to present the limited ban first, with successive votes on the additional restrictions. The moderates hoped this tactic would reduce the likelihood of a full moratorium. They expected that once the new members felt the exhilaration of imposing their power on the builders, reason would prevail against making stronger moves. But mysteriously, in the confusion and noise that swirled around the crowded council chamber, the mayor mistakenly offered the full moratorium first. As a local reporter described it, "Before a screaming, applauding crowd of several hundred proponents," mostly from COPS, the city council voted 6 to 4 to adopt the total ban on aquifer development. Henry Cisneros, the aspiring mayoral candidate, abstained.[76]

Business Reacts

Reaction to the decision was swift and angry. One member of the planning commission threatened to resign, crying, "This is not government, but an anarchy." Councilman Hartman called the action "completely foolish," and Judge Reeves, long a supporter of strict rules for groundwater protection, announced that the county would decide subdivision platting around the fringe of the city. The council was "puffing in the wind," he said. Business reaction was even more hostile. The president of the Greater San Antonio Home Builders Association warned that the council should not expect "certain magical things" to happen in other parts of the city just because northside growth has been stopped. "All businessmen work where the climate is conducive to their development and when it's not, they leave." The president of Datapoint Corporation, a fast-growing northside computer company, announced cancellation of plans to enlarge its operations in the city. "The climate for business expansion in San Antonio appears to be rapidly deteriorating because of actions being taken in the public sector." Banner headlines in the tabloid *San Antonio News* screamed of "Job Losses Feared Over Aquifer Ban." The city manager proclaimed, "We can forget about economic development." But the best summary was furnished by the headline in the *Express*: "No Expansion." [77]

The local capitalists once again supplemented their threats with lawsuits. One involved a $750 million class action filed in the U.S. Federal Court charging an unconstitutional taking of private property. Another, brought in state court by eight local developers, was aimed at the six council members who voted for the moratorium. All told, the suits claimed damages of $1.5 billion. [78]

Within weeks, both state and federal courts issued temporary injunctions against implementation of the moratorium. According to Bernardo Eureste, one of the most outspoken of the pro-moratorium council members, this injunction came as no surprise. He had fully expected the suits, admitting he would do the same if he were a landowner. However, by forcing the construction interests to respond to an extreme action, he insisted, the council was in a far stronger position to achieve its real goal of controlled growth. [79]

Although Eureste may have anticipated the explosion of criticism, other members of the council were more surprised. Some wanted immediate repeal of the ordinance; others suggested carefully worded amendments to bring it into conformity with law. Councilman Cisneros, however, who had been arguing for an interim ordinance since the mall referendum eighteen months earlier, saw that the court's restraining order gave the city time to start the policy-formation process anew. He agreed with the radicals to keep the present ordinance and go ahead with the lawsuits, but he convinced them to look outside San Antonio for legal help. He recommended the services of the prestigious Chicago land-use law firm of Ross, Hardies, O'Keefe, Babcock and Parsons. They would both defend the city against the developers' suits and assist the council in formulating a land use plan capable of controlling growth and protecting the aquifer. [80]

Within weeks the Chicago lawyers confirmed the analysis and advice offered by the planners in May: the limits on utility extensions and subdivision plat approval were illegal. But that part of the ordinance governing zoning and building permits was enforceable. With the injunctions on the illegal portions of the ban in place, the city's new lawyers went to work on a defensible ordinance to remain in effect until the technical studies and master-planning process were completed. The chance of obtaining a new set of rules allowing existing contracts to be fulfilled and new projects to be undertaken inspired the developers to agree to a delay in their federal suit pending the writing of a new ordinance.

In August, the lawyers advised the council to repeal its total moratorium in favor of a limited, interim ordinance and suggested that the council impose a series of rigid controls on development inside the city's portion of the recharge zone. They proposed a five-acre-minimum lot size and a requirement that all applicants for building permits furnish a detailed natural-resource-disclosure statement, including engineering surveys demonstrating that construction would not adversely affect the aquifer. They also urged the City Water Board to refuse water to subdivisions if promoters did not meet the standards. The Chicago lawyers urged passage of an interim ordinance that came close to being a moratorium in effect.[81]

Although COPS and APA preferred to leave less room for growth over the aquifer, and representatives of the builders continued to complain that "the majority of this Council is trying to do everything in its power to stop growth to the north," the council decided to accept the firm's proposal. On September 8, 1977, the total moratorium was repealed. In its place the modified version drawn up by the Chicago lawyers was enacted.[82]

The moratorium victory was aquifer protection's greatest moment. Since then its proponents have entered a dismal time warp, an embittering return to the days of frustration, uncertainty, and defeat that marked their earliest encounters with the Texas Water Quality Board. In January 1978 the Fourth Court of Texas Appeals overturned the super-mall referendum vote, just as the builders predicted.[83] It held that zoning ordinances enacted under state authority could not be vetoed through referenda unless the state constitution provided machinery for direct democracy. Since the constitution of Texas had no such provision, the national precedents were irrelevant, and the variance stood. Appeals to the Supreme Courts of Texas and the United States were fruitless.

Since the decision, commercial interest in the recharge zone has been rekindled. New "super-malls" have been announced for construction in the recharge zone, and subdivisions continue to spill north.[84] Local landowners have much cause to celebrate, and they do. May 21–27, 1978, was declared Private Property Week by the San Antonio Board of Realtors. Endorsed by the mayor as a "time of recognition of the right of all people to own property," it is now an annual affair.

No firecrackers were set off, however, when the outside studies of the Edwards aquifer were finally submitted a year later. The report, produced by the Massachusetts engineering firm of Metcalf and Eddy, did little to clarify the situation, except to emphasize once again the danger of reliance on a regional water resource without a regional authority to guard it. It concluded that although "development can occur on the recharge zone . . . only with proper controls and preventive measures, can the risks to contamination . . . be sufficiently reduced to be acceptable." But because rural counties opposed such controls, the metropolitan governments "may be helpless in protecting the health, welfare, and safety of their citizens."[85]

The situation today is remarkably like that in 1971 when the battles began. Local elites have patched differences and reestablished a new citywide front called United San Antonio. Though Mexican-Americans are much more politically prominent today than a decade ago, COPS learned self-restraint after it unsuccessfully challenged the rights of business to make economic-development policy.[86] Fortunately, the groundwater remains pure, protected more by a decade of economic stagnation than by comprehensive public control. Not a spade of dirt has been turned on any of the "super-malls." The city still has time to take stronger steps, but ultimately it remains dependent on those taken by others. The Aquifer Protection Association persists, of course, in trying to maintain the alert, but city officials are diffident. Several years ago, in fact, several suggested dropping the collective-landowner role altogether, arguing that private owners in the subdivisions should be forced to "organize homeowner associations which would then have to correct . . . pollution" problems after they move in. City attorneys advised, however, that public governments lack powers to compel membership in private ones.[87] Meanwhile, attorneys for area landowners continue to warn of lawsuits, reminding the citizenry that "someone will have to come up with $160 million" if expansion is prohibited.[88] Metcalf and Eddy's conclusion seems reasonable: San Antonio's population must continue to place faith in the aquifer's resilience, for the city otherwise remains "helpless" in the face of forces beyond its control.

Leaving the Scene

San Antonio's experience suggests that zoning can turn out to be a porous and shaky fence; it doesn't necessarily fare well in the face of regional pressures, toxic pollutants, intergovernmental domination, and well-entrenched business power. A brief review may allow a clearer understanding of the local limits of land use control.

Localities, even huge ones that stretch over 260 square miles, are poorly suited to regulate the use of resources that cut through many different jurisdictions. Political geography and physical geology rarely fit snugly together. When fragile lands extend across neighboring borders, local excluders should not count on neighborly cooperation; they may encounter expansionists. Urban interests already know what happens when suburbs are asked to cooperate in housing the poor.

But zoning is frustrated not only by geological forces. Corporate chemistry is at work, too. A major result of the petrochemical industry's fantastic success in proliferating synthetic products from oil has been redepositing the toxic consequences in the ground, where subsoil water is especially vulnerable to pollution. San Antonio's crisis was hardly unique in this respect. About half the country's urban drinking water flows from beneath the land, while 80 percent of rural water needs are supplied by groundwater. And, as Rochelle L. Stanfield notes:

> An increasing amount of toxic chemicals are ending up in this water supply as a result of pesticide spraying, improper disposal of hazardous wastes and conventional disposal of industrial and residential wastes. The Council on Environmental Quality has found serious groundwater contamination in 34 states. The Congressional Research Service reported 4,000 wells nationwide damaged or closed by contaminants. Public wells have been closed in 25 Pennsylvania cities, 22 cities each in New York and Massachusetts and 16 cities in Connecticut. EPA has found chemical contamination of a third of the larger public water systems dependent on groundwater that it studied.[89]

But the problem of toxicity is much more pervasive even than this. For, as one report notes, "the products of the chemical industry are everywhere in modern society," especially in the home where they are found in "plastics, textiles, construction materials, paints, adhesives, fertilizers, pesticides, and medicines, to name a few." [90] Like capital, only more insidiously, they "nestle everywhere, settle everywhere, establish connections everywhere," sometimes refusing to expose themselves until long after their residence has been ruinously established. Moreover, according to the Environmental Protection Agency, over 90 percent of industrial hazardous waste has already been "disposed in a manner actually or potentially harmful to the environment." Love Canal, New York, and Times Beach, Missouri, are now familiar symbols of the new forms of silent degradation.[91]

The outpouring of federal and state policies concerning air, water, and toxic pollution represents intergovernmental efforts to compensate for the inadequacies of local land use controls.[92] Though poorly administered in all too many cases, these policies embody second steps toward enlarging the scope of social control of economic change. But the continuing absence of a national policy for groundwater protection remains the most dangerous vacuum in environmental law.

Expansionists, however, are wary of more protection. The Reagan administration's tawdry handling of the toxics issue is only the tip of much deeper corporate concern over larger-scale democratic efforts to regulate capitalist action. As Robert Nelson complains, "The basic incentive behind protection of regional and state environmental quality is much the same as that behind protection of neighborhood and community quality. . . . While this purpose may seem laudable, it in fact has radical implications" favoring "feudal tenure trends" and "opposition to the market verdict." [93] Thus the transition from zoning to wider strategies for social control of development is bound to cross a treacherous path of corporate opposition.

Not the least of the issues is corporate influence in the intergovernmental arrangements themselves. Frank J. Popper's studies of six regional and state land use programs led him to conclude that the new "agencies are under-staffed and underfinanced," leaving them exposed to strong corporate pres-sures to modify regulations and procedures in pro-expansionist directions. Thus "improvements have been slighter, slow to arrive, and more difficult to achieve than reformers . . . might have hoped." [94]

Certainly San Antonio's experience in trying to win assistance from re-gional and state bodies shows that higher levels of government do not neces-sarily favor environmental values. The Texas Water Quality Board felt entirely free to oppose land use control in open violation of its legal responsibilities. And the Edwards Underground Water District was sufficiently impressed by local business power that it refused to accept nominal authority to regulate land use, out of fear of harsh corporate reactions.

Within San Antonio, the builders' political power was extremely well ap-plied—directly through local government, as well as through the courts—to prevent action at odds with the "positive push to laissez-faire." The legal bias favoring growth was especially important in checking majority rule inside the city. Real estate forces dictated the policy options and limits. Public action was forced into a commercial cage. As a draft of the city's proposed mas-ter plan states, "the City has limited direct influence on economic benefit to its citizens." To gain environmental protection for its citizens San Antonio must "cooperate with the private sector" and "assist all new and existing in-dustries in meeting environmental regulations." [95] San Antonio's junior status is unmistakable.

Given San Antonio's limited powers of self-protection, the aquifer's multi-jurisdictional reach, the conservative bias of the Texan intergovernmental framework, and the power of business at all levels of the state's political sys-tem, Lone Star capitalists feel little need for centralized controls or for admin-istrative planning as the condition of corporate access. National land policies make little sense where freedom to expand is so amply endowed by regional governments. But in other sections of the United States, land clearance is not so facilely accomplished. Suburban homeowners, neighborhood activists, and environmentalists fight their battles to control economic change with greater rates of success. In these less compliant settings, the struggles for land use control have been seedbeds of frustration for big capital. And it is this frustra-tion that has driven the efforts to expand the scope of land use conflict, push-ing the fight upward in the governmental system, all the way to the Congress and the White House. The remainder of this study follows the rising trajectory of land use conflict into debates over a national land use policy and the Energy Mobilization Board. But it is the essence of land use policy, as well as American politics in general, that tensions at the grass roots are never very far removed from the heights of national decision. Excluders have voices in Washington, too.

This country is in the midst of a revolution in the way we regulate the use of our land. It is a peaceful revolution, conducted entirely within the law. It is a quiet revolution . . . a disorganized revolution with no central cadre of leaders.

Fred Bosselman and David Callies

Zoning is a very confused area.

Senator Henry Jackson

For communities eager to control the scope of economic change, zoning is an imperfect but essential tool. The San Antonio story exposed some of its important limits. In the smaller, more affluent settings of suburbia, however, zoning has proven to be a more formidable weapon, which has significantly helped to maintain the status quo. Low-cost housing, waste dumps, factories, and other undesirables have all been duly barred, a fact of considerable annoyance to government and corporate planners for whom such projects are necessary components in the industrial network. From the vantage point of high-level command posts, local zoners can often appear to be archaic and parochial, the wielders of a tool whose geographic frame bears little objective relationship to the economic facts of life. In this view, local land use control is like a rusty old cog in a dynamic social engine. Technocrats see it as functionally disruptive; its political opponents call it "feudal." Exclusion often has a bad name in the higher circles.

Of course, elite land managers are not habituated to feelings of rejection, and big institutions are not well designed to suffer frustration; they are rather more used to getting things done. The forces of "creative destruction" have, as we have seen, been given legal room for maneuver. Expansion has never been contained for long. Thus zoning has come in for its share of criticism and attack, never more forcefully than in the battle to establish a national land use policy in the 1970s. Important social interests thought it high time that the local zoners be checked by higher-level viewpoints and broader concerns.

149

Clashing Views of Land Use Reform

Students of land use policy have paid remarkably little attention to the political patterning of the national land use fight. Only one brief monograph, by Noreen Lyday, claims to tell the story in any detail.[1] Like most other students of land use, she tends to attribute the introduction of national land use policy legislation to the rising environmental awareness of the 1960s and its defeat to the increasing power of business in the 1970s.[2] But conventional wisdom notwithstanding, the roots of such legislation can be found in some of the weightier institutions of American expansion, not only in the new environmentalism. Indeed, historical parallels are evident in the pro-development shifts of the 1820s and 1830s as much as in the zoning movement of the 1920s. But the expansionist push for national land use policy was no more a simple phenomenon than were any of the other examples reviewed in this study. Environmentalists were not the originators of land use reform, but neither was it forced into prominence by high-pressure corporate lobbyists.

The political dynamics of land use reform were governed by other, less obvious forces. One of the most important was the patterning of class and policy consciousness at the highest levels of American society. The best way to see this is to consider for a moment how some theorists have dealt with the larger issue of how general business needs—what Marx called the class interests of capital—come to be established as public-policy recommendations.

Business Needs and Corporate Consciousness

The Italian theorist Antonio Gramsci argued that organic intellectuals play key roles in working out the longer-range organizational needs of capitalism. The story of the development of today's property and land controls, told in chapter 3, showed how a scattering of legal and planning intellectuals shaped the law of property to accommodate the growth of capital and the rights of landowners to resist. Today, adds G. William Domhoff, Gramsci's organic intellectuals have themselves increasingly been organized in an institutional pattern Domhoff calls the "policy planning network."

For Domhoff, as for Gramsci, "social cohesion and common economic interests are not enough in themselves to lead" capitalists "to agreed-upon policies without research, consultation, and deliberation." The corporate economy, Domhoff insists, "is too big and diverse for the new policies that are often required to be deduced from some storehouse of wisdom on the functioning of corporate capitalism or to arise implicitly from the fact of a common social environment."[3] In other words, policy experts and planners intervene between business's workaday production problems and its need to have the longer-range requirements of accumulation and legitimacy identified and acted on for the system as a whole. Between the corporate giants, then, which control most of the production system, and the organs of government, where final policy decisions are made, "there is a complex network of people and institutions that plays an important role in sharpening the issues and weighing the alternatives," a network including "policy groups, foundations, think tanks, and university research institutes," whose main job is to think about what capitalism needs for its good health over the long haul.[4]

To study how the idea of land use reform won its place on the national agenda, it is extremely helpful to use the Domhoff thesis of the "policy planning network" in conjunction with our working hypothesis of the exclusion-expansion dialectic.[5] The question is, How did policy planners interact with the deeper currents of expansion and exclusion and initiate the politics of national land use reform? It is best to begin by meeting some of the main policy planners themselves and the larger political economic forces with which they contend.

The Land Use Policy Network

In his study entitled *The Politics of Land-Use Reform,* Frank J. Popper described this network very broadly. Following the lead of Fred Bosselman and David Callies—who insisted that land use reform was a "disorganized revolution, with no central cadre of leaders"—Popper saw the reformers as a "loose coalition of environmentalists, city planners, land-use lawyers, some state and federal officials, a few progressive business people, and citizen activists of all sorts" whose prime goal was to encourage more centralized planning and regulation, "particularly from an environmental perspective."[6]

Looking somewhat more closely at the actual figures who drafted most of the key national reform documents and proposals—the people who sat on or advised the major public and private study commissions on land use and who had the greatest influence in actually bringing the issue to the attention of national political leaders—Richard A. Walker and Michael Heiman arrived at a much narrower conception of the land use reform network, finding a distinct "central cadre of leaders." For them, "a select group has directed the mainstream reform movement," a "small network" of leading land-use lawyers, with close ties to big construction firms, blue-ribbon research organizations, and elite foundations.[7] Walker and Heiman believe that the land use reformers were indeed concerned with the environmental aspects of land use. But they contend that this factor was only one part of the reformers' general interest in standardizing the overall development regulation process so that it could be made more responsive to a battery of national corporate priorities, including large-scale industrial and commercial projects and open housing for black workers. In their view, economic interests, particularly large-scale urban booster capitalists and their national allies in the prestigious policy institutes, were the motor behind land use reform. A close look at the organic intellectuals involved in land use policy turns up people who bear a much greater resemblance to Walker and Heiman's policy elites than to Popper's loosely grouped environmentalists.

The main voices of land policy included, among others, Charles Haar, Harvard law professor and assistant secretary for metropolitan development in the Department of Housing and Urban Development in the Johnson administration; Richard F. Babcock, author of *The Zoning Game,* president of the American Society of Planning Officials, and chairman of the American Law Institute (ALI) Model Land Law advisory committee; Fred Bosselman, author of several key reform studies for the Council on Environmental Quality, consultant to the Douglas Commission (a key Johnson-era housing and land use study group), and coauthor of the ALI's model land law code; and William K. Reilly, who served on the staff of the Council for Environmental Quality, where he helped draft land use legislation during the Nixon administration, and the Rockefeller Task Force on Land Use, where he edited that group's influential study *The Use of Land: A Citizens' Policy Guide to Urban Growth.* Babcock, Bosselman, and Reilly were at one time all members of the same Chicago law firm—Ross, Hardies, O'Keefe, Babcock and Parsons—the same firm, it will be remembered, that helped San Antonio prepare its revised aquifer protection ordinance in 1978.[8]

Tied to wider circles of intellectual, corporate, and political power through organizations such as the American Law Institute, the Urban Institute, and the Rockefeller, Ford, and Conservation foundations, these and a handful of other people helped to frame the issues in terms of lawyers' traditional concerns with conflict resolution, although they were also strongly influenced by advances in academic regional-planning theory. Their activities—which included writing books, articles, and reports; serving on, or as advisers to, presidential and private study commissions; and spreading the gospel to other advocates in government—laid the intellectual groundwork for the reform of land use policy.

The lawyers never worked outside the current political context. Their activities were heavily influenced not only by the troubles of their clients but also by the confluence of other, more systemic forces, especially changes in the housing industry, environmental abuse, and the urban riots of the mid-1960s. Reformers believed in an economic theory of land use that held that expansion was best conducted by large, efficient development enterprises, big capitalist corporations that could afford to operate on a large scale and to remember social and ecological values in their planning. They strongly favored the increasing concentration of the construction industry in a few large firms. But to seize the advantages of scale, corporate builders needed access to the big suburban lots that many communities wanted left untouched. Although the construction firms did not themselves make the case for it, reformers plugged land use centralization as the appropriate answer. Industrial advancement made land use reform seem economically logical.

The land use reformers drew support from another side as well. Federal construction agencies, such as the U.S. Army Corps of Engineers and the Interior Department's Bureau of Reclamation, angrily complained to the congressional Interior committees that too many groups were fighting their projects. The obstructors, it was said, stymied progress, raised costs, and created intergovernmental turmoil, impeding the efficiency of the national government and economy by delaying necessary additions to the economic system, such as airports, highways, and transmission lines. As Washington experienced its own internal pressures to straighten out the mess of land use decision making, the land use reformers found allies in the public works agencies of the federal government and among their congressional supporters.

The national land use reformers came largely from the cream of the American legal and planning professions, from the organic intellectuals of big urban capital, and, to a lesser extent, from the traditionally growth-oriented federal development bureaus and Interior committees. Their policy network drew strength from the broader metropolitan restructuring that has characterized postwar urban capitalism. It was in this context that the reform network quietly placed on the national agenda a matter whose traditional bailiwick lay in local courthouses and city halls. This chapter will explore how this process unfolded and how it set the stage for the legislative fight discussed in the next.

A Political Science of Expansion

The early 1950s saw big-city commercial and real estate interests in recession. Millions of consumers had taken flight to the suburbs, leaving behind only gloomy prospects for downtown merchants. Real estate values were unsettled; many expansion plans were quietly retired;[9] slums spread. In this discouraging climate creative destruction seemed pointless. Since the New Deal, though, national Democratic party leaders had viewed the longer process of urban decline as a fruitful opportunity to secure the future of their organization. As John Mollenkopf argues, the Democrats—from Franklin Roosevelt's New Deal to Lyndon Johnson's Great Society—conceived of urban decay as a seedbed for the growth of support for activist federal policies, especially urban renewal. Such programs would stimulate downtown business and, in the bargain, glue local constituencies to the party with contracts, subsidies, and jobs. Downtown revival programs, Mollenkopf writes, "provided a means by which diverse local constituencies, all of which had a stake in stepping up the rate of urban development, could be brought together in new 'progrowth' coalitions" that would, in turn, furnish "organizational and political support for the national Democratic political entrepreneurs who had established them."[10]

But if downtown redevelopment had a substantial political rationale, the partisan benefit was officially muted. The publicized motivations were those of urban uplift and economic revival, goals that were legitimized as matters of rational planning and purely administrative moves toward regional integration. As central-city boosters and pro-growth mayors allied themselves with national Democrats, social scientists developed new theories of regional development. In the seemingly neutral language of regional science and economic geography, they warned of the inevitability of urban deterioration—unless government took bold steps to manage expansion. Planners gave the new politics of expansion the imprimatur of expertise and the gloss of science.

Economists and planners such as Walter Isard, Charles Tiebout, and John Friedmann led the way in producing new, "realistic" studies of the spatial diffusion of capital.[11] They treated the market as an inexorable geographic force that spread wealth across the open, national economy while pocketing stagnation and decay in backward regions and spent cities. Terms such as "spatial structure" and "functional integration" were projected as the objective categories of the new scientific geography. People and places became variables in mathematical equations of the higher corporate logic.

But in accepting the market's terms and incentives as the only reasonable forces behind "spatial development," social scientists also shared in its boundless optimism about what could be accomplished given the appropriate mix of scientific foresight and profit-making opportunity. By developing plans that followed the logic of "functional integration" of existing institutions, sound arguments could be made for consciously targeting incentives so that the more progressive development forces of modern architecture and planning could be joined with public and private capital to rebuild the cities and improve the life of the poor. What Jane Jacobs called "super-blocks and park promenades" became the planners' vision of a new "ideal of order and gentility" in the cities, one linked directly to hopes for an expanding economy.[12] Economists and planners helped to establish a rational scientific context for coupling market forces to new administrative designs. It was objectively possible, as well as socially just, to renew the cities and rationalize the metropolis.

The whole conception of land use control now began to change. Expansion, especially in its urban capitalist form, was coming to be seen not only as a process whose basic features could be classified, located, and spatially separated according to plan, as in the old zoning format, but also as a process that required planning out the smoothest possible merger of economic functions and land uses. Planners thought they could preconceive the most efficient connections between the major metropolitan functions and recommend appropriate mixtures of public investment, private accumulation, and land use control to bring it all about. They argued that blueprints for the scale and form of development across large metropolitan areas could be related to some notion of "integrated development," which, in practical terms, meant the creation of regional mechanisms for joining major public-sector investments, such as sewers, roads, and mass transit, with the objectives, outlooks, and private master plans of large corporations and the land use plans of local governments. The restructuring of the metropolis was not something that would just happen; it would be made to happen, according to plan.

Urban restructuring, it was insisted, would greatly improve overall economic efficiency by raising corporate profits and lowering government budgets. As the Committee for Economic Development (CED) argued in 1960, "The concentration of population in metropolitan areas and of economic activity outside the limits of the central city have reduced the effectiveness of existing procedures of allocating resources. . . . An integrated approach to area-wide problems such as transportation is, over the long run, more efficient and economical per unit of service provided." But, as the CED stressed, "The heart of our problem is the use of land . . . in the most efficient manner." [13]

Obviously, the new planning was as different from zoning as it was from what the CED disparagingly called "unpremeditated growth." [14] Land use policy was now appreciated as a potentially crucial tool for unifying people, processes, and things within the dominant structure of capitalist class relations and exclusions. Thus, it was argued, if geographic links between functions, resources, and labor were seen and ordered in relation to the profit and ecological potentials of regions as wholes, then battles such as the Edwards aquifer fight in San Antonio could largely be avoided. The cities could be restored by big business, and middle-class suburbanites could be relieved of the constant threat of unexpected disruptions. Much more land could be saved from speculative development, and the poor could find new chances on the urban border. However, as long as land use policy was viewed as an administrative projection of large-scale investment across jurisdictions, rather than as a device for social control within them, the centralization of authority for land use control was axiomatic. This was the rub of regional-planning theory.

Naturally, serious consequences followed for existing ties between individual landownership rights and local political power. In modern regional-planning theory, David Ricardo's contempt for the land interest clearly shone through. Individual ownership and local land use control were not taken as ends in themselves; they were changeable institutions, which had to show new flexibility within the more dynamic and dominant macroeconomic system. Individual or neighborhood versions of exclusion and expansion, versions geared to local pocketbooks and neighborhood custom, were necessarily subordinate. The scattering of landownership rights in the cities, and the splintering of land use controls in the suburbs, were merely different forms in space of the old tendency of landed property to lag behind and resist the centralizing thrust of capitalist industrial property. Each needed to be consolidated: the divisions of land-based power—political as well as economic—had to be overcome and subjected to greater political and economic control—through eminent domain and reform of land use policy. A new kind of corporate liberalism was emerging that threatened to give modern content to Marx's observation that "the division of landed property corresponds to the movement of competition in the sphere of industry." [15]

The Science of Taking

The first problem facing urban renewal planners was the parcelization of landownership in America's slum districts and skid rows. In Charles Abrams's words, the "rationalization of disparate plots" was an essential precondition for efficient, large-scale planning and redevelopment. "The power of land assemblage," he wrote, "makes possible the establishment of contiguity between plots and the bringing into use of land with unmarketable titles that have held up development of whole sections; it facilitates the synchronization of public and private improvements as well as the planning of cohesive shopping centers." Mollenkopf states the point more bluntly: government needed "the muscle to shape urban development patterns." [16]

For Abrams and other proponents of urban renewal, the power of eminent domain was seen as the indispensable tool of rational development, an instrument of technical and social progress in modern city construction. It presupposed an important step beyond the already widely accepted ideas that urban development was a social process and that the forces of private expansion and exclusion were incapable of producing socially beneficial outcomes on their own. Renewal implied an enlarged positive role for government in the capitalist development of cities, not merely the old collective landowner task of interfering with private decisions when they "adversely affect neighboring properties." [17] It embraced the exercise of the state's most powerful economic instrument to fashion new spatial and property frameworks, much as government did on the fenceless frontier in the nineteenth century. Not for nothing did Abrams entitle his study of urban renewal *The City Is the Frontier*.

Congress eagerly threw its weight behind this idea. With the Housing Acts of 1949 and 1954, a massive federal commitment was made to finance urban land clearance. [18] Over one billion dollars was authorized between 1949 and 1957. Most of this money was used to lay the groundwork for investment in what one real estate textbook calls "facelifting operations." [19] Among the notable beneficiaries were New York City's Lincoln Center, the civic centers in Hartford and St. Paul, and the Independence Hall area in Philadelphia. According to a 1967 survey, 67 percent of the areas affected were primarily residential before urban renewal, but only 43 percent remained so after their reconstruction. And most of the new housing units were priced above the means of low-income renters, who formed a majority of those displaced. As one federal study concluded, "Instead of a grand assault on slums and blight as an integral part of a campaign for 'a decent home and a suitable living environment for every American family,' renewal was . . . a federally financed gimmick to provide relatively cheap land for a miscellany of profitable or prestigious enterprises." [20]

Legal skeptics and some among the dispossessed, always the bane of urban boosters, raised touchy questions. They challenged the legitimacy of applying powers of eminent domain for the purpose of enriching central-city land values. The issue reached its head in the U.S. Supreme Court in the justly famous case of *Berman* v. *Parker* (1954).[21] The test involved the District of Columbia Redevelopment Act of 1954, in which Congress gave broad authority for land clearance to the district's planning agency. Berman sued the agency when it seized his department store. He contended that since his land was slated to be turned over to other private entrepreneurs, the planning department's goals failed to meet the demands of the "public use" test. For Berman, urban renewal illegally extended the state's power when it envisioned a partnership of public takers and private receivers. He wanted the court to fix the power of eminent domain squarely within a strict construction of public use and necessity.

As noted in chapter 2, Justice William O. Douglas was not in a fixing mood the day he authored the defeat of Berman. Instead, Douglas declared a sweeping entitlement of state power both to seize and to regulate private property. He argued that Congress's vision of the public good may extend very broadly and that "any attempt to define its reach or trace its outer limits is fruitless, for each case must turn on its own facts. . . . The concept of the public welfare is broad and inclusive. The values it represents are spiritual as well as physical, aesthetic as well as monetary. It is within the power of the legislature to determine that the community should be beautiful as well as healthy, spacious as well as clean, well-balanced as well as carefully patrolled." There is, concluded Douglas, "nothing in the Fifth Amendment that stands in the way." [22] Quiet citizens would be well advised to beware; the exuberant were once more showing signs of restlessness.

Although some state judges continued to apply strict interpretations of the "public use" test even after *Berman* v. *Parker,*[23] the Supreme Court's ruling strongly fortified the 1954 Housing Act, lending local officials and entrepreneurs ample power to rumble about in the nation's downtowns. By 1967 more than 37,000 acres of real estate, over thirty-five square miles, was stripped of its buildings and residents. The total was not great by the standards of frontier land policy—where Indians were driven off millions of square miles—but it should not be overlooked that this space was of very high density. In the end, over 400,000 apartments, 129,000 buildings, and tens of thousands of Americans gave up their place for "urban renewal." [24]

Metropolitan Divisions

Berman considerably eased problems of urban land assembly. But it left the issue of suburban land-use controls even more clouded than before, for Douglas's broad interpretation of the police power also gave suburbs new room to set land apart for community defense purposes. It took a generation for the exclusionary implications of *Berman* to become clear, but when the opportunity presented itself, Douglas once again led the Court in a strong assertion of community land use powers. The case was *Village of Belle Terre* v. *Boraas* (1974), and it was the first major zoning dispute to be heard by the Supreme Court since the late 1920s.[25] A small community on Long Island, New York, was charged by a group of local college students with violation of their constitutional rights to travel and their liberty to differ from the majority through its enforcement of a land use ordinance that barred any but conventionally defined families from living inside its borders. Douglas invoked his earlier reasoning to restate the municipality's power to determine its internal land use patterns and thus its prevailing social relationships. "The police power," wrote Douglas, "is not confined to elimination of filth, stench, and unhealthy places. It is ample to lay out zones where family values, youth values, and the blessings of quiet seclusion and clean air make the area a sanctuary for people." [26] The American suburb could not have won a more resounding judicial endorsement. But only the words were new: as Douglas was careful to make clear, the logic of community exclusion was embraced "within *Berman* v. *Parker.*"

The Court's ironclad consistency was received with less than delight by regional planners, developers, and lawyers, for although *Berman* efficiently hitched eminent domain to the cause of large-scale expansion in cities, the broad scope it implied for exclusion powers in the suburbs began increasingly to frustrate corporate hopes of achieving functional integration of key facilities in the metropolis as a whole. As San Antonio's experience showed, political constituencies, physical ecologies, and regional economies were anything but neatly aligned in and around the nation's cities. Whatever sense of order and limit American cities may have inherited from eras of horse-and-buggy technology and traditional common law was cracked by the twin drives toward suburban expansion and urban rebirth. Local governments, for example, were mass produced with abandon. By the early 1960s the Chicago metropolis abounded with 1,214 separate governments, followed by 852 in Philadelphia, 698 in Pittsburgh, 531 in New York, 483 in St. Louis, and 304 in Houston. As many as 84 distinct governments dotted the average metropolitan landscape.[27] Complaints of "balkanization" rang out from the legal and business fraternities. By 1966 the prestigious Committee on Economic Development was calling for abolition of fully "eighty percent" of the little polities and their replacement by more businesslike, centralized systems.[28]

The gripes reflected more than aesthetic displeasure. Systemwide needs to deploy resources and people efficiently were stymied by an urban layout that reeked of waste. Even untrained social accountants could see the toll. Huge quantities of still usable urban housing decayed while subdivisions leapfrogged over big chunks of farmland that speculation drove out of production. Public utilities stretched across cow pastures to reach outlying settlements where fitful taxpayers grumbled at the bill. The new metropolitan distances strained mass transit and sewage systems. Commuters opted for spacious automobiles but were forced to accept congested, time-wasting highways. Pollution of air and water rotted the landscape, and the races grew ever farther apart. And in the midst of all this, governments regulated land and taxed incomes with minimal coordination and utter indifference to areawide implications. But as the CED stressed, "Overemphasis on waste, inefficiency and incompetence may obscure the point: most American communities lack any instrumentality of government with legal powers, geographic jurisdiction, and independent revenue sources necessary to conduct self-government in any valid sense." [29] This was, for the big-business group, a technical question of bringing government institutions into line with new economic, social, and mechanical realities. Politics did not figure in their administrative equations, at least not explicitly.

Presidential Support

In 1961, however, the newly elected Democratic president, John F. Kennedy, was quickly sensitized to the issues of urban growth and policy fragmentation. Friction between exclusion and expansion interests was generating new political heat, but the overriding context was shaped by the larger economic doldrums of the late 1950s. Dwight Eisenhower had presided over an "affluent America," but not all quarters shared in the goods. Three recessions in the decade left construction wanting, despite the great infusions of suburban and city development contracts. Nonfarm housing starts in 1960 slumped 18 percent to their lowest level in ten years. Unemployment among construction workers jumped 25 percent. Indeed, throughout the Eisenhower years, housing starts declined an average of 2 percent annually. Home builders pressed for subsidies to encourage new starts. For the first time since its founding in 1942, the National Association of Home Builders omitted from their annual "policy statement their traditional attack on public housing." [30] Big-city Democrats, meanwhile, fearing political disasters as a result of the loss of white working-class votes to the suburbs, sought special representation in a new cabinet-level department for housing and urban affairs. Blacks, on the verge of revolt for civil rights, pressed demands for open housing. Suburbanites, meanwhile, called for more open space. [31]

Experienced attorneys saw unifying explanations in the failures of urban land use policy. Suburban exclusion was quickly identified as a main culprit; it blocked racial integration of the society and stymied necessary growth. In 1961 Richard Babcock, a distinguished member of the land use bar, was asked by the American Society of Planning Officials to produce a careful analysis of the situation. Funding was provided by the Ford Foundation, an institution much interested in urban reform and civil rights causes. Babcock's report, later published as *The Zoning Game,* was a caustic indictment of local control: "Land-use planning is in chaos. . . . I doubt that even the most intransigent disciple of anarchy ever wished for or intended the litter that prevails in the area of land-use regulation." [32]

Babcock urged creation of statewide authorities to oversee the local excluders. His work, plus other criticism from reformers such as Charles Haar of the Harvard Law School, linked the rising cause of civil rights with economic growth and land use reform. [33] Strongly influenced by the informed legal opinion that racial segregation and land use controls were inseparable, the Ford Foundation now granted the American Bar Association's research arm, the American Law Institute, $500,000 to draft a replacement for the old Model State Land Use Code, originally written in the early 1920s when zoning was first taking root. Gradually, builders and lawyers took on roles as the tail wagging the dog of the open-housing issue and equal access to the suburbs.

The accumulated grievances guided Kennedy's lieutenants in the Housing and Home Finance Agency toward an urban policy that attempted to confront metropolitan realities. But critiques of local control were kept understandably subtle. Poor planning took the brunt of the attack. The local pattern was said to be organizationally archaic and out of step with modern pressures demanding wider, metropolitan views. Central cities needed suburban cooperation to fulfill their new function as "service centers" for activities conducted around the metropolitan fringe. In Kennedy's words, "Urban renewal programs to date have been too narrow to cope effectively with the basic problems facing older cities. We must do more than concern ourselves with bad housing—we must reshape our cities into effective service centers for expanding metropolitan areas. [We require] the establishment of an effective and comprehensive planning process in each metropolitan area embracing all major activities, both public and private, which shape the community." [34]

Of course, if cities were "reshaped" to fit the economic realities, the logic of urban renewal dictated that many working-class people, especially non-whites, would continue to be displaced. Suburbs were expected to take their share. As the president warned, "Bold programs in individual jurisdictions are no longer enough. Increasingly, community development must be a cooperative venture toward the common goals of the new metropolitan region as a whole." [35]

The president restated these ideas in his 1962 message to Congress requesting establishment of a new Department of Urban Affairs. "There must be expansion," he said, "but orderly and planned expansion, not explosion and sprawl."[36] Kennedy stressed unregulated growth as the main danger in metropolitan development. But his calls for large-scale planning implied an unstated corollary: exclusion too must be "orderly and planned," that is, subject to review from above. For if each community could, in the words of a later, more explicit report, "maximize its tax base and minimize its social problems . . . caring less what happens to all the others," then Kennedy's "cooperative venture" would inevitably fail.[37] Expansion would continue to spill out over the countryside, beyond the reach of metropolitan controllers.

The stakes of metropolitan planning reform were, of course, thoroughly political. At bottom, they involved the power to veto decisions on local siting and community protection by higher levels of public authority. In short, Kennedy's officials wanted capital geographically steered from *above,* not below. Brakes and accelerators were to be applied by experts in the public sector, but not at the grass roots. As CED explained, with purely municipal control of land use, "positions requiring knowledge of modern technology are frequently occupied by unqualified personnel."[38]

Land Use Reform and the Great Society

After Kennedy's death, President Lyndon B. Johnson made the planning themes a centerpiece of the Great Society. Unregulated expansion was once again questioned, but now for "eroding the precious and time-honored values of community." Laissez-faire growth caused "the decay of the urban centers and the despoiling of the suburbs." The nation had a common interest in beautification. "Today," Johnson declared, "we must act to prevent an ugly America."[39]

Like Kennedy, Johnson saw no need to upbraid the middle class for its exclusionary posture. Rich and poor alike shared the goal of a more beautiful America, and voluntary cooperation in regional planning would lead to the achievement of this goal. But Washington, insisted the president, "cannot and should not require the communities which make up a metropolitan area to cooperate against their will."[40] Yet he failed to explain how sprawl could be prevented as long as localities reserved rights to veto regional plans.

Rebellions in the ghettos in the mid-1960s forced the White House to take a second look at problems of "metropolitan cooperation." Even superficial readers of public opinion could see the flames of Detroit, Newark, and Watts as something less than beacons of metropolitan brotherhood.[41] A host of presidential commissions were commanded to study the urban question. One after another, beginning in 1968, they turned in their findings. Invariably, suburbia was labeled the villain, and with it, the system of local land use control.

The most famous of the urban studies, the Kerner Commission Report of the National Advisory Commission on Civil Disorders, blamed suburban practices for "restricting the area open to a growing population," thus giving incentives to slumlords "to break up ghetto apartments for denser occupancy, hastening housing deterioration" and embittering blacks. The "two societies, one black, one white, separate and unequal" could not exist, after all, if government refused to sanction racial and class segregation. It concluded that "areas outside of ghetto neighborhoods should be opened up to occupancy by racial minorities." [42]

Similarly, the President's Committee on Urban Housing, chaired by Edgar F. Kaiser of Kaiser Aluminum Corporation, a company eager to experiment in mass-produced housing, reported that it was "convinced . . . that widespread abuses of zoning techniques and their inherent defects as a land-use control make it necessary for local prerogatives to yield to the greater good." [43]

Capping the anti-suburban critiques was the Report of the National Commission on Urban Problems, a group asked by President Johnson in 1965 to generate "better and more realistic standards for suburban development." Widely known as the Douglas Commission Report, in honor of its chairman, Senator Paul Douglas of Illinois, its study, *Building the American City*, was the most comprehensive attack yet on local land use practices. Like Richard Babcock's earlier study, the Douglas Commission in its report called on the states "to assure that local governments exercising regulatory authority are responsive to the needs of broad segments of the population and are competent to exercise land-use controls in a fair and effective manner." Furthermore, it urged the "establishment of state or regional machinery to reconcile conflicts among local governments and special purpose agencies, and to plan and act on matters demanding a broader than local perspective." Specifically, residential space for all income classes should be provided by all governments "exercising the zoning power." The "regulatory conspiracy against low-income housing must be broken," for "the power of government should not be used for the purpose of creating social or economic segregation." [44]

It is important, of course, not to overstate the influence of the Johnson-era studies. Their call for more centralized control of location decisions may have been clear, but they had no authority to command action. As Lipsky and Olson note, "riot commissions and public officials" tended to answer urban rebellion by directing their "reform recommendations at branches of government *other* than those over which they presided." [45] Nonetheless, as Domhoff points out, a latent role of such commissions is "to legitimate and make 'official' the ideas that have been developed in the private-sector network," in effect, to translate corporate suggestions into public proposals. [46] In this sense, the urban commission reports deserve substantial credit for bringing land use reform to the national attention.

Large-Scale Profits and
Land Use Reform

As a group, the Johnson-era reports identified the prevailing style of "urbanization" as "of course, inevitable," a "natural comcomitant of an increasing technological age." Centralized land use policy could "mitigate certain adverse affects" of this process, such as race and class segregation, by accelerating the kind of large-scale development and planning that worked so efficiently and profitably in the corporate sector and that played such a big part in urban renewal.[47] Indeed, suburban integration was really just the logical extension of the philosophy of centralized-development planning that was unfurled in the 1950s. Besides, it was arguably easier and more commercially rational to relocate and rehouse the poor than to eradicate poverty directly. Moreover, free entrepreneurs were ready to do the job if only the suburbs would permit them to.

"By the mid-1960's," writes William Lilly, "the homebuilders had moved from neutrality to active collaboration with the big city mayors and with the Johnson administration in pushing for enactment of Great Society programs."[48] But more than the National Association of Home Builders was behind the push to build low-income housing. Giant industrial companies, with big pools of surplus cash accumulated after years of postwar expansion, were gearing up for entry into land and construction operations. As one government study reported, some of the new corporate movements into real estate were dictated by "a desire for product sales stimulation." Heavy-appliance makers, such as General Electric and Westinghouse, envisioned new marketing strategies in planned communities built around their products. Others, such as the cement and aluminum manufacturers, were "characterized by over-capacity and a limited number of major processors." They had reached the point where continued reinvestment in their present lines no longer made business sense. And antitrust policy blocked outright monopoly. By adding new markets, avoiding further overcapacity, and preempting Justice Department inquiries, "vertical integration" strongly appealed to these companies. Thus Kaiser Aluminum formed a land-development subsidiary called Westwood Properties, and major cement manufacturers undertook similar ventures in Colorado and California. Finally, other corporations, notably in the oil industry, were simply awash with "excess funds to invest because of favorable profit positions and special tax treatment arising from depletion allowances." Land development became a commercial sideshow for the petroleum giants: Humble Oil, of the Exxon family, became primary developer of Clear Lake City, Texas, near Houston; and Gulf Oil was a major backer of the planned town of Reston, Virginia (after gaining an agreement giving it first option on service station sites in the town). Dozens of smaller enterprises also spun real estate subdivisions off their oil profits.[49]

The new blue-chip interest in housing signaled major changes in the corporate structure of the development business. They also portended new threats to community control of land. Historically, the construction business lagged well behind the march of creative destruction. An industry firmly ensconced in what James O'Connor calls the competitive sector, home building was, from a big corporate perspective, overly competitive, inefficient, and narrow in outlook.[50] Its orientation to local and regional markets and heavy reliance on labor-intensive production left it nearly as archaic as the "feudal" suburban markets it served. These enduring facts disqualified the industry from ascendancy into the higher corporate ranks.

In the postwar era, however, technological prospects brightened. As builder William Levitt explained: "We tried to copy the automobile industry. A fellow would come to one house and go bang, bang, bang, and then go to the next one."[51] Similarly, the National Association of Home Builders informed the Douglas Commission that over 150 improvements in construction technology had been achieved since the end of World War II, and even more could be expected. Prefinished siding, component wall panels, ready-mix concrete, increased use of power tools, and many other innovations raised hopes of increased efficiency and profits based on new economies of scale.[52]

This was language that corporations understood, and the giants were impressed. Economist Leo Grebler found at least forty-seven instances where "generally large or rapidly growing construction firms" were taken over by national businesses interested in organizing "multi-area" construction work.[53] And these examples did not include the internally generated land operations of companies such as General Electric, Kaiser, and Exxon. As one IT&T executive put it, "You can no longer accuse this of being a Mama and Papa [sic] industry. You will have the best of American industry attacking the problems, and the dynamics of the business itself will change."[54] The Douglas Commission cheered them on: "It is important that the government and public-spirited private organizations take action to encourage and promote research and experimentation" in "new materials and new production techniques," including the search for "advanced systems approaches" to home building.[55]

But economies of scale depended on access to large chunks of space. Corporations found that it was easy enough to purchase large parcels of land but not the rights to use the land as they saw fit. This problem was quickly understood as being something more than a trivial issue. One business study warned that the "bewildering variation in local regulations may very well mean that potentially profitable innovations are . . . illegal in many jurisdictions."[56] Another advised that "urban space-making technology will be advanced most when we can creatively organize new ways of doing things on a scale commensurate with the size of our spaces and our problems." Land use control by "an overall administrative body [is] an essential basis for technological innovation."[57]

Nonetheless, there is very little evidence that the large construction outfits did much as an industry to make a "federal case" out of zoning. Their political muscle was not heavily applied nationally to press the reform cause. Nor is this particularly surprising. The corporate giants, after all, had a number of other political and economic options. In many instances, such as in San Antonio's Ranchtown, the sponsors of big projects tried, more or less successfully, to cooperate with or cajole local power brokers to make their way. In still others, they made sure to site their investments in places where the welcome mat was already laid out. As multistate enterprises, the national builders could easily afford to scan the horizon for the best, and least troublesome, opportunities. As Richard Babcock put it, "The capital aggregates . . . entering the housing market have resources to counter the municipal gambit." [58]

The major exception to the corporate builders' relative quiet was the voice of the Urban Land Institute (ULI), which was, according to Walker and Heiman, "the research and policy-generating arm of the big developers." The ULI's many reports and studies showing the economic rationality of land use centralization became an important source for the argument that land use reform made business sense. [59] In this respect, however, the centralization of the housing industry was less important to the cause of land use reform as a matter of direct political pressure than as an economic development whose fulfillment reformers could invoke as a reason for centralization.

The Small-Builder Perspective

Traditional home builders—who numbered over 100,000 in the mid-1970s—took a very different political stance on local exclusion. Operating on a much smaller scale, bound by the opportunities of the hometown market, they found that land use restrictions were a much more immediate and dangerous threat to them. And they needed no lessons from reformers on its economic impact. In two of the nation's most lucrative markets, Florida and California, developers complained that land use controls contributed to as much as a one-third drop in new housing starts during the early 1970s. Things were so bad that some companies even began to profit from exclusion by packaging sites for other builders. As *Business Week* explained, "The situation seems made to order for a company that can find land, steer it through the official thickets and deliver it in a ready to use state." The small builders countered with direct political action. As in the San Antonio case, they took on the local city councils and went into the courts: they tried to control the municipal political and legal institutions that still had jurisdiction over land use policy and property rights. By 1973, for example, the National Association of Home Builders had accumulated a $200,000 legal fund to aid members in antiexclusion court battles, while the National Association of Realtors helped out with pleas in national magazines to "save the endangered American bungalow" from an "anti-housing philosophy . . . that says build it somewhere else." [60]

For the small home builders, in other words, centralization of land control was, at the very least, beside the point. As Walker and Heiman explain, "They have little need for zoning and administrative assistance for large-scale development and . . . they have experience and considerable success in influencing local politics." [61] Thus, in the ranks of competitive construction, enthusiasm for land use reform was conspicuous by its absence. But Walker and Heiman understate the potential of small builders and other petty land capitalists to move from passive indifference on land use reform toward outright opposition. After all, what made the local land business tick for decades was local control of community zoning boards by builders and the real estate industry. In construction, the forces of expansion were as solidly connected to local controls as the forces of exclusion. Intimate knowledge of and access to local land regulation was a key force of production in small home building, especially for suburban property capitalists such as San Antonio's northside developers. As Marion Clawson once summarized the local scene: "Not only is fragmentation the order of the day, but there are powerful forces anxious to keep it that way so that there will be no unit of government strong enough to take coordinated action on suburban development." [62] Local home builders, in short, were happy to have the controls remain just where they were; they only wanted the "keep out" signs removed. When they took to the courts for aid, however, the judicial system flashed red lights.

Judicial Brakes

For decades, the U.S. Supreme Court had remained silent on the zoning issue, reluctant to cut through the "litter" of local policy and vested interests. *Euclid* v. *Ambler* was permitted to cast a long shadow in the field of land use control. In the early 1970s, however, the justices found their voices. Challenged by the civil rights implications of an ever-lengthening agenda of suburban land use fights, the Court tried its hand at drawing lines. Its first vehicle was a California battle that clearly marked off democratic aspirations to community self-protection from civil and economic rights to equal-opportunity expansion. [63] The citizenry of California, in 1950, had adopted a constitutional amendment providing that low-income public-housing projects could not be built in any community without the approval of local majorities. After several projects were rejected in San Jose and in San Mateo County, poor blacks brought suit claiming, as one of several inequities, a denial of equal protection of the laws. As was noted in the earlier San Antonio study, the Supreme Court in 1971 upheld the referendum power because it was duly situated in the California constitution. [64] Here, though, it is worth adding that *James* v. *Valtierra* did more than embrace local democracy; it also reaffirmed the view that economic discrimination is not forbidden by the U.S. Constitution. Justice Hugo Black proclaimed that the California statute was "a law seemingly neutral on its face," because it required "approval for any low-rent public housing project, not only for projects which will be occupied by a racial minority." That the poor were hurt as a result did not in itself warrant a legal remedy, since "of course a lawmaking procedure that 'disadvantages' a particular group does not always deny equal protection." Justice Thurgood Marshall rejected Black's definition of economic class as "a totally benign, technical classification," but he could persuade only two of his colleagues, Brennan and Blackman.[65] Exclusionary referenda stood, as long as they were sanctified by state constitutional law and were aimed at the poor, not at racial minorities. The *Village of Belle Terre* decision, noted above, only tightened the suburban locks in 1974.

Developers were perplexed. In some places whole sections and neighborhoods could be razed to let in a skyscraper, whereas in others, small communities could keep out the slightest interference with their quiet. Suburbanites could wrap themselves in the logic of *Berman,* but urbanites were left naked against it. Secondhand land in the cities was "up for grabs"; virgin suburban land was "behind closed doors." Land use policy seemed to be a function of the accidents of municipal organization, not economic or even ecological rationality. The suburb remained, in the view of the modern Supreme Court, what it appeared to be in 1926: "a separate municipality, with powers of its own and authority to govern itself as it sees fit." Public and private governments at higher levels had little choice but to accommodate themselves to that fact, unless, of course, they could persuade Congress to implement a new administrative system for making land use decisions.

Federal Impatience

Corporations were not the only ones experiencing weariness with the obstructions of local land use controls; government development agencies had their share as well. In the 1960s public construction often met the same obstacles as private capital. Excluders made no distinctions between state- and corporate-sponsored expansion. Industrial projects were questioned regardless of source. Major public enterprises such as airports, power facilities, and highways seemed everywhere to run into walls. The Tocks Island Dam in New Jersey, the Miami–Dade County Jetport in Florida, San Antonio's North Expressway, and the Bridge Canyon Dam in Colorado were among the dozens of projects that were halted as federal agencies tried to wire the industrial system with strategic transportation and energy connectors. The "Build We Must" theme, made famous by New York City's Consolidated Edison Company, had lost its charms. A useful illustration is the case of Miami's Dade

County Jetport, which went hand in hand with development around the Florida Everglades.

Backed by a grant from the U.S. Department of Transportation, the Dade County Port Authority began in 1968 to construct a "super jetport" within six miles of the Everglades National Park, which had been established by Congress thirty-four years earlier. During the years between these two seemingly unrelated events, the Corps of Engineers had developed nearby a flood control project (1948). According to the Senate Interior Committee chairman, Henry Jackson, the water project "threatened the park's very life and existence." So did the jetport, not least because, in Jackson's words, "it would encourage . . . residential, commercial, and industrial developments . . . in direct conflict and totally incompatible with maintenance of the park as a great national recreation and scientific asset."[66] National, state, county, and local agencies, each connected with its own corps of private allies, pressed to impose their own particular stamp on the Everglades region. Collaboration was nonexistent; the agencies went their own way. The result, naturally, was collision.

The National Park Service, the Department of Transportation, the Corps of Engineers, local officials, private groups, and the state of Florida were trapped in one another's nets. But as in San Antonio, no forum proved adequate to the range of interests involved. The Senate Interior Committee, congressional overseer of the Park Service, found itself swamped by a host of similar conflicts around the nation. Extensive hearings were invariably held. Their product was a new sense by the committee that something was seriously wrong in the nation's system of making decisions on land use. Jurisdictional walls bore little correspondence to regional realities. Government agencies were blocked by nothing less than their own tunnel vision. Obvious conflicts were, as Jackson explained, "totally unanticipated and unintended." Rather, "the increased size, scale, and impact of private actions" and the many "needless and costly" intergovernmental conflicts "created a situation in which many, if not most, land-use management decisions [were] not being rationally made." Instead of orderly planning, development decisions were decided on the basis of "expediency, tradition, archaic legal principles, short-term economic considerations, and other factors . . . unrelated to what the real concerns of National, State and local land-use management should be." A substantial need existed, said the senator, for "a specific plan of Federal and State action for meeting the challenge of the land, the competing demands which are made upon it, and the needs and future aspirations of present and future generations." Conflicts between expansion and exclusion interests now warranted a "national land use policy" to reconcile them.[67]

Senator Jackson's Theory
of Planning

The Senate Interior Committee was an unlikely setting for metropolitan land use debates. It was an organ far removed from the insular world of the suburb or the cosmopolitan world of urban real estate. Its historic field was the fenceless America, the public domain. By the same token, though, Interior was hardly a novice at managing land use conflict; by some standards it was a past master. It is no accident that until recently there have been relatively few texts examining the politics of the public lands. One would think that American politics stopped not only "at the water's edge" but also at checkpoints to the public domain. An occasional scandal aside, the Interior committees of Congress were astute managers of public-domain issues. Until the advent of Interior Secretary James Watt the better known symbols of the national wealth consisted of Smokey the Bear and the "Friendly Forest Ranger"; the Conservation Foundation had appropriately entitled a recent study *The Lands Nobody Wanted.*[68]

While its troubles with the numerous interagency battles over land use increasingly focused the committee's attention on developments in the metropolis, the staff brought its traditional perspectives on public-land management to bear. From Interior's viewpoint, said staffer William Van Ness, the debate on land use "manifested itself in specific controversies over particular pieces of land."[69] Or, as Senator Jackson explained, "these conflicts have simply been the result of poor planning procedures" and a "lack of coordination."[70] High-level management and multiple-use doctrine served well in dealing with the public lands. There seemed little reason to believe they would not be equally effective in the private realm.

What the experts tended to overlook, however, was a rather fundamental difference between multiple-use theory and zoning policy. The former encouraged expansionists to share development rights to the public lands. It divided land among capitalists and presupposed a consensus about the value of industrial action. But zoning was implemented to keep excluders and expanders apart, to sequester industry and labor from middle-class residential preserves. It presupposed the separation of land use combatants. Multiple-use theory employed science to promote economic cooperation; zoning invoked science to maintain social segregation.[71]

Indifferent to the political distinctions, Interior's staff hoped to apply techniques with proven effectiveness to what seemed to be familiar problems. Thus traditional conservation practices would be combined with contemporary regional-planning theory to generate a national land use policy imbued with the logic of science. A first step was taken in 1969 when Congress enacted the National Environmental Policy Act (NEPA), a measure drafted principally by the Interior staff. NEPA was based on the classic conservation principle that land use decisions should rest on empirical analysis of natural-resource features. Federal development agencies were now instructed to "identify and develop methods and procedures . . . which will insure that presently unquantified environmental amenities and values may be given appropriate consideration before undertaking major projects." [72] But NEPA's environmental impact statements neither prohibited environmental abuses nor clearly defined substantive guidelines for agencies to follow in applying their procedures. As one senator noted, NEPA promised "an exposé . . . but we still go ahead with some unhealthy projects." [73] A similar strategy guided the committee's approach to national land use policy. As Noreen Lyday points out, the committee's staff director, Dan Dreyfus, thought that "the development of a data base was the key to resolving land-use conflicts" and the key to the data problem was development of a land classification system. [74] For Dreyfus, William Van Ness, and Senator Henry Jackson, reform of land use policy could best be accomplished by paying states to accumulate data and sharpen their planning tools. Thus Jackson's National Land Use Policy bill, introduced on January 29, 1970, authorized grants-in-aid of $100 million to the states to be used for the establishment of land-use planning agencies. These agencies would be required to prepare comprehensive inventories of natural resources and prevailing economic trends. They would form the "data base" for comprehensive growth plans defining the states' industrial, commercial, residential, and recreational land use needs for the next fifty years. [75]

National guidelines were included to guarantee space for corporate and public investments in "new towns," transportation facilities, and "heavy commercial and industrial development," and those areas of the state were identified "where ecological, environmental, geological and physical conditions dictate that certain types of land-use activities are incompatible and undesirable." After a three-year start-up period, the land agency would have to demonstrate "authority to implement the Statewide Environmental, Recreational and Industrial Land Use Plan." Federal oversight would be provided by a Land and Water Resources Planning Council made up of a corps of executive-branch officials. [76] Noncompliant states could expect to suffer the loss of federal assistance at an annual rate of 20 percent for programs "to be designated by the President." The end result, argued Jackson, would be a "more efficient and comprehensive system of national and statewide land use planning." Economic, social, and environmental values would be balanced scientifically against the carrying capacity of the land. All this, said one Interior staffer, was "policy neutral." Washington intended "no value judgments about the outcome." [77]

The Interior Committee's emphasis on objective land use planning tended to cut across the grain of the common law's traditional preoccupation with conflict regulation. But Jackson's bill was far from innocent of power implications: S. 3354 did not fail to remind states of their authority to "acquire interests in real property if deemed necessary under the State-wide Land Use Plan" and "to place restrictions on . . . land use . . . in areas designated for a special use under the Plan." That is, for the committee, state planning goals were to be enforceable through exercise of the eminent domain and police powers. And these would be governed by the direction of the plan itself, not the ad hoc responses to individual conflicts typical of local zoning and court decisions. As Jackson explained during early hearings on S. 3354, the point was to connect "Statewide zoning" with "machinery for comprehensive land use planning which would incorporate environmental as well as economic considerations." This "would not thwart material progress, but . . . guide it." [78] But since local landowners and local government presently controlled the boundaries of expansion and exclusion, Jackson's approach involved much more than technical adjustments of governmental "machinery." It implied important shifts in the power to foster and resist economic change in the United States.

Early Reactions

The initial Senate hearings on the National Land Use Policy bill were neither extensive nor combative. Jackson wanted to corral support for the principle of a national presence in private-sector conflicts; details could be worked out later. Witnesses were carefully selected to represent the states, the land-related industries, and the lawyers and planners who regularly defended private expansion and exclusion interests. Many were anxious for even stronger measures. Governors John Love of Colorado and Winthrop Sargent of Massachusetts, for example, called for strong state powers of enforcement. "I think you can't avoid the stick . . . the stick has to be available," said Sargent. [79] Allison Dunham and Fred Bosselman of the American Law Institute's Model Land Development Code Project also called for substantial state regulatory powers. "The important thing," said Dunham, "is that the state have a way of saying to the local community you must, or you cannot, as the case may be." [80] This call was echoed by utility-company executives who were increasingly frustrated by opposition to power-plant sitings. [81] The committee's lone environmental witness agreed that successful land policy must rely on more than moral suasion, but Peter Borrelli of the Sierra Club insisted that enforcement must be linked to "the priority status of ecological and environmental considerations." [82]

Not all voices sang Jackson's tune. Timber producers, the National Association of Manufacturers, and the National Association of Home Builders expressed fears that state planning might itself turn dangerously exclusionary. A spokesman for the National Forest Products Association explained: "Our culture is like an inverted pyramid with land at its apex. . . . Removal of the

basic ingredient, access to material resources has a domino effect." Yet "the
pressures for withdrawals of lands . . . are relentless";[83] they must be checked,
he warned.

Planners were concerned, too. Those employed by large national or regional development firms argued that fifty state plans would merely com-
pound the disarray of local controls. Initial steps should be taken toward a
national land use plan that would culminate in the power "to direct the location of economic and urbanizing activities." But county planners opposed the
elevation of authority to jurisdictions "much too extensive and too greatly
separated" from the diverse needs of local government.[84]

The Nixon administration, meanwhile, was understandably cautious about
the issue. Russell Train, chairman of the newly formed Council on Environmental Quality, supported Jackson's land-policy explorations but reserved
judgment about whether S. 3354 offered "exactly the right stick or carrot."
The White House, as the senator noted, wanted to "preserve its options."[85]

Toward a National Land Use Policy:
A Summary

The 1950s and 1960s saw increasing business disaffection with the scattered powers of urban and metropolitan land use control. Suburban land was
too often kept off-limits to corporate and state plans. There were, in Richard F.
Babcock's words, "powerful and conservative commercial forces" ready to
"welcome an erosion of local land use control."[86]

Top-rank lawyers and policy planners from presidential study commissions
looked to the states to provide administrative land clearance for their clients.
Centralization hardly intimidated this group. Inheritors of the liberal progressive outlook, they saw power as a tool to be used by the able and efficient for
the good of the whole. Centralization provided useful strategic positions for
guiding orderly action and needed social change. A wise society defers to its
best citizens, after all, and responsibly accords them the resources to achieve
big things. Similarly, large corporations, whether new entrants to the housing
trade or experienced in the ways of energy and raw materials, effectively de-
ferred to the professionals in the American Law Institute to find ways around
the exclusionary law of land use. Reform of land use policy was thus deemed
a technical, legal matter. Lawyers were paid well to scribble so that business
could find the room to grow.

But other interests remained wild cards in land use reform. The emerging
movement of environmentalists certainly saw value in regional approaches to
land management, but they were also suspicious of the expansionist influence
in land use reform. By contrast, small builders and realtors were troubled by
increasing government regulation in development policy: top land-use attor-

neys seemed to make sense when they voiced criticism of local regulations, but all the talk about centralized control seemed more dubious and threatening. Many builders were on convivial terms with local politicians; in San Antonio, for example, they needed little help from the state capital to control local government. And there would be little need for big administrative changes if the courts would live up to their obligations and repay landowners whose rights were "taken" without "just compensation." Still, if builders could be persuaded that expansionist rights might be reestablished without bringing down on their heads the wrath of state environmental commissioners, then local construction interests might well come along in support.

Everything hinged on what E. E. Schattschneider would call "the mobilization of bias" at higher levels of the political system. Noreen Lyday concisely describes the conundrum: "Interest groups were decidedly not concerned that conflicts simply be resolved. They wanted to know *how* and in whose favor." [87] Given the unbreakable ties of exclusion and expansion, however, any bill that furnished more than hazy answers was bound to deprive reformers of half their potential support.

The Frustration of Reform 6

*The architects of power in the United States must
create a force that can be felt but not seen. Power
remains strong when it remains in the dark; exposed
to the sunlight it begins to evaporate.*

Samuel P. Huntington

By early 1971 the reform of land use policy was an idea that had popped up
in a series of presidential reports and speeches. The idea was well publicized
in the legal fraternity, too, and among blue-chip corporate think-tanks. It had
even won the status of a congressional proposal, carrying the sponsorship of
one of the Senate's most distinguished committee heads and a possible Democratic candidate for the presidency in 1972. Yet, for all the support they had
garnered, the land use reformers had not yet picked up the one last ingredient
necessary to get the measure through: the direct, forceful, and personal backing
of the president himself. Without the political steam of strong White House
support, Congress was unlikely to move against rights so precious to the folks
back home.

At the same time, Congress was not feeling any anti-reform pressure, either. Potential opponents—local land capitalists, homeowners, and government officials—remained passive on the national scene, though they struggled
fiercely over hometown issues, such as the fate of the San Antonio aquifer.
Even potential allies of reform in the environmental movement—land use
reform "sounded" like a conservation idea, after all—had failed to rally
strongly behind the idea. Until now the corporate lawyers and planners enjoyed a virtual monopoly of the terms of the debate. For an issue so deeply
affected by the dialectical forces of exclusion and expansion, the politics of
national land use reform were oddly nonantagonistic. What would happen
when the issue was posed clearly for the interests in local land use controls?

This was an especially sensitive question for the Nixon administration.
Strongly committed to a conservative agenda on domestic policy, with loyal

constituencies among suburbanites as well as builders, the president proclaimed the goal of a "new federalism" that was supposed to return power to
the states and localities. This stance conflicted with the centralizing drift of
land use reform and the administration's desires to rationalize development
and cut federal costs. As James O'Connor argues, such conundrums are the
rule in the executive branch of capitalist government. High-level officials in
the policy agencies are compelled to address numerous conflicting political
issues and constituencies all at once. Hence there are powerful incentives for
"the President and his key aides . . . [to] remain independent" of specific interests as they try to make policy.[1] But the autonomy is always relative: individual officials come into office with enduring career and constituency perspectives intact; these are not easily shed. Moreover, many interest groups
from the various classes and strata are more than sufficiently well organized to
push their case at all necessary points in government, including the executive
agencies. And, to win their place on national agendas, the various unofficial
policy-planning elites press their advantages with familiar faces in every administration.

All these forces terribly complicate policy making in the executive and legislative branches; thus the larger translation of what O'Connor calls "class
corporate interests into action" is anything but automatic. In other words, the
definition of class needs must not be confused with their satisfaction; these are
very different matters. This chapter is a tale of caution about the limited
power of even the most prestigious policy-planning institutions to work their
will in the face of political-economic crisis and powerfully organized resistance emanating from the lower ranks of capitalism.

Land Use Reform and
the Nixon White House

The Nixon administration showed much greater sensitivity than the Senate
Interior Committee to the special qualities of private land use conflicts. This
sensitivity resulted less from the president's watchful interest in land use
matters than from the presence of land use reformers in the top ranks of his
administration. According to William Ruckelshaus, the first administrator of
the Environmental Protection Agency (EPA), Nixon hardly took resource
issues seriously. "Nixon thought the environment was a lot of nonsense. He
never tried to learn anything about it." But the president did read the polls,
and they showed that environmental worries rankled the public. According to
John Quarles, Ruckelshaus's deputy at EPA, Nixon directed aides to "prepare
a program that would put him on the right side of the issue."[2]

But more than partisan politics led the newly formed Council on Environmental Quality (CEQ) to the subject of the reform of land use policy. The

organization, bristling with bright young lawyers, was socially connected to key organs of the corporate "policy formation network," the topflight foundations, research institutions, and law firms that, in G. William Domhoff's words, "are best categorized as the policy planning and consensus seeking organizations of the power elite."[3] As its first chief, for example, Russell Train brought impressive credentials and elite ties to the CEQ. Before accepting a position as undersecretary of the interior in the Nixon administration, he had served in high posts for a number of conservation organizations, most recently as president of the Rockefeller-backed Conservation Foundation. Train assigned the land use issue to two young lawyers: Boyd Gibbons, who followed Train over from the Interior Department after developing a coastal zone planning proposal; and William K. Reilly, who had earlier served with the civil-rights–oriented National Urban Coalition and the distinguished Chicago law firm of Ross, Hardies, O'Keefe, Babcock and Parsons. This firm, it will be remembered, not only produced San Antonio's interim aquifer-protection plan but also contributed Richard Babcock and Fred Bosselman to the American Law Institute's model land law project, as well as to numerous other ventures in land use reform.[4]

Gibbons and Reilly all too neatly personified the paradoxical themes of corporate land use reform. For Gibbons, on the one hand, the task was to centralize the police powers as a way of eliminating the worst environmental effects of local growth-mania. "We thought the states, free of the property tax concerns, could take a broader perspective on the matter," he observed. Reilly, on the other hand, emphasized the problem of exclusionary zoning that preoccupied the American Law Institute in its search for a new model land-use law. Open housing was his keen interest. Thus Gibbons and Reilly labored to centralize the powers of exclusion on the assumption that modern business and rational public regulations could transcend the old contradictions between growth, nature, and property.[5]

Within the Nixon administration, support for this view was not limited to the idealistic quarters of the Council on Environmental Quality. Hardheaded realists also shared it, including one with direct access to the Oval Office. The president's domestic policy chief, John Ehrlichman, was himself a Seattle land lawyer and well versed in the tribulations of suburban exclusion. Noreen Lyday reports that "according to John Whitaker, . . . then deputy assistant to the President for Environmental and Natural Resources, when the bill first came up, the President said, 'John, you're a land use lawyer and you know what's needed. You handle the bill.' "[6]

With Ehrlichman's backing, CEQ transmitted its second annual report to Congress, accompanied by a strongly worded presidential statement on the need for reform of national land use policy:

Today, we are coming to realize that our land is finite while our population is growing. The uses to which our generation puts the land can either expand or severely limit the choices our children will have. The time has come when we must accept the idea that none of us has a right to abuse the land, and that on the contrary, society as a whole has a legitimate interest in proper land use. There is a national interest in effective land use planning all across the nation.[7]

Nixon's remarks gave land use reform a clear environmental accent. For suburbanites and conservationists, he seemed to come down on the right, that is, the exclusionary, side of the issue. Reilly and Ehrlichman, however, knew very well that the idea of land use planning could, in Lyday's words, also be "interpreted so as to allow states to override exclusionary local zoning," that it was a principle equally important for the siting of large-scale industrial installations and housing developments. But the expansionist aspect was played down.[8] Land use policy was publicly identified with the currently popular, though one-sided, environmental perspective.

Expansionist Impulses Behind Reform

Just as it sought ties with middle-class conservationists, the Nixon White House was also under considerable pressure from the National Association of Home Builders to get behind the construction industry. The president's economic policies, designed to suppress demand and lick the inflation ignited by the Vietnam War, hurt builders severely. Though Congress, in the 1968 Housing Act, called for 2.6 million new private-housing starts annually, the actual number produced barely reached 1.5 million in 1968, dipping even below that number in 1970, after a severe credit crunch.[9] Lyday's analysis of the legislation on land use policy tends to understate this aspect of the story, but it is in fact crucial to an understanding of the contradictions in reform.

According to Charles Colson, special counsel to the president, "When things were looking bad for housing" in January 1970, President Nixon invited the leadership of the National Association of Home Builders to the White House. The president assured the construction representatives that housing would "be given top priority." As an aide to George Romney, the housing secretary, explained, "We had no problems taking care of the homebuilders. Both HUD and the homebuilders are moving in the same direction." As it turned out, this direction was toward the suburbs.[10]

Their vehicle was named, appropriately enough, Operation Breakthrough. The allusion was to assistance from the Department of Housing and Urban Development (HUD) in stimulating what Michael Danielson describes as "the large-scale production of factory built housing by large corporations." One optimistic builder predicted, "We are going to produce three million housing units a year, each with headlights." With a helping hand from Washington, he

assumed that builders would have little difficulty mounting the frames in suburban backyards. But as the Johnson era made clear, the extension of "space
age technology" to home building was likely to be crippled by "bewildering . . . local regulations." In Danielson's words, "Intended or not, 'Operation Breakthrough' inevitably brought Romney face-to-face with suburban
exclusion." [11]

At first, HUD officials thought that offers of federal grants would induce
excluders to open their gates. However, Danielson writes, "substantial local
opposition materialized to some of the projects when it became known that
Breakthrough would involve subsidized housing and blacks." Indeed, after the
program's race and class implications became evident, HUD was left with just
one project site. Over two hundred urban competitors had vanished in a rush
to close their doors. The agency's planners returned to their policy drawing
boards to invent more potent methods for penetrating suburban walls. Their
next attempt was called the Open Communities Program. Under this more
punitive approach, federal grants for community development were to be
selectively withheld from cities that practiced discrimination against low-
income projects. [12]

After a few successes, HUD once more faced hard resistance, this time in
Secretary George Romney's own backyard, the Detroit suburb of Warren—a
big industrial community, hardly an example of the snobbish parlors lived in
by the middle and upper classes. But for many of its 180,000 inhabitants, it
represented a step up from the old neighborhoods, such as Poletown, and
a step away from Detroit's black ghetto. Sociologically speaking, Warren
seemed to be a logical place to test corporate and bureaucratic hypotheses
about large-scale construction of housing for the black poor. George Romney,
a recent chief of American Motors Corporation, returned to the neighborhood
of some of his former employees with reminders of their civic obligations.
What followed was a classic replay of industry's historic use of poor blacks as
battering rams against the resistance of white workers, except that in this case
the white workers were organized not as union members but as landowners. [13]

Warren's population quickly became incensed at the prospect of a former
corporate chieftain brandishing public authority, forcing them to live with
blacks, and presuming to tell them how to run their city. When HUD threatened to suspend funds for urban renewal unless the city's discriminatory housing regulations were lifted, local officials demanded a meeting with the secretary. They got no sympathy; Romney warned the city leaders that "you can try
to hermetically seal Warren off from the surrounding areas if you want to, but
you won't do it with Federal money." [14]

The conflict received national attention after banner headlines in the Detroit Press proclaimed Richard Nixon's intention to "Integrate All Suburbs." [15]
Romney was soon forced to back down. The community's bitter reactions, and
the president's anxiety over potential damage to his standing among middle-

class whites, were too much for the secretary. In the following months, numerous White House statements were proffered to explain the administration's firm opposition to "forced integration" of the suburbs and its equally strong commitment to local land use control.[16]

Legal Perspectives: The ALI Model

The trials of HUD confirmed the wisdom of Ehrlichman's silence on the open-housing implications of land use reform. But from the standpoint of the builders and lawyers, this experience also confirmed the need to do something about suburban exclusion and metropolitan fragmentation. It was imperative, said Allison Dunham of the University of Chicago Law School and the American Law Institute (ALI), that "state agencies be given the power to intervene in major land-use decisions of local governments," those with "an important impact on the State as a whole or a Region." Attorneys Fred Bosselman and David Callies also stressed the need to concentrate "state efforts on major land use issues" and to exercise controls only over the big decisions. Regulatory reform and centralization were the keynotes of the American Law Institute's work on a new model state statute for land use. And these themes dominated its advice to the policy planners of CEQ.[17]

Like Henry Jackson, the ALI experts thought that many of society's most serious land use conflicts were avoidable, resulting only from a mismatch between the scale of decision and the scope of modern development pressure. Much of the stress could be relieved if society would simply realign the power to control land so that it reflected the breadth of major land use impacts. Naturally, such changes would appear unsettling at first; but as the big siting decisions were routinely made in state capitals, citizen landowners would gradually come to forget that they ever had veto powers over jumbo projects. Like nineteenth-century farmers who finally gave up their struggles against the Mill Acts, the children of today's resisters would come to accept state-steered expansion and exclusion—what Richard Babcock would call "a programmatic way of public life"—as an ordinary part of the environment, as unremarkable as state regulation of telephone service or liquor sales.[18]

The important point for the lawyers was that bureaucratic control of land use did not require fifty-year plans, as Henry Jackson imagined. Regulations needed only to categorize the main areas and functions requiring state controls. Most local decisions would not even be affected. As Fred Bosselman explained, "One of the important issues [is] to separate the major decisions from the minor so that State officials are not bogged down with gas station applications when they should be considering power plant sites." Russell Train agreed; the task, he said, is to go "beyond planning to the central issues of controls," to "a fundamental reallocation of responsibilities between state and local governments where regional issues are involved." [19] In effect, the argument went, local governments should continue to supervise the twin processes of exclusion and expansion, except where community decisions contradicted the interests of wider jurisdictions—as defined by state-level managers, corporate developers, regional environmentalists, and other, more broadly organized interests.

To guide the state regulators, the ALI planners suggested the appropriate geographic and functional categories of land use requiring top-level oversight. These were "areas of critical concern" and "development of regional benefit." The former category included sites for large government projects, such as "new towns"; especially fragile regions, such as aquifers or wetlands; or places not yet subject to existing development ordinances, such as metropolitan borderlands. "Development of regional benefit" took in projects sponsored by nonlocal governments, those intended for area-wide religious or educational facilities, regional public utilities, and housing "for persons of low and moderate income." The ALI model was clearly intended to protect regional environmental resources; but the textual emphasis was just as clearly on reserving space for big public and private enterprises. [20]

The Nixon Administration Bill

Following the lead of the ALI, the executive branch drafted a version of national land use legislation that stressed regulation, not planning. Reform was seen as the elevation of authority and the creation of new procedures for decision-making. The states were to be given grants-in-aid to establish "land use programs" aimed at "decisions of more than local significance." The "programs," to consist of "unified authorities, policies, criteria, standards, methods, and processes," would be determined by the states but would remain subject to review by the secretary of the interior. Although federal policy guidance was kept to a minimum in deference to Nixon's "new federalism," the familiar geographic and functional categories were intended to focus the regulatory process. States had to ensure that special attention was paid to "areas of critical concern," "key facilities," and "development of regional benefit." For Lyday, the "critical areas" provision was the "core of the bill" and indelibly stamped it as environmental legislation. In her view, reform of land use policy was preeminently about the rescue of nature from overdevelopment. [21]

But there was much more to the bill. The expansionist aspect shone through in the "key facilities" and regional-development provisions. These sections of the bill controlled the states' obligations to clear the way for big public and private development projects, from airports and highways to low-income housing and waste facilities. [22] Thus, despite John Ehrlichman's suggestions to play down the measure's expansionist implications, Interior Secretary Rogers Morton argued that

> the Administration's bill is not simply exclusionary or protectionist—designed to tell developers where they *cannot* develop. It is also designed to assist development and land use projects of regional benefit to *overcome* exclusionary ordinances and to find places where they can develop.[23]

Thus every state program was to contain "a method for assuring that local regulations do not restrict or exclude development and land use of regional benefit." This provision was aimed explicitly at limiting the power of local government to exclude "unwanted regional growth," defined as "land use and private development for which there is a demonstratable need affecting the interests of constituents of more than one local government which outweighs the benefits of any applicable restrictive or exclusionary regulations."[24] However, because the administration offered no yardstick for measuring regional needs in the absence of regional-development plans or resource inventories, as Jackson's bill did, suburbs could argue that no basis existed in fact for identifying regionally necessary growth. An important exclusionary loophole seemed to be opened.

Futhermore, the administration did not require the states to take direct charge of land use policy. Although they were invited to establish statewide regulatory programs as one means of enforcement, the states could satisfy Washington merely by drafting criteria to be used by high-level administrators and judges in reviews of local decisions. The reviewers, however, would have to have "full powers to approve or disapprove" municipal actions.

Obviously, the meat of the ALI–White House approach to land use reform lay in the standards to be enforced by state officials—whether administrators or judges. But as the bill was nominally concerned only with procedures, not substantive policies, no land use criteria were actually spelled out. The bill, S. 992, authorized the secretary of the interior to review the state programs for their procedural adequacy, but without specifying how the states should "exercise their full authority over the planning and regulations of non-Federal lands" when, for example, "developments of regional benefit" clashed with "areas of critical environmental concern" or "important . . . cultural, historic, and aesthetic values." If the programs failed to meet the Secretary's approval, then state plans for future federal projects, such as interstate highways, would be delayed by an extra round of administrative reviews in Washington. Moreover, federal grant approvals could not be given until the secretary of the interior ascertained, to the satisfaction of the secretary of housing and urban development, that those aspects of a state's land use program dealing with large-scale development, key facilities, development and use of regional benefit, and new communities were "in conformity with national commitments to growth and development of more than local significance."[25] Thus, although the Nixon administration did not openly make the call for national land use planning or clearly articulate the states' land use obligations to the nation as a whole, its definition of areawide land use categories as the basis of state regulation placed it squarely on the side of state centralization as the main instrument of land use reform.

With the White House bill placed on the table in February 1971, the legislative debate over national land use policy finally began to take shape. Three issues dominated the deliberations: standards, sanctions, and takings.

Standards

The administration's land use reformers made their bid to rationalize the system by asking states to judge local decisions. Judicial review had also been the basic theme of legal reformers since Babcock's 1961 report to the American Society of Planners.[26] For Henry Jackson, judicial oversight was a reasonable strategy, except that it obligated the states to clarify the "procedural and substantive" criteria behind their decisions—otherwise, what would the judges evaluate? And standards could not be developed without a lot of hard work devoted to research, data gathering, and planning. But because the administration failed to require states to do their preregulation homework, Jackson saw the end result as a kind of regulatory nominalism. By merely labeling an area "critical," or an activity of "regional benefit," states could make whatever decisions they pleased. Land use categories could be enlarged or shrunk at will: "The distinct possibility exists," said Jackson, "that one category would be defined very broadly and another very narrowly." One state might call its whole territory "critical," whereas another could swallow all the development it was offered by insisting that each project was of "regional benefit." The administration's approach was thus decidedly suited to interest-group bargaining and manipulation, not what *Business Week* called "rational planning of land use on a broad scale." As Jackson put it:

> Pressure from environmentalists would evoke sudden state assumption of control over the proposed sites of power plants. Pressure from transportation interests could result in effective control over highway and air sites. The exercise of control to solve immediate issues and to meet immediate pressure invites narrow consideration of the important problems at hand.[27]

Jackson was not alone in wishing to know in advance the values and interests the executive branch expected the states to support; the oil industry wanted signals, too. Bedeviled by opposition to their proposed Alaska pipeline as well as other facilities, energy companies sought clear statements that expansion of fuel supplies would be a top priority of land use regulation. An Exxon official stated that "it would seem appropriate either to state federal goals . . . in the bill or to require the Secretary of the Interior to develop such goals and present them to Congress so they can be ratified as lawful national policy." [28]

Naturally, this sort of talk worried environmentalists. They couldn't shake recurrent fears that reform of land use policy was really a euphemism for an industrial-siting program. The Sierra Club advised that their anxieties could easily be put to rest by writing environmental protection standards into the law. It insisted, for example, that "new land use legislation must be weighted toward environmental concerns, lest accelerating growth and development continue as the dominant factors in land use policy considerations." Conservationists were anything but convinced that their values dominated the reform impulse; as one predicted, the proposal could well lead to "more ad hoc peddling, too much of the local zoning game, simply removed one level higher." Bernard Siegan, a well-known conservative maverick among land-use lawyers for his opposition to all public controls, urged environmentalists to look twice before supporting changes in the locus of authority. "The big owners and developers . . . will frequently defeat regulations," he said; "they will easily succeed against those who cannot fight back." [29]

By far the sharpest critic of standardless regulation was Senator Edmund S. Muskie of Maine. Chairman of the Public Works Subcommittee on Air and Water Pollution, Muskie was strongly protective of his jurisdictional prerogatives and of his reputation as Congress's "Mr. Environment." Muskie was irritated that Jackson had not allowed him sufficient input into a bill whose "implications" were "perhaps greater than any domestic legislation we have yet considered in this session." (The two were also rival Democratic candidates for the presidency.) But Muskie's analysis was more telling than his pique. "This bill," he charged, "creates an outline for national land use policy with no substance. . . . Legislation of this magnitude with far-reaching impact on many Federal programs . . . must provide some Federal policy guidance." Criteria are essential, he argued, to distinguish good planning from bad, to coordinate the many land-related public policies, to prevent the states from undermining national environmental goals, and to protect the states and localities from federal bureaucratic arbitrariness. Indeed, he argued, criteria would be applied whether they were written or not: "The question raised by the issue is whether we establish the guidelines for . . . bureaucracy in the legislation, or whether we leave it to an ad hoc process." [30]

The administration—reluctant to spell out the expansionist implications of any more Operation Breakthroughs—carefully chose the latter course. Secretary Morton explained that the matter of standards was best left to "negotiation with the State as opposed to putting standards . . . in the legislation. [I think] there should be a dialogue." State resource planners, experts in the regional topographies of power, also supported flexible approaches. The president of the Council of State Planning Officials advised that it was best to let professional land managers and interest groups negotiate the standards after the bill was passed. "Get the framework, the policy, the direction in the bill," it was argued, "and allow the development of the guidelines for the implementation." Reconciling expansion and exclusion rights required bargaining, not law.[31]

At first Jackson held his ground, refusing to trade planning for negotiation. But the legislative process shaped the substantive policy in its own image. Eager for White House support and impressed by the state planners' reluctance to plan, Jackson soon came around to the view that negotiation (i.e., bargaining) was the appropriate strategy of reform. In June 1972 the Senate Interior Committee reported a new bill patterned almost entirely on the executive's draft. This version included titles requiring state planners to gather data and make economic and environmental forecasts, but provisions requiring "State Environmental, Recreational, and Industrial Land Use Plans" were dropped.[32]

Jackson called on the Senate to help establish a new political system of land use at the state level. Showing little mark of his earlier planning commitments, though, Jackson told his colleagues that federal guidelines were not "workable." They would "create mischief" and "were not in accord with the basic philosophy of the land use bill." When Muskie introduced an amendment that offered specific environmental standards to guide policy, Jackson successfully urged their defeat, arguing that they would lead to "Federal zoning."[33]

Sanctions

The debate on standards illuminated the White House's refusal to signal its intentions in land use policy. The contradictory cat was left in the bag; but sharp-eyed conservatives and local officials still noticed a protruding federal tail. The Senate Interior Committee bill, for example, despite White House opposition, included sanctions to force states into compliance with Washington's procedural requirements. Federal aid for three major public investment programs—the Land and Water Conservation Fund (which financed state parkland acquisitions) and airport and highway construction grants—would be cut unless states established new land-use management agencies. According to the Interior Committee report, these penalties were "carefully chosen . . . because of their extraordinary impact on land-use patterns." These were also highly popular programs, which few state officials would be likely to trade just to protect local control. As Jackson put it, "There is a real question in my mind whether simply providing for grant-in-aid funds [to finance state regulation] is ample to induce the States to do this job, because it is a tough one. Let's face it."[34]

Squabbles naturally ensued. For example, only one of the grants, the conservation fund, fell directly under the Interior Committee's control. Chairman

Jennings Randolph (D-West Virginia) of the Senate Public Works Committee, which traditionally held the rights to disperse most federal construction aid, objected to Jackson's intervention. Jackson politely retreated, agreeing to introduce an amendment changing the sanction back to a freeze on all large-scale projects. John Ehrlichman, meanwhile, forced the CEQ to drop similar sanctions from its bill. This tempered criticisms from the Office of Management and Budget (OMB) that the whole land use enterprise conflicted with the president's desire to cut federal strings on the states. It also avoided a bruising fight with the highway lobby.[35]

But local officials and conservative Republicans, frequent allies in issues of national land use reform, were the most adamant fighters against forced compliance. Strong lobbying efforts by local government organizations (the U.S. Conference of Mayors, the National Association of Counties, and the National Service to Regional Councils), plus testimony by dozens of individual officials, reinforced beliefs in the sanctity of local landowner authority and municipal rights to exclude. Numerous amendments were added to the Senate bill to strengthen the community say in state regulation. But none was equal to the local resistance against sanctions.[36]

Jackson quickly became exasperated with the opposition. All he wanted, he said, was to ensure that states establish "methods" to control the big land use conflicts: "This is not a subjective thing where the Federal Government can intercede and substitute its subjective judgment for the State's judgment. As long as the plan covers the principal areas . . . then the Federal Government is required to accept it."[37] Reform of land use policy was merely a logical extension of business rationality to the governmental process. After all, said the *New York Times*, "no well-run business would undertake a major expansion or a big construction project without relating it to the corporation's long term plans."[38]

But Jackson and the *Times* tended to understate the significance of land use control for local property owners. Although environmentalists wanted more regulation of large construction projects, and many corporate managers were eager to rationalize expansion, few Americans outside what might be termed "the land use elite" were anxious for basic change in the rules or the level of decision making. On the contrary, in thousands of U.S. cities and towns, the politics of land use was a highly stabilized and ritualized form of activity, with well-settled patterns of access for local power groups. In some places these traditions favored excluders; in others, expansionists. But whatever the case in particular jurisdictions, local contenders had little cause to abandon familiar institutions or to trust new absentee controllers of community development, especially where future directions were uncertain. One of San Antonio's top builders might have been speaking for suburbanites when he observed that "it is imperative to keep regulations at the lowest possible level—so we can maximize our access to the controls." From the perspective of middle-class land interests, the sanctions proposed by Senator Jackson appeared not as an instrument of rationalization but as a threat to land use democracy. Wyoming Republican Clifford P. Hansen clearly articulated the anti-centralist argument during Senate debate:

> What this bill demands of the States is that they shall come up with a plan which satisfies not the people in the State government, not the State legislature, not the Governor, not the county commissioners, not the city, not the school board, but the Secretary of the Interior because he is all wise, all knowing, and knows best. It is up to the States to satisfy him.[39]

Jackson, unable to overcome local fears, finally relented and announced his support for Hansen's amendment, which deleted the sanction provision, noting only his hope "that at least this will expedite action on the bill." The amendment was adopted by voice vote. At this point in the legislative process, the proposed national land use policy—an idea born in the think-tanks of America's best lawyers—lacked both clear standards and the authority to enforce them. It was now truly a framework for bargaining.

Takings

When the CEQ lawyers originally took their proposal to the Office of Management and Budget for legislative clearance, they met a chilly reception. William Reilly notes that to the OMB staff, the philosophy of the bill seemed "fundamentally antithetical to private property and the philosophy of John Locke." Only John Ehrlichman's influence managed to extract it from an early demise at the hands of OMB.[40]

Others had similar reservations, especially western Republicans. These reservations came into focus with an amendment offered by Len Jordan of Idaho. Along with Hansen, Jordan saw in the "critical areas" provisions the potential for massive suppression of land use rights without requirements for "just compensation." His proposal permitted individuals to sue for compensation if "the State has prohibited or restricted the full use and enjoyment of their property."[41]

To the degree that individuals already possessed rights to sue against unjust takings, the amendment was innocuous and changed nothing. The reference to compensation rights, however, was much more portentous. Under existing precedents, notably *Euclid* v. *Ambler* and *Pennsylvania Coal* v. *Mahon,* illegal regulations were subject to invalidation by the courts, but owners could not sue for compensatory damages.[42] But Jordan's amendment could easily be read to place localities and states in financial jeopardy if they experimented with controls later determined to be unconstitutional. This position, close to that taken by Justice Brennan in the *San Diego Gas & Electric* case, represents a notable departure from the traditional case law. Jordan argued—less than precisely—that he only wanted to prevent regulators from issuing controls that had the effect of "limiting and prohibiting the use of land." [43]

Regulators issued dire warnings: passage of Jordan's amendment, they said, would explode the whole system of land use controls. "If this route becomes available," charged Russell Train, "we could just about kiss any effective regulatory systems goodbye [for it] would involve compensating almost every owner of land all over the country." Similarly, in 1973, Colorado state legislator Richard Lamm warned that such a provision "would tie the States' hands and set land use planning back to before the first U.S. Supreme Court case in this area." Fred Bosselman was quickly recruited by CEQ to write a definitive reply, *The Taking Issue,* published in 1973. [44]

Most senators read the provision to reflect only an endorsement of the status quo and not the foundation for an enlargement of existing rights. Henry Jackson argued that the bill as a whole was consistent with the precedents: it "does not change anything," hence neither would the amendment. [45] In a colloquy between Jackson and Senator Hansen, however, the conservatives' desire to expand the rights of individual property owners was clear. Jackson tried to rephrase Hansen's position as a question about whether the federal government could interfere in local zoning decisions. Hansen replied:

Mr. Hansen: No, just give them the right.

Mr. Jackson: The right?

Mr. Hansen: The landowner the right.

Mr. Jackson: The landowner has all the rights he had before.

Mr. Hansen: If the Senator can cite one example where so far a landowner has been adversely affected and has been entitled to a judgment on account of a zoning ordinance, I would be interested . . .

Mr. Jackson: Look, we are not involved in that.

Mr. Hansen: As a landowner, I am involved in it. [46]

Despite extensive debate on the real meaning of the amendment, no consensus was reached. Liberals interpreted it as a statement of existing principles, conservatives as a new bulwark for property rights against what Hansen termed "the Federal coercion . . . this bill supposes." The amendment passed by a vote of 58 to 14, the nays coming from a handful of liberal Democrats. Yet little was actually resolved. Hansen summed it up best when he said, "Well, I suspect we must leave it to the courts to determine what was intended by Congress." [47]

Senate Passages and
Conservative Doubts

As befits the responsibility assigned to it by the Founding Fathers, the Senate modified S. 632 to protect the status quo. This was nicely symbolized by passage of an administration-backed amendment that sliced authorizations for the program from $800 million over eight years, as originally proposed by Senator Jackson, to $170 million for five years. Finally, on September 19, 1972, the bill was easily passed by the Senate 60 to 18, fourteen conservatives joining four liberals in opposition.[48]

The smashing reelection of Richard Nixon in 1972 augured well for another Senate triumph in the new, 93d Congress. "I will urge passage again, this year," said the president, "of legislation designed to encourage states to establish effective means of controlling land use." The din of Watergate was still distant thunder. Jackson accepted the president's invitation and led the Senate through another round of hearings, debates, and compromises, once more delivering a majority for the lawyers of the CEQ and the ALI.

No basic changes were made during land use reform's second passage. One amendment was added by Senator Gaylord Nelson (D-Wisconsin), toughening controls on interstate sellers of leisure homes, and James Buckley (R-New York) tacked on another that gave communities the right to set environmental standards more rigorous than those of the states. But sanctions were once again rejected, and save for Nelson's leisure-home amendment, substantive standards were again kept out of the package. Henry Jackson applauded the Senate's work, calling the bill a "careful balance" between the need for a "more efficient system of land use planning and decision making" and the obligation to "protect the existing rights and responsibilities of State and local government," that is, the existing rights of expansion and exclusion.[49]

But conservative Republicans continued to assail land use reform for "preempting local responsibilities" in order "drastically" to "alter the traditional system." [50] Strikingly, most reformers refused to deny this; indeed, they boasted of it. Reformers were rarely modest about the changes they sought. Thus Russell Train called national land use policy "a basic institutional reform in the political institutions of this country." The undersecretary of the interior, John Whitaker, predicted that it would push states toward "zoning" of their regions "into different types of growth rates." And Gladwin Hill of the *New York Times* announced in a front-page story that it symbolized "a fundamental change in the American way of life." Then, just in case conservatives and local-control advocates failed to get the message, the Rockefeller Task Force on Land Use published its findings in the summer of 1973.[51]

The Task Force report, edited by William K. Reilly, was in many ways the loudest shot yet in the battle to modernize U.S. land policy, for it not only brought into the open the long-veiled though oft-applied social theory of property, but it also dramatically enunciated the full implications of that theory for centralized land use reform. Explicitly rejecting the individualist view that "urbanization rights arise from the land itself," that is, from the ownership of discrete parcels of real estate, the Task Force report said that development rights roll "down from the top" of society: they are "created by society and allocated by it to each land parcel." All landowner rights are thus inextricably connected by a network of social privileges and obligations. Property rights possess no autonomy save that established by government. Centralization of land use policy was merely the logical fulfillment of legal theory and social fact. Local property interests—developers and protectionists alike—must expect that "tough restrictions will have to be placed on the use of privately owned land." Expansionists will "be fairly required to bear [such restrictions] without payment by government," while the states will "establish governmental entities" with "the full range of powers, including the power of eminent domain, the power to control local land-use regulations, and the power to control the provision of public utilities, when necessary, to overcome the barriers that now prevent developers from operating at the larger scales that the public interest requires." [52]

With this proclamation, the political struggle over land use reform was set into new relief. The point was not really whether the bill tilted toward environmental protection or growth, because for reformers this was a matter best left to official discretion. Nor was it really an ideological struggle between defenders of conflicting theories about property, for the social theory had always been the real underpinning of both zoning and eminent domain. The question was ultimately about which version of "society" governed the rights of property—the rationalized, corporate "society" of land use reformers, or the more traditional, geographic "societies" of local landowner and real estate forces, where property rights were directly exercised.

Undoubtedly, most citizens were oblivious to the conceptual issues and to the bill itself. National television and local press gave the matter scant attention. But important private interest groups observed the Senate debates, carefully appraising the scene for an appropriate moment to act. As the administration persuaded Senator Jackson to replace Senator Jordan's "takings" amendment with safer language, the Idaho Republican blasted what he called "boilerplate disclaimers" and "so-called safeguard provisions," language taken directly from publications of the U.S. Chamber of Commerce. It was a telling sign, for once legislative activity shifted to the House of Representatives, after the Senate passed the bill on June 21, 1973, the chamber turned its legislative guns full blast against land use policy reform. [53]

The Stall in the House

Senate action on land-policy reform struck the *Wall Street Journal* as a strangely subdued affair. The bill aroused "surprisingly little opposition considering the amount of controversy the subject usually generates." It enjoyed the kind of intellectual reception accorded by bankers' conferences and university colloquia, not the working-over typical of a public legislature. Significant interests seemed reticent. But none of this reflected a deep well of tacit support. The quiet was more like the uneasy silence that grows out of ignorance and indifference, or uncertainty. Not all the shoes had dropped. If the bill enjoyed the open backing of some business and environmental groups, this support was nourished by vague understandings that it would be a good idea to build machinery for making better decisions. Although the measure embodied the regulatory impulses of corporate reform, most interest groups perceived it in terms closer to those originally set out by the Interior Committee staff. It was a "relatively innocuous piece of 'good government' legislation that threatened no one," what William Van Ness called "a policy neutral" bill.[54]

While the Senate quietly went about its deliberations, the House Interior Committee was prevented from even discussing the issue. For two years its chairman, Wayne Aspinall (D-Colorado), adamantly refused to act on legislation for the use of private-sector land. He demanded action first on a bill to answer business demands for surer access to the public lands, after Congress gave environmentalists the Wilderness Act of 1965 and an endorsement of single-use zoning for public-land preservation.[55]

Aspinall was a congressional chairman of the old school: he was used to getting his way. "I've had over 1,000 bills before Congress," he liked to boast, "and never lost a one." But environmentalists crowded him closely on the public-lands issue; indeed, they helped to defeat him in 1972, permitting Morris Udall of Arizona to take over the Subcommittee on Environment and play catch-up on land use policy reform.[56]

Udall was a liberal, with much stronger environmental affinities than his Colorado predecessor. "Having witnessed the abuse of some of Arizona's most beautiful and scenic land," he once said, "land use reform has become a kind of personal cause with me." But he was also a pragmatist, a man acutely sensitive to the needs for compromise that are the keys to legislative achievement. Ralph Nader's report on the Interior Committee notes that some conservation groups were "wary" of "Mo" because of his willingness to trade with expansionists.[57]

In the case of land use, Udall's practical bent showed through in a broad view of the implications of reform. Although it could help in treating "the serious environmental questions of the day," Udall thought it also had important implications for "housing, poverty, discrimination. . . . [It] could halt the deterioration of the inner city and the urban sprawl of the outer." [58] In short, he approached the issue with the outlook of a Great Society planner. But by the time Udall took control of the issue in 1973, the national political economy was in flux, the optimism of the Great Society was dying, and average Americans were dusting off school-book Constitutions to read the impeachment clause.

Bertram Gross once observed that "the history of American legislation reveals cyclical trends as sharp as the rise and fall in the level of business activity and employment." [59] Because of economic crisis and Watergate, the prospects of land use legislation suddenly began to run against a new cycle. Morris Udall needed all his skills as a compromiser to eke out one last victory for the Great Society and liberal reform.

The Bad Tidings of Watergate

At first the bad news swirling about the White House seemed to bear no relation to the progress of land use legislation. In the spring of 1973 Morris Udall took hold of the land use issue by immediately defusing the row over disposal of the public lands. He incorporated into the framework of the Senate's bill a separate title mandating that all public-land agencies should inventory and plan for the use of the areas under their jurisdiction, while clearly stating that existing reserves such as the national parks and forests "are vital national assets . . . dedicated to the benefit of both present and future generations." [60] With the public-lands issue tucked away, he led the Environment Subcommittee into detailed hearings on private land use regulation, once again thrashing over questions of standards, sanctions, federalism, and property rights.

The presidential misery went unnoted in the House Interior Committee hearings. But then, on April 30, 1973, less than a month after their completion, John Ehrlichman resigned as Nixon's chief domestic adviser. Land use reform had suddenly lost its chief White House patron. Now no one close to Nixon was powerful enough to protect the reform from the OMB hatchet or the president's insensitivity to resource issues. Land use became "just another issue" at the White House, to be favored or dumped as the political winds shifted. And with a full-blown gale blowing toward impeachment, the president was forced to see the direst political implications in every move. Nixon courted with extra gentle care the few friends that remained.

The president's allies were not distributed evenly across the political landscape. Nixon preserved his ties only with the most conservative political and economic groups. Southwestern rural and suburban capitalists and their representatives in Congress were notable among the few who continued to chant "four more years." Sunbelt entrepreneurs, as the San Antonio case illustrates, were used to a bright business climate and unfettered growth. As these interests became sensitized to the dangers of land use reform, the president was subtly encouraged to see ties between his fate and theirs.

During the Senate debates, small and middling capitalists who anchor much of the American urban and rural economies, and whose profits are closely hitched to local governmental control of development, were largely invisible. Most were simply unaware of the national discussions. The "revolution in land use control" was, after all, conducted quietly. But local business did not want for eyes on the Senate.

Suspicious Eyes

Dan Denning, an able young lobbyist for the Chamber of Commerce, closely watched the land use deliberations. At first he was merely uneasy. Like many other business advocates, he called for mechanisms to assure "balanced decision-making." [61] Unimpressed by arguments that planning would rationalize controls or further opportunities for developers, and speaking less for big national corporations than for middle-sized manufacturers, real estate interests, and small property owners, Denning knew that local controls worked well for average business owners. Change wasn't needed. Of course, home builders had real land use problems and a different view of the issue than many other small businesses; they were willing to bargain with Udall for special considerations. Denning conceded that exclusionary zoning warranted criticism and reform. Thus he didn't interfere with the builders' efforts to gain footholds in the Udall bill. Indeed, the Chamber of Commerce did little to oppose land use reform in the Senate because, in Denning's words, "the Senate was a no-win situation. . . . What we tried to do was get the bill amended. But as far as outright defeat, there was not enough awareness in the country or in the Senate at that point to oppose it." [62]

Land use was an abstract subject with little "sex appeal"; and there was little in the complex Senate bill, packed as it was with reassurances of continued support for private and local land rights, to suggest a "clear and present danger" to major groups. But publications such as *The Use of Land* and *The Taking Issue* changed all that. With the appearance of these studies, Denning explained, "all my vague fears about the bill crystallized. These guys were proposing a massive assault on private property rights to protect nature. I had listened to the perfunctory debate in the Senate when the bill first passed and I knew those guys didn't understand the implications of the bill they were voting for. I decided that if we're going to make revolutionary changes in the traditional concept of property rights, we should at least have a public debate." [63]

In November 1973, as Udall readied H.R. 10294—essentially the same bill that had passed the Senate a few months before—for presentation to the Interior Committee, Denning met with a handful of conservatives to spin a strategy aimed at the bill's defeat. His trusted allies were Republicans Steven Symmes of Idaho, William Ketchum of California, and most important, Sam Steiger, an Arizona cattleman with little but contempt for environmentalists.

The plan was straightforward and direct: to arouse local and regional land-owners to the threat of centralized regulation, forcing the liberal reformers to state their case before a jury of affected interests. Denning, like E. E. Schatt-schneider, knew that "the audience determines the outcome of the fight." [64] One segment of the property audience was especially crucial. Rural land-owners, such as those we met earlier in Uvalde County, Texas, are by far the most stubborn defenders of individual exclusion and expansion rights. For them, even local zoning is frequently unacceptable. If the Rockefeller Task Force and the *New York Times* wanted to define the issues in terms of individual rights versus public rights, that was fine with Denning. He knew where most of rural and small-business America would come down.

But it was important to touch base with more sophisticated capitalist interests as well. For a decade corporations had been intrigued with land use reform as a means of land clearance without conflict. But as Denning knew from conversations with trade association lobbyists, as well as from the public hearings, individual industries such as energy, mining, and utilities were not really devoted to overall land use reform. They only wanted administrative land clearance for *their* businesses. The lawyers among the business elite were most strongly committed to reform in general; land use policy was their fight. It was enough for Denning to remind business lobbyists that corporate needs could be taken care of industry by industry. Allegiance to land use reform was unnecessary. [65]

Economic Collapse and Political Resistance

Current events helped Denning to make the point. October 1973 brought the Yom Kippur War and its climax, the OPEC oil embargo, an event of catastrophic proportions for global capitalism. [66] The price of a barrel of oil exploded 400 percent. Suddenly an industrial system based on endless supplies of cheap fuel was rendered sorely inefficient and unprofitable. At the very same moment, "energy independence" became a national battle cry. With an oil-thirsty public crying for an end to gasoline lines, energy executives grew optimistic that land clearance policies could be tailored to their unique specifications. "Policy-neutral" approaches would not be necessary. But the severe recession that followed in the wake of the embargo changed more than the oil executives' outlook. The construction industry crashed, too.

Recession devastated the land business, including the once optimistic corporate builders. The giants lost millions in real estate and were struggling to get out. In 1973 alone, Alcoa lost $74 million, American Cyanamid $5.5 million, IT&T $14 million, and Bethlehem Steel $15.7 million on development ventures. Real Estate Investment Trusts and "new towns" collapsed. Over $400 million in loans were defaulted by the REITs, and nearly $20 million of public money was spent to make interest payments on behalf of failed "new town" builders. The bankruptcy expert replaced the land-use lawyer as the corporate advocate in real estate. As one national executive confessed, "We have come to the conclusion that homebuilding is really a local business." [67]

But local business was also decimated. New housing starts dropped from nearly 2.4 million in 1972 to barely a million by 1974, leaving the industry in what President Ford would later call "the longest and most severe . . . recession" since the end of World War II. Compounding their ills, home builders also lost federal subsidies that contributed to the production of more than 1 million low- and moderate-income units between 1971 and 1974. In January 1973 President Nixon announced a freeze on housing subsidy programs in preparation for new experiments with housing vouchers for the poor. Coupled with court rulings that upheld timed-growth ordinances such as that of Ramapo, New York, the Nixon policy and the economic collapse backed home builders to the outer limits of tolerance for anything smacking of environmental controls. [68] Regulations such as the recently passed Clean Air and Water Acts were widely inspected for price tags. Members of Congress, especially those with union ties, went on the offensive against policies that seemed to threaten jobs. Growth was something to be ignited, not managed. Seeds were planted that later sprouted as supply-side economics.

Denning understood perfectly the implications of the new climate. Environmental protection and social exclusion were no longer values to be "balanced," but anti-business forces to be pushed aside in favor of expansion. He rounded up an army of trade associations, called the Coordinating Committee on Land Use Control, to spread the fight against land use reform. [69] Most of these groups had earlier testified, as had Denning, that the land use bill should be balanced more evenly in favor of development. But not all were committed to stopping it. Some, like the home builders, bartered with Udall for special considerations. Denning wisely kept these more moderate, or perhaps desperate, groups on his side, persuading them of the need to trade from strength. By early 1974, however, with the Udall measure under study by the full Interior Committee, most of the potential opposition was convinced that reform must and could be stopped. One lobbyist who still refused to oppose the bill recalls that Denning accused him of being "naive. . . . He told me we would just be sold out in conference." [70]

But the Chamber of Commerce itself was the largest and best organized pro-expansion group in Washington, with a huge network of contacts and connections. More than 70,000 firms and individuals claimed membership along with more than 1,000 trade and professional associations, carefully organized along federal lines in neat parallel to the political system. Over 2,500 local, state, and regional chambers were influential in communities across the nation. The grass-roots chapters were alerted by "Action Lines" that asked local business people to consider the implications if "the government . . . says you may continue to own your own land, but you may not build anything on it." Denning recounts that he "stayed on the phone a hell of a lot making sure [business owners] did things. If I heard of somebody in San Antonio or Shreveport that had an interest in this, I made sure they were energized. People need to be told what to do sometimes. You have just got to point a direction. They did their jobs." [71] Indeed, Congress was inundated with letters protesting this "unconstitutional" bill, this "threat to freedom and individual liberty." One Vermont newspaper warned that "if Congress should adopt such a bill, it may well be seen years from now as perhaps the one most significant action of the century in destroying the institution of private property." [72]

Given the barrage of grass-roots lobbying, it became essential for Udall to produce a package that, in the words of an Interior aide, "could be objectively viewed as a balanced bill." Amendments soon abounded to solidify expansionist rights under the proposed state regulations. Requirements to "protect" critical areas were changed into obligations to "consider" them. And such "considerations" could not exclude "the production, conversion, transportation, use and storage of energy," even in "areas of critical environmental concern." The bill's findings were also adjusted to reflect the new priorities. Enhancement of the environment was at the bottom of the list of social causes justifying reform, below material needs "to secure a . . . balanced allocation of resources" and "advance social and economic well-being." The Interior Committee's report to the House concluded with the statements that "every effort was made to take a balanced approach. . . . We are considering the use of land . . . and are not proposing a non-growth policy." [73]

Nonetheless, the committee's minority report continued to assail the bill's "lopsided . . . concern for the physical environment" while "almost ignoring the needs of our citizens for economic development." [74] Nevertheless, after winning twenty-six votes in favor of reporting the bill, including eleven Republicans, Chairman Udall looked forward to routine clearance by the Rules Committee. On the eve of that committee's decision of February 26, however, Congressman Sam Steiger and House Minority Leader John Rhodes met with the president and persuaded him to switch his support from the Udall measure—much stronger versions of which his administration had backed since 1971—to a sham substitute offered by Steiger. Meanwhile, Rules Committee members were heavily lobbied by the Chamber of Commerce to view land use reform as a threat to energy independence. Economic crisis, intense business pressures, and the president's need to maintain support among conservative Republicans during the late days of the Watergate scandal, now took their toll of the land use bill: the Rules Committee elected not even to permit House debate on the measure.[75]

Morris Udall joined a tradition when he accused Richard Nixon of double-dealing. Journalists counted anti-impeachment votes. The *New York Times* capped its editorial with the headline: "Land Use Bill Knifed." Lyday, however, suggests that Udall's real problem "was massive confusion about the bill's intent and concern about . . . private property rights." Clearly, though, impeachment politics and conservative opposition to land use reform were mutually reinforcing. Whether Richard Nixon's change of mind carried much weight at this point in his presidency is really beside the point. Watergate left a huge power vacuum in the governmental system, and with the executive branch reduced to a scattering of agencies, highly aligned and well-financed interest groups such as the Chamber of Commerce were beautifully positioned to exploit the uncertainties of elected officials at all levels. Denning took full advantage of the new conditions.[76]

The End of Land Use Reform

But Udall did not give up the fight. To retrieve his bill from the Rules Committee he agreed to hold additional hearings so that rural capitalists could make their case against land use policy. The "audience" of landowners filed into the meeting room of the Subcommittee on Environment in April 1974. There were southwestern loggers and cattle ranchers, farmers and oil wildcatters, along with suburban construction executives, real estate developers, and the Liberty Lobby, nearly all opposed in principle to land use reform. L. L. "Moon" Mullins, for example, a Mississippi tree farmer, urged the committee to understand that where he came from "the most effective land-use planning is an agreement worked out by neighbors." Another witness, a member of the Oklahoma Conservation Commission, expressed greater sympathy with the goals of the bill but indicated that its sponsors didn't understand the continued grip of frontier attitudes in America. He told Udall this story to make his point:

> I was in your state, Mr. Udall, about a year and a half ago. . . . And that is where I first found out that Goodyear Farm was going into a housing development. I had been on this farm many years ago several times, and knew what a great piece of agricultural land it was. So I asked my friend Deswood . . . I said, "What are you going to do, carving up all this good land?" He said, "Ah hell, when we need it for food, we will take a bulldozer and scrape it off, and put it back into production."

That, he concluded, "is the way we operate in this country." Udall reassured his critics that, by itself, land use reform would do nothing to change such practices: "If a community wants to choose sprawl constitutionally and openly after having public hearings and involving the citizens and local government, they can damn well choose sprawl under this." But one cattleman bluntly replied, with words that stood well for the general view of local business, "We do not want any interference." [77]

A few weeks later, his promise to hold hearings fulfilled, Udall barely secured his rule for a floor debate. But now the White House was behind Steiger's substitute. In the words of domestic policy aide Kenneth Cole, this legislation "minimized the role of the federal government." Still, the Interior Department's lobbyist, Lance Marston, ignored the new White House policy and continued to press for land use reform down to the final floor vote. Meanwhile, as one business lobbyist put it, "Sam Steiger didn't want any bill at all, but he was afraid he would look bad" if he took the floor without one. [78]

Just as important, key interest groups reconsidered their earlier pro-reform views. At its convention, for example, the National Association of Home Builders rebelled against its Washington staff. The organization's new president, Lewis Cenker, instructed its representatives "to act fast to stop" the Udall proposal. [79] Environmentalists had their own second thoughts. Although they didn't reverse field and oppose Udall outright, few actively pitched in to help the cause. Early suspicions that the proposal was a shrewd cover for corporate siting policy were strengthened by Udall's many steps toward "balance," an "even-handedness" conservationists rejected because, as one argued, "there is no market force which represents environmental values." Udall scolded them for staying out of the fight; so did the *New York Times*. But environmentalists had difficulty backing the multiple use of the same land for protection of "critical environmental concerns" and "the production of energy." [80]

Not all of Udall's support evaporated, though. A few stragglers still marched with him: the National Mortgage Bankers Association, the League of New Community Developers, and groups representing parking-lot owners and builders of industrial parks, for example. But the Chamber of Commerce spread anxiety among the greater ranks of middle and small business, who responded with a powerful "No!" to land use reform. "There has been so much fear" about the bill, Udall observed, "people are just frightened about it." Before the House debate, on June 11, he circulated a "Dear Colleague" letter, asking the members to see through "the flood of misrepresentation." More amendments were promised to "remove any possible interpretation that the Secretary of Interior or any other federal agency will have any authority over state and local land use decisions" or that the bill "will lead to any infringement of property rights." [81]

Udall hardly exaggerated his willingness to bargain. Among his new offers were provisions sharply restricting federal reviews of state decisions and policies as well as state interference in local decisions. These amendments, he concluded, will "answer any remaining concerns." [82] They didn't. As the

House met on June 12 to decide whether to debate land use reform at all, the conflict was well out of Udall's control. He was charged with trying to write the bill on the floor, with offering a measure based on "collectivist theory," and with trying to push "agrarian reform" in America. Congressman William Randall (D-Missouri) stated the conservatives' central point: "This legislation is so objectionable that it simply should not be debated." Steiger twisted the knife, adding that "a vote against the Rule is responsible . . . and besides that, it will let us go home early." [83]

Given the mood on the floor, the final tally was amazingly close. Land use reform was defeated by only seven votes, 204 to 211.[84] A traditional coalition of Republicans and country Democrats, most from the South, combined to reject the rule permitting House debate. As the conservatives had argued throughout, procedural decisions do have substantive implications, and formal requirements are instruments of substantive power. Thus land use reform was killed without ever winning the honor of formal discussion on the House floor, and by forces its backers had never really factored into their strategic equations; indeed, over half the forty-six Republicans voting *for* the rule represented affluent suburbanites, the archetypical excluders.[85]

Conclusion

Committed to the goals of increased efficiency in the location of public and private capital, racial and class integration of the suburbs, and professional management of environmental resources, land use reformers expected strong opposition mainly from middle-class homeowners and local planning officials. Thus, John Ehrlichman's political strategy for the passage of a national land use policy was based on muting the growth implications of reform in favor of an accent on the environment. This strategy made sense in 1971, when ecology was a popular new issue, but it badly damaged the bill's chances in the post–oil-embargo era of the mid-1970s.

But the economic situation notwithstanding, many land use reformers never really anticipated, or understood, the social resistance to central planning and regulation that was rooted not only in the suburban homeowner associations but in the ranks of small business as well, especially in rural America. As Frank J. Popper notes, reformers did not want "direct government control of the market;"[86] they were fully committed to capitalism. But they envisioned a regulated and coordinated capitalism, organized and managed from above by expert, public-spirited administrators, in close cooperation with corporate technicians and environmental scientists. Their world view, however, left little room for the petty expansionists of real estate and construction, of agriculture, ranching, mining, and timber, who play such prominent roles in the urban and rural political economies of land use and whose political influence is especially great in the locally oriented House of Representatives. Thus, just as in the San Antonio case, an alliance of town and country capital proved to be a formidable adversary of new, more centralized land use controls, especially those identified with exclusion and the environment. In short, the elite legal and corporate backers of land use reform were blindsided by petty capital.

From this point of view, the battle for land use reform was not a struggle between environmentalists and developers. Rather, it represented an attempt by the best of the American land-use lawyers to "rationalize the system" in the interests of large-scale development and the kind of "state of the art" environmental management appropriate to modern accumulation. In simple terms, regulatory power over crucial growth questions would no longer be dominated by local voices. Wider system perspectives would come to prevail against parochial ones. For this reason centralized regulation aroused both the suspicions of environmentalists and the outright opposition of smaller business interests.

In substance, the fight for land use reform was really a struggle over the locus of authority for managing the expansion-exclusion contradictions of capitalist development. In form, it was a battle over the social, economic, and environmental implications of change in the federal system. In the end, it was a fight over modernization of the capitalist state, and it is one that continues. Predictably, even in the growth-conscious era of the 1970s and 1980s, central industrial-siting policies have not won warm welcome among the ranks of rural and local business, any more than they have among environmentalists. To the contrary, new alliances have been forged between environmental, local government, and regional capitalist interests in defense of "local control." The energy industry's struggle for a national Energy Mobilization Board furnishes a useful illustration, one explored in the pages ahead.

The Defeat of the Energy Mobilization Board   7

When this Nation critically needs a refinery or a pipeline, we will build it.

President Jimmy Carter

The refusal of the House Interior Committee to prolong the debate over the reform of land use policy conveniently removed the issue from the national agenda. This action, however, did not remove either the problem of land use conflict or the tensions in the political economy that lay at its root. Congress, unable to reconcile the contradictions, merely gave its tacit support to continued reliance on local controls. If individual states wanted to risk the political costs and carry on the fight to regionalize or centralize land use power, that was fine—but Washington was not going to pay the tab. The land fights of worker-owners, small business, and big capitalists were best settled at the grass roots. Private-sector controversies over exclusion and expansion did not need national spotlights. The corporate giants of industry and housing would have to haggle for space along with everyone else, down in the trenches, where, it could be safely assumed, enough communities were in want of jobs and taxes that room would be found, sooner or later, even for the dirtiest work and the poorest of the poor.

But rules are made to be broken, and Congress was not altogether convinced that it should leave land-clearance issues to the locals. At least one industrial exception attracted its attention. Nearly everywhere embattled in their efforts to expand the nation's fuel supply, the oil companies straggled into Washington seeking special aid and comfort. After the long discussions over land use planning, few in the industry had patience for further explorations along academic lines. This time, oil executives went straight to the point. Local and regional rights of resistance were being exercised without sensitivity to the industry's vision of the national interest: they must be made subject to the national oversight. And, argued the executives, when the parochial forces refuse to budge, they must be made to budge—by a federal agency

201

with the authority to enforce the industrial and land use preferences of the national government.

The oil companies' bid for a national energy mobilization board (EMB) offers a very different kind of opportunity to study the politics of expansion than does the national land use legislation, for we are dealing here with a very different kind of capitalist political power. Whereas the land use proposal originated in an unofficial policy network of lawyers and policy planners, one formally separated from the main business of capitalist production, the large energy firms operated at the core of modern capitalism. Their interests in land clearance were not diffuse but highly specific. Oil executives did not have to worry about the impact of their needs on the whole system—they just needed access to land. Identifying the industry's interest was not difficult in this case; indeed, it happened almost automatically. Thus the EMB proposal itself was originally broached by a major industry trade association, the Edison Electric Institute, in 1975. Within four years, the proposal had become a presidential initiative.

This kind of success in gaining access to the national agenda is the rule for energy capital, which has long sported a reputation for political power unmatched by other sectors of American industry. As Robert Engler's studies of the politics of oil fully demonstrate, it is a reputation richly deserved.[1] The energy industry has regularly watched its version of policy become law at every level of U.S. government, and its success in foreign political settings has been no less impressive. This is an industry habituated to political control.

With the EMB case, then, we have the chance to study the politics of expansion as pursued by an enormously influential corporate sector, in a context where it is relatively unconstrained by obligations to wider class interests. Nevertheless, because this is a case study, the normal reservations must be counted against tendencies to generalize. Indeed, given the industry's historic success, some may be tempted to read this chapter as a study of those exceptional conditions that allow vast industrial and political power to be outweighed by well-organized countervailing forces. But this reading would overlook the unifying theme of the study: expansion is never found without its opposite; and the forces of exclusion are pervasive. In the underlying movements of capitalist development, counterpoint and dissonance are the norms. This is the more enduring structural clue to the defeat of EMB.

Frontier Crude

Even before the oil cutoff of 1973, the energy industry in the United States was gearing up for enlarged ventures into the great American storehouse. Easy habits of dependence on cheap Arabian crude, stimulated by corporate arguments for free trade in fuel, were correctable with massive new efforts to re-

cover domestic supplies on the frontier.[2] Alaska was the preferred target for
the new explorations, but it was only one component in a larger industrial
plan that included probes in the outer continental shelf, giant excavations of
western coal, and a new system of "infrastructure" to bring it all "on line."

Alaska's promise was great. America's northland held an estimated 9.6 billion barrels of oil at Prudhoe Bay, and upwards of 100 billion additional
barrels throughout the state. Natural gas supplies were calculated at over 400
trillion cubic feet, nearly 11 percent of the national total. But getting the resources to faraway metropolitan markets meant crossing vast, cold stretches
of the continent. According to federal estimates, approximately 7,500 miles of
new pipelines and 6,000 miles of new highways were needed to bring out the
wealth.[3] By the late 1970s, one 800-mile line had been built across Alaska,
and three more were slated to distribute the fuel throughout the United States.
Standard Oil of Ohio, for example, urged the construction of a 1,000-mile
line across the Southwest, from Long Beach, California, where Alaskan oil
would be picked up at the port, to Midland, Texas, where it would be connected with existing pipelines to the Midwest. Two additional lines were later
proposed to carry Alaskan oil and natural gas over 4,000 miles across Canada
to the United States.

Closer to home, the industry looked toward the riches of the Outer Continental Shelf (OCS) as well as to western coal and shale. Since the mid-1960s,
offshore oil production in the United States had exceeded the take from land-
based wells, and optimism abounded over the future haul along the California,
New England, and mid-Atlantic coasts. Plans were afoot to lay a belt of drilling installations around the perimeter of the United States, covering potential
finds in over 800,000 square miles of offshore lands. In 1973 and 1974 alone,
for example, Washington leased over 2.8 million acres for oil and gas explorations.[4] Western coal held similar attractions for the American power industry.
With over 225 billion tons in the ground, including 75 billion tons of relatively
clean, low-sulfur coal, the West held over half of the nation's recoverable reserves. Nearly all the shale supply was there, too, over 80 percent of it on
federal land. Energy planners expected that the region would rapidly increase
its contribution to the national stores, rising from around 10 percent in the
1970s to over half the country's total by 1985.[5]

In 1975 President Gerald R. Ford summed up the extraordinary vision of
concrete and steel that was to connect the energy fields and factories. He saw
coming no less than "200 major nuclear power plants, 250 major new coal
mines, 150 major coal-fired plants, 30 major new refineries, 20 major new
synthetic fuel plants, the drilling of many thousands of new oil wells" and "increased production from new frontier areas on the Outer Continental Shelf."
The costs of this program in capital and land were to be immense. By 1975
energy investments were already consuming up to 35 percent of total capital
spending in the United States, up from 21 percent in 1970 and 16 percent in

the mid-1960s. And, according to an estimate by the Congressional Research Service, siting the proposed new facilities would require a land area the size of Missouri.[6]

Viewed historically, the industry's current appetite for land and capital was anything but out of line with its traditions. Oil companies in the United States were accustomed to operating in a big way. Their multinational structure and activities are well known; less familiar, perhaps, is their control of domestic lands. At one time or another, oil corporations have held leases on territory equal to 25 percent of the national estate.[7] The demands of the 1970s, then, were just part of the oil business as usual. But operations in this decade were interrupted by new and uncontrollable factors. In the Middle East, the Organization of Petroleum Exporting Countries (OPEC) took substantial charge of production planning. In the United States, an irascible and distrustful public became increasingly skeptical of the corporations' patriotic claims and no longer welcomed their traditional freedom to control raw materials. In this less-compliant environment, the companies' need for land became a sore point of industrial vulnerability to grass-roots political and economic power.

Frontier Skirmishes

Public favor and support had long been carefully cultivated by the major oil companies. In Engler's words, "public relations" was the "first line of defense of the organized economic power of the oil industry."[8] Energetic tigers and trustworthy "men who wear the star" were made familiar figures, widely displayed on television screens to remind the public of the corporate concern for its welfare. Heavy investments were placed to ensure that if the going ever got rough, the citizenry would be on the side of the industry. Mass faith, however, was less easily captured than natural resources. When the gallons stopped flowing in 1973, the corporations, along with the desert kings of OPEC, bore the brunt of public indignation. "No matter how you word the question," remarked a pollster in 1976, "55 percent to 65 percent of the American people have always believed the energy crisis was just a matter of price-rigging, a kind of hocus crisis created for the profit of the oil companies." Indeed, even after President Jimmy Carter, a man elected on the pledge of restoring credibility to government, declared that the energy crisis was "the moral equivalent of war," 57 percent thought that the fuel situation was not "as bad as the President said," and 49 percent believed that the shortage was an outright myth. Just as important, the same *New York Times* poll revealed that, by a 5 to 3 margin, Americans considered environmental protection "more important" than energy production. These were not the statistics of public compliance—they were the data of incipient resistance.[9]

The industry indeed met trouble wherever it poked in the political system.

In Washington its profits were assailed as "obscene" and its tax benefits reduced.[10] Across the country, wherever it attempted to drill, mine, or build, it seemed that angry publics threw up roadblocks and "Keep Out" signs. Paths of least resistance were difficult to find.

In Alaska, for instance, ecologists eagerly tested their strength by invoking the newly passed National Environmental Policy Act (NEPA) to slow down construction of the Trans-Alaska pipeline. Their troublesome questions were enough to persuade Congress that NEPA's procedures were best waived in connection with this key project. Later, the conservationists were more successful in persuading the Carter administration to withdraw from corporate entry 161 million acres of rich Alaskan land, a resource shed the size of California. From the industrial perspective, this was exclusion with a vengeance. And if that were not enough, Alaskans demanded their own pound of economic flesh. Refusing to repeat the mistakes of Kentucky, the state hiked taxes on energy producers some 900 percent between 1968 and 1979. By 1979 industry profits equaled its payments to the state—a novel balance for companies accustomed to friendlier receptions in the Lower Forty-eight.[11]

Just as much of the Alaskan frontier was excluded from development, oil companies faced tough fights to defend their claims to the Outer Continental Shelf. States on both coasts brought lawsuits to halt exploration, and Congress undertook a major effort to reform coastal leasing practices, including steps to increase the state role in leasing decisions. As Tom Arrandale points out, Californians, like their northern counterparts, made their opposition felt by maintaining "that the Coastal Zone Management Act of 1972 required that federal OCS leasing be consistent with state coastal management plans drafted under the statute."[12] Local interests also sought to block construction of the onshore facilities that were essential to coastal development. In Maine, for example, environmentalists and fishing interests joined forces to stop construction on the Pittston Company refinery at Eastport, while in California, citizens threw enough legal obstacles in the way of the Long Beach-to-Midland pipeline that Standard Oil of California decided to cancel the project in 1979, after a slip in demand cut its commercial viability. The delays, it was announced, had rendered the line unprofitable. Up the coast, in Washington State, the proposed Alaska gas pipeline was halted in 1982, when the governor refused to issue a permit necessary for construction under Puget Sound.[13]

Similar battles roiled in the West. The world's largest coal-fired power plant, the Kaiparowitz project in Utah, was dropped in 1976 after a ten-year fight by local ranching and environmental interests anxious about its effect on the area's air, water, and land. In Montana and Wyoming, cattle ranchers and ecologists allied to battle the massive strip-mining of coal. Protesting that "we will not become the nation's slag-heap," Governor Richard Lamm led Colorado in opposition to shale-oil development. The struggle was felt in Washington, too, as westerners demanded and finally won a comprehensive strip-mine control policy in 1977. And earlier in the decade, sufficiently serious questions were raised about the federal government's coal-leasing policies that sales were suspended in 1971, not to be renewed until the arrival of the Reagan administration ten years later.[14]

Midwesterners, too, battled for their land. Minnesota farmers used guerrilla tactics to knock down 765 kv power lines. Ohio citizens used less coercive strategies to fight the lines cropping up in their neighborhoods. And when coal-slurry-pipeline companies announced plans to construct their facilities across the Midwest and the South, farmers, ranchers, environmentalists, state officials, and railroad representatives journeyed to Washington to fight their appeals for eminent domain authority to clear the way.[15]

Altogether, according to industry figures, no fewer than twenty major projects were canceled, and dozens of others suspended, because of regulatory delays and seemingly interminable political conflicts over access to land.[16] Although economic stagnation and conservation cut demand, making several of these projects less rational economically, the land battles contributed by complicating the long-range commercial calculations of industry planners. More important, they reflected the striking change in the political standing of the energy business. Not since the old muckraking days, when the name Rockefeller was a curse, had the petroleum giants faced such abuse. Oil companies appealed for public understanding. Mobil, among the most outspoken, pleaded for national attention to focus on "the paramount issue of development . . . of U.S. energy supplies." Texaco promised the uncertain that it was "working to keep your trust." And Exxon, in a series of beautifully photographed commercials, showed that, unlike pigs and parlors, swans and refineries could exist in harmony. In Congress, however, executives adopted more pointed arguments. The regulatory process had gone haywire, they exclaimed. Procedures seemingly unfolded without end: "There are no deadlines in the decision-making process," observed one increasingly impatient manager. In a world of rapidly rising interest costs, procedural delays threatened death by mortgage for projects essential to the national survival.

But corporate leaders were anxious about more than the duration of conflict; it was the loss of autonomy that most embittered them. Power to direct economic change now had to be shared with an undisciplined public. As one executive explained, corporate managers retained fiscal but not "operational control" of new plants because of the "many government regulations that determine how [the plants] are built." Backing the industry's cause, James Schlesinger, secretary of energy, put the problem squarely at the door of democracy: "We have reached the stage of participatory democracy where almost everyone in the society can say 'no,' but no one can say 'yes.'"[17] At this level, of course, the complaint was less about the process of regulation than its substance, about the public's oversight of corporate planning and industry's loss of freedom to engineer change with few questions asked. Popular control of land use policy, among other avenues of "participatory democracy," loomed large as an exclusionary limit on capitalist power, and the managers were growing restless with its implications.

Exclusion Aside

Tough battles for land had given the industry substantial incentives to join the earlier fight for a national land use policy; indeed, energy corporations were among its most ardent supporters. When this opportunity was lost in 1975, attention shifted to more limited strategies. The states, for example, were encouraged to pass new power-plant-siting laws to limit local resistance and expedite construction. By 1975 Connecticut, Florida, Maryland, Minnesota, New Hampshire, Oregon, and Rhode Island had enacted various forms of centralized authority over plant siting. Five years later, thirty-two states had power-siting boards to oversee the location of plants and transmission lines. The programs varied, of course. In Connecticut, local control of plant siting was not substantially reduced, although municipal decisions could be appealed to the state public utility commission, which was not bound by local zoning policies. Minnesota's Environmental Quality Council was directed by the state's Power Plant Siting Act to develop an inventory of potential energy locations for which utilities could apply. In Maryland, the law permitted the state to purchase sites for what amounted to an energy land-bank program geared to utility company plans. The states used a host of techniques, but the variation was bunched along a graph line pointing toward consolidated authority over energy-siting decisions.[18]

But despite all the state action, the dilemmas of energy and land use were larger than the scope of reform in particular jurisdictions. Power plants, after all, were not the only type of facility needing clearance. The biggest headaches, aside from nuclear power, arose from the mammoth multistate and transstate projects requiring licenses from a variety of subnational authorities, as well as from the national government itself. These included the four Alaskan oil and gas pipelines, the midwestern coal-slurry pipelines, offshore drilling projects, and mineral development in the intermountain West. For these tasks, the industry needed larger openings to ease its claims for land and raw materials. Although it received relatively little notice in the country, national policy makers were increasingly receptive to company pleas for help in clearing the way.

The Ford Administration Bill

An important clue lay in the Ford administration's answer to the National Land Use Planning Act. It proposed a more limited, specialized land use policy, one designed to expedite construction of the big energy projects. Like the energy multinationals, the White House wanted the states' energy programs to be efficiently integrated with corporate plans. To accomplish this, it proposed in 1975 a national plant-siting bill that would finance state efforts to make room for energy.[19]

In the Ford approach, the Federal Energy Administration (FEA) was authorized to write a National Energy Site and Facility Report indicating "the number, type and general location of energy facilities required to meet national energy objectives." States would be expected to produce locations that accommodated the FEA's plans and to provide a facility "review and approval process" lasting no longer than eighteen months.[20] Federal intrusion was prohibited, except in cases where states failed to submit a program within one year after publication of the FEA report. In these instances, the national administrator was authorized to "prepare and promulgate a . . . management program for the State." Moreover, the FEA chief was empowered to ensure that the national program take precedence over "any statute, rules, or regulations . . . of such State or . . . municipality . . . which relate to energy facility planning, or which affect the siting, construction and operation of energy facilities."[21]

This proposal was far more draconian than anything ever imagined by the architects of the national land policy. The range of local rules potentially affected was vast, encompassing a whole litany of environmental and community protection controls, as well as economic regulations concerned with rate setting, taxation, and other commercial implications of power production. Any of these could be preempted by the FEA. In effect, the Federal Energy Administration was being offered up as a credible candidate to fill the industry's need for a national energy zoning board, with powers to overcome any local or state ordinance that barred the development of energy resources. The FEA, in short, would have the power to "say yes."

Ford adminstration representatives vigorously denied that the White House intended to "make individual siting decisions." They only wanted to ensure that the states had "adequate mechanisms to make the decisions" at "some minimal level of performance."[22] But because Washington would define the terms of "performance," with further decisions to impose federal plans and variances made on the basis of its judgments, such reassurances were less than candid. As the fate of national land use legislation illustrated, it took much less than this to outrage local interests. Sensing the likely reactions, Senator Henry Jackson recoiled, though not against the proposal itself. On the contrary, he vented his anger at those he termed the "extremists" and "wild crackpots" who travel the country trying "to scare" citizens into believing "that Uncle Sam is going to come in and start dictating locations." Refusing to commit himself to the Ford bill, Jackson nonetheless called for "firmness on the part of responsible people in both political parties."[23]

Corporate Suggestions

Utility executives, representing an industry in increasingly serious financial and political difficulty, also urged the administration to be sensitive to the political dangers of trying to force compliance on unwilling constituencies. The present "lack of institutional confidence . . . makes preemption difficult," warned one executive. Another cautioned that attempts to push central energy plans in the present climate of popular suspicion would be a "divisive and needless source of contention." [24] Others, representing the nuclear industry, felt it was worth a try. [25] But by far the most provocative response to the Ford proposal came from the Edison Electric Institute (EEI), the trade association of "investor owned" utilities.

Just as the Nixon administration had urged Henry Jackson to drop planning for regulation in the land use fight, the EEI called on Ford to sacrifice planning for control in energy siting. Because the problems were immediate, remedies had to be direct and concentrated. Thus the EEI recommended the use of waivers against all regulatory obstructions to major new facilities. It called for passage of a bill "under which the President, after finding a particular energy facility is urgently needed to meet national . . . requirements, could direct the FEA to assert jurisdiction." After consulting with the relevant agencies at all levels of government, the FEA would be authorized to "license the facility expeditiously, granting waivers of particular Federal, State or local laws and regulations if found necessary in the public interest." Strikingly, EEI did not foresee grave opposition to such moves: "We believe . . . that much could be accomplished by a relatively simple authorization for the FEA to act as expediter and coordinator." [26]

In essence, the EEI was urging Congress to scrap everything in the Ford bill except the power to supersede existing regulations. Its tool was to be the federal sword. This call "to cut through . . . existing statutes" seemed unusually bold, even for an industry as accustomed as energy was to getting its way. But in 1975, the call went largely unheard. Facing hard battles over fuel taxes and pricing, the Ford team had scarcely any political capital to invest in a fight for a vast new waiver authority. Besides, getting caught in the morass of local exclusion would have done little to aid the president's reelection appeals to states' righters and suburbanites. Thus the energy-siting issue languished. But signals had been given; the forces of energy mobilization were gathering.

The Semi-Organized Stalemate of Carter's Energy Policy

Jimmy Carter's administration continued the battle begun by his predecessors for a comprehensive national energy policy. Like Nixon and Ford, he hammered at the themes of national security, conservation, and the need to encourage more abundant domestic supplies. The struggle to achieve energy independence was defined as a matter of national survival. But, at bottom, Carter offered nothing new. His planners stressed only the familiar arithmetic of higher prices and taxes as the most efficient means to reduce consumption and lift production. The skeptical population reacted predictably, and their representatives in Congress reflected their doubts. David Howard Davis describes the morass of legislative stalemates: Carter, he writes, "found little support in Congress. Oil-state congressmen wanted price regulation ended. No congressman was eager to tax his constituents. Some congressmen wanted to tap the new petroleum tax to pay for social welfare programs or to balance the budget. Both geography and ideology divided Congress." [27] Energy policy had become another agonizing illustration of what C. Wright Mills called "the semi-organized stalemate of the middle levels of power," or what James MacGregor Burns named the "deadlock of democracy." But the population at large had little cause to celebrate their powers of resistance, for the world price of oil remained at Olympian levels and consumers were bearing its weight. Americans were learning to live with colder winters, hotter summers, fewer long-distance vacations, higher prices, fewer jobs, and the knowledge that their standard of living was inextricably connected to the uncontrollable swirls of international politics. For those yet to be convinced, the events of the spring of 1979 repeated the bitter lessons of 1973.

Spring Training

Revolution in Iran seemed to set the stage for the miserable replay of the decade's earlier power crunch. As Davis notes, "In December 1978, Iranian oil workers struck, completely halting production in the Kingdom which supplied 5.5 million barrels a day to the United States, Europe, and Japan." [28] While Iranian imports trickled, fears grew of spot shortages and, worse, a devastating cutoff resembling the events of autumn 1973. In fact, however, as the *Oil and Gas Journal* later reported, in the first six months of 1979, worldwide crude oil production reached record levels. Moreover, U.S. oil imports increased 9 percent over the same period a year earlier. Similarly, a Federal Trade Commission study found that in the first two quarters of 1979, gasoline supplies in the United States rose between 4 and 8 percent over 1978 levels. Other studies made by the Central Intelligence Agency and the U.S. Customs Service revealed similar patterns. [29] Whatever domestic turbulence was set loose by the overthrow of the Shah of Iran, the international petroleum implications were less than critical. Nonetheless, by late April 1979, Americans were feeling the pinch: their service station lines were lengthening and energy prices were jumping.

The shortages first cropped up in California, then spread quickly eastward, hitting Texas, moving up to Pennsylvania, and then into New York and New England. By June most regions of the country were facing energy-supply difficulties. Angry truckers and farmers organized wildcat strikes to protest the price hikes, while service station owners took to carrying shotguns to protect their property from impatient motorists. The president was advised of "sporadic violence over gasoline."[30] But the public was unbelieving as well as angry; nearly 75 percent told national pollsters that "the oil companies have created the shortage . . . so they could raise prices and increase their profits."[31]

Industry leaders and the White House pointed accusatory fingers at Iranian revolutionaries and panicky consumers. But suggestions were also made that selective shortages taught useful lessons. Oft-heard arguments about the need to boost domestic production and to increase conservation efforts would now, it was said, be taken more seriously. As the president observed in defending the case for fuel rationing authority, "We may have to have a few demonstrable shortages to show that it is necessary." Standard Oil of California made similar arguments for the utility of coercion: "It's simply not realistic to believe that people will voluntarily opt for lowered standards of living and reduced employment to accommodate future needs." As *Business Week* noted early in the crisis, "The oil companies seem to expect the California panic to spread—and so does the President." Perhaps they knew something.[32]

It is difficult even now to determine just what combination of actual shortfall, mismanagement, and planned restriction triggered the 1979 energy crisis—and this is not the place to make a detailed inquiry. But one thing is clear: the Carter administration tried to capitalize on the situation by presenting still another "comprehensive energy package" to Congress, one that included its own major assault on the siting question. With the publication of domestic adviser Stuart Eisenstat's famous memo of June 1979, we have a remarkably clear picture of administration thinking.

As the president departed for a June summit meeting in Tokyo, where promises would be renewed to cut petroleum consumption in the United States, Carter's assistant warned of severe political damage resulting from the "domestic energy problem. . . . Nothing else has so frustrated, confused, angered the American people—or so targeted their distress at you personally." His counsel was "to shift the cause for inflation and energy problems to OPEC." By targeting wily Arabs as the cause of American distress, support could rapidly be built for the kind of large-scale action the executive branch had been struggling toward for six years. Hitherto impossible objectives could now be achieved under the gun of imminent threats. For example, the industry's long-sought national siting authority was now within reach. Labeled an Energy Mobilization Board, recalling the earlier War Mobilization Boards of World Wars I and II, such an agency, said Eisenstat, could designate essential national facilities for rapid construction, thus "eliminating all of the normal regulatory tangle that slows such projects down." Moreover, the idea had already been broached "on the Hill," where it found "an enormous receptivity." [33] It was time to take it to the country.

Laying Down the Fast Track

After returning from Japan, the president called a "time out" in the energy crisis, sequestering himself at Camp David for secret discussions about new directions in policy and leadership style. Meeting over a span of nearly two weeks with dozens of "national leaders," including many with ties to oil, the president learned that the people had lost confidence in his stewardship and that they longed for a firmer hand. [34]

Carter replied to the country with his now famous "malaise" speech. The nation's troubles were traced back to what the president called "a crisis of confidence . . . that strikes at the very heart and soul and spirit of our national will," one that is reflected "in the growing doubt about the meaning of our own lives and the loss of a unity of purpose for our Nation." This want of public identification and commitment, with roots in an undisciplined private materialism, was at the bottom of the inability of the political system to govern the energy dilemma and of the public's refusal to sacrifice for the national good. But the very danger of the power shortage offered a dramatic opportunity to reverse the national drift and to show the world that Americans could still lead the way toward technological mastery and national power. "On the battlefield of energy," said Carter, "we can win for our Nation a new confidence and we can seize control again of our common destiny." [35]

Every war, of course, has its strategies and its command posts. In the energy battle, conventional weapons would be used to stimulate market forces. Carter called for the creation of a new Energy Security Corporation to funnel up to $5 billion to the oil industry to promote frontier technologies in synthetic fuels. Shale oil, coal liquefaction, and coal gasification would be rapidly introduced, while foreign imports would be held down. But the general staff of the war would be located in a separate new institution, an Energy Mobilization Board, "to make sure that nothing stands in the way of achieving these goals." Like the earlier war-production agencies, the new EMB would "have the responsibility to cut through the red tape, the delays, and the endless roadblocks to completion of key energy projects." And it would accomplish this while protecting the environment. "But when this Nation critically needs a refinery or a pipeline, we will build it." [36]

The speech included no further details. A day later in Kansas City, however, at a meeting of the National Association of Counties, a group with natural sympathies for the rights of exclusion, Carter brought his proposed EMB into slightly clearer focus. For example, "port facilities" and "production plants" were added to the list of "critical projects." EMB was no longer merely to "cut" red tape: now it would "slash" through "bureaucratic obstacles" to "set absolute deadlines for action." Finally, the president made it clear for the first time that EMB would not limit the use of its rapier to the national government's schedules; state and local timetables would feel the swipe, too. Just as he had warned environmentalists a day earlier, Carter reminded the local officials:

> We are leaving with state and local authorities the first line of responsibility to remove roadblocks . . . but our energy crisis is so severe that if any level of government fails to act within a reasonable time, this board will see to it that action is taken. . . . It is time for us to take this bold action, and we will.[37]

The Substance-Process Conundrum

Carter called for his Energy Mobilization Board to take charge of "accelerating development of non-nuclear energy resources" and of coordinating intergovernmental "actions necessary for approval of . . . facilities." These tasks would be accomplished "without altering substantive Federal, State or local standards established prior to the commencement of construction" on key installations. In short, EMB's job was "to eliminate or modify procedural impediments to the construction of non-nuclear energy facilities."[38] Leaving aside for the moment the question of industry complaints about the substance of regulatory policy questions not directly answered through procedural shortcuts, Carter's approach left open the key issue of how it was possible to determine when a "responsibility" to uphold state and local law became a "roadblock" to the national interest in energy. The only available clues were to be found in a "description of specifications" sent to Congress as a guide for its deliberations. But a close look at these suggests that the White House was itself unsure of the distinction; indeed, that it presupposed precisely what had yet to be defined.

According to White House instructions, the new EMB was authorized to designate projects for "fast-tracking," to devise binding Project Decision Schedules of not longer than one year, and to issue waivers of "procedural requirements imposed . . . by Federal, State, or local law." These would include, but not be limited to, "timetables and requirements for hearing and notice." The failure of agencies at any level of government to comply with a Project Decision Schedule would be penalized by yielding decision-making authority to EMB. This "bump-up" or "in lieu" power would have to be exercised in line with relevant statutes. However, the Board could suppress substantive and procedural rules enacted by any level of government, following the commencement of construction on a "critical energy facility." This grandfather waiver was intended to limit the ability of local and state governments to harass project sponsors with ex post facto laws. But it also meant that unforeseen dangers might not be corrected through legal remedy if EMB officials deemed rapid construction of the plant essential. Finally, judicial review of agency actions was to be curtailed. The designation of priority projects would be exempt from review altogether, and other agency decisions would not be reviewable until after EMB certified that the permitting processes were complete. Suits could be entered no later than sixty days following such certification.[39]

Superficially, Carter's plan exhibited confidence, even daring, traits rarely visible in the president's earlier moves. Widely criticized for indecisiveness, the president was finally showing his nerve. Democracy's deadlock would no longer cripple the power elite. But careful study suggests a less than audacious leap. Nothing in the specifications indicated how agency executives were supposed to decipher the difference between substantive standards to be preserved and procedural red tape to be waived. To the extent that "red tape" was a slogan and not an administrative theory, the administration seemed to be begging the question.

In failing to define what he meant by "red tape," Carter risked losing the offensive on his bill, for the paradox of procedural waivers was inescapable. Either the variances were to have real substantive implications, or EMB would be irrelevant to the goal of overcoming local resistance. But if the agency did push the resisters aside, then the distinction was meaningless and the administration was playing a dangerous and deceitful game. For real energy mobilization implied a shift of the land use system's bias from exclusion to expansion. Just as in the earlier national land use battle, the provocative issue threatened to become the legislative reluctance, or perhaps inability, to define clear standards for federal action against the opponents of large-scale capital investments.

Given the widespread distrust of the nation's energy managers, and his own sympathies with the environmental cause, Jimmy Carter understandably felt compelled to understate the implications of EMB. Caught between commitments to energy expansion and consensus politics, he naturally wanted to avoid head-on collisions and angry conflicts. But, given his goals, conflicts were unavoidable. Contradiction, after all, is at the core of land use politics. If the White House was afraid to admit this, others in the legislative process would be less diffident. Indeed, while the homeowners and small land capitalists who would be most affected by the changes continued to wage their local struggles, the organized interest-group and congressional reaction focused precisely on the implications of EMB for the representation of their exclusion and expansion rights. Once more, as in the case of the national land use fight, the distinction between substance and process dominated discussion. Energy policy placed a distant second in the politics of EMB. Although most groups tended to agree about what was really important in the proposal, the distribution of opinion about what should be done about it was much greater.

At least four reasonably distinct groupings clustered around the issue. Environmental groups and organizations of state and local officials were the most active defenders of existing exclusion rights; they wanted as little change in the current rules as possible. Executives from the big energy corporations and trade associations tended to believe that an EMB with substantive waiver powers was the most effective means of increasing their expansionist powers within the limits of existing environmental law. Conservative Republicans, especially from the West, argued for basic changes in the environmental law. They wanted to open much wider fields for general business expansion. Caught in the middle were the mainstream liberals, mostly Democrats, who struggled to defend the president's policy. It was their job to hold the forces of exclusion and expansion together within the narrow focus of procedural reform.

These distinctions, however, were not hard and fast; overlaps abounded in the politics of energy mobilization. For example, some liberals, especially from areas likely to get some of Carter's projects, were very sympathetic to exclusion, whereas others, especially from pro-energy states such as Louisiana and Texas, came much closer to the industry view. As we shall see, committee membership joined political geography as key factors in determining the relative inclinations of Democrats. Similarly, some very conservative Republicans also opposed EMB for exclusionary reasons, fearing its impact on farm and ranch interests in their home districts. Thus the following breakdown of "sides" on the EMB fight is intended more as a suggestive outline of the main patterns of political division than a rigid description of sharp cleavages.

The Excluders

Environmental groups and organizations of state and local officials publicly agreed with the president's main point that the regulatory system needed streamlining. They were unwilling to concede much more than this, however. Conservationists strongly criticized centralized schedule making and procedural shortcuts whose effect was likely to limit the serious analysis of the effects of a project. They warned of a "full-fledged panic in progress," of "normally prudent people . . . stampeding to endorse solutions which have the apparent short-term advantage of being quick and the probable long-term drawback of being wrong." Besides, as one sympathetic member of Congress pointed out, "One of the jobs of government is throwing up roadblocks so that the innocent public is not trampled on." Or as one Senate aide put it, "In our laws, the procedure is the substance."[40]

Environmentalists recommended two alternatives to EMB. First, the president was urged to continue using the previously established mechanisms of informal interagency coordination, such as the Critical Energy Facility Program under the Office of Management and Budget, which fostered integrated scheduling and review, but not at the cost of existing statutory requirements.[41] More important, environmentalists insisted that the energy debate should concentrate not on rules for bypassing other rules but on discovering how to stimulate alternative technologies, such as solar and geothermal power, that would make the big and dangerous fossil-fuel projects unnecessary. Environmentalists, in other words, challenged the president's most fundamental assumption. For them, the emerging forms of energy production need not be governed by the capacities of private corporations, institutions whose vast sunk capital in petroleum-based facilities crippled the promise of technological innovation. "The nation," argued Jonathan Gibson of the Sierra Club, "is now facing [a] fairly simple and stark decision—do we want to take public regulatory and investment actions to begin the transition to an era of energy efficiency and renewable energy use, or are we going . . . to continue to satisfy America's gluttonous and unabated appetite for ever more energy at whatever the price?"[42] Given the reluctance of Congress to accept Gibson's characterization of the American standard of living as "gluttonous," the invitation to serious debate about alternative patterns of economic change was not eagerly accepted.

Local officials also paid lip service to rationalization. Although polite support was given to the idea of improved coordination with federal decision-makers, groups such as the National Governors Association demanded extensive interlevel consultation concerning project designations and scheduling. The governors insisted that state and local decisions should "be strictly voluntary and consistent with State statutes and regulations."[43]

The Conservative Republicans

Like the excluders, conservative Republicans also rejected the terms of the EMB debate. For them, administrative delay was only the symptom of a more basic problem: the existence of numerous public policies that opposed economic activity. Representative Steven Symmes (R-Idaho) put it this way: "To really make the energy dilemma disappear in the United States, all this Congress would have to do is repeal a few laws and people would look back upon the energy crisis as something they used to talk about."[44] For the conservatives, EMB was an unnecessary bureaucratic sop; it merely reflected the administration's unwillingness to accept the discipline of environmental retrenchment. Conservatives saw the path to energy abundance marked "deregulation." Letting market forces determine resource allocation would not only increase output, but it would also avoid the problem of federal intrusion into states' rights. Most conservatives argued as if land use and other protectionist controls were unconnected to exclusionary property rights and political interests in economic stability, as if environmental policy were a kind of socially disembodied bureaucratic interest. They tended to assume that an automatic harmony existed between capitalism, federalism, and landed property. But not all the conservatives were so sure of a benign relation between capitalism and local rights. Representatives such as Manuel Lujan (R-New Mexico) and James Santini (D-Nevada), and Senator Malcolm Wallop (R-Wyoming), all from areas targeted as major energy-production sites, were among those on the Right who remained extremely sensitive to exclusionary inclinations back home.

The Corporate Perspective

Unlike the national land use legislation, which affected companies in many fields and in many places, EMB was perceived by business leaders as a narrow, single-industry bill, the kind of limited proposal best advanced by those firms most intimately affected. Moreover, important regional industries, such as agriculture, fishing, tourism, and real estate, could be expected to oppose EMB as a direct threat to their economic interests in secure environments. In cases of such divided corporate loyalties, the all-encompassing business groups such as the Chamber of Commerce tend to remove themselves from the fray, leaving it to the parties at interest to battle it out.[45] Besides, EMB represented a formidable example of government coercion, and on this ground alone it left some business representatives more than a little uncomfortable. In the words of one especially nervous construction executive, "Fundamentally, what the President is doing is confirming the end of capitalism. . . . This nation apparently has come to the conclusion that it would rather be told what to do . . . than have it happen by fundamental economic principles." Other executives were noticeably less pessimistic—the heads of General Motors, General Electric, Monsanto, and Ford, for example, all praised Carter's plans—but the major national business associations nonetheless kept out of the EMB battle. Energy companies were left to fight their own battles for land.[46]

Energy industry executives were pleased, if not enthusiastic, about the proposed EMB—at least the issue was finally on the national agenda—but they were uncertain. How much of a difference would it really make? It was true that Carter's specifications mandated a strong agency capable of fixing schedules for the entire political system. But unlike the Ford administration's earlier bill and the EEI proposal of 1975, the White House remained suspiciously vague on the question of substantive local and state powers to resist. For all the president's new-found eloquence on the needs of expansion, his EMB guidelines did not include an explicit statement of national primacy in matters of energy-plant siting. If waivers were all that could be gotten from a Democratic administration, then it was critical that they embrace substantive as well as procedural rights of refusal. Industry lobbyists believed, quite reasonably, that the courts would closely scrutinize the board's constitutionality. And unless Congress clearly mandated EMB's national preeminence, a preeminence that included the will of Congress to bypass environmental commitments when necessary, the courts would almost surely force EMB to respect the exclusionary bias of existing law. Ramming the big projects through would remain as difficult as ever. The American Petroleum Institute, the Interstate Natural Gas Association, the National Coal Association, and similar trade groups pushed hard for a measure that included authority to waive substantive law when required by "national security." This was seen as the only sure basis for gaining what one executive called "a favorable regulatory attitude."[47] As a lobbyist for the coal industry added, there was, practically speaking, "very little difference between procedural and substantive issues," although judges have always insisted on this distinction. He advised Congress "to find a way around the constitutional problem and certainly to provide language withdrawing those requirements imposed pursuant to Federal law."[48]

This position was far more unequivocal than any statement by the president. But given the ambiguity of Carter's working distinction, the question was how far his administration was willing to go in following the substantive implications of procedural waivers. In testimony before the House Commerce Committee, the chairman of the Federal Energy Regulatory Commission, Charles B. Curtis, suggested an executive branch perspective identical to the corporate view. Insisting that it would be impossible both to protect the environment and to expedite decisions, he concluded that EMB must be "equipped with substantive powers to cut through the generic substantive requirements."[49] Still, the president continued to stress that the "Board could not waive substantive environmental standards."[50]

The Corporate Liberals

Most congressional Democrats backed the president's initiative, but even within the president's party, important differences surfaced over the meaning and implications of the distinction between procedure and substance. Liberal Democrats, especially those with ties to the environmental lobby, insisted on the strictest separation of form and content. Led in the House by Morris Udall of Arizona, now Chairman of the House Interior Committee, and Timothy Wirth of Colorado, and in the Senate by Edmund Muskie of Maine and Abraham Ribicoff of Connecticut, these liberals hoped to establish a waiver system that would not undermine the exclusionary power of federal, state, or local agencies. Many of these legislators, of course, represented areas of the nation already experiencing serious energy-expansion pressures.[51] By contrast, more conservative Democrats—led by Representative John Dingell of Michigan, chairman of the Commerce Subcommittee on Energy and Power;

the House Democratic Majority Leader, Jim Wright of Texas; and Senators Henry Jackson of Washington, chairman of the Energy and Natural Resources Committee, and his lieutenant for EMB legislation, J. Bennett Johnston of Louisiana—wanted a clearer commitment to rapid development. More inclined to concede industry arguments that substantive exemptions were sometimes necessary, they worked to place the power on a firmer legal footing.

Democrats of all persuasions agreed with the president that administrative rationalization was crucial for improved national energy policy and national security. For example, in opening hearings on the EMB bill, Udall complained that "paralysis all too often overtakes the Government when evaluating major energy projects." It is perfectly reasonable, he urged, to press for a more predictable decision-system that would "minimize business uncertainty, expedite . . . applications, and still protect the rights of affected citizens and their communities." EMB had an appropriate role to play as a "schedule expediter." [52]

Conservative Democrats described the situation much more graphically. Jackson spoke of an "institutional crisis" in which "you can't get anything done in this country." Majority Leader Wright lamented that "government [was] tied down like Gulliver by the Lilliputians." [53] Furthermore, these Democrats charged, paralysis was stimulating a severe right-wing reaction against environmental policy. Excluders were warned that unless they joined in accepting some form of substantive variance, then, in the words of Senator Howard Metzenbaum of Ohio, "the steamroller is going to go over you." [54]

Exclusion-minded Democrats answered that strictly limited procedural waivers were enough. Udall said that we only need to "knock heads together" to obtain a fast-track schedule, but that "our energy problems must not be used as an excuse to make an end run around all the existing laws." [55] Consistent with this logic, Udall's committee produced a bill that was faithful to the president's wish not to change legal standards "established prior to the commencement of construction" on priority projects. According to the Interior Committee's report, EMB was authorized to modify "the time taken to reach decisions, not the basis upon which decisions are made." [56]

Senate Democrats went noticeably further. Senator Johnston failed to win support for a full substantive waiver; but he did manage to add language to his committee's report that established the panel's intention to authorize administrative "changes . . . whether or not they can be categorized as procedural or substantive and whether or not they have substantive or procedural implications." [57] It was in the House Commerce Committee, however, that the waiver power was most clearly etched.

Dingell was persuaded, in part by corporate lobbyists and in part by a growing personal skepticism about the virtue of tough environmental regulation in a stagnant economy, that substantive variances must be made a permanent feature of policy if expansion and exclusion interests were to be harmonized.[58] The Commerce Committee, naturally, was quite sympathetic to this view. Committee support quickly galvanized behind the power to waive all legal obstructions, at any level of government, whether passed before or after the commencement of construction on priority projects.

To justify this step, the committee argued that, historically, Congress showed no reluctance to issue legal waivers when faced with roadblocks to the completion of key facilities, such as the Alaska pipelines. However, these actions tended to be characterized by "last minute decisions" to attach "a barely germane amendment to an unrelated piece of legislation." If particularism was inevitable in regulating the affairs of a modern industrial society, it was all the more important to base the making of exceptions on predictable, general processes. In this way, the substantive meaning of due process, protection against arbitrary state action, would be preserved by the requirement that waivers be treated as a form of legislation. "Problems are more likely to be resolved in a rational and desirable fashion if a generic process is adopted which will permit orderly review of waiver proposals . . . pursuant to a clearly defined process." [59] This could be achieved by adding a legislative veto provision to the waiver authority. Without it, excluders would sue on the ground that executive actions to change the law were an unconstitutional violation of the right of Congress to make the law. In Dingell's words, "The only way [to] avoid the most appalling case of litigation would be to permit action subject to Congressional veto." [60]

When Representative Wirth announced that he would offer an amendment to strike the waiver, President Carter was invited to confirm, once and for all, his commitment to the exclusionary bias. After all, Carter himself had declared that it was "vitally important" that the administration "speak and act with a single voice" on energy policy. In fact, however, White House lobbyists joined industry representatives in opposing Wirth. After the amendment was twice rejected by the Commerce Committee, excluders became incensed at what they regarded as Carter's duplicity.[61] Instead of balancing corporate power with a concern for the environment, the administration merely joined hands with the big oil companies. But Carter's aides demurred; they replied that the White House opposed Wirth not because Jimmy Carter favored substantive waivers but because he feared that a House bill without waivers would increase pressure on the Senate to delete its procedural waiver, leaving the administration with a weak, useless agency. Excluders found little to cheer in this explanation.

Congressional Action: The First Round

By autumn, Udall, Jackson, and Dingell submitted essentially similar bills for consideration by Congress. Each bill offered a new executive agency authorized to designate priority energy projects, set binding decision schedules for regulatory agencies, and enforce fast-track schedules by restricting the scope of environmental analysis, including judicial review. Their differences centered on enforcement. The Jackson and Dingell bills either indirectly or directly permitted waivers of substantive law, whereas the Udall bill only allowed the abbreviation of schedules.

In each house, excluders mounted challenges to the stronger bills. In the Senate Muskie and Ribicoff introduced a counterproposal employing court orders as the Energy Mobilization Board's main enforcement tool.[62] A similar alternative was offered in the House. In late summer, Morris Udall read the Commerce Committee vote for full waivers as a warning that his colleagues desired a stronger EMB than the Interior Committee promised. Joining forces with Wirth and conservative Republican Don Clausen of California, Udall prepared a substitute modeled on the Ribicoff-Muskie bill, with the exception that his plan included authority for EMB to act "in lieu" of other federal agencies and to issue grandfather waivers.[63]

Pro-EMB forces answered by moving to weaken, at least somewhat, their bolder conception of the agency. On the Senate floor a compromise was hastily arranged after the Ribicoff-Muskie amendment was narrowly defeated.[64] Under this provision, the administrator of the Environmental Protection Agency and the secretary of the interior were authorized to reject proposed waivers of laws enacted after commencement of construction on a priority project. Having successfully added one more veto to the energy decision system as the price of gaining a "fast-track" agency, the Senate proceeded to reject a last effort to include substantive waiver authority. Finally, the Senate passed the Energy Mobilization Board legislation by a vote of 68 to 25, on October 4, 1979, less than three months after President Carter's television address.[65]

John Dingell also tempered his legislation. Seeing many members inclined to accept the Udall-Wirth-Clausen substitute, the Commerce Committee chairman let it be known that he was disposed to accept an amendment revoking EMB waiver authority over state and local laws. This amendment, proposed by conservative westerners James Santini (D-Nevada) and Manuel Lujan (R-New Mexico), also added the grandfather waiver and bump-up authority to Dingell's measure.

Among members of the House this turned out to be an extremely popular reply to the bill's critics. Nevertheless, local and state officials continued to oppose Dingell strongly, despite his embrace of the Santini-Lujan amendment. Following the nearly unanimous adoption of the amendment, the National League of Cities issued a statement predicting that the amendment would return "to haunt members who voted for it in good faith, not realizing the impact of such sweeping power on local communities and states."[66]

Their concern stemmed from a fundamental fact about post–New Deal federalism. Much of state and local administrative power is tightly interlocked with organic federal law. For dozens of policies, including education, transportation, health, welfare, housing, and environmental protection, state action depends on congressionally mandated national requirements, not to mention national funding.[67] Under Santini-Lujan, the decision of Congress to waive national environmental standards could effectively nullify regional enforcement powers.[68] Thus, Udall and Wirth insisted, unless the federal mandates were secure, states and local communities would be vulnerable to suppression of their regulatory and exclusionary powers—precisely because those powers were already, to a considerable degree, national in character.[69]

Dingell responded wisely by shifting the debate onto his proffered terrain of red tape. Labeling Udall's substitute the "Slow-Track, Sidetrack, Massive Litigation and Lawyer's Full Employment and Enjoyment Act of 1979," he cited administration charges that the measure would cause up to seven years delay in making decisions on energy projects. Protectionists fought back by attacking what Udall called a "phony letter" by "some junior lawyer down at the Justice Department" who "assumes that every judge is stupid."[70] But enough doubt had been planted about the efficiency implications of judicial enforcement. By a narrow majority, 192 to 215, the House rejected Udall's substitute. Almost immediately, Representative Bob Eckhardt of Texas moved to rally support for deletion of the federal waiver provisions, but his amendment also failed, and by an even wider, 100-vote, margin. The House of Representatives now decisively moved toward the Commerce Committee bill, accepting it by a vote of 299 to 107 on November 1, 1979.[71]

Shutting Down the Fast Track

After four weeks of wrangling over appointments to the EMB conference committee, thirty-six members were given the responsibility to engineer a compromise. Predictably, the conferees deadlocked over the variance issue. Senate members struggled to preserve whatever semblance remained of the procedure-substance distinction, while their House counterparts, a majority representing the Commerce Committee, demanded full waivers.[72] The stalemate lasted until late April 1980, when the necessary bargains were struck. The committee recommended that the agency be authorized to propose for presidential consideration the suspension of any federal statute or rule presenting a "substantial impediment" to critical projects. With presidential concurrence, the recommendation would be forwarded to Congress where it would be referred "immediately . . . to the committee having jurisdiction over the relevant statute or requirement."[73] But this meant that the proposed variance could now be killed without ever reaching the floor of Congress. As one utility executive lamented, "There's no jumping for joy" about climbing onto this fast track.[74]

When the House of Representatives finally took up the Conference Committee report in late June, the energy worries of the previous spring had been displaced by higher prices, increased supplies, and a new national focus on American hostages in Iran. Ironically, the Ayatollah Khomeini now provided just the kind of unifying symbol Stuart Eisenstat had envisioned a year earlier. Unfortunately, it conveyed an image of presidential impotence as much as foreign intrigue. Meanwhile, as the presidential election campaign sped toward the summer conventions, the Republicans' top candidate, Ronald Reagan, missed few opportunities to savage Carter's record. Reagan's Republican congressional allies, whose votes had proved crucial to passage of the original House bill, now had precious little interest in giving Jimmy Carter a political victory. Energy mobilization was better left to a Reagan administration, where it could be accomplished without "Even More Bureaucracy." [75]

Despite the months of debate, doubts about EMB were more pervasive than ever. Early opponents of the variance power, such as Udall and Clausen, were joined by former Dingell allies such as Manuel Lujan. Corporate lobbyists criticized the waiver process as overly politicized. Adding vetos to waivers of other vetos only deepened the problems of regulatory miasma and legal deadlock and attracted few adherents. Nonetheless, Dingell pleaded for votes, once more warning liberals and environmentalists that only EMB could hold back the impending conservative assault on the environmental laws. [76] The House rejected this appeal, voting 232 to 131 to recommit the bill to a conference committee. No effort was ever made to bring it back to life.

As the *Congressional Quarterly* summarized the outcome, "Republicans clearly played the key role" in EMB's defeat. Only 9 out of 134 Republicans voting sided with the president. Instead, 123 Republicans joined 109 mostly liberal Democrats in defeating the establishment of an Energy Mobilization Board. [77]

Conclusion

Once again the walls held. Backed by the Republicans' partisan self-interest, community protectionists managed to ward off another high-level assault. But as in the case of the national land use policy, this battle was essentially a battle of evasion and avoidance. Society's need for energy and other forms of economic development persists, as does the need to undertake all human activities in ways that allow the larger network of ecology and community to be preserved rather than shattered. In Barry Commoner's words, "everything must go somewhere"; siting is compulsory. If these tasks are not accomplished thoughtfully, with respect for the limits of nature and the needs of other human beings, then backlashes such as the EMB battle are inevitable. The consequence is always some awful crisis of discovery: the sudden encounter with institutional demands for space or, even more brutally, the shocking appearance of a toxic substance in the land or even in the body.

It is doubtless a corollary of Commoner's law that the more complex and sophisticated industrial activity becomes, the more terrifying and demoralizing the consequences of failing to plan for its impact on people and nature. Scientist Harrison Brown put it well when he noted that stability in industrial settings does not arise accidentally; it depends on subtle understandings of cause and effect, and on the "desire to create a stable situation."[78] It is equally true, of course, that just as the land map must be redrawn to accept the industries of advancing capitalism, so the development of technology must itself be adapted to the profit logic of the corporations. Capitalist planning is essential to the creation and selection of technologies so that they fit the preexisting industrial framework. Thus, when recession suppressed demand for energy in the early 1980s, the argument for syn-fuels became markedly less compelling.

Lessons are not hard to find. Technology and economic change are not given; they are socially produced within class relationships and institutions to serve the interests of those in charge. Technologies embody political interests; they end up governing people and resources in the interest of those who have power. As environmentalists tried to argue, syn-fuels were not an automatic necessity of economic development, an objective force naturally arising as the next stage of energy development. They only seemed to be inevitable because the president's whole approach depended on the critical assumption that existing capital investment must determine future technical change. In Carter's view, corporate readiness dictated public necessity. Society must adapt to industry; there is no other way.

But if capitalism itself depends on conscious planning and legal intervention to ensure its technical development and social acceptance, its growth is not a matter of natural law or Adam Smith's invisible hand. It is the end result of human choices, choices that often must be imposed against the will of others. Looked at in this way, the production system appears as what it really is—an ideological contrivance inseparable from the political institutions in which it is embedded. Is it necessary, then, that the needs of exclusionary expansion should control and dominate the choices of techno-politics? Doesn't this very limitation of what is industrially possible feed the narrow-minded, defensive politics of "keep out"? From this angle, the question is not how the people may better resist planning, but how they may more humanely control it for their informed democratic purposes. In what other ways can planning and intervention be organized and for what ends? In reviewing the main themes and implications of this study in the next chapter, we shall try to face these issues.

A Reagan-Era Postscript

The election of Ronald Reagan in November 1980 did little to raise the hopes of the energy industry for early establishment of a national land-clearance agency. Reagan promised oil companies not another bureaucratic outpost, but a return to freedom for their private government of energy. In fact, however, he presided over the worst recession of the postwar era, leading to sharp cuts in demand for current as well as future supplies of oil. The land hunger of oil giants has temporarily abated. As one former Energy Department official put it, "At the moment, the economics have changed . . . [the] hysteria to get these projects on line" has been supplanted by "a deep sense of complacency." [79] This was clearly reflected in the Reagan administration's 1984 budget proposals for the Department of Energy, where conservation and renewable-fuels programs were slashed by 400 percent and 100 percent, respectively. [80] It is also reflected in corporate hesitancy to undertake the massive production of syn-fuels envisioned by President Carter in 1979. At least six projects were canceled between January 1982 and May 1983, leaving only two projects actually under construction. And three years after Congress created the U.S. Synthetic Fuels Corporation in 1980—to help finance construction of eighty new plants capable of producing the equivalent of two million barrels of oil per day—the agency had not yet committed a single dollar in loan or price guarantees. In December 1985, Congress simply abolished the agency. [81]

The oil industry, meanwhile, uses its time and big chunks of its capital to "rationalize" its affairs. With prices, profits, and consumption down, major companies have not only begun to advertise their gasolines once again, but they have also sought to secure supplies for the long haul by merging with erstwhile competitors. Socal's recent acquisition of Gulf, Texaco's of Getty, and Mobil's of Superior Oil mark a vast rearrangement of assets—some 30 billion dollars worth—but little advance in basic energy philosophy or technology. These were essentially businesslike gestures toward a stronger position in the markets of tomorrow.

Energy observers continue to warn of a day of reckoning ahead, for energy and national security remain linked. Instability in the Middle East invites attention to the need for what Daniel Yergin calls "a credible ability to respond quickly and in sufficient force to protect the integrity of the oil supply system." And Charles Ebinger of Georgetown University's Center for Strategic and International Studies writes of "the illusion that with the emergence of the oil glut the energy crisis is behind us and that we can relax and let market forces alone solve our energy dilemma." A strong state presence must remain; the point will be to strengthen and direct it for productive purposes. As Ebinger concludes, "Parochial interests must not be allowed to continue to thwart the formulation and implementation of a coherent national energy program." Thus, the pressures underlying the battle over the EMB persist. [82]

Overviews and New Views 8

Reformers kid themselves if they believe that many of the problems . . . can be solved by replacing a local official with a state or regional official.

Richard F. Babcock

As the administrative liberalism of the Thirties has been swallowed up by economic boom and military fright, the noisier political initiative has been seized by a small group of petty conservatives.

C. Wright Mills

Hermes asked Zeus how he should impart justice and reverence. . . . Should he distribute them as the arts are distributed; that is to say, to a favored few only? . . . "To all," said Zeus, "I should like them all to have a share; for cities cannot exist, if only a few share in the virtues."

Plato

The defeat of EMB foretold the outcome of the presidential election six months later; astute observers could have read the handwriting on the walls. Jimmy Carter was surely wiser to celebrate the "ethnic purity" of American neighborhoods in 1976 than to lament American moral standards in 1979, especially in a context designed to favor the oil giants. But, then, shrewd onlookers will note the masterful performance of Carter's successor, for whom corporate imperatives and community values have gone hand in hand. So effectively have the equations been drawn that resource issues now seem anachronistic. Like throwbacks to a decade of misbegotten fears, they are out of bounds in the Reagan era.

Still, elites continue to be vexed by local land politics. Housing shortages, industry-siting conflicts, the waste and abuse of fragile areas, chemical pollution of land and water, and the lack of metropolitan coordination all continue to draw criticism. For reformers from the Left and the Right, the land-control system needs institutional upkeep, a little modernization, or some deregulation. But for each side, the problems of land use, however aggravating, represent only flaws in a balanced social order. Collisions between rival interests are the lifeblood of a competitive society, it is said. Inherent in the clash and clamor of competition for land are outcomes beneficial to the community as a whole. Informed tinkering is all that is needed to elicit the underlying common good.

A critical analysis of land-policy development leads to more pessimistic conclusions. The purpose of this closing chapter will be to trace the larger theoretical and political implications of the struggle for land use control as the setting for work toward more progressive, democratic directions.

History, Structure, and Ideology

If one follows Herbert Marcuse's injunction to search history for "the factors that made the facts," it becomes clear that the development of American land policy has featured not only more disorder than the reform model assumes but also a specific social patterning that reflects, however awkwardly, the needs of property owners and entrepreneurs, not the needs of society as a whole. It is useful, in this light, to think of policy as working on two, interrelated levels. On the level of social structure, regulation can be seen as an evolving, historical response to dynamic contradictions within the capitalist property system. A main result is the increasing government control of private property and attempts to enlarge that control through measures such as the national land use bill. This control is typically justified on the second, ideological, level with the claim that policy deals with the efficient separation of incongruent uses and functions, not vested interests; it is a matter of technical "process," not substantive "rights," of inanimate objects, not people.

The social form of conflict and the apolitical form of ideology are structurally interconnected. Capitalism, after all, is a "social form of economy in which the relations among people are not regulated directly, but through things." [1] Strain and denial condition and reinforce each other, furnishing both the context and the rationale for political intervention in the property system. More than any other features of the land situation, these patterns establish the dynamics, limits, and alternatives of policy. Increasingly, however, the regulators find themselves in situations where their claims to be dealing with things fly in the face of popular understandings to the contrary. No matter how valiantly they tried, the proponents of centralization failed to persuade their adversaries that land-management issues could be separated from questions of property rights and political power. In this sense, the recent battles over land use control and centralized siting programs highlight a widening gap between the two levels of policy, a gap that needs to be explained both historically and politically.

Property's Inner World of Conflict

The long-simmering inner theme of land use conflict is the clash of exclusion and expansion forces unleashed by capitalist development. Exclusion and expansion, pressures structured directly into the makeup of capitalist property rights, form the dominant but double-sided claims of private property. They frame the capitalist social organization, supplying it with defensive strength and offensive momentum. Exclusion defines the social relations of the basic classes and channels investment through narrow routes: it keeps the rights of individual competitors at one remove from the society. Expansion is the prime motivator of entrepreneurial action and the leading edge of business's version of social progress. But exclusion and expansion are themselves incapable of self-government within the system of private competition for land. Unfettered expansion threatens the fixed interests of land and community; the immovable right of landed property cripples the circulation and growth of capital. By looking at the struggles of exclusion and expansion in land use, we can see how capitalism is really a system of private power in motion and at rest, all at once.

It has been left to capitalist governments to make sense of the economy's defiance of physical law, to keep rights moving while defending rights at rest. The problem of land use policy has been, in a nutshell, to rationalize the ir-rational. To do this, to keep rights moving, or to keep them from caving in on the rights of others, government not only tunnels into the very core of owner-ship, defining and preempting rights to exclude and expand, but also creates the relative invincibility of the private core in the very process of gouging it. Milton Friedman is on target, then, when he writes that property rights are "complex social creations."[2] He fails, however, to give due notice to the fact that the legal upkeep of property requires periodic invasions of those rights. In the wider field of capitalist law, land use policy is an especially dirty busi-ness. Seventeenth-century political theorist Thomas Hobbes stepped much closer to the uncomfortable truth when he observed that "the Propriety which a subject hath in his lands, consisteth in a right to exclude all other subjects from the use of them; and not to exclude their Soveraign, be it an Assembly, or a Monarch."[3]

In many ways, this book has been a study of the permeability of property to political power. It reveals the property owners' inability and even reluctance "to exclude the Soveraign." Capitalists want the state to intervene to clear the way for expansion, just as landowners desire such intervention when the law can protect them from expansion. The contradictory needs of property demand that government play a double role in land use policy: the collec-tive capitalist who accumulates land for investment must also be the collective landowner who locks private pantries against the land hunger of free enter-prise. Despite much private-sector ballyhoo about the dangers of big gov-ernment, neither capitalists nor landowners really act as if the public control of private property were a matter of unyielding principle. General Motors thought no less of the city of Detroit, when it gobbled up the property rights of the Poletowners, than the worker-owners thought of suburban Warren, when they used their town's power to keep out the developers of low-income housing for blacks.

Land use policy is a euphemism for the political control of contradictory private property rights, and it is an extremely powerful tool in the competitive struggle for power and wealth that is the essence of capitalist activity. Admittedly, wider interests *are* sometimes served by the political control of land use, fragile lands and resources are sometimes saved, and housing opportunities are sometimes opened. Important ties between local land use policies and the growth of democratic control of change do exist. But in the battle for the control of land use, general interests in the use of land have to tag along behind the more formidable interests and the more legitimate claims of the property owners and capitalists. Land use policy is property policy, as it must be where private property is the guiding institution of economic action.

To play its dual roles in the battles for land use control, government in the United States has needed much of what Marxist political theorists like to call "relative autonomy" from the contending interests. But this study also shows that this autonomy has been very relative indeed. Precisely to the extent that capitalists and landowners know how important political strength is to their cause, each struggles to control the state as a means of regulating the bias of intervention. Thus, the relative autonomy of capitalist government is everywhere challenged by economic pressures to instrumentalize government, to turn government into a tool of interests. The story of the development of land use policy can be read as a continuing struggle to diminish and enlarge the relative autonomy of government, to tighten and loosen connections between political institutions and the owners of land and capital.

Policy Change and Political Power

In the early nineteenth century, when entrepreneurs commenced their creative destruction of the land, courts took the lead in defining away many of property's traditional rights of self-protection. Judges slanted the common law heavily in favor of expansion, and the legal system itself narrowed the conflict to the individuals at odds. No wars were declared against landed property. Unfolding without much explicit organization or direction, the larger social rationality of legal change remained immanent. Wider implications for the general mass of landowners were kept discreetly concealed in the creeping process of legal change. Property rights were first taken, then transformed, as policy moved behind the backs of the landowners. Thus, in the formative years of the U.S. political economy, not only did land policy support the growth of juvenile capitalism, but the form of legal change itself paralleled what Jürgen Habermas calls "the unplanned nature-like movement of economic development" that is typical of early market society.[4]

Urban Resistance

But the historical circumstances of conflicts between land and capital did not remain static. Industrialization and urbanization compressed huge populations into small working spaces. Friction between and among classes and property owners increased, as did the awareness that something had to be done to limit the destructiveness of capital. This process was strengthened by major ideological and social changes in the nature of property and ownership. As single-family houses became available to ever greater numbers of more affluent workers, old and simple connections between property and production were complicated by new residential consumption interests in land and housing. For most people, property gradually lost its ideological affiliation with economic power over the means of production, only to resurface as an institution of home-based consumption. The ideological shifts in the understanding of property solidified the legitimacy of American capitalism, but they expanded the defensive exclusionary consciousness of property well beyond the neighborhoods of the new corporate rich and the old independent middle class. Worker-owners became pugnacious about their communities, too. The siege mentality took over at all income levels; land use conflict intensified.

In Gramsci's terms, capitalism spawned a cadre of organic intellectuals to help rearrange the increasingly strained relations of urban capitalism. Planners, architects, designers, and scientists, who took the system's class and property relations for granted, showed that keeping people and functions apart in space was a reasonable way to pacify the turmoil. They helped to educate both land and capitalist interests to their shared interests in more perfected means of collective exclusion. Working closely with the more traditional functionaries of law, the planners gave capitalism a new recipe for stability: zoning.

Zoning collectivized the landed right to exclude, just as big corporations in the early years of the twentieth century collectivized the exclusionary control of industrial property. Once again, legal change corresponded to the general movement of capital. But there was a big difference now: the concentration of corporate power was an oligarchical tendency; the collectivization of exclusion rights was a more democratic one.

Community zoning controls became vital mechanisms for the regulation of unwanted social and economic change. Through powers to veto industrial and governmental decisions on siting, worker-owners and the middle class possessed important leverage over managers of the society's leading institutions. In the absence of more direct pathways into the control of production, pathways barred as much by the consumerist ideology of the workers themselves as by the system's own force, land use controls represented some of the deepest inroads of the underlying population on the structuring of economic development. Next to the control of labor itself, it is hard to imagine what other channel provided as much power at points of strategic vulnerability in the corporate system as the fragmented control of land.

With all the limitations of narrow-mindedness, racism, and class prejudice duly weighed, it remains crucial to see that a step had been taken toward conscious, democratic regulation of capitalist economic change. The price was considerable for free enterprise, however. Capital faced new land barriers that were difficult to surmount. Scores of legal scholars complained about what Richard Babcock called "the litter" of local, exclusionary law.

The troubles of lawyers are not necessarily the troubles of society; but when they arise out of the internal debilities of property, and those debilities are themselves accentuated by larger changes in capitalist development, the lawyers' travails become clues to more important transformations. In the 1950s and 1960s, the legal critique of land use policy was catapulted from the law reviews to the Congress by just such a change: the massive restructuring of postwar urban industrial capitalism.

The Pressures to Centralize

The transformation of metropolitan capitalism gave structural force to the lawyers' complaints; it made the effort to change zoning all but inevitable. Accompanying the advanced mechanical order of petroleum and synthetic chemicals were the cool ideas and impersonal ideology of modern technocracy; older planning notions of "system integration," "regional efficiency," and "functional rationality" were lent new force and power. In this world of interconnected parts and smoothly working processes, premiums were placed on administrative arrangements and economic activities that linked people into the system. The country abounded with power lines and superhighways. Enormous capital investments were made to bring people and things together and under control. The consequent erosion of privacy has been widely noted. In Marcuse's words, overwhelming pressures built up "to prevent autonomy even in a small, reserved sphere of existence."[5]

Local control of land seemed to be one of the "small, reserved" spaces that had to go, for it exaggerated the power of tiny units in a system dominated by corporate and governmental mammoths. When asked to make way for the new restructuring, too many communities said no. By the mid-1960s, even the poor refused to move; urban renewal had to be abandoned, only to reappear a decade later in the private form of "gentrification." Legal arrangements were not well synchronized with accumulation.

A new generation of planners and lawyers revealed schemes to adjust the system. Centralization of land use control was promoted as the logical instrument of regional planning, the rational answer to widening gaps between the scale of production and the locus of land use power. It would ensure that communities could no longer exclude the absentee developers and land regulators who were restructuring metropolitan capitalism. For land reformers, the decisive question was well stated by Marion Clawson, former chief of the U.S. Bureau of Land Management. "How," Clawson wondered, "can public participation in . . . land management be made more efficient?"[6] However obliquely, Clawson's query made the appropriate connection: land use management was really people management, and efficiency implied the relative de-representation of the local interests in exclusion and expansion. This would increase government's regulatory freedom in controlling the endless conflicts over metropolitan restructuring.

The land use reformers saw all this as objectively necessary, apolitical, and nonpartisan, a reasonable and efficient step forward. The lawyers and reformers had no personal interests to defend, no axe to grind; as Gramsci suggests, they were external to the production system and thus saw themselves as neutral managers of the conflicts between capital and community. They did not debate the issues of exclusion and expansion; they suggested how the issues should be debated. They did not seek private control of land; they sought new systems of control. But just as they were external to the production system, they were without formal political power. Operating mainly in a detached world of think-tanks and law firms, they could not bring their ideas into action without coming to grips with the real world of capitalist politics.

Political Complexities

This study has suggested throughout that capitalist politics is a very complicated world indeed. As Fred Block has argued, there is great reason to doubt the existence of coherent political outlooks and long-term class consciousness within the higher circles of economic power.[7] For one thing, large companies do not necessarily leap to the support of intellectuals who seek to advance their long-term interests. Although elite executives may rest more or less comfortably with a big government that plans and regulates overall economic affairs—as Irving S. Shapiro, former chairman of DuPont said, "It's healthy to keep business and government at arm's length"[8]—the distance does little to enliven corporate capital's consciousness of its secular interests or its appetite to fight for them. Moreover, as the EMB case shows, even when the giants do gear up for political action, there is nothing automatic about their ability to call the shots of public policy.

By contrast, as all the cases discussed here suggest, the political power of big capital in the United States is matched in no small measure by the ability of small and medium-sized firms to influence and control locally and regionally elected officials. As practically all officials in the federal system are elected by subnational constituencies, including all members of the House and Senate, small capital is extremely well positioned to voice its opinion and see it carried into action.

For small businesses, what Marxists like to call the instrumental theory of the state—the tendency of government to become a tool of discrete capitalist interests[9]—is no theory at all: it is an indispensable strategy for economic survival. The direct conquest and control of officials and agencies at all levels is not a choice; it is a necessity if the more competitive firms are to control labor, capital, and land within a system dominated by economic and political giants. They must try to live out the theory of economic determinism because the most crude economic determinism is applied against them, in cyclical swings of the economy, by absentee controllers of credit and capital and in the demands of labor and consumers. As Poulantzas notes, the small capitalists, "being fiercely attached to their property," develop a strongly proprietary attitude toward government. Small business sees the state "as being by rights its state, and its rightful representative and political organizer." Edward Greer was surely correct, therefore, when he concluded his study of power in Gary, Indiana, with the observation that "political power in the United States is in large measure shared between competitive and monopoly capital." [10] If the community-based power of worker-owners and the middle class is added to the analysis, as this study suggests it must be, it becomes clear that the contradictions and complications of political power in the United States are indeed vast.

Such complications do little to enlarge the relative autonomy of capitalist government in America. Even the courts, the traditional forum of land use justice, are besieged by litigious communities and capitalists. Yet since the defeat of the national land use legislation, the U.S. Supreme Court, offered several opportunities to limit the exclusionary land powers of local government, has demurred each time, preferring the limited rough-and-tumble of the status quo to the roaring national outcry that would follow a serious legal crackdown on the suburbs.[11] Similarly, former stalwart backers of centralization, such as attorney Richard Babcock and Harvard law professor Charles Haar, have pretty much given up on the battle to open the suburbs. Babcock, tempered by the resistance to centralization, acknowledges that "reformers kid themselves if they believe that many of the problems plaguing the administration of land use controls can be solved by replacing a local official with a state or regional official." But in place of liberal technocracy he can only recommend a return to liberal politics, a "balancing of conflicting . . . interests and objectives" that sidesteps the very problems of bias, scale, and jurisdiction he so clearly identified in *The Zoning Game*. Haar, by contrast, sees new promise in the legal system, though not as an opener of suburban doors. In his most recent book, *The Wrong Side of the Tracks*, Haar eloquently calls for use of the old common-law principle of equal and adequate service to bring equality of public goods to separate and unequal neighborhoods. In his view, metropolitan social inequality may yet be compelled to yield to a greater measure of justice in the allocation of public wealth, but not by bringing people together. The basic class separations that mark American urban life—America's economic apartheid—will not soon be changed, not even by a court system several times removed from direct public control.[12]

The judiciary's reluctance to tackle the contradictions of exclusion and expansion should come as no shock. The restraint seems wise, for what one jurist called "the deep social antagonisms" aroused by land use conflict no longer seem easily converted into what another called "questions which arise at the margins of ownership." [13] The contradictions of organized power befuddle the legal system. Community protectionists, writes Sondra Berchin, have so effectively entrenched themselves in the development process that in many places individual landowners may no longer assume an automatic entitlement to use their property. For her, and for others as well, "land ownership has been redefined so that it no longer entails a constitutional right to develop." [14] But turn the pages of the law journals, and remarkably opposite conclusions may be found close by. Seeking larger lessons from the Poletown case, Peter Millspaugh wondered whether excluders had any rights at all when cities joined corporations in the hunt for space. His readers were left to wonder, "What now remains within the fabric of the law with which to curb the growing use of this intrusive power?" [15]

Readers have the right to be confused. Trains seem to be passing in the night; but the fact remains that they depart from the same station. In an extended review of the zoning issue several years ago, the *Harvard Law Review* made a crucial point in connection with an attempt to specify the real divisions of land use conflict. In its words, "the political clash at the core of private property" is over "simultaneously securing regulatory freedom to the state as well as safeguarding a regime of entitlement to property holders." [16] The contradictions between expansion and exclusion rights, compounded by the mutually organized forces of industrial capital and community protection, generate increasing pressures for "regulatory freedom," and also resistance to it.

The land use case thus illustrates one of the most pervasive and important themes in the theory of the capitalist state: the contradiction between rationalization and legitimation, between increasing system needs for control of private life and the defense of the private by highly organized interest groups from all classes. As Habermas writes, in the face of these contradictory imperatives, "the state vacillates between expected intervention and forced renunciation of intervention, between becoming independent of its clients in a way that threatens the system and subordinating itself to their particular interests." [17] A government relatively autonomous of the main property classes is essential to keep the class structure intact—as Ralph Miliband has written, the capitalist state "*must* have that high degree of autonomy and independence if it is to act as a class state"—but this function is crippled by the political organization of the affected interests and the extent of representative democracy: "What emerges as a result is always very battered." [18] Back and forth the state lurches, incapable of integrating the interests in conflict, incapable of abandoning them to private competition. Uncertainty becomes the hallmark of policy, and struggle the result of any effort to straighten things out. Paradoxically, pluralism leads toward the very instrumental relationships between the state and key interest groups which Marxists were once, not unfairly, accused of oversimplifying. Today, however, such tendencies are more correctly seen as a major strain on the state's capacity to manage the system.

Fighting for Time

The collision of interests and powers in land use politics adds up to much more than just another illustration of pluralist equilibrium: the result is decidedly not a political draw of balanced forces. Nothing in the defeats of individual projects or the resistance to centralization of control directly alters the fact that the capacity to define economic and technological directions remains in the hands of the few. But by the same token, the bitter opposition to centralized decisions and procedures means that the consequences of corporate and state power are increasingly repelled by average people; the quick and efficient spread of domineering institutions and processes is blocked; the functioning of the system is delayed and interrupted; capitalist and state autonomy are restricted. In struggling to protect their lives and neighborhoods, in creating dysfunctions, in refusing to submit, citizens give the system trouble. They also give themselves and society something else: the precious time to make different kinds of decisions about what ought to be done with resources and capital and to fight for new arrangements in which to make the decisions. In effect, their battles give democracy time. The point was effectively made by Karl Polanyi: "The rate of change," he wrote, "is often of no less importance than the direction of change itself." Whether people can adjust to changing conditions "without fatally damaging their substance, human and economic, physical and moral," ultimately depends on whether they can slow the process down and bend it to their will. While the degree to which humans can consciously regulate the forces of economic and technological change is an open question—and the experience with nuclear power must lessen our optimism— "it is the rate at which we allow change to occur," concludes Polanyi, "which may well depend on us." [19]

But establishment liberals and conservatives are impatient with democracy's demands for time. They want to speed the movement of capital, to quicken the forces of change. That is why they heap so much praise on the free market: capitalist markets depoliticize issues of change, confining the democratic powers of resistance behind thick walls of respect for the rights of private property and the supposed virtues of free competition. But the free land market never worked without political assistance and judicial support; sometimes subtly, at other times forcefully and unmistakably, the power of government has always been there, deeply involved with the capitalist development of land in America. As the Reagan administration rediscovers every time it probes for a hole in the ground to fill with nuclear waste or nuclear missiles, the real estate market is helpless to clear the land. Battles are inevitable with outraged homeowners, environmentalists, small business owners, peace advocates—all the local and regional forces desperate to preserve their communities against the dangers of imperial technology and absentee control. And there is no reason to believe that the fervor behind the protest will abate soon. As one Connecticut citizen explains, the opposition endures because it springs from venerable American traditions: "The concept of people being able to determine the use of their town's land—that's got to be the first consideration," for "part of the idea of the American Revolution was to give local people more say than people from outside the area." [20]

In the absence of judicial commitments to tackle the "deep social antagonisms" of land use controversy and in the presence of well-organized and well-represented land interests in Congress, state legislatures, and city halls, it is difficult, in the waning days of the Reagan administration, to believe that a return to "free markets" in land is imminent. More battles over increased administrative control of land use at higher levels of the state seem unavoidable. Although neither a national land use policy nor comprehensive state controls are in the offing, less explicit, functionally targeted forms of centralization are good bets. Frank J. Popper notes that "single-purpose or single area land-use legislation tends to arouse less opposition, to be easier to pass, and to result in more demanding environmental legislation than comprehensive state laws." [21] Much the same could be said for specifically targeted industry-siting laws, such as the various power-plant acts, and of pressures only now emerging to create centralized programs for hazardous-waste siting. As Sondra Berchin concludes, "Growing judicial and scholarly opinion supports the view that the state must be given broad power to control development." [22]

Moving On

This has not been an altogether reassuring summary of basic themes. But a serious inquiry into the politics of land use cannot fail to confront the issue of whether there can be a common good at all in a society where class-based exclusions are a basic feature of everyday life. This basic contradiction between general and particular interests is, finally, where reform fails. For social irresponsibility in land use is not a "problem" of the greed or short-sightedness of builders and landowners, but the very logic of capitalist development itself. The one-sidedness of exclusion and expansion interests represents the competitive system in action: owner versus owner, and all owners against the claims of society. Social alienation, the view of the other as the enemy at the gates, is built into the rivalrous logic of private advantage. It is not the external defect but the norm of the capitalist market system. Entrepreneurs and landowners alike adopt the role of cost-shifter, not because they are morally deficient, but because it is economically rational, indeed necessary, in the competitive marketplace. Both are in society for the value it brings to their property, but both are against society in struggling to shift the costs of production over the private wall into the fenceless commons. In the words of biologist Garrett Hardin, "Ruin is the destination toward which all men rush, each pursuing his own best interest in a society that believes in the freedom of the commons." [23]

The problems of land use—class exclusion in housing, local refusals to accept collective responsibilities for the siting of key facilities, overuse of unregulated land, and underuse of territory already geared to urban expansion—reflect the normal and predictable motivations of an exclusionary form of economic development, namely, capitalism itself. Reform can modify and deflect such tendencies, perhaps, but cannot replace them with socially responsible patterns. To make the private-property system of capitalism socially responsible is, as Robert S. Lynd once observed in a related context, "like trying to drive a car forward with the gears set in reverse." [24] Is society stuck, then, with an unbreakable contradiction? The answer is yes, of course, if the existing social relations of production and exclusion are maintained. But can nothing be done to change the existing patterns, at least somewhat, so that first steps can be taken toward a more humane form of economic change?

The radical's answer is that much can be done. As long as action is informed by an understanding of its limitations within the established context, an appreciation of the nature of the society we are dealing with, many things can be done to advance toward a more socially responsible form of development. The starting point is to recognize that exclusion and expansion are not natural forces, but the specific patterns through which a capitalist society organizes the social relations of development. Once this is understood, it becomes possible to imagine a future society in which growth and community protection need not be pitted against each other; where they could be integral elements of a community in control of its material as well as political destiny; where work, nature, and economic security are regarded as mutually reinforcing aspects of human existence. Here, expansion and exclusion would be stripped of their socially alien forms. Nothing would be left but basic human needs for material progress and security to be met through nonexploitative, nondestructive, nonexclusionary forms of cooperation and conflict.

This vision, it should be emphasized, is linked inextricably to the end of the capitalist class organization of production relations and their replacement by what Marx called a "classless society." Need it be said that this country is a very long way from believing in or fighting for the realization of such a vision? But that is not such a terribly crippling admission. For there are such things, even within the Marxist tradition, as "transitional demands," which can be used to bridge what Hal Draper calls "the gap between minimum demands (for immediate reforms) and maximum demands (involving the realization of socialism)." [25] Even within the present situation, policy and institutional changes can be made—some quite familiar, others less so—to enlarge the scope of democratic action and gradually broaden the possibilities for more thoroughgoing changes in social structure and ideology. Seemingly small moves can have big consequences, especially if they are consciously related to larger programs and visions. It is precisely the task of political leaders—community organizers, labor activists, party politicians, journalists, intellectuals—to blend carefully and sensitively an understanding of what should be done here and now with a keen appreciation for what people in the society may want at a given historical moment, and both of these together with a concept of a more humane, unalienated social order.

The middle element in the equation—public opinion—is crucial. It stands between the activist's immediate policy goals and his or her political vision. It keeps the activist conservative when the penchant is to be more radical. Sometimes this works in reverse. But in either case, conservatism can have a progressive role: the very frustration it arouses should inspire challenges and debate between the leader and the led. That educators should themselves be educated was one of Marx's most important lessons; that it was never meant to preclude the educators' responsibility to shed theoretical light on immediate circumstances is equally worth remembering.

Land Use and Economic Democracy

In this spirit, we can return to the theme of liberal reform and see what might be extracted from it as a basis for more democratic options. A good way to begin is to stress that the trouble with land use reform is not its tendency to increase the social control of land use. This tendency is inevitable in complex industrial orders, regardless of their property system. Indeed, social control of land is a condition of ownership in all settings, from the simplest societies to the most advanced. The issue is not whether society will regulate use, but what interests and values are served by it and the extent to which ordinary people have access both to the controls and to the land. In this light, we can see that the problem with liberal centralization is that it promises less popular access to the controls without more equal access to the land. It accelerates centralization while suppressing one of the few means of effective community protection.

The liberal land use reform model assumed that decisions of major economic and technological consequence are best decided by corporate and state experts. Average citizens, to the extent they have any role at all, should enter the decision stream only when the big projects need sites. In a real sense, then, a critical look at the liberal reform model shows how the administrative system of the modern capitalist state organizes the rules of capitalist expansion and exclusion into its own operations, into its own regular way of doing things. The central government attempts to manage the populace by incorporating the assumptions of private exclusionism into the processes of public review. As Poulantzas writes, "It is within the capitalist State that the organic relationship between intellectual labour and political domination, knowledge and power, is realized in the most consummate manner." And central to this relationship, as he adds, is the "permanent exclusion" of the majority of citizens from the knowledge and decisions that shape their industrial future.[26] Alienated from the procedures of decision, trapped by ignorance of mysterious technologies, communities exact their due—they refuse the projects whose presence they did not request; they exclude the excluders.

But the issues may be defined very differently. The liberal understanding that development is a legitimately social matter can be joined with the progressive, democratic idea that the form and the content of economic development are also too important to leave to private controllers. In other words, the social control of land can be coupled with democratic control of investment to produce a genuinely inclusionary form of development. In this approach, liberal land use reform would be modified in two fundamental ways. First, authority to plan the economic and social future of communities would not be organized from the top down, as in the National Land Use Policy and EMB models. Rather, it would be organized from the bottom up, with local citizens and their representatives making the key decisions about economic directions. Second, community planning would be established in the context of national economic and environmental policies that stress security as the basis of economic growth. National programs would aim at establishing a protective framework within which citizens could work to shape the substance of their local economies without abusing their land and without fear of sudden economic or social dislocation. Community production and consumption would be consciously joined and harmonized.

The key assumptions of this model are that increased democratic control of the economy will bring greater economic, social, and ecological protection and that these forms of security are essential if exclusion is gradually to be replaced by more socially responsible attitudes toward others. Here, economic, social, and environmental security are seen, not as distinctly different needs or separate issues, as in the conventional wisdom, but as different aspects of the same yearning for protection that is one of the primary values of organized social living. The interests of workers in protecting their jobs, of homeowners in securing their neighborhood, and of environmentalists in the guardianship of nature are essentially alike in their mutual opposition to the logic of "creative destruction."

These now often-warring groups should begin to see job, home, and nature as coordinate elements of the land and the community they all really share.

Protection of the community could thus become what it deserves to be: the organizing theme for a movement of trade unions, minorities, the unemployed, neighborhood associations, and ecologists in pursuit of democratic development. With this movement, the national Democratic party might be pushed by its hundreds of local and state organizations to sponsor a National Community Security Act to further the legitimate protection interests of the unemployed, workers, homeowners, taxpayers, and nature itself.

Five recommendations are made here for inclusion in such a measure. These by no means represent an exhaustive program. Their collective point is mainly ideological, to expose some of the issues that may be used to move beyond the exclusionary patterns that currently bar democratic community growth. If they merely clarify the importance of the exclusion issue to the cause of economic and ecological democracy, they will have more than served their purpose. The five steps include efforts to

- achieve full employment
- control oligopoly prices
- value housing for use
- control corporate mobility
- establish integrated community planning and investment controls

Full Employment and Price Controls

At least two familiar elements would have to be present to make the inclusionary economy feasible. First, national policy must embrace full employment as its top economic priority. All citizens who want a job at decent wages should have ready access to one. Otherwise, the population of surplus people, what Marx termed "the reserve army of the unemployed," will continue to mount outside the main gates of society and be stigmatized by their dependence as unfit neighbors. Sustained full employment is the primary condition for attacking waste in human lives.

Second, in order to protect against inflationary tendencies resulting from a vigorous full-employment program, the prices and profits of oligopoly-sector corporations must be controlled by the federal government. Because the large companies have such disproportionate leverage in the economy, an incomes policy aimed at their pricing decisions can have great impact on overall cost levels without saddling federal regulators with the impossible job of scrutinizing every price tag. This policy would do much to rid the society of the ruinous uncertainty of inflation. Full employment and incomes policy are hardly novel proposals. Though still stridently opposed by free-marketeers, such proposals have been supported by many liberals, off and on since the early days of the New Deal, who have recognized these policies as essential components of a balanced national economy. The last three elements of our program, however, are less familiar.

Housing

Housing is the third plank in our program. In the politics of exclusion, housing interests are central. The politics of land spins around housing issues, especially concerns for economic security and social standing. Locational privileges, heavily protected by land use controls, have been relied on to boost prestige, inflate real estate values, increase speculation, and drive up the price of housing for middle- and low-income workers. In short, the placement of housing in the real estate market has strengthened tremendously those factors tending to divide groups against one another while encouraging faith in the "magic of the marketplace" to create something from nothing.[27]

A National Community Security Act should seek to guard housing opportunities by insisting that housing is a fundamental necessity, much too precious to be treated as a speculative commodity.[28] Housing should be valued for its use as shelter, not for its speculative exchange value. As a starter, Congress could require that the price of houses built or purchased with the aid of federal assistance—either directly or through the help of federal tax benefits—must be controlled.[29] Prices might, for instance, be indexed to the average rate of economic growth during the period of ownership, plus the value of whatever capital improvements might have been added by the owner. Sellers would keep the sum of the original purchase price plus the growth increment. But any surplus would have to be invested in development trust funds controlled by local community-planning entities, who would determine interest rates on the surplus accounts.[30]

Such a strategy would have several benefits. It would diminish the speculative drive in housing and real estate and replace it with a measure of economic security and predictability pegged to the real economic progress of the society. And because locational advantages would have much less relevance to long-term housing values, the price of new housing would probably diminish, too. An important economic cause for exclusion would thus be eliminated. In essence, exclusionary patterns in the housing market could no longer be directly translated into exchange values. Property taxes would, of course, also be much lower; indeed, they too would effectively be linked to the rate of real economic growth. The potential for equalizing access to community services such as education, and to the so-called amenities, such as a healthy environment, would also be enhanced, as neighborhoods would tend to be less divided along income lines. Changing housing from a commodity into a use-value might diminish middle-class environmental activism somewhat but might also increase it among poorer workers.

Controlling Corporate Mobility

The placement of price controls on the housing market is critical to the enhancement of the economic security of families and to the reduction of the exclusionary forces in community politics. But unless efforts are made to strengthen the economic independence of the communities in which individuals live, the rapid movement of capital may well undermine the ability of many American towns to survive. To answer this need, many in the labor movement have urged Congress and state legislatures to pass plant-shutdown legislation. Most such bills include provisions requiring advance notification of company plans to abandon local operations, and some require enterprises to provide greater or lesser amounts of severance pay to help workers adjust to the shock of lost jobs and wages, as well as community-assistance funds to help the locality over the hump of fiscal strain due to vanishing tax payments.[31]

Such proposals deserve support. But they are weakened by their essentially reactive response to the issue of corporate flight. The time to establish the responsibility of a private firm to a community is not when the firm is about to make a hasty exit, but when its operations are fresh and full of the potential for profits. Until now most communities have fought against one another for new business. Numerous privileges are granted to corporations as the price for their agreement to move in. Typically, this assistance is seen as public benevolence, a gratuity with no strings attached—which it does not have to be.

A major goal of a Community Security Act must be stabilization of the relationships between local government and the community's major private employers. To combat capital flight and help protect communities against their environments being held hostage to threats of corporate abandonment, cities must strive for economic equality with business. They must be empowered to exact enforceable commitments from companies to remain in the community for a designated period. In effect, the kind of contractual relationship that exists between professional sports teams and municipalities should be extended to urban relations with business in general—with several notable additions.

First, any firm that violates its contract by leaving or shutting down a substantial portion of its operations early, should be liable for the losses its abandonment would cause the locality, plus—and this is very important—triple damages for violating the public trust. In addition—and this is equally important—on termination of the contract the company should be obligated to repay the community the value of all public grants made to benefit its operations, tax abatements, any specially provided public utilities, land, and so forth. With renewal of the contract, such obligations would be "rolled over" to the end of the next contract period. Finally, any firm that failed to meet its payments to the local government would have this amount credited against a city take-over under eminent domain proceedings.[32] The city would then be free to run the plant or to sell off its assets, with the proceeds going to a local community-development corporation as investment capital for new enterprises. Corporate responsibility for the privilege of using the public space and facilities would now be a legal obligation. Community rights would gain enhanced legal standing. To institutionalize this approach, Congress should prohibit distribution of federal development assistance to any local government that conferred public subsidies on private firms without first establishing the legal obligation of companies to their hometowns.

Obviously, all this depends on action at the national level. Corporate manipulation of local government cannot be restricted without action by the central government. Washington must support local political power against private economic power, for in the present world of divide and conquer, municipalities are heavily disadvantaged from the start. Without this enforced equality, localities will remain under tremendous pressure to meet the prevailing terms of business—in Aaron Wildavsky's words, to "choose to be richer with fewer environmental amenities or poorer with a more pleasant environment." [33]

But what is to prevent corporations from abandoning the United States itself? Capitalism is a world system, and corporations can park their plants anywhere on the global lot. George Gilder is undoubtedly right when he warns that "all governments, regardless of political ideology, are necessarily caught up in a global rivalry" for business locations. [34] But Congress could apply the logic of corporate municipal responsibility to the corporations' national responsibility. In other words, companies that could be shown to have left U.S. cities and towns in order to avoid the terms of public accountability could be prohibited from selling their wares in U.S. markets.

Given the tremendous losses this would entail for even the biggest firms, it is unlikely that many would risk the penalty of exclusion. A lesser but still unpleasant sanction might be prohibition from federal, state, or local government contracts. These steps would not, of course, reverse the fundamental logic of capital mobility, but at least they would illuminate the fact that, given the present workings of the system, industrial patriotism is halfhearted, fleeting, and not at all to be taken for granted. By taking the logic of exclusion to its outermost limits, such steps can make industrial patriotism an embarrassing and perhaps provocative and illuminating issue.

Democratic Investment

The containment of capital mobility is crucial to the strengthening of community economies. But unless localities begin to exercise direct influence over the substance of investment itself, they will continue to find themselves hamstrung by the need to react to surprise proposals of corporations and state development agencies. Indeed, perhaps the greatest single force working to intensify land use conflict today, apart from economic insecurities surrounding the decline of real estate values, is the fact that most citizens enter the debate over economic change long after the key decisions have been made by absentee planners. Workers, homeowners, and ecologists have practically no voice in the formation of industrial alternatives. Land use democracy thus becomes every neighborhood's last stand to save its preferred vision of the future. Barry Casper and Paul David Wellstone offer an excellent capsule description of the standard procedure for introducing new projects in a community:

> Planners, looking ahead, conceive projects that promote institutionalized objectives. Experts are hired to decide on the technical details and to write the required reports. Monies, public and/or private, are acquired from sympathetic sources. Only then does word reach beyond the tight circle of planners and benefactors.[35]

Communities are then implored to either accept the installation or produce an alternative. As one federal manager asked the New Hampshire opponents of a national nuclear waste dump in their backyard, "What do *you* propose to do with the existing waste?" (emphasis added). Although local residents were not consulted about the big question of whether the society should adopt nuclear technology in the first place, they were dutifully expected to educate the experts about how to cope with its terrifying consequences. "It is one measure of the absurdity of our situation here," responded one activist, "that ordinary citizens have been put in the position of coming up with answers to that question." [36] In fact, the absurdity stems from the rationality of the established procedures of investment. It is the irrationality of the rational. Systematically excluded from the original production and investment decisions, citizens and landowners are randomly included in the locational decisions only because their land must be conscripted for industrial purposes. Local people enter the process as extraneous and dependent variables; economic and technological expansion, by contrast, looms as an independent force, whose rationality needs no rationale.

Plainly, the root of the problem is the fact that most citizens are not in a social position to regulate the major economic and technological decisions that affect their lives. To make the politics of land use responsible and democratic, this position must be changed. As Joshua Cohen and Joel Rogers argue, the most direct lever over the future is the control of industrial investment itself. Indeed, "investment is effectively the only guarantee of a society's future." Without open, democratic discussion of capital investment patterns, the public is stuck in a reactionary rut. Its planning remains "fundamentally constrained and incomplete," its claim to "home rule" an empty slogan.[37]

With community planning and control of investment, especially the increasing use of community enterprises, the on-the-job experience of local workers can be coupled with that of engineers and ecologists in the public service, to fashion issues of industrial and technological change with a view to their impact on real communities, not the abstract space of the real estate market. The shaping of technology can thus be restored to what David Noble calls "its actual site and social context," the everyday life of workers and citizens, their needs, capabilities, and aspirations.[38]

Under these circumstances, land use control need no longer be a separate social function. Questions of land use and location could be part of larger debates over the form and content of industry and technology, not last-minute issues raised after all the key planning matters have been decided. Inclusionary planning would not permit millions to be spent on lethal boondoggles, such as the MX missile or nuclear power, unless the land use and locational issues were worked out—one way or the other—within the debate over the feasibility and desirability of the project to the various public constituencies. Thus public concerns, including environmental and safety issues, would be directly integrated into considerations of industrial and technological design, architecture, and siting. These would be discussed and examined in the planning process, not afterward when expansionist commitments have hardened and local resistance has been stiffened by the element of surprise. Battles would be fought where they really count, at the drawing-board stage, rather than at the community walls where the options are invariably reduced to yes or no. The inclusionary economy, in short, would be part of the society it served, not an engine out in front, blind to the wreckage it leaves behind.

Many proposals have recently been published by American progressives describing, often in great detail, how steps might be taken toward community economic planning. Writers such as Samuel Bowles, David Gordon, and Thomas Weisskopf, Barry Bluestone and Bennett Harrison, Derek Shearer, Gar Alperovitz, Maurice Zeitlin, and others have laid out schemes and blueprints for democratic control of investment.[39] Most involve the establishment of new public-investment funds, through control of savings and insurance institutions and union pensions, and increased oversight of private investment decisions as a condition of production. Bowles and his colleagues urge local governments to "establish democratically elected community investment boards to determine investments from personal savings and insurance reserves." And Maurice Zeitlin suggests that the creation of a system of public-investment reserves at the state level, based largely on control of pension funds, could have sufficient capital "to influence the industrial location strategies and investment policies of private capital by allocating funds regionally."[40]

A National Community Security Act could facilitate progress along these lines in several ways. Grants-in-aid should be made available to cities interested in establishing industrial-planning entities. Regional Academies of Technology (RATs) should be established in connection with the great public universities, with free tuition for students agreeing to commit themselves to public service. The RATs could help structure community and regional technological issues for public debate and provide the essential technical base for challenges to the private experts, as well as provide the research and experimentation necessary for new, regionally oriented technologies. They could be financed, at least in part, through corporate patent fees; these might be pegged to a progressive scale, with the largest firms paying substantially higher rates for the public protection than small firms or individual inventors. Their essential point, however, would be to provide communities with the knowledge necessary for the development of an independent, public-centered technology.

Facing Up to Exclusion

This survey of possibilities cannot be concluded without one last encounter with the exclusion issue. Any serious appeal for unity among workers of all colors, homeowners, and environmentalists must face the present realities of social division. Would these divisions not get in the way of a movement for the kind of changes necessary to bring about inclusionary development? What has the Left had to say about the relationships between property rights, exclusion, and the promise of social change?

The short answer is "not enough." It is not surprising, perhaps, that most of the community-planning literature has been mute about the negative relationship between private property, exclusion, and democratic control. Frank Popper's conclusion about the liberal land-use reformers might well apply to many radical arguments today, including the ones advanced above: they do not face up to the idea of how different, even alien, their approaches are from those that most Americans would prefer.

In fact, much of the localist planning literature does tend to work with an abstract and romantic image of the American community. As the land use case all too clearly illustrates, and as most radicals themselves understand, this institution is ripe with class and racial tensions. Still, as Mike Cooley notes, "Seldom does it seem to be admitted that within a community there will be conflicting class and cultural interests."[41] Similarly, there are strong tendencies to overlook the organizational and social irrationalities of local government structures: when radicals discuss "community," do they mean Scarsdale as well as New York City? And what is to be done with the thousands of independent agencies and boards, such as the Edwards Underground Water District discussed in the San Antonio case, which have such great influence over resource and education politics? What are the boundaries of "community," and what constituencies will have authority to decide these issues? Will the states continue to hold the dominant legal power over community structure? Or should "communities" have the right to go their own way? The Left needs to develop its own theory of intergovernmental relations if it is to advance the cause of community planning, as well as a legal theory of community protection. And these need to be couched in much more explicit class terms.[42]

Many on the progressive Left seem so intent on drawing popular support that they tend to overlook some of the less benign realities of American community life. Rooting their analysis in populism, rather than in an explicit critique of capitalism, they end up evading the issues of class and race division in the United States. In this sense, the focus on community planning is crucial but insufficient, for it fails to confront the fact that the issue of exclusionary development is bigger and deeper than the corporation's centralized economic power. Exclusion arises from the capitalist system in which the corporation is embedded and according to whose logic it behaves. Here is to be found the locus of the privately controlled dynamics of expansion and exclusion—the driving forces behind the endless resistance to needs greater than those encompassed by the local zoning map.

Unless radicals openly challenge workers of different strata to see through the paradoxes of capitalist property itself, people will continue to behave as though they were separate from an alien society, using the defense of individual property rights to keep society out. Labor historian David Montgomery makes the point unmistakably clear: "No style of struggle and no militant 'fight-back' will lead out of the crisis of capitalism unless it evokes widespread popular debate about the basic nature of our society and what sort of life we wish to create."[43] Ideological issues, in short, must frame the effort to build a different, inclusionary social order.

Thus within the context of short-range policy recommendations, options should be carefully weighed from the perspective of their power to shed light on exclusionary patterns that need to be changed within the working class as well as in corporate capitalism itself. The point deserves heavy emphasis. Trade unions and American workers more generally should support limitations on corporate power. Community-based actions can and should be used to expose what Bluestone and Harrison call the "fundamental struggle between capital and community."[44] But at the same time, workers should be urged to debate the exclusionary values within their communities that are derived from the same system that gives the corporation its huge power.

The end result of this logic can be a shift away from the simplistic definition of property as a "sole and despotic dominion" over the land. As this study has suggested throughout, such a change is happening now, though under capitalist auspices that threaten citizens with loss of one of the few powers they command to protect their community. Looking ahead, we can see that the most reasonable future for secure possession is community ownership, with long-term leaseholds held by families, associations, and enterprises. Long leases can provide fences and walls for privacy, but in a context that recognizes the overlapping claims of the community and the future to the earth. Under their legal protection, and with the combined power of social control over investment, citizens can feel genuinely secure in their homes and possessions. Private life can be nurtured without fear of the sudden disruption of periodic "bad times."

With the drives toward decommodification of land and housing, and the increasing public role in investment planning, the social relations of exclusion can have room to change. The category of "outsider" can gradually become alien to a society ever more committed to patterns of inclusionary development. Greater understanding of social interdependence will help to overcome the irrational belief that we can simply heap unwanted troubles and unwanted people behind distant fences. We may learn finally that there really is no such thing as waste, for the products of an inclusionary economy will no longer be distinguished into "goods" and "bads." The entire output of the production system will be recognized as the product of human action, the result of a social process in which all communities participate and for which they share a common responsibility.

Similarly, increasing knowledge of environmental-industrial interactions could turn resource recycling into a major facet of industrial design. The impressive spread of energy co-generation, for example, signals greater possibilities for other areas of renewal and recovery. As the population comes to exercise greater control of the production system, and as technological understanding is enhanced and made available to the public at large, many of the most serious and hazardous of today's "waste" and "pollution" issues can be bypassed, or at least substantially modified by alternative productive processes and decisions to produce less-toxic substances.

There will always be communities that find themselves confronted with difficult locational choices. Battles will still be fought to resist something deemed dangerous or undesirable.[45] But individuals will know that they or their representatives have joined in the formation of economic alternatives and that locational implications have been factored into planning equations, thus eliminating the sense of powerlessness that so often accompanies economic change today. Hard decisions will still have to be made and coercion applied; and not every citizen, neighborhood, or community will be pleased at the outcome of every battle. Nor will the social good always prevail. But the fights will no longer have to be the last stands of communities struggling against unrepresentative decisions made elsewhere. The battles will be fought at earlier stages in the development of technology and industry, when community members can place their stamp on the very design of facilities and functions. Inclusionary development can erode the social basis of exclusion as we know it. The defensive compulsion to shout "Keep out!" can then be replaced by the less alien, though still dutifully skeptical, "Let's see."

Notes

Introduction

1. *New York Times,* 18 December 1982; Felix Rohatyn, "The Coming Emergency and What Can Be Done About It," *New York Review of Books* 4 (December 1980): 24, 26; George Gilder, *Wealth and Poverty* (New York: Bantam, 1981), p. 279; Robert B. Reich, *The Next American Frontier* (New York: Times Books, 1983), p. 279. Such views are not the monopoly of eastern voices. In a recent look at Seattle, the *New York Times* economics editor, Leonard Silk, quotes James R. Ellis—"regarded . . . as the informal chairman of the Seattle establishment"—as observing that "we have seen a drift from general to special interests—to groups who take blocking actions and are not progressive." Local elites were especially frustrated by successful efforts to block the Westlake Mall (*New York Times,* 22 April 1983). For a look at another community's struggle against a mall—this time unsuccessful—see chapter 4 for a case study of land use San Antonio style.

2. Peter Bachrach and Morton Baratz, *Power and Poverty: Theory and Practice* (New York: Oxford University Press, 1970), p. 11.

3. Some readers, intimidated by the very mention of "method," may wish to skip this section and proceed directly to the next. This can be done without sacrificing an understanding of the main analysis. What I have to say concerning method, however, should not overwhelm general readers and may in fact help them to evaluate the work as a whole.

4. Robert H. Nelson, *Zoning and Private Property Rights: An Analysis of the American System of Land-Use Regulation* (Cambridge: MIT Press, 1980). More typical of the field are Richard F. Babcock, *The Zoning Game: Municipal Practices and Policies* (Madison: University of Wisconsin Press, 1966); Boyd Gibbons, *Wye Island: The True Story of an American Community's Struggle to Preserve Its Way of Life* (New

York: Penguin, 1979); and Frank J. Popper, *The Politics of Land-Use Reform* (Madison: University of Wisconsin Press, 1981). Robert C. Ellickson, "Suburban Growth Controls: An Economic and Legal Analysis," *Yale Law Journal* 86 (January 1977): 385–511, is a good introduction to the market approach to land use conflict.

5. E. E. Schattschneider, *The Semisovereign People: A Realist's View of Democracy in America* (New York: Holt, Rinehart & Winston, 1960); Bachrach and Baratz, *Power and Poverty.*

6. Robert S. Lynd, "Power in American Society as Resource and Problem," in *Problems of Power in American Democracy,* ed. Arthur Kornhauser (Detroit: Wayne State University Press, 1957), p. 22; Schattschneider, *Semisovereign People,* p. 71.

7. Bachrach and Baratz, *Power and Poverty,* chap. 3.

8. John Dewey, *The Public and Its Problems* (Chicago: Holt, 1927), p. 31.

9. Sidney Plotkin, "Keep Out: Land Use Controls and Political Conflict in American Development," Ph.D. dissertation, City University of New York, 1978.

10. Lynd, "Power in American Society," pp. 3, 23–28.

11. John Holloway and Sol Picciotto, eds., *State and Capital: A Marxist Debate* (London: Edward Arnold, 1978); Nicos Poulantzas, *State, Power, Socialism,* trans. Patrick Camiller (London: Verso / New Left Books, 1980); Thorstein Veblen, *The Theory of the Leisure Class* (New York: New American Library, 1953).

12. See, for example, Holloway and Picciotto, *State and Capital;* and Poulantzas, *State, Power, Socialism.* For an unusually literate exception to this rule, see Ralph Miliband, *Marxism and Politics* (New York: Oxford University Press, 1977).

13. Kenneth M. Dolbeare, *Democracy at Risk: The Politics of Economic Renewal* (Chatham, N.J.: Chatham House, 1984), p. 141.

14. C. Wright Mills, *The Sociological Imagination* (New York: Oxford University Press, 1959), chap. 8.

15. K. William Kapp, *The Social Costs of Private Enterprise* (New York: Schocken, 1971), p. 16.

16. "In the Suburbs, Backyard Politics Comes Naturally," *New York Times,* 10 June 1984, p. E6.

17. Kent A. Price, "Introduction and Overview," in *Regional Conflict and National Policy,* ed. Kent A. Price (Baltimore: Resources for the Future, 1982), p. 15.

18. Robert B. Reich, "Industrial Evolution," *Democracy* 3 (Summer 1983): 17. See also Ira C. Magaziner and Robert B. Reich, *Minding America's Business: The Decline and Rise of the American Economy* (New York: Random House, 1983), p. 362; Pat Choate and Susan Walter, *America in Ruins: The Decaying Infrastructure* (Durham, N.C.: Duke University Press, 1981), pp. 51–55.

19. Samuel Bowles and Herbert Gintis, *Democracy and Capitalism: Property, Community, and the Contradictions of Modern Social Thought* (New York: Basic Books, 1986), p. 29.

20. Herbert Marcuse, *One-Dimensional Man: Studies in the Ideology of Advanced Industrial Society* (Boston: Beacon, 1964), pp. 99–100.

21. Bowles and Gintis, *Democracy and Capitalism,* p. 64.

22. In Marx's words, "The essential condition for the existence and sway of the bourgeois class is the formation and augmentation of capital; the condition for capital is wage-labor" (Karl Marx and Friedrich Engels, *The Communist Manifesto* [New York: International Publishers, 1948], p. 21).

23. Claus Offe provides a good working definition of Marx's notion of contradiction: "A *contradiction* is the tendency inherent to a specific mode of production to destroy those very preconditions on which its survival depends" ("Introduction to Part III," in *Stress and Contradiction in Modern Capitalism*, ed. Leon N. Lindberg et al. [Lexington, Mass.: D. C. Heath, 1974], p. 246).

24. Karl Marx, "The Eighteenth Brumaire of Louis Bonaparte," in *The Marx-Engels Reader*, ed. Robert Tucker (New York: W. W. Norton, 1972), p. 519.

25. C. Wright Mills, *The Power Elite* (New York: Oxford University Press, 1956), p. 24.

26. Sheldon Wolin, "Editorial," *Democracy* 3 (Summer 1983): 3. For general theoretical statements of this view, see Lynd, "Power in American Society"; Michael Parenti, *Power and the Powerless* (New York: St. Martin's, 1978), pp. 12–13; John Westergaard and Henrietta Resler, *Class in a Capitalist Society: A Study of Contemporary Britain* (New York: Basic Books, 1975).

27. Marx and Engels, *Communist Manifesto*, p. 12. Also see James O'Connor, *The Fiscal Crisis of the State* (New York: St. Martin's, 1973).

28. Alan Wolfe, "The Rise of Logo America," *The Nation*, 26 May 1984, p. 642. Kapp, *Social Costs of Private Enterprise*, pp. 16–17; Karl Polanyi, *The Great Transformation* (Boston: Beacon, 1971).

29. John Friedmann, "Life Space and Economic Space: Contradictions in Regional Development," manuscript (University of California at Los Angeles, 1981), cited in Barry Bluestone and Bennett Harrison, *The Deindustrialization of America: Plant Closings, Community Abandonment, and the Dismantling of Basic Industry* (New York: Basic Books, 1982), p. 20.

30. Poulantzas, *State, Power, Socialism*, p. 191.

31. Excellent reviews of the contemporary Marxist theories of the state include Martin Carnoy, *The State and Political Theory* (Princeton, N.J.: Princeton University Press, 1984); and Bob Jessop, *The Capitalist State: Marxist Theories and Methods* (New York: New York University Press, 1982). See also Poulantzas, *State, Power, Socialism;* Nicos Poulantzas, *Political Power and Social Classes*, trans. and ed. Timothy O'Hagan (London: Verso / New Left Books, 1978); Miliband, *Marxism and Politics;* and Jürgen Habermas, *Legitimation Crisis*, trans. Thomas McCarthy (Boston: Beacon, 1975).

32. Alan Wolfe, *The Limits of Legitimacy: Political Contradictions of Contemporary Capitalism* (New York: Free Press, 1977), p. 259. For an exhaustive summary and analysis of Marx's own extremely complex and often rich views of politics, see Hal Draper, *Karl Marx's Theory of Revolution*, 2 vols. (New York: Monthly Review Press, 1978).

33. San Antonio's population grew 20 percent between 1970 and 1980, making it the twenty-fifth fastest growing city in the country. The metropolitan area grew at a similar rate, ranking twenty-ninth on the list of fast-growing American metropolises. However, it should also be noted that when examined as a metropolitan area, or what the U.S. Census Bureau calls a Standard Metropolitan Statistical Area (SMSA), San Antonio ranks thirty-fifth in population, with 1,071,000 inhabitants; the city proper numbers 785,000 people (John Tepper Marlin and James S. Avery, with Stephen T. Collins, *The Book of American City Rankings* [New York: Facts on File Publications, 1983], pp. 34–37).

34. Leonard Goodall, ed., *Urban Politics in the Southwest* (Tempe: Arizona State University Press, 1967), p. 159, cited in John H. Mollenkopf, *The Contested City* (Princeton, N.J.: Princeton University Press, 1983), p. 247. The observation about the paucity of political conflict in Sunbelt cities is Mollenkopf's (p. 242).

35. "Fast-Growing Suburbs Act to Limit Development," *New York Times*, 2 December 1985; "Florida, Battling History, Tries to Rein in Growth," *New York Times*, 15 July 1986.

Part One

Chapter 1

1. Robert Frost, "Mending Wall," in *The Pocket Book of Robert Frost's Poems* (New York: Pocket Books, 1956), pp. 94–95.

2. D. H. Lawrence, *Studies in Classic American Literature* (New York: Viking, 1964), p. 3. Ironically, Lawrence's opening chapter is entitled "The Spirit of Place." Sheldon Wolin offers a similar view, although he adds: "To be an American is not merely to flee, but to flee optimistically" ("Carter and the New Constitution," *New York Review of Books*, 1 June 1978, p. 18).

3. As Wilson Carey McWilliams notes, early American sensibilities about place were contradictory. Although colonists longed to run and build a vast nation, their affections were nourished "within the boundaries of locality." Their intense localism bred a respect for walls protective of regional interests and outlooks. But their desires for expansion implied restlessness with fences and stirrings of "diffuse national sentiments of fraternity" (*The Idea of Fraternity in America* [Berkeley and Los Angeles: University of California Press, 1973], pp. 200, 222). For a very different view of this paradox, one stressing the difficulties of reconciling empire and republicanism, see William Appleton Williams, "Is the Idea and Reality of America Possible Without Empire?" *The Nation*, 2–9 August 1980, pp. 99–119.

4. Henry Nash Smith, *Virgin Land: The American West as Symbol and Myth* (New York: Random House, 1950); Frederick Jackson Turner, "The Significance of the Frontier in American History," in *The Frontier in American History* (New York: Holt, Rinehart & Winston, 1962), p. 1. For the mobility thesis, see George W. Pierson, "The M-Factor in American History," *American Quarterly* 14 (Summer 1962): 275–289; Everett S. Lee, "The Turner Thesis Re-Examined," *American Quarterly* 13 (Spring 1961): 77–87; Alexis de Tocqueville, *Democracy in America*, ed. Philips Bradley (New York: Random House, 1945), 2:109. A rarely heard stanza of Guthrie's tune celebrates an encounter with a "no trespassing" sign:

> But on the other side
> It didn't say nothin'
> That side was made for
> You and me.

(Woody Guthrie, "This Land Is Your Land" [New York: TRO, Ludlow Music, 1970])

5. "The Unwelcome Mat Is Out For Ideological Undesirables," *New York Times*, 15 July 1984; "Homosexual, a U.S. Resident 19 Years, Faces Deportation," *New York Times*, 3 June 1984; "33 Haitians Drown as Boat Capsizes off Florida," *New York Times*, 27 October 1981. Others recently denied visas to speak in the United States

have included Hortensia Allende Gossens, widow of Chilean president Salvador Allende Gossens; Nino Paste, a retired Italian general who opposes the spread of U.S. missiles in Western Europe; and three hundred Japanese citizens who planned to participate in a 1982 U.N. disarmament conference. A handful of rightist radicals have also been excluded, such as Rev. Ian Paisley, leader of Northern Irish Protestants, and Roberto d'Aubuisson, militant leader of the Salvadoran right. In contrast, eight members of the sanctuary movement, a loose network of religious groups committed to the protection of Central American refugees in the United States, were convicted in 1986 of smuggling aliens into the country ("Sanctuary Movement: New Hopes After Trial," *New York Times,* 6 May 1986).

Another illustration may be found in President Ronald Reagan's remarks on the occasion of the twentieth anniversary of the great 1963 civil rights demonstration and the memorable speech by Dr. Martin Luther King, Jr. After invoking King's "cherished ideals" of "human dignity . . . and brotherhood," Reagan could not help but turn the universal into a particular, remarking that America was "a special place, a place where so many dreams have come true." The president, however, did not pursue the implicit theme of moral superiority. Perhaps he remembered the thirty-three dead Haitians who washed up on Miami's shore trying to enter the "place where . . . dreams come true." Although their drowning was an "act of God," the policy that closes the national estate is not. But, then, as the Soviet press agency, TASS, observed after the Soviet attack on a Korean jetliner, "It is the sovereign right of every state to protect its borders." See "A Statement by the President," *New York Times,* 28 August 1983; "Text of Statement by Soviet Government," *New York Times,* 7 September 1983.

6. See Michael N. Danielson and Jameson W. Doig, *New York: The Politics of Urban Regional Development* (Berkeley and Los Angeles: University of California Press, 1982), p. 67. See also National Commission on Urban Problems, *Building the American City* (Washington, D.C.: GPO, 1968); President's Task Force on Suburban Problems, *Final Report,* ed. Charles Haar (Cambridge, Mass.: Ballinger, 1968); Anthony Downs, *Opening Up the Suburbs: An Urban Strategy for America* (New Haven: Yale University Press, 1973). The vision of "separate and unequal societies" was widely publicized from the *Report of the National Commission on Civil Disorders* (New York: Bantam, 1968), p. 1. This theme is developed in chapter 5.

7. "Shelter for Men Opened by City at Brooklyn Site," *New York Times,* 22 October 1981; "Problems Grow in Sheltering Homeless in City," *New York Times,* 18 November 1981; "The Need of the Nation's Homeless Is Becoming Their Right," *New York Times,* 20 July 1986; CBS News, "60 Minutes" (broadcast), 29 August 1982; "Trouble in Paradise," *Time,* 23 November 1981; Kim Hopper and Jill Hamberg, "The Making of America's Homeless: From Skid Row to New Poor, 1945–1984," in *Critical Perspectives on Housing,* ed. Rachel G. Bratt, Chester Hartman, and Ann Meyerson (Philadelphia: Temple University Press, 1986), pp. 12–40.

8. Michelle J. White, "Self-Interest in the Suburbs: The Trend Toward No-Growth Zoning," *Policy Analysis* 4, no. 2 (1978): 185. These pressures are reflected in a recent decline of American mobility. During the twenty-five years following World War II, about 20 percent of the population changed addresses annually. In 1976, however, the figure declined to 17.7 percent. According to the U.S. Census Bureau's chief migration specialist, the United States "is very unlikely to return to the mobility of the 1950s and 1960s" ("America's New Immobile Society," *Business Week,* 27 July 1981, pp. 58–62).

During the height of the oil crunch in 1979, economics editor Robert J. Samuelson observed that "the real issue . . . is not gasoline, but the automobile. It creates mobility, and mobility underpins our economic and social life. Lose it and the country is in deep trouble" ("You Asked for It, You Got It," *National Journal*, 5 May 1979, p. 831). Elites, anxious to stimulate a national reawakening after the stagnant seventies, are critical of popular resistance to change and movement. See, for example, the President's Commission for a National Agenda for the Eighties, *A National Agenda for the Eighties* (New York: New American Library, 1981), pp. 181–183. For the New York survey, see "Poll of Suburbanites Shows a Growing Sense of a Separate World," *New York Times*, 13 November 1978. On timed growth controls, see William K. Reilly, ed., *The Use of Land: A Citizens' Policy Guide to Urban Growth*, a task force report sponsored by the Rockefeller Brothers' Fund (New York: Thomas Y. Crowell, 1973); Robert H. Freilich and Davis T. Greis, "Timing and Sequencing Development: Controlling Growth," in *Future Land Use: Energy, Environmental, and Legal Constraints*, ed. Robert W. Burchell and David Listokin (New Brunswick, N.J.: Center for Urban Policy Research, Rutgers University, 1975), pp. 59–106; and Nelson, *Zoning and Private Property Rights*.

9. *New York Times*, 22 June 1985. After the city's streetside eaters rallied in support of expansion, Mayor Koch backed off and the measure was dropped. For the *Time*'s editorial disappointment, see the edition of 21 July 1985. On no-children housing complexes, see, e.g., "Adults-Only Enclaves Find Wider Market," *New York Times*, 25 October 1981; "Adults-Only Housing in California Causing Hardship for Some," *New York Times*, 26 June 1983.

10. *New York Times*, 16 May 1985.

11. Peter Wolfe, *Land in America: Its Value, Use, and Control* (New York: Pantheon, 1981), p. 140; John Delafons, *Land-Use Controls in the United States* (Cambridge: Joint Center for Urban Studies of the Massachusetts Institute of Technology and Harvard University, 1962), p. 23.

12. Tocqueville, *Democracy in America*, 2:104, 146.

13. Veblen, *Theory of the Leisure Class*, pp. 38–39. As Veblen adds, "It is extremely gratifying to possess something more than others."

14. Philip Slater, *The Pursuit of Loneliness: American Culture at the Breaking Point* (Boston: Beacon, 1970), p. 7.

15. Robert S. Lynd, *Knowledge for What? The Place of Social Science in American Culture* (Princeton, N.J.: Princeton University Press, 1967), p. 68.

16. *The Federal Convention and the Formation of the Union of the United States*, ed. Winton U. Solberg (New York: Liberal Arts Press, 1958), p. 176. Also see Francis Fox Piven and Richard A. Cloward, *The New Class War: Reagan's Attack on the Welfare State and Its Consequences* (New York: Pantheon, 1982), chap. 3.

17. There are, of course, illustrative exceptions to this statement. George Henry Evans's National Reform Association sought, in the 1840s, to gain not only free land for labor but also limits on free trade in land; Henry George's Single-Tax movement aimed to curb speculation by heavily taxing land instead of structures; and an isolated effort was made during the Civil War to deliver on promises of "sixty acres and a mule" by carving up plantations. For background on these efforts, see Helen Zahler, *Eastern Workingmen and National Land Policy* (New York: Columbia University Press, 1942); Henry George, *Progress and Poverty* (New York: Robert Schalkenbach Founda-

tion, 1948); Steven J. Ross, "Political Economy for the Masses: Henry George," *Democracy* 2 (July 1982): 125–134; Willie Lee Rose, *Rehearsal for Re-Construction: The Port Royal Experiment* (New York: Random House, 1964). It should be emphasized that none of these efforts involved promoting the goal of land redistribution as a tenet of national policy.

18. These amounts were deduced by Peter Meyer, in "Land Rush: A Survey of America's Land," *Harper's,* January 1979, pp. 48–49, from data supplied by U.S. Department of Agriculture economist Gene Wunderlich, who studied U.S. landownership patterns for a decade. In the absence of any comprehensive national ownership inventory, they represent what Wunderlich calls "rationalized estimates." Meyer calls his own deduction a "generous interpretation" of Wunderlich's figures and suggests other data showing even greater concentration of ownership by corporations. He notes, for example, a study by the Economic Research Service, "Corporate Land Holdings: An Inquiry into a Data Source," which discovered that 568 firms controlled, through either outright ownership or lease, 301.7 million acres of U.S. land, or more than 11 percent of the total national land area, and 23 percent of all privately held land. Worldwide, these same corporations were found by the ERS to own land in amounts greater than the size of Europe, almost 2 billion acres (p. 49). The oil industry alone, meanwhile, has had under lease lands amounting to one-quarter of the nation's acreage (Robert Engler, *The Politics of Oil* [Chicago: University of Chicago Press, 1967], p. 80). Exxon, to take an example, owns approximately 3 percent of Harris County, Texas—or, in other words, Houston (Jim Chiles, "Who Owns Texas?" *Texas Monthly,* June 1980, p. 129). *Business Week* estimates that "20 percent of all corporate assets lie in real estate," adding that after the recent rounds of inflation, "some companies may be sitting on gold mines" ("Why Sale-Leasebacks Are Booming," *Business Week,* 7 February 1983). The data come primarily from journalistic sources; official or scholarly reports are lacking. Except for the late Lee Metcalf of Montana, a rare populist voice in the Senate, few have devoted effort to learning "who owns America."

19. Meyer, "Land Rush," p. 48.

20. Danielson and Doig, *New York,* pp. 67–68.

21. Ellickson, "Suburban Growth Controls"; also "Zoning for the Regional Welfare," *Yale Law Journal* 89 (March 1980): 748–768. The latter article argues for a regional market system in socially necessary uses. Exclusionary communities would thus have to purchase exclusion rights from other towns willing to accept the costs. Segregation, like anything else in market systems, should have its price.

22. *San Diego Gas & Electric Co.* v. *City of San Diego,* 450 U.S. 621, 101 S. Ct. 1287 (1981). Although given several opportunities to uphold the Brennan doctrine over the last few years, the Supreme Court remains hesitant to take the final step. In its most recent opportunity, in 1986, the Court was asked to decide whether Yolo County, California, had seized private property rights without just compensation when it blocked a land company's plans for the construction of residential housing, limiting the use of the corporation's forty-four acres to farming. Justice John Paul Stevens carried a slim 5–4 majority with the view that the basic issue must remain undecided because the lower courts' rulings in the case "leave open the possibility that some development will be permitted." The minority included Justices Rehnquist, Powell, Burger, and White, who wrote the dissent. The appointment of another conservative, Antonin Scalia, to the Court and the elevation of Rehnquist to the position of Chief Justice

suggest that a majority favoring greater restrictions on local land use powers may soon be in place. See *MacDonald, Summer, & Frates—A Partnership* v. *The County of Yolo and the City of Davis,* No. 84–2015, decided 25 June 1986; "Decision on Loss in Land Use Rules Avoided," *New York Times,* 26 June 1986.

For a critique of Brennan's dissent in the San Diego case, see Robert N. Freilich, "Solving the 'Taking' Equation: Making the Whole Equal the Sum of the Parts," *Urban Lawyer* 15 (September 1983): 447–485. The questions of police powers, takings, and eminent domain are reviewed below in chapters 2 and 3.

23. "Reduction of Housing Development Costs: Excerpts from the Report of the President's Commission on Housing," reprinted in *1983 Zoning and Planning Law Handbook,* ed. Fredrick A. Stom (New York: Clark Boardman, 1983), pp. 369, 368.

24. Ibid., pp. 365, 362; *Berman* v. *Parker,* 348 U.S. 26 (1954), reprinted in Charles M. Haar, ed., *Land-Use Planning: A Casebook on the Use, Misuse, and Reuse of Urban Land,* 3d ed. (Boston: Little, Brown, 1976), p. 637.

25. Robert R. Wright, "Constitutional Rights and Land Use Planning: The New Era and the Old Reality," *Duke Law Journal,* no. 4 (October 1977): 845.

26. "Developments in the Law, Zoning," *Harvard Law Review* 91 (May 1978): 1590.

27. Popper, *Politics of Land-Use Reform;* Fred Bosselman and David Callies, *The Quiet Revolution in Land Use Control* (Washington, D.C.: GPO, 1971); Richard A. Walker and Michael K. Heiman, "Quiet Revolution for Whom?" *Annals of the Association of American Geographers* 71, no. 1 (1981): 67–83. Also see Sidney Plotkin, "Policy Fragmentation and Capitalist Reform: The Defeat of National Land-Use Policy," *Politics and Society* 9, no. 4 (1980): 409–445.

28. For overviews of these efforts, see Popper, *Politics of Land-Use Reform;* Robert Healy and John S. Rosenberg, *Land Use and the States,* 2d ed. (Baltimore: Johns Hopkins University Press, 1979); Richard H. Jackson, *Land Use in America* (New York: Wiley, 1981).

29. U.S. Senate, *Congressional Record* (hereafter cited as *Cong. Rec.*), 91st Cong., 2d sess., 29 January 1970, pt. 116, p. 1758, and 10 August 1970, pt. 116, pp. 28–40; Senate Committee on Interior and Insular Affairs, *Land Use Policy and Planning Assistance Act of 1973. Hearings Before the Subcommittee on Environment and Land Resources on S. 268,* 93d Cong., 1st sess., 1973, pt. 2, p. 87.

30. *New York Times,* 4 April 1976.

31. *New York Times,* 3 October 1981. The church was apparently less upset at the prospect of new weapons in the neighborhood than at the likelihood of "social dislocation from having thousands of construction workers and military move into the region." Nor were all local entrepreneurs pleased with the veto; as a local storeowner put it, "The area could have stood the growth that would have come with the missile."

32. *New York Times,* 18 November 1981; "Slurry Backers Outfox the Rails," *Business Week,* 2 August 1982; Dawn P. Jackson, "Preserving Western Water Rights— A Key to Coal Slurry Pipeline Bill," *National Journal,* 8 May 1982, pp. 820–821; "Slurry Pipelines Gain White House Support," *Power Line,* August–September 1983, p. 9. The bill was defeated by the House of Representatives, 235–182, in September 1983.

33. See U.S. Congress, House Committee on Interior and Insular Affairs, *Nuclear Waste Facility Siting. Hearings Before the Subcommittee on Energy and the Environment,* 96th Cong., 2d sess., pt. 5, 1979; Harold P. Green and Marc Zeil, "Federal-

State Conflict in Nuclear Waste Management: The Legal Bases," in *The Politics of Nuclear Waste*, ed. E. William Colglazier, Jr. (New York: Pergamon, 1982), pp. 110–137; "Congress Clears Nuclear Waste Legislation," *Congressional Quarterly Weekly Report*, 25 December 1982, pp. 3103–3104. Of course, the Supreme Court's recent decision overturning the legislative veto seems to improve the states' position in the legislation, as their veto stands "unless both houses of Congress voted to override it."

Communities are blocking the transport of such materials, too. Bans have been enacted on the shipment of wastes through such cities as New York; New London, Connecticut; and Missoula, Montana; and into Marin County, California, in the San Francisco Bay Area. Louisiana fences out all shipments into the state. See Sarah Scott, "Nuclear Wastes: Local Governments Up in Arms over U.S. Transport Rule," *National Journal*, 20 December 1980, pp. 2162–2164. The "rule" in question would have preempted such restrictions by requiring shipment on urban interstate highways where no circumferential route is available. In addition, the U.S. Supreme Court compounded the contradictions when it reinforced the states' exclusionary rights against nuclear power, ruling in 1983 that states may ban nuclear plants as long as the prohibitions are motivated by economic concerns, not safety—determinations of the latter are the province of national authority, the Court held. Only a day earlier, however, the Court ruled that the U.S. Nuclear Regulatory Commission was not required to take psychological stress into account in deciding whether to permit operations at the undamaged Three Mile Island Unit 1 nuclear plant. See "High Court Rules a State May Ban New Atomic Plant," *New York Times*, 21 April 1983; and "Court Rules Psychological Stress Is Not Guideline on Nuclear Plant," *New York Times*, 20 April 1983.

34. See "The Airports' Space Squeeze," *Business Week*, 29 March 1982; *New York Times*, 19 and 21 February 1982. Meanwhile, the Department of Transportation narrowed its environmental outlook by eliminating its Office of Environment. Secretary Drew Lewis noted that the change was meant "to increase efficiency," although a definition of this critical term was not supplied (*New York Times*, 28 February 1982).

35. *New York Times*, 16 September 1983.

36. Lawrence S. Bacow and James R. Milkey, "Overcoming Opposition to Hazardous Waste Facilities: The Massachusetts Approach," *Harvard Environmental Law Review* 6, no. 2 (1982): 269. Also see "Industrial Wastes with Nowhere to Go," *Business Week*, 8 March 1982, pp. 32–34; William Schneider, "Public Ambivalent on Nuclear Power," *National Journal*, 21 June 1986, p. 1563.

37. "The Reindustrialization of America," *Business Week*, 30 June 1980, pp. 86–88. The journal adds that at "the center of the new consensus must stand the recognition that each social group will be measured by how it contributes to economic revitalization." Also see Lester C. Thurow, *The Zero-Sum Society: Distribution and the Possibilities for Economic Change* (New York: Penguin, 1981), p. 11; Michael J. Crozier, Samuel P. Huntington, and Joji Watanuki, *The Crisis of Democracy: Report on the Governability of Democracies to the Trilateral Commission* (New York: New York University Press, 1975), p. 2; and Reich, *The Next American Frontier*, pp. 273, 139. The Schlesinger quotation is cited in "Controversy Abounds over Authority of the Proposed Energy Mobilization Board," *Congressional Quarterly Weekly Report*, 29 September 1979, p. 2134.

38. Popper, *Politics of Land-Use Reform*, pp. 210–211; Wolfe, *Land in America*, p. 140.

39. Danielson and Doig, *New York*, p. 68; Bernard J. Frieden, "The Environmental

Attack on Home-Building," in *The Prospective City: Economic, Population, Energy, and Environmental Developments,* ed. Arthur P. Solomon (Cambridge: MIT Press, 1980), p. 301. See also Babcock, *The Zoning Game;* Downs, *Opening Up the Suburbs;* and Edward C. Banfield, *The Unheavenly City Revisited* (Boston: Little, Brown, 1974). Thurow (*Zero-Sum Society*) and Ronald E. Müller (*Revitalizing America: Politics for Prosperity* [New York: Simon & Schuster, 1980]) argue along similar lines.

40. Karl Polanyi brilliantly analyzes this tendency for the nineteenth century, when "in effect, the great influence wielded by landed interests in Western Europe and the survival of feudal forms of life in Central and Eastern Europe . . . are readily explained by the vital protective function of these forces in retarding the mobilization of the land" (*The Great Transformation,* p. 183).

41. Anthony Downs, *Neighborhoods and Urban Development* (Washington, D.C.: Brookings Institution, 1981), p. 5. Banfield calls this "the logic of metropolitan growth" (*Unheavenly City Revisited,* chap. 2).

42. An excellent illustration of this dimension in protectionism is Gibbons, *Wye Island,* which describes rural opposition to an upper-income housing development on Maryland's Eastern Shore, an opposition stamped by elitist and racist as well as traditionalist motives.

43. For examples, see Louise B. Young, *Power over People* (New York: Oxford University Press, 1973); Barry M. Casper and Paul David Wellstone, *Powerline: The First Battle of America's Energy War* (Amherst: University of Massachusetts Press, 1981); Michael Brown, *Laying Waste: The Poisoning of America by Toxic Chemicals* (New York: Washington Square Press, 1981); Chester Hartman, *Yerba Buena: Land Grab and Community Resistance* (San Francisco: Glide Publications, 1974); "On Staten Island, Mothers Fight Against Dumping of Toxic Waste," *New York Times,* 16 April 1982.

44. William Worthy, *The Rape of Our Neighborhoods* (New York: Morrow, 1976); Lynne Sharon Schwartz, *We Are Talking About Homes: A Great University Against Its Neighbors* (New York: Harper & Row, 1985); Brian Anson, *I'll Fight You for It: Behind the Struggle for Covent Garden* (London: Jonathan Cape, 1981); Matthew Edel, "Urban Renewal and Land Use Conflicts," in *Problems in Political Economy: An Urban Perspective,* ed. David M. Gordon, 2d ed. (Lexington, Mass.: D. C. Heath, 1977), pp. 519–527; John Rex and Robert Moore, *Race, Community, and Conflict* (London: Oxford University Press, 1967); Martin Meyerson and Edward Banfield, *Politics, Planning and the Public Interest: The Case of Public Housing in Chicago* (New York: Free Press, 1955).

45. The poll data and Nader statement are quoted from Harry C. Boyte, *The Backyard Revolution: Understanding the New Citizen Movement* (Philadelphia: Temple University Press, 1980), pp. 3, 40; Mark Green, *Winning Back America* (New York: Bantam, 1982), pp. 326–327; "Activist Neighborhoods Are Becoming a New Political Force," *New York Times,* 18 June 1979, p. 1. For a more elaborate theoretical and historical discussion of this idea, see Manuel Castells, *The City and the Grassroots: A Cross-Cultural Theory of Urban Social Movements* (Berkeley and Los Angeles: University of California Press, 1983).

46. Thorstein Veblen, *Absentee Ownership: The Case of America* (Boston: Beacon, 1967), p. 78; Max Weber, "Class, Status and Party," chap. 7 in *From Max Weber: Essays in Sociology,* ed. Hans Gerth and C. Wright Mills (New York: Oxford University Press, 1948).

47. J. David Greenstone, *Labor in American Politics*, 2d ed. (Chicago: University of Chicago Press, 1969), p. xxxvi.

48. Boyte, *Backyard Revolution*, p. 36.

49. Martha A. Ackelsberg, "Women's Collaborative Activities and City Life: Politics and Policy," in *Political Women: Current Roles in State and Local Government*, ed. Janet A. Flammang, Sage Yearbooks in Women's Policy Studies, vol. 8 (Beverly Hills, Calif.: Sage, 1984), pp. 242–259; Cynthia Cockburn, *The Local State* (London: Pluto, 1977); Castells, *City and the Grassroots*, p. 68.

50. Ackelsberg, "Women's Collaborative Activities," p. 249.

51. Weber, *From Max Weber*, pp. 183–184. See also Peter Saunders, *Social Theory and the Urban Question* (New York: Holmes & Meier, 1981); Castells, *City and the Grassroots;* Rex and Moore, *Race, Community, and Conflict;* Roy Pahl, *Whose City? And Further Essays on Urban Society*, 2d ed. (Harmondsworth: Penguin, 1975).

52. Ira Katznelson, *City Trenches: Urban Politics and the Patterning of Class in the United States* (Chicago: University of Chicago Press, 1981), chap. 3.

53. Saunders, *Social Theory and the Urban Question*, p. 275; Peter Saunders, "Domestic Property and Social Class," *International Journal of Urban and Regional Research* 2 (June 1978): 233–251. For an excellent discussion of Saunders's theory—including an effort to save it after Saunders himself abandoned it in favor of the view that housing differences are formed through political, not class, struggles—see Geraldine Pratt, "Class Analysis and Urban Domestic Property: A Critical Reexamination," *International Journal of Urban and Regional Research* 6 (December 1982): 481–501.

54. As Saunders put it, "Those whose primary concerns lie in furthering the conditions for the development of socialism will derive little return from either analysis of or activity in urban politics" (*Social Theory and the Urban Question*, p. 276).

55. Matthew Edel, "Homeownership and Working Class Unity," *International Journal of Urban and Regional Research* 6 (June 1982): 205–221; Kevin R. Cox, "Capitalism and Conflict Around the Communal Living Space," in *Urbanization and Urban Planning in Capitalist Society*, ed. Michael Dear and Allen J. Scott (New York: Methuen, 1981), pp. 431–455; Robert M. Rakoff, "Ideology in Everyday Life: The Meaning of the House," *Politics and Society* 7, no. 1 (1977): 85–104; Jim Kameny, "A Critique of Homeownership," in Bratt, Hartman, and Meyerson, *Critical Perspectives on Housing*, pp. 272–276; J. A. Agnew, "Homeownership and the Capitalist Social Order," in Dear and Scott, *Urbanization and Urban Planning*, pp. 457–480.

56. "Using 1980 census data, the National Low Income Housing Coalition estimates that for very-low-income renter households there is a gap of 1.2 million units between the number of such households and the number of rental units" (Bratt, Hartman, and Meyerson, *Critical Perspectives on Housing*, p. xiii). Meanwhile, according to the U.S. League of Savings Institutions, the percentage of Americans owning their own homes declined to a seventeen-year low of 63.9 percent in 1985. The U.S. Conference of Mayors reported that for the same year, in twenty-two of twenty-five major U.S. cities, the demand for emergency shelter for the homeless rose by an average of 25 percent ("House and Home and the American Dream," *National Journal*, 1 February 1986, p. 294). See also n. 27, chap. 8.

57. Joe Feagin, *The Urban Real Estate Game: Playing Monopoly with Real Money* (New York: Prentice-Hall, 1983), p. 60; Cox, "Capitalism and Conflict," p. 431; David

Harvey, "The Urban Process Under Capitalism: A Framework for Analysis," in Dear and Scott, *Urbanization and Urban Planning*, pp. 91–121.

58. Robert S. Lynd and Helen Merrell Lynd, *Middletown: A Study in Modern American Culture* (New York: Harcourt, Brace & World, 1956), chap. 7.

59. Enzo Mingione, *Social Conflict and the City* (New York: St. Martin's, 1981), p. 24.

60. Seymour Toll, *Zoned American* (New York: Grossman, 1969).

61. O'Connor, *Fiscal Crisis of the State*, p. 83; Edward Greer, *Big Steel: Black Politics and Corporate Power in Gary, Indiana* (New York: Monthly Review Press, 1979).

62. Cox, "Capitalism and Conflict," pp. 439–440; Mollenkopf, *The Contested City*, chaps. 1, 4; Feagin, *Urban Real Estate Game*, chap. 9.

63. Walker and Heiman, "Quiet Revolution for Whom?" pp. 72–83; O'Connor, *Fiscal Crisis of the State*, pp. 135–137.

64. Cox, "Capitalism and Conflict," pp. 439–440. A useful study by James Lorimer of the land development industry in Canada offers striking evidence that local land capitalists are wise to oppose political centralization (*The Developers* [Toronto: James Lorimer & Co., 1978]). Lorimer found that in the postwar era, the size of Canadian land development companies grew substantially in most major urban markets. Competitive entrepreneurial firms gave way to large corporations, as they have in the United States; but in Canada the process of concentration went much further, transforming the industry more radically. In practically every case, moreover, economic concentration was accompanied by centralization of urban political power, including power to regulate land use. In Lorimer's words, "Alongside the process of corporate concentration in land development has gone a parallel process of political concentration," one that has been "unpopular and widely opposed" (p. 78). In one instance, though, he discovered that economic centralization did not occur. In Montreal, thirty small municipal jurisdictions maintained the decentralized and fragmented pattern of government familiar in the United States. Here, the parcelization of land use powers discouraged the growth of scale in the development industry. Fragmentation of political authority favored small builders, who enjoyed "greater success in ensuring that the servicing of lots proceed[ed] in advance of supply and that there [was] always an ample supply of lots ready at current prices" (p. 124).

65. Castells, in *City and the Grassroots*, makes the point this way: "Urban social movements are aimed at transforming the meaning of the city without being able to transform society. They are a reaction, not an alternative: they are calling for a depth of existence without being able to create that new breadth" (p. 327). See also Saunders, *Social Theory and the Urban Question*, p. 276; and Francis Fox Piven and Richard Cloward, *Poor People's Movements: Why They Succeed, How They Fail* (New York: Random House, 1979), chap. 1.

66. Barry Commoner, *The Closing Circle: Nature, Man and Technology* (New York: Knopf, 1971), p. 39.

67. Slater, *Pursuit of Loneliness*, p. 15.

68. Weber, *From Max Weber*, pp. 230–231.

69. Samuel P. Huntington, *Political Order in Changing Societies* (New Haven: Yale University Press, 1968), pp. 98, 126.

70. Robert Goodman, *The Last Entrepreneurs: America's Regional Wars for Jobs*

and Dollars (New York: Simon & Schuster, 1979), pp. 3–4. See also "The Second War Between the States," *Business Week,* 17 May 1976.

71. Bryan D. Jones and Lynn W. Batchelor, with Carter Wilson, *The Sustaining Hand: Community Leadership and Corporate Power* (Lawrence: University of Kansas Press, 1986), chaps. 5–10. Also, for good, if legalistic, accounts, see Emily J. Lewis, "Comment: Corporate Prerogative, 'Public Use' and a People's Plight: *Poletown Neighborhood Council* v. *City of Detroit,*" *Detroit College of Law Review* 4 (Winter 1982): 907–929; Barry Bennett, "Eminent Domain and Redevelopment: The Return of Engine Charlie," *DePaul Law Review* 31 (1981): 115–151. See also "Neighbors Lose and Detroit Wins in Court Ruling on New Auto Plant," *New York Times,* 10 December 1980; and "The Last Days of Poletown," *Time,* 30 March 1981.

72. *The Book of the States, 1976–77* (Lexington, Ky.: Council of State Governments, 1976), tables 2–5, pp. 465–468; "Employment Outlook in High Technology," *New York Times,* Special Supplement, 27 March 1983, p. 6.

73. "Excerpts from President's Message to Congress on Urban Enterprise Zones," *New York Times,* 24 March 1982. See also William W. Goldsmith, "Bringing the Third World Home: Enterprise Zones for America?" in *Sunbelt/Snowbelt: Urban Development and Regional Restructuring,* ed. Larry Sawers and William K. Tabb (New York: Oxford University Press, 1984), pp. 339–350. For an evaluation of the plan that argues against its use "to dismantle the local land use management system," see David L. Callies and Gail M. Tamashiro, "Enterprise Zones: The Redevelopment Sweepstakes Begin," *Urban Lawyer* 15 (Winter 1983): 288. In Reagan's view, if a citizen fails to appreciate the benefits of reduced protection, then he retains "the right . . . [to] vote with his feet" and "go someplace else." See "Reagan to the Nation's Governors—The Federal Aid Cupboard is Bare," *National Journal,* 28 November 1981, p. 211; cf. the editorial "Voting with Your Feet," *Wall Street Journal,* 29 April 1976, where the *Journal* criticized a New York City clergyman for urging firms not to abandon the city. Such pleas were described as being like Moses trying to keep "the Israelites in Egypt. People and corporations will always leave political jurisdictions while costs exceed benefits as long as they believe the spot over the horizon is better." The felicitous calculus explains all; Moses must have owned a calculator. Also, cf. President Carter's attempt to "induce" business to stay put through direct grants and low-cost loans (*New York Times,* 8 March 1978).

74. *New York Times,* 1 April 1982, 19 February 1982; Mobil Corporation, "Fair, Warm, and Not at All Sticky," national advertisement, 1981. In Dallas, to cite another instance, the city planned to establish a $357 million rapid transit system to be financed partly by public taxes and the rest by three private developers. The line would connect "major residential and commercial projects owned by the three developers." As one local official put it, severe cuts in federal aid justified acceptance of the "freebie that will benefit the public. I don't care if it's a bit self-serving to anybody" (*New York Times,* 28 March 1982). For many other examples, see Rochelle L. Stanfield, "Reagan Urban Policy—Count Us Out of Public-Private Partnerships," *National Journal,* 3 July 1982, pp. 1172–1175.

75. Carol Steinbach, "Tapping Private Resources," *National Journal,* 26 April 1986, pp. 993, 996.

76. *Village of Euclid* v. *Ambler Realty Co., * 272 U.S. 365, in Haar, *Land-Use Planning,* p. 201.

77. Alfred Bettman, *City and Regional Planning Papers,* ed. Arthur C. Comely (Cambridge: Harvard University Press, 1946), pp. 55–56.

78. Popper's *Politics of Land-Use Reform* notes this idea but fails to develop its implications (p. 8); cf., however, Manuel Castells, *The Urban Question: A Marxist Approach,* trans. Alan Sheridan (Cambridge: MIT Press, 1979); and David Harvey, *Social Justice and the City* (Baltimore: Johns Hopkins University Press, 1973).

79. "Developments in the Law, Zoning," p. 1487. The *New York Times* architecture critic, Paul Goldberger, calls this "urban Darwinism—the survival of only the most lucrative use of any given plot of land" ("The Limits of Urban Growth," *New York Times Magazine,* 14 November 1982, p. 47). In fact, however, the law is not entirely preoccupied with "given plots." Environmental lawyers and defenders of community land-use powers more generally stress needs to maximize "the output of the entire resource base upon which competing claims of right are dependent, rather than maintenance of the profitability of the individual parcels of property" (Joseph Sax, "Takings, Private Property and Public Rights," *Yale Law Journal* 81 [December 1971]: 172). As we shall see, the distinction between concerns for "given plots" and "the entire resource base" forms the basis of two quite different approaches to metropolitan land: a radical capitalism in cities and a conservative capitalism in the suburbs; see below, chapters 2, 3, and 5.

80. Marx and Engels, *Communist Manifesto,* p. 12; Joseph A. Schumpeter, *Capitalism, Socialism, and Democracy,* 3d ed. (New York: Harper & Row, 1962), p. 83.

81. On devaluation as a basic effect of capitalist competition, see David Harvey, *The Limits to Capital* (Chicago: University of Chicago Press, 1982). Obviously, the threat of devaluation applies with equal force to the value of consumption property such as residential housing, too, and it is a main factor behind zoning; thus the endless concern with protecting property values.

82. Gilder, *Wealth and Poverty,* chap. 19.

83. Dana L. Thomas, *Lords of the Land* (New York: Putnam, 1977), p. 13.

84. James C. Hite, *Room and Situation: The Political Economy of Land Use Policy* (Chicago: Nelson-Hall, 1979), p. 2. Defying "the laws of nature," New York City's builders added seventy-seven million square feet to Manhattan Island between 1960 and 1979, giving the city a staggering total of 40 percent of the seven hundred million square feet of office space in the nation's major cities. But others scrambled to keep up; predictably, scarcity soon turned to overproduction. By 1983 most major cities faced office-space gluts, the average big-city vacancy rate equaling 10.8 percent; see "Commercial Real Estate Report," *New York Times,* Special Supplement, 15 May 1983, p. 6. Naturally, the *Times*'s totals do not include additional space created by arson, abandonment, unemployment, factory closings, or the generalized processes of impoverishment that are the unprized products of urban capitalism. On the role of land speculation in capitalist development, see Harvey, *Limits to Capital,* esp. pp. 367–372.

85. Castells, *The Urban Question,* p. 115.

86. "Buying Land: The Dangers," an interview with Peter Wolf, "consultant on land planning and land-asset management," *New York Times,* 15 September 1981, p. D2; Julian L. Simon, "Are We Losing our Farmland?" *Public Interest* 67 (Spring 1982): 51; John R. Commons, *Legal Foundations of Capitalism* (Madison: University of Wisconsin Press, 1968), p. 368; Hite, *Room and Situation,* p. 2.

87. The *New York Times,* 13 March 1983, reported that between 1976 and 1981

real estate showed the "largest proportionate growth" as a percentage of national income, rising from 7.8 to 9.2 percent. That this was an otherwise stagnant economic period which saw massive property tax increases around the country dims the glow of these figures, however. Land speculation became a hot substitute for real production, an example of what Robert B. Reich calls "paper entrepreneurialism" (*The Next American Frontier*, pp. 140–172); see also Veblen, *Absentee Ownership*, pp. 142–143. As a particularly grotesque example of Veblen's point, consider the recent arrest of a Chicago real estate broker "on charges that he offered $1 million to have [Mayor Harold] Washington assassinated." The land trader's justification was that "Washington's fiscal strategy would have ruined the city's real estate business" ("Downgraded," *Time*, 19 September 1983, p. 29).

88. Nelson, *Zoning and Private Property Rights*, p. 145.

89. Poulantzas, *State, Power, Socialism*, p. 104.

Chapter 2

1. Charles Abrams, *Revolution in Land* (New York: Harper, 1939), pp. 3–4.

2. "What Is a Home," Guy Chipman Co. Realtors, San Antonio, *Express News*, 21 May 1978, Special Section, "Private Property Week," p. 3J. Those interested in "a reproduction" of the complete ode, "without obligation and suitable for framing," are urged to write the company. The *New York Times* is equally optimistic about the land trade: in a recent ad campaign aimed at expanding its real estate pages, it offered "an inspiring message for area developers. . . . It's a big broad, buzzing land, this nation of ours. Ripe with potential. All it takes is enterprise, and profit is yours. Practically for the asking." Readers are urged to test the hypothesis.

3. One English historian notes, however, that although "many thousands of small farmers and cottagers were displaced, enclosure did not necessarily have adverse effects on the rural population, especially where it led to improved cultivation." Besides, "even when pasture did replace tillage and farms were engrossed, there was not necessarily a depopulation of the countryside. In some areas expanding industrial employment absorbed those displaced from farming." The standards of judgment used here are, of course, those of profit and capital productivity. See G. E. Mingay, *The Gentry: The Rise and Fall of a Ruling Class* (London: Longmans, 1976), pp. 41–42. As Barrington Moore notes, enclosures were far from "the main device" by which the peasantry was undermined. They were rather "the final blow," the last slam of the hammer, in a more diffuse process of "creative destruction" dominated by the commercialization of English social relations in the towns, and only later in the country (Barrington Moore, Jr., *Social Origins of Dictatorship and Democracy: Lord and Peasant in the Making of the Modern World* [Boston: Beacon, 1967], pp. 20–21).

4. Karl Marx, *The Economic and Philosophic Manuscripts of 1844*, ed. Dirk J. Struik, trans. Martin Milligan (New York: International Publishers, 1964), p. 101. Cf. E. P. Thompson, *Whigs and Hunters: The Origin of the Black Act* (New York: Pantheon, 1975). Thompson traces the reasons for the use of capital punishment against poachers in eighteenth-century England. He finds them in the inability of peasants to grasp the fact that property rights had changed and in the desire of the new holders of "absolute" property rights to make the lesson stick. The "rural idiocy" quote is, of course, from Marx and Engels, *Communist Manifesto*, p. 13. Cf. Draper, *Marx's The-*

ory of Revolution, 2:344–348, where Draper argues that the "idiocy" reference should be understood in the Greek sense of an isolated existence outside the mainstream of public life.

5. Adam Smith, *An Inquiry into the Nature and Causes of the Wealth of Nations,* 2 vols. (Homewood, Ill.: Irwin, 1963), 1:199–201.

6. David Ricardo, *The Works of David Ricardo, with a Notice of the Life and Writings of the Author by J. R. McCulloch* (London: John Murray, 1852), p. 35.

7. John Stuart Mill, *Principles of Political Economy* (New York: Appleton, 1864), 1:296. Mill accepted the legitimacy of landownership only where owners produced goods for society: "When private property in land is not expedient, it is unjust" (p. 295).

8. Karl Marx, "The Elections—Tories and Whigs," *New York Daily Tribune,* 21 August 1852, reprinted in *Selected Writings in Sociology and Social Philosophy,* trans. T. B. Bottomore (New York: McGraw-Hill, 1956), pp. 191–192.

9. Marx, *Capital,* 3 vols., ed. Friedrich Engels (New York: International Publishers, 1967), 3:761–762.

10. Ricardo, *Works,* p. 35. John Roscoe Turner's study of *The Ricardian Rent Theory in Early American Economics* (New York: New York University Press, 1921) concludes that the "doctrine . . . could not hold in the United States because we had no distinct class supported by wages, and because a growth of population here caused increasing returns and lower prices" (p. 197). The U.S. problem was labor, not land shortage. Cf. Walter Prescott Webb, *The Great Frontier* (Austin: University of Texas Press, 1951).

11. "Extract from the Report of Mr. Rush, Secretary of the Treasury, December, 1827," *Appendix No. 1 to S. Rept. 145,* Senate Committee on Public Lands, 22d Cong., 1st sess., 18 May 1832, in *Bounty Lands, Revenues,* vol. 4 of *The New American State Papers: The Public Lands,* 8 vols. (Wilmington, Del.: Scholarly Resources, 1973), pp. 293–294. Cf. Marx, "The Modern Theory of Colonization," chap. 33 in *Capital,* vol. 1; and the interesting discussion in Draper, *Marx's Theory of Revolution,* 2:419–422. Clearly there are differences among landlords, who extract income (e.g., rent) from the need of others to use land; self-employed entrepreneurs and capitalists, who profit from the use of land by setting it into production themselves or through wage-labor; and modern worker-owners, who seek to reap unearned increment through changes in the market value of land and housing. It is the latter two groups, the land businesses and worker-owners, who occupy the stage for most of this study of American patterns.

12. Cited in Turner, "Significance of the Frontier," p. 26.

13. Ibid.

14. Curtis P. Nettles, *The Roots of American Civilization: A History of American Colonial Life* (New York: Appleton-Century-Crofts, 1963), pp. 329–354, 516–542; Charles A. Beard, *Economic Origins of Jeffersonian Democracy* (New York: Macmillan, 1915); Jackson Turner Main, *The Antifederalists, Critics of the Constitution, 1781–1788* (Chapel Hill: University of North Carolina Press, 1961); Ray Allen Billington, with James Blaine Hedges, *Westward Expansion: A History of the American Frontier,* 4th ed. (New York: Macmillan, 1974); Paul Wallace Gates, *The Farmer's Age, 1815–1860* (New York: Holt, Rinehart & Winston, 1960); John D. Hicks, *The Populist Revolt: A History of the Farmers' Alliance and the People's Party* (Lincoln: University of Nebraska Press, 1961).

15. Billington, *Westward Expansion*, p. 323. As Paul Wallace Gates notes, "The term squatters applied to all settlers who anticipated the government land sale and after 1853 to those who anticipated the government surveyor"; squatting was legalized for surveyed land by the Preemption Act of 1832 (*The History of Public Land Law Development* [New York: Arno, 1979], p. 116). Also see Malcolm J. Rohrbough, *The Land Office Business: The Settlement and Administration of American Public Lands, 1789–1837* (New York: Oxford University Press, 1968), who notes that "squatting on lands was as old as settlement in the New World, and illegal settlements . . . plagued the proprietors of colonial America" (pp. 14–16).

16. The fullest account of Evans's efforts is found in Zahler, *Eastern Workingmen*. But see also George Stephenson, *Political History of the Public Lands, 1840–1862* (New York: Russell and Russell, 1917); Roy Robbins, *Our Landed Heritage: The Public Domain, 1776–1936* (Lincoln: University of Nebraska Press, 1962), pp. 94–104; Gates, *History of Public Land Law Development*, pp. 170–171, 390–391; Arthur M. Schlesinger, Jr., *The Age of Jackson* (Boston: Little, Brown, 1945), esp. pp. 347–348.

17. U.S. Congress, House Committee on Public Lands, *Graduation, Reduction and Disposition of the Public Lands*, H. Rept. 732, 30th Cong., 1st sess., 1848, in *Land Prices and Preemption Rights*, vol. 3 of *New American State Papers*, p. 454. As the report also noted, a policy of entails "would render the land of little or no value as it would have no exchange value." For "no man would ever lay out money in making expensive erections and improvements on land, which he could never sell to replace such money when his circumstances required." Farmers favored the more conservative land reformers who sought land grants with full rights of ownership, including the right to sell. Thus a noted liberal, George Julian, argued in favor of the Homestead Act that "the friends of land reform claim no right to interfere with the laws of property of the several States, or the vested interests of their citizens"; cited in Eric Foner, *Free Soil, Free Labor, Free Men: The Ideology of the Republican Party Before the Civil War* (New York: Oxford University Press, 1970), p. 29. As Veblen summarized the farmers' view, they wanted only "a democratically equal opportunity of seizure" (*Absentee Ownership*, p. 122).

18. Veblen, *Absentee Ownership*, p. 130. Would-be farmers, of course, sugared their pleas. One group asked "that the Poor industrious people may obtain a sufficient quantity of land . . . to enjoy the sweets of liberty and so become useful and loyal citizens." But warnings were also issued: wider ownership would "remove animosities" and "prevent rebellions," contributing to "loyalty in each citizen." See "Memorial for Revision of Public Land Laws," to the U.S. Senate, 28 February 1811, in *New American State Papers*, 3:20.

19. George, *Progress and Poverty*. For background, see Charles Albro Barker, *Henry George* (New York: Oxford University Press, 1955); and Arthur Nicholas Young, *The Single Tax Movement in the United States* (Princeton, N.J.: Princeton University Press, 1916). For a recent effort to revive democratic respect for George, see Ross, "Political Economy for the Masses." As Ross points out, *Progress and Poverty* "outsold every other book in the nineteenth century except the Bible" (p. 125). And Eric Foner adds that the book "became the most widely read economic treatise ever written in this country"; see his interesting essay, "Class, Ethnicity, and Radicalism in the Gilded Age: The Land League and Irish America," reprinted in Foner, *Politics and Ideology in the Age of the Civil War* (New York: Oxford University Press, 1980), p. 185.

20. Hite, *Room and Situation,* p. 69.

21. Allen Tate, "Notes on Liberty and Property," in *Who Owns America? A New Declaration of Independence,* ed. Herbert Agar and Allen Tate (Boston: Houghton Mifflin, 1936, reprinted by University Press of America, Washington, D.C., n.d.), p. 82.

22. Marcuse, *One-Dimensional Man,* p. 3; and Doreen Massey and Alexandrina Catalano, *Capital and Land: Landownership by Capital in Great Britain* (London: Edward Arnold, 1978), pp. 25–26.

23. Benton MacKaye, *Employment and Natural Resources,* a report written for the U.S. Department of Labor (Washington, D.C.: GPO, 1919), pp. 13–14.

24. Veblen, *Theory of the Leisure Class.*

25. Thorstein Veblen, *The Theory of Business Enterprise* (New Brunswick, N.J.: Transaction Books, 1978); Veblen, *Absentee Ownership.* Cf. Adolf A. Berle, Jr., "Property, Production, and Revolution—A Preface to the Revised Edition," in *The Modern Corporation and Private Property,* ed. Adolf A. Berle, Jr., and Gardiner C. Means, rev. ed. (New York: Harcourt, Brace & World, 1967), p. xi; and C. Wright Mills, *White Collar: The American Middle Classes* (New York: Oxford University Press, 1951), pp. 13–14.

26. Between the new forms of consumer leisure and the more distant background world of industry, there stood the new power of business enterprise. Motivated neither by a lust for leisure nor by the old "instinct of workmanship," the managers of the big corporations sought only "an advantageous discrepancy in the price of the capital which they manage" (Veblen, *Theory of Business Enterprise,* p. 159).

27. Matthew Edel, Elliot D. Sclar, and Daniel Luria, *Shaky Palaces: Homeownership and Social Mobility in Boston's Suburbanization* (New York: Columbia University Press, 1984), p. 194. Indeed, as Leonardo Benevolo has argued, Marx and Engels did little to aid radical thought on urban questions, such as housing, because they saw the question of the city as best left to the deliberations of a future socialist society. In this sense, the fathers of communism wrongly separated consumption and production issues and, in the process, invited reformist conservatives to appropriate urban planning and housing themes for capitalist purposes. See Leonardo Benevolo, *The Origins of Modern Town Planning* (Cambridge: MIT Press, 1971), pp. xii–xiii; cf. Friedrich Engels, *The Housing Question* (Moscow: Progress Publishers, 1979).

28. Saunders, *Urban Politics: A Sociological Approach* (London: Hutchinson, 1979), p. 100, cited in Pratt, "Class Analysis and Urban Domestic Property," p. 484.

29. Harry Braverman, *Labor and Monopoly Capital: The Degradation of Work in the Twentieth Century* (New York: Monthly Review Press, 1974); David M. Gordon, Richard Edwards, and Michael Reich, *Segmented Work, Divided Workers: The Historical Transformation of Labor in the United States* (Cambridge: Cambridge University Press, 1982).

30. Alfred D. Chandler, *The Visible Hand: The Managerial Revolution in American Business* (Cambridge: Harvard University Press, 1977).

31. Martin Oppenheimer, *White Collar Politics* (New York: Monthly Review Press, 1985), p. 9. See also Erik Olin Wright, *Class, Crisis and the State* (London: New Left Books, 1978).

32. See, for example, Anthony Giddens and David Held, eds., *Classes, Power, and Conflict: Classical and Contemporary Debates* (Berkeley and Los Angeles: University of California Press, 1982).

33. John Kenneth Galbraith, *The New Industrial State* (Boston: Houghton Mifflin, 1967), p. 55. Matthew Edel and his colleagues put it well when they note that in land use conflicts, the "struggles are, in a sense, secondary to more global contradictions between capital and labor over living standards, working conditions, and the control and use of economic surplus. But being secondary, they are not necessarily unimportant" (Edel, Sclar, and Luria, *Shaky Palaces*, p. 384).

34. On the multiple meanings of modern bourgeois culture and its resistance to corporate-state control, see Habermas, *Legitimation Crisis;* and Harvey, *Social Justice and the City*, pp. 79–86. See also Cox, "Capitalism and Conflict," p. 432.

35. Reich, *The Next American Frontier*, p. 254; and "Rising Cottage Industry Stirring Concern in U.S.," *New York Times*, 13 May 1986.

36. David Noble, "Present Tense Technology," *Democracy* 3 (Spring 1983): 8.

37. See Lawrence Gene Sager, "Insular Majorities Unabated: *Warth* v. *Seldin* and *City of Eastlake* v. *Forest City Enterprises, Inc.*," *Harvard Law Review* 91 (May 1978): 1373–1425.

38. Writing of the land use reformers of the 1970s, Frank J. Popper notes a clear tendency to avoid questions of economic organization, power, and rights. "The movement's supporters shy away . . . from measures involving direct government control of the market" and "have shown little interest in such issues as the concentration of private ownership." Land use reform, whether understood from economic or environmental perspectives, is not seen as a question with egalitarian implications beyond, perhaps, the concern for low-income housing in the suburbs (*Politics of Land-Use Reform*, p. 14).

39. Georg Lukács, *History and Class Consciousness*, trans. Rodney Livingstone (Cambridge: MIT Press, 1971), p. 10. Also see Westergaard and Resler, *Class in a Capitalist Society*, pp. 143–144.

40. Offe, "Introduction to Part III," in Lindberg et al., *Stress and Contradiction*, p. 246.

41. Frank I. Michelman, "Property, Utility, and Fairness: Comments on the Ethical Foundations of 'Just Compensation' Law," *Harvard Law Review* 80 (April 1967): 1212.

42. Franz Neumann, "The Change in the Function of Law in Modern Society," in *The Democratic and the Authoritarian State: Essays in Political and Legal Theory*, ed. Herbert Marcuse (New York: Free Press, 1957), pp. 28–43; Michael E. Tigar, with Madeleine R. Levy, *Law and the Rise of Capitalism* (New York: Monthly Review Press, 1977), p. 280.

43. Friedrich A. Hayek, *The Road to Serfdom* (Chicago: University of Chicago Press, 1944), p. 75.

44. Ibid., p. 73.

45. Babcock, *The Zoning Game*, p. 12; Duncan S. McAffer, "What Constitutes a Public Use?" in *Valuation for Eminent Domain*, ed. Edwin M. Rams (Englewood Cliffs, N.J.: Prentice-Hall, 1973), p. 17. Also see "Developments in the Law: Zoning," pp. 1437, 1464.

46. Haar, *Land-Use Planning*, p. 124.

47. Poulantzas, *State, Power, Socialism*, p. 72.

48. Fred Bosselman, David Callies, and John Banta, *The Taking Issue* (written for the Council on Environmental Quality) (Washington, D.C.: GPO, 1973), p. v.

49. Boyd Gibbons suggests that "owning land is the most effective way in which people keep their distance from others. Land is the ultimate means of exclusion" (*Wye Island*, p. 90). Of course, it is the social institution of private ownership, not land, that embodies the powers of exclusion.

50. Sir William Blackstone's *Commentaries, with Notes of References to the Constitution and Laws of the Federal Government of the United States and of the Commonwealth of Virginia*, ed. St. George Tucker, 5 vols. (New York: Augustus M. Kelly Publishers, 1969), 3:1.

51. Ibid., 2:139. But Blackstone also believed that owners must not harm others in their use of land. Cf. Morton J. Horwitz, *The Transformation of American Law, 1780–1860* (Cambridge: Harvard University Press, 1977), p. 31.

52. Berle and Means, *The Modern Corporation*, p. 8.

53. *Corpus Juris Secundum*, ed. Francis J. Ludes and Harold L. Gilbert (St. Paul, Minn.: West Publishing, 1951), vol. 73, Property, no. 1, p. 136 (hereafter cited as *CJS*).

54. "By proximity I mean the effects of being close to something people do not make any direct use of. A household may thus find itself proximate to a source of pollution, to a source of noise, or to a run-down environment. This proximity tends to impose certain costs upon the household (for example, cleaning and laundry bills, sound-proofing, etc.)." By contrast, the economic cost of access to superior locational advantages is termed, not surprisingly, the "price of accessibility." In effect, these are the negative and positive sides of interdependence in land use. As Harvey points out, much of urban politics can be understood in terms of neighborhood and business struggles to lower proximity costs by keeping their producers away and to lower prices of accessibility by bringing good things near (Harvey, *Social Justice and the City*, pp. 56–57, and chap. 2 passim).

55. Tocqueville, *Democracy in America*, 2:311, 343.

56. Grant McConnell, *Private Power and American Democracy* (New York: Random House, 1966), chap. 5. For an economic theory of this tradition, see Mancur Olson, Jr., *The Logic of Collective Action: Public Goods and the Theory of Groups*, rev. ed. (New York: Schocken, 1968). The causes of this blindness to the social basis of private institutions are most cogently analyzed by Lukács (see n. 39, above).

57. Haar, *Land-Use Planning*, p. 124.

58. William H. Rodgers, Jr., "Bringing People Back: Toward a Comprehensive Theory of Taking in Natural Resources Law," *Ecology Law Quarterly* 10 (1982): 219.

59. Ibid.

60. John Locke, *Two Treatises of Government* (New York: New American Library, 1960), p. 375.

61. Wright, "Constitutional Rights," p. 843.

62. Neo-classical economic theory has begun to recognize, long after Locke, that for owners, "establishing and protecting property rights is very much a productive activity to which resources can be devoted" (Terry L. Anderson and P. J. Hill, "From Free Grass to Fences: Transforming the Commons of the American West," in *Managing the Commons*, ed. Garret Hardin and John Baden (San Francisco: Freeman, 1977), p. 202. For attempts to develop the neo-classical view from a Left, critical perspective, see Margaret Levi, "The Predatory Theory of Rule," *Politics and Society* 10, no. 4 (1981): 431–465; and Margaret Levi and Douglass C. North, "Towards a Property Rights Theory of Exploitation," *Politics and Society* 11, no. 3 (1982): 315–320.

63. Sax, "Takings, Private Property, and Public Rights," p. 152.

64. The fact that formal land use authority resides with the states explains, at least in part, why congressional efforts to legislate a national land use policy aimed at strengthening state regulatory powers. It also helps explain the Supreme Court's tendency to leave most land use issues to the state courts for resolution, thus safely avoiding the land use, property rights tangle.

65. See *Nectow* v. *City of Cambridge*, 277 U.S. 183, 48 S. Ct. 447, 72 L. ED. 842 (1928). This was the Supreme Court's first major zoning case after it had upheld the power to zone two years before. In this instance, however, the local ordinance was overturned because the restriction in question did not seem "indispensable to the general [land use] plan" and thus to the overall community interest. The Court insisted that land use controls "cannot be imposed if [they do] not bear a substantial relation to the public health, safety, morals or general welfare." The case is reprinted in Haar, *Land-Use Planning*, pp. 205–207, quote above at p. 207.

66. 72 *CJS* Police, 1:207–208.

67. *Gardner* v. *Michigan*, 199 U.S. 325, 330 (1905), cited in Sax, "Takings and the Police Power," *Yale Law Journal* 74 (November 1964): 39. Only "unoffending property" may not be "taken" without just compensation. See *Mugler* v. *Kansas*, 123 U.S. 623, 679 (1887), cited in ibid.

68. *Mugler* v. *Kansas*, 123 U.S. 623 (1887).

69. *Berman* v. *Parker*, 348 U.S. 26, reprinted in Norman Williams, Jr., ed., *American Land Planning Law: Cases and Materials*, 2 vols. (New Brunswick, N.J.: Rutgers University, Center for Urban Policy Research, 1978), 2:1691. The case and its implications are discussed at greater length in chapter 5 below.

70. Ibid.

71. Lewis, "Comment: Corporate Prerogative," pp. 920–921.

72. *U.S.* v. *5,324 Acres of Land*, D.C. Cal., 79 F. Supp. 748, 760, cited in 30 *CJS* Eminent Domain, 1:162.

73. Weber, *From Max Weber*, p. 78.

74. Theodore J. Lowi, *Incomplete Conquest: Governing America*, 2d ed. (New York: Holt, Rinehart & Winston, 1981), p. 7. Although it is true that the U.S. political system lacks the degree of centralization typical of most Western European states and that "from its founding the very term 'state' has had an odd ring in the United States," the federal divisions and checks-and-balances machinery limit, but do not preclude, the ultimate powers of statehood. It is as reasonable to use the term *state* to describe the U.S. political system as it is to use it to describe the British, French, or Soviet regimes, however much political scientists have generally avoided the term. See Katznelson, *City Trenches*, p. 63; and Theodore J. Lowi, "Decision Making vs. Policy Making: Toward an Antidote for Technocracy," *Public Administration Review* 30 (May–June 1970): 314–325. For an argument that places eminent domain in the context of social contract theory, see Arthur Lenhoff, "Development of the Concept of Eminent Domain," *Columbia Law Review* 42 (April 1942): 599.

75. Poulantzas, *State, Power, Socialism*, pp. 93–107.

76. Lowi, *Incomplete Conquest*, p. 99.

77. Bosselman, Callies, and Banta, *The Taking Issue*, pp. 1, 318.

78. Ellickson, "Suburban Growth Controls," p. 419.

79. *San Diego Gas & Electric Co.* v. *City of San Diego*, 450 U.S. 621, 101 S. Ct.

1287 (1981), at p. 1305. The procedural question turned on the fact that SDG&E had failed to make an application to the city to use or develop the property, or to press the city to determine "what development might be permitted." Because numerous issues of fact remained open, the Court suggested that the corporation go back to the city and start the process anew. In 1980 the U.S. Supreme Court held in another California case, also arising under the state's open-space law, that owners deprived of substantial land use rights are entitled not to damage awards but only to invalidation of a statute that unconstitutionally restricts use rights. In this instance, *Agins* v. *City of Tiburon,* 447 U.S. 255, 100 S. Ct. 2138 (1980), the owners' pleas were rejected on the grounds that the ordinance did not cut off all expansionist rights since it permitted construction of up to five residences on their property. A similar judgment informed the Court's ruling in *MacDonald, Summer & Frates—A Partnership* v. *The County of Yolo and the City of Davis,* No. 84–2015 (1986).

80. Freilich, "Solving the 'Taking' Equation," p. 485.

81. *San Diego Gas & Electric Co.* v. *City of San Diego,* 450 U.S. 621, at p. 652, 101 S. Ct. 1287 (1981), at p. 1304.

82. *Just* v. *Marinette County,* 56 Wis. 2d 7, at p. 16, 201 N.W. 2d 761 (1972), at p. 768, in Williams, *American Land Planning Law,* 2:1204.

83. Reilly, *The Use of Land,* p. 23.

84. Sondra Berchin, "Regulation of Land Use: From Magna Carta to a *Just* Formulation," *UCLA Law Review* 23 (June 1976): 904.

85. Lawrence Berger, "The Public Use Requirement in Eminent Domain," *Oregon Law Review* 57 (1978): 243. For one of the rare examples of a state court acting to block a major downtown project on constitutional grounds, see *In Re Seattle,* 96 Wn. 2d 616 (1981). In this instance, the Supreme Court of the State of Washington blocked condemnation of private land for the city's Westlake Project, a major central city shopping complex. In the words of the majority, "It may be conceded that the Westlake Project is in the 'public interest.' However, the fact that the public interest may require it is insufficient if the use is not really public. A beneficial use is not necessarily a public use." Such views are rarely heard in urban land condemnation cases, which helps to explain why, for one of the foremost critics of suburban zoning—attorney Richard F. Babcock—the land use policies of large cities are in substantially less need of regional oversight than those of their more exclusionary suburban neighbors. See Clifford L. Weaver and Richard F. Babcock, *City Zoning: The Once and Future Frontier* (Chicago: American Planning Association, Planners Press, 1979), pp. 243–255.

86. Laura Mansnerus, "Public Use, Private Use, and Judicial Review in Eminent Domain," *New York University Law Review* 58 (May 1983): 428.

87. Michelman, "Property, Utility, and Fairness," p. 1169.

88. Tigar and Levy, *Law and the Rise of Capitalism,* p. 283; Thompson, *Whigs and Hunters,* pp. 258–269.

Chapter 3

1. Harvey, *Limits to Capital,* p. 409.

2. Gilder, *Wealth and Poverty,* p. 283.

3. Antonio Gramsci, *Selections from the Prison Notebooks,* ed. and trans. Quintin Hoare and Geoffrey Nowell Smith (New York: International Publishers, 1971), p. 6.

4. Bosselman, Callies, and Banta, *The Taking Issue*, p. 83.

5. Ibid., p. 84. Early New England towns exerted even tighter controls by restricting population growth. As Lewis Mumford writes, the villages "ceased to grow beyond the possibility of socializing and assimilating [their] numbers: when near crowding, a new congregation would move off under a special pastor, erect a new meeting house, form a new village, lay out fresh fields" (*The Culture of Cities* [New York: Harcourt, Brace, Jovanovich, 1970], p. 140). Restrictions on growth, of course, were the essence of feudal urban policy, and the first American towns merely carried their theme forward. See Henri Pirenne, *Medieval Cities* (Princeton, N.J.: Princeton University Press, 1948); and Murray Bookchin, *The Limits of the City* (New York: Harper & Row, 1974). Bosselmann, Callies, and Banta (*The Taking Issue*, pp. 54–81) also cover some of this ground with respect to English common-law controls.

6. Horwitz, *Transformation of American Law*, pp. 31–32.

7. Rush Welter, *The Mind of America, 1820–1860* (New York: Columbia University Press, 1975), p. 107.

8. Louis M. Hacker, *The Triumph of American Capitalism* (New York: Simon & Schuster, 1940), pp. 141–142. Not surprisingly, entrepreneurial lusts turned toward the land trade. As Shaw Livermore discovered, land speculation companies were our first models of big business organization (*Early American Land Companies: Their Influence on Corporate Development* [New York: Commonwealth Fund, 1939]; see also Thomas P. Abernethy, *The Western Lands and the American Revolution* [New York: Appleton-Century, 1937]). Thus, when the British Privy Council in 1774 placed its infamous restrictions on western settlement and land disposal, they "hit hard . . . at cherished policies that local authorities were not prepared to surrender," especially squatting and government land grants to the well-placed (Gates, *History of Public Land Law Development*, p. 47). What particularly incensed the Americans were suspicions that British entrepreneurs were planning to take the land for themselves; see Nettles, *Roots of American Civilization*, p. 660.

9. *Encyclopedia of American History*, Bicentennial Edition, ed. Richard B. Morris (New York: Harper & Row, 1976), pp. 720–723.

10. Hacker, *Triumph of American Capitalism*, pp. 227–234; Carter Goodrich, *Government Promotion of American Canals and Railroads, 1800–1890* (New York: Columbia University Press, 1960).

11. Benjamin Horace Hibbard, *A History of the Public Land Policies* (Madison: University of Wisconsin Press, 1965), pp. 228–268; Gates, *History of Public Land Law Development*, pp. 384–385; Frederick Cleveland and Frederick Powell, *Railroad Promotion and Capitalization in the United States* (New York: Longmans Green, 1909), esp. pp. 101–148; and Lewis Haney, *A Congressional History of Railways in the United States to 1850*, 2 vols. (Madison: Bulletin of the University of Wisconsin, no. 211, 1908). The railroads and canal companies received more than land. As Frank Smith notes, in 1824 Congress passed a General Survey Act authorizing "studies of both canals and roads." This obligation was interpreted loosely; before long, the U.S. Army Corps of Engineers "was furnishing a major part of the technical skill for the first American railroads." Indeed, the first rail line in the United States, the Baltimore & Ohio, "was surveyed and laid out, and its first section constructed by Corps of Engineers Officers." Corps officers were sometimes even "paid directly by the railroads." Not until 1838 were such formal ties severed and army men prohibited from joint em-

ployment by private companies. The roots of the military-industrial complex run deep (Frank E. Smith, *The Politics of Conservation* [New York: Harper & Row, 1966], pp. 10–15). Of course, formal distinctions did not prevent continuing "cooperation" between the Corps and the corporations; cf. Arthur Maass, *Muddy Waters: The Army Engineers and the Nation's Rivers* (Cambridge: Harvard University Press, 1951), esp. chap. 2, "Adjustment of Group Interests."

12. James Willard Hurst, *Law and the Conditions of Freedom in the Nineteenth-Century United States* (Madison: University of Wisconsin Press, 1956), p. 3 and passim.

13. Quoted in Bennett, "Eminent Domain and Redevelopment," p. 116.

14. Hurst, *Law and the Conditions of Freedom,* pp. 9–10; Tocqueville, *Democracy in America,* 1:170. Tocqueville, for all his subtle grasp of the American case, was largely oblivious to changes in the law of property. "Inside of the frontiers of the Union," he observed, "profound peace prevails." He might have thought otherwise if he had looked inside the frontiers of landed property.

15. James Kent, *Commentaries on American Law,* 2d ed., 4 vols. (New York: O. Halstead, 1832), 3:48.

16. Debates and Proceedings in the New York State Convention for the Revision of the Constitution (Albany, 1846), p. 805, quoted in Hurst, *Law and the Conditions of Freedom,* p. 13.

17. Thomas Jefferson, Letter to John Jay, Paris, 23 August 1785, in *The Portable Thomas Jefferson* (New York: Viking, 1975), p. 384; 1 Beven, *Principles of the Law of Negligence,* 679 (2d ed. 1895), quoted in Horwitz, *Transformation of American Law,* p. 99.

18. Albert K. Weinberg, *Manifest Destiny: A Study of Nationalist Expansion in American History* (Chicago: Quadrangle, 1963), esp. chap. 5, "True Title"; Locke, *Two Treatises,* pp. 327–344; Richard Schlatter, *Private Property: The History of an Idea* (New Brunswick, N.J.: Rutgers University Press, 1951), pp. 151–161; William Leiss, *The Domination of Nature* (Boston: Beacon, 1974), chap. 2. For contemporary Middle Eastern illustrations, see Edward Said, *The Question of Palestine* (New York: Times Books, 1979).

19. Quoted in Weinberg, *Manifest Destiny,* p. 74.

20. Quoted in ibid., pp. 77, 80.

21. Representative Dixon H. Lewis (D-Ala.), 21st Cong., 1st sess., *Congressional Debates,* p. 506, quoted in Robbins, *Our Landed Heritage,* p. 47.

22. Hibbard, *History of the Public Land Policies,* p. 198.

23. "Report of the Commissioner of the General Land Office," House Executive Documents, 49th Cong., 1st sess., 11, pp. 155–156, 217–218, reprinted in *The Making of American Democracy: Readings and Cases,* ed. Ray Allen Billington, Bert James Loewenberg, and Samuel Hugh Brockunier (New York: Rinehart, 1950), 2:45–46.

24. Welter, *The Mind of America,* p. 133.

25. Billington, *Westward Expansion,* pp. 323, 563–581; Dee Brown, *Bury My Heart at Wounded Knee* (New York: Random House, 1971); Imre Sutton, *Indian Land Tenure: Bibliographical Essays and a Guide to the Literature* (New York: Clearwater, 1975), pp. 44–50 (a good bibliographical guide to the literature of Indian removal); and Gates, *History of Public Land Law Development,* pp. 219–224 passim.

26. Gates, *History of Public Land Law Development*, pp. 221–247; Hibbard, *History of the Public Land Policies*, pp. 92–98.

27. Veblen, *Absentee Ownership*, p. 122.

28. Webb, *The Great Frontier;* Maurice Dobb, *Studies in the Development of Capitalism* (New York: International Publishers, 1947), pp. 184ff. K. William Kapp (*Social Costs of Private Enterprise*, esp. chaps. 1–3) goes further and argues that the market system works as a giant economic shovel that continuously dumps costs onto society, while entrepreneurs boast of their "efficiency."

29. Haar, *Land-Use Planning*, p. 124.

30. Locke, *Two Treatises*, p. 340: "And that Prince who shall be so wise and godlike as by established laws of liberty to secure protection and encouragement to . . . honest industry . . . will quickly be too hard for his neighbours." See also Commons, *Legal Foundations of Capitalism*, pp. 19–20.

31. Veblen, *Absentee Ownership*, p. 48.

32. See n. 11, chapter 2, above.

33. Karl Marx and Friedrich Engels, *The German Ideology*, parts 1 and 3, ed. R. Pascal (New York: International Publishers, 1947), p. 22.

34. Elie Halévy, *The Growth of Philosophic Radicalism*, trans. Mary Morris (Boston: Beacon, 1955).

35. James Mill, *Analysis of the Phenomena of the Human Mind*, vol. 2, pp. 187–188, quoted in Halévy, *Growth of Philosophic Radicalism*, p. 362.

36. Jeremy Bentham, *The Works of Jeremy Bentham*, ed. J. Bowring, vol. 4, pp. 362–363, quoted in Halévy, *Growth of Philosophic Radicalism*, p. 168.

37. Jeremy Bentham, *An Introduction to the Principles of Morals and Legislation* (New York: Hafner, 1948). For the implications of the utilitarian view in its modern technocratic guise, see Marcuse, *One-Dimensional Man*.

38. Commons, *Legal Foundations of Capitalism*, p. 20.

39. Marx, *Capital*, 1:761–762.

40. Quoted in Welter, *The Mind of America*, pp. 114–115.

41. Horwitz, *Transformation of American Law*, pp. 31ff.

42. *Palmer* v. *Mulligan*, 3 Cai R 307, 314 (N.Y. Sup. Ct. 1805), quoted in ibid., p. 37.

43. *Platt* v. *Johnson*, 15 Johns. 213, 218 (N.Y. 1818), quoted in Horwitz, *Transformation of American Law*, p. 37.

44. Noble, "Present Tense Technology," p. 10.

45. Bennett, "Eminent Domain," p. 116; and Horwitz, *Transformation of American Law*, chaps. 2 and 3.

46. Bennett, "Eminent Domain," p. 116; Harry N. Schreiber, "Property Law, Expropriation and Resource Allocation by Government, 1789–1910," *Journal of Economic History* 33 (March 1973): 232–251; Errol E. Meidinger, "The 'Public Uses' of Eminent Domain: History and Policy," *Environmental Law* 11 (1980): 1–66.

47. *Monongahela Navigation Co.* v. *V. Coons*, 6 Watts and S. 101 (Pa. 1843) at 115, quoted in Joseph M. Cormack, "Legal Concepts in Cases of Eminent Domain," *Yale Law Journal* 41 (December 1931): 228.

48. Lenhoff, "Development of the Concept of Eminent Domain," pp. 612–613; Horwitz, *Transformation of American Law*, pp. 76–77 (the Blackstone statement [*Commentaries* 3:219] is quoted on p. 76).

49. *Brick Presbyterian Church* v. *The City of New York,* 5 Cow. 538 (N.Y. 1826); *Commonwealth* v. *Tewksbury,* 12 Pick. at 194, cited in Bosselman, Callies, and Banta, *The Taking Issue,* pp. 106–111.

50. *Pumpelly* v. *Green Bay Company,* 13 Wall. 166 (1871) at 177.

51. Cormack, "Legal Concepts in Cases of Eminent Domain, pp. 225–231; Lenhoff, "Development of the Concept of Eminent Domain," pp. 606–607.

52. Cormack, "Legal Concepts in Cases of Eminent Domain," pp. 224–225.

53. In the slaughterhouse cases, see 16 Wall. 36 (1872); the Court upheld Louisiana's grant of a corporate monopoly on slaughter operations. *Munn* v. *Illinois,* 94 U.S. 113 (1876), found the Court in support of state powers to regulate warehouse pricing. And *Mugler* v. *Kansas,* 123 U.S. 623, resulted in the validation of a state law proscribing the manufacture of alcoholic beverages. In each instance, physical conceptions of individual property prevailed over the view of property as a bundle of exchange values caught up in market relations. See Commons, *Legal Foundations of Capitalism,* pp. 11–21. Commons does not discuss *Pumpelly* or *Mugler,* although they clearly fit into his general line of analysis.

54. *Eaton* v. *B. C. and M. Railroad,* 51 N.H. 504 (1872), quoted in Cormack, "Legal Concepts in Cases of Eminent Domain," p. 238. A few years later, another New Hampshire court went considerably further in defining individual property rights in terms of the overall, social interest of landowners: "Property in land must be considered for many purposes not as an absolute, unrestricted dominion" but as the "correlation of rights and obligations necessary for the highest enjoyment of land by the entire community of proprietors" (*Thompson* v. *Androscoggin Co.,* 54 N.H. 545, 551, quoted in ibid., p. 239).

55. Lenhoff, "Development of the Concept of Eminent Domain," p. 610.

56. Mel Scott, *American City Planning Since 1890* (Berkeley and Los Angeles: University of California Press, 1969), p. 3; Cormack, "Legal Concepts in Cases of Eminent Domain," pp. 241, 244.

57. *Chicago, Minneapolis and St. Paul Railway Co.* v. *Minnesota,* 134 U.S. 418 (1890), cited in Commons, *Legal Foundations of Capitalism,* p. 15.

58. Ernst Freund, *The Police Power: Public Policy and Constitutional Rights* (Chicago: Callaghan, 1904), p. 550.

59. *Pennsylvania Coal Co.* v. *Mahon,* 260 U.S. 393. The discussion here follows Bosselman, Callies, and Banta, *The Taking Issue,* pp. 124–138.

60. For graphic descriptions of coal's impact on land, people, and communities, see Harry Caudill, *Night Comes to the Cumberlands: A Biography of a Depressed Area* (Boston: Atlantic Monthly–Little, Brown, 1963); Caudill, *The Watches of the Night* (Boston: Atlantic Monthly–Little, Brown, 1976); Kai T. Erikson, *Everything in Its Path: Destruction of Community in the Buffalo Creek Flood* (New York: Simon & Schuster, 1976); John Gaventa, *Power and Powerlessness: Quiescence and Rebellion in an Appalachian Valley* (Urbana: University of Illinois Press, 1980).

61. Brief on Behalf of the City of Scranton, Intervenor, in the Supreme Court of the United States, October term, 1922, p. 1, cited in Bosselman, Callies, and Banta, *The Taking Issue,* p. 128.

62. Bosselman, Callies, and Banta, *The Taking Issue,* pp. 130–131.

63. 260 U.S. 393, at p. 413, quoted in ibid., p. 134.

64. Ibid. Justice Brandeis's dissent returned to traditional distinctions between direct seizure and regulation and warned against the emerging conception of property as a bundle of rights, or "sticks," as Holmes called them. "The sum of the rights in the parts cannot be greater than the rights of the whole. . . . No one would contend that by selling his interest above one hundred feet from the surface [an owner] could prevent the State from limiting by the police power, the height of structures in a city." No, Brandeis insisted, "coal in place is land; and the right of the owner to use land is not absolute. He may not so use it as to cause a public nuisance" (U.S. 393, at pp. 419, 417 [dissenting opinion], quoted in Bosselman, Callies, and Banta, *The Taking Issue,* pp. 244–245, 247).

65. Toll, *Zoned American,* p. 87; Nelson, *Zoning and Private Property Rights.* Cf. Friedrich Engels, *The Condition of the Working Class in England,* trans. W. O. Henderson and W. H. Chaloner (Stanford: Stanford University Press, 1968), p. 54.

66. Burton J. Bledstein, *The Culture of Professionalism: The Middle Class and the Development of Higher Education in America* (New York: W. W. Norton, 1976), p. 64; and David Gordon, "Capitalist Development and the History of American Cities," in *Marxism and the Metropolis: New Perspectives in Urban Political Economy,* ed. William K. Tabb and Larry Sawers (New York: Oxford University Press, 1978), p. 43. But cf. Engels, *Condition of the Working Class:* Engels writes of Manchester that "he who visits . . . need never see the slums, mainly because the working class districts and the middle class districts are quite distinct. The division is due partly to deliberate policy and partly to instinctive and tacit agreement between the two social groups" (p. 54).

67. Robert Wood, *Suburbia: Its People and Their Politics* (Boston: Houghton Mifflin, 1958), pp. 55–56, 60; John C. Bollens and Henry J. Schmandt, *The Metropolis: Its People, Politics, and Economic Life,* 4th ed. (New York: Harper & Row, 1982), p. 38; Blake McKelvey, *The Urbanization of America, 1860–1915* (New Brunswick, N.J.: Rutgers University Press, 1963), chap. 1.

68. McKelvey, *Urbanization of America,* p. 51.

69. Lewis Mumford, *The City in History: Its Origins, Its Transformations, and Its Prospects* (New York: Harcourt, Brace & World, 1961), p. 429; Wood, *Suburbia;* Patrick J. Ashton, "The Political Economy of Suburban Development," in Tabb and Sawers, *Marxism and the Metropolis,* pp. 64–89; Frederick M. Wirt et al., *On the City's Rim: Politics and Policy in Suburbia* (Lexington, Mass.: D. C. Heath, 1972), pp. 3–23; Oliver P. Williams, *Metropolitan Political Analysis: A Social Access Approach* (New York: Free Press, 1971), esp. chap. 6. Cf. McConnell, *Private Power and American Democracy,* esp. chap. 4, which discusses the general problem of private appropriation of public government as a typically American solution to the question of power. In two early cases, the Supreme Court overturned private exclusionary controls on land use. In *Eubank* v. *City of Richmond,* 226 U.S. 137 (1912), a local ordinance was rejected which gave two-thirds of the landowners on any street rights "to require the city street committee to set a building line past which no construction on individual lots was permitted." And in Washington, *Seattle Title Trust Co.* v. *Roberge,* 278 U.S. 116 (1928), the law in question was a zoning amendment permitting charitable homes for the poor in residential districts only with the written consent of two-thirds of the adjoining property owners (i.e., those within 400 feet). In each

instance, the Court frowned on legislative delegations that lacked clear standards to control the exercise of power over "reasonable" land use activities. By contrast, in *Thomas Cusack Co.* v. *City of Chicago*, 242 U.S. 526 (1917), the Court upheld against due process challenges an ordinance prohibiting billboards in residential areas without the approval of a majority of the affected landowners. Because billboards were considered by the Court to be nuisances per se, and thus subject to outright bans by local governments, this law was seen as "benefitting potential billboard erectors," since it involved a legitimate restriction that was made subject to waiver by those affected. See Sager, "Insular Majorities Unabated," pp. 1405–1406.

70. Kenneth T. Jackson, "Metropolitan Government Versus Suburban Autonomy: Politics on the Crabgrass Frontier," in *Cities in American History,* ed. Kenneth T. Jackson and Stanley K. Schultz (New York: Knopf, 1972), pp. 442–462; Ann Marcusen, "Class and Urban Social Expenditure: A Marxist Theory of Metropolitan Government," in Tabb and Sawers, *Marxism and the Metropolis,* pp. 90–111.

71. Nelson, *Zoning and Private Property Rights,* p. 112.

72. David Gordon, "Capitalist Development," pp. 47–48. See also Richard A. Walker, "A Theory of Suburbanization: Capitalism and the Construction of Urban Space in the United States," in Dear and Scott, *Urbanization and Urban Planning,* pp. 399–401.

73. Bollens and Schmandt, *The Metropolis,* pp. 242–243. Private, restrictive convenants were overturned by the Supreme Court in *Shelley* v. *Kramer,* 334 U.S. 1 (1948). The grounds centered on the unconstitutionality of limiting the rights of blacks "to acquire, enjoy, own and dispose of property" (Williams, *American Land Planning Law,* 1:313).

74. See *St. Louis Poster Advertising Co.* v. *City of St. Louis,* 249 U.S. 269 (1919); *Barbier* v. *Connolly,* 113 U.S. 27 (1885); *Soon Hing* v. *Crowley,* 113 U.S. 703 (1885); *Reinman* v. *Little Rock,* 237 U.S. 171 (1915). The laundry cases, Barbier and Soon Hing, deserve special mention. They involved Chinese shopowners imprisoned "for violating local laws regulating the location of shops and prohibiting night work" (Toll, *Zoned American,* p. 29). However, the fact that the shops were also used as Chinese social clubs made them especially "noxious." These cases supplied early proof for the idea that "land use control" is really social control, control over the spatial relationships between different races and classes. As Toll observed, "The immigrant is in the fiber of zoning" (p. 29).

75. *Welch* v. *Swazey,* 214 U.S. 91 (1909).

76. *Hadacheck* v. *Sebastian,* 239 U.S. 394 (1915), in Williams, *American Land Planning Law,* 1:329–335.

77. Ibid., p. 333.

78. Ibid. "And the only limitation upon the power [is] that the power could not be exercised arbitrarily or with unjust discrimination."

79. Ibid.

80. In 1891 Congress passed the General Revision Act, which among other things gave the president authority to withdraw public land from entry in order to create forest preserves. See Gates, *History of Public Land Law Development,* p. 484; Craig W. Allin, *The Politics of Wilderness Preservation* (Westport, Conn.: Greenwood, 1982), pp. 34–36; Robbins, *Our Landed Heritage,* pp. 296–297. This law set the precedent for subsequent reservations and creation of a permanent public-land system.

81. Engler, *Politics of Oil;* Robert Engler, *The Brotherhood of Oil* (Chicago: University of Chicago Press, 1977); John Ise, *The United States Forest Policy* (New Haven: Yale University Press, 1920); John Ise, *The United States Oil Policy* (New Haven: Yale University Press, 1926); Wesley Calef, *Private Grazing and Public Lands: Studies of the Local Management of the Taylor Grazing Act* (Chicago: University of Chicago Press, 1960); Philip O. Foss, *Politics and Grass: The Administration of Grazing on the Public Domain* (Seattle: University of Washington Press, 1960); Marion Clawson and Burnell Held, *The Federal Lands: Their Use and Management* (Baltimore: Resources for the Future series, Johns Hopkins University Press, 1957); Samuel P. Hays, *Conservation and the Gospel of Efficiency: The Progressive Conservation Movement, 1890–1920* (New York: Atheneum, 1969); Louise E. Peffer, *The Closing of the Public Domain* (Stanford: Stanford University Press, 1951); Marion Clawson, *The Federal Lands Revisited* (Baltimore: Resources for the Future series, Johns Hopkins University Press, 1983); Paul J. Culhane, *Public Lands Politics: Interest Group Influence on the Forest Service and the Bureau of Land Management* (Baltimore: Resources for the Future series, Johns Hopkins University Press, 1981); Tom Arrandale, *The Battle for Natural Resources* (Washington, D.C.: Congressional Quarterly, 1983).

82. George Perkins Marsh, *The Earth as Modified by Human Action: A New Edition of Man and Nature* (New York: Scribner, Armstrong, 1874). Marsh's work was central to the later development of physical conservation policies, but he was thoroughly impressed by the close interrelationships between social domination and ecological exploitation. "Next to ignorance" of the physical laws of nature, Marsh also explained the destructiveness of early Roman resource policy by "the brutal and exhausting despotism which Rome . . . exercised over her conquered kingdoms." Similarly, exploitation of American raw materials was linked to the fact that "joint-stock companies have no souls; their managers, in general, no consciences" (pp. 5, 53, note); cf. Gifford Pinchot, *Breaking New Ground* (New York: Harcourt, Brace, 1947); Norman I. Wengert, *Natural Resources and the Political Struggle* (New York: Doubleday, 1955); Hays, *Conservation and the Gospel of Efficiency.*

83. Clawson and Held, *Federal Lands*, p. 10. The authors add: "This is especially true for those uses which produce salable products. Those who enjoy the gains from federal land use should pay a reasonable price for that use." But cf. Engler, *Politics of Oil* and *Brotherhood of Oil;* Lynne Milne et al., *The Great Giveaway: Public Oil, Gas and Coal and the Reagan Administration*, Sierra Club, Natural Heritage Report no. 1 (San Francisco: Sierra Club, 1982).

84. Hays, *Conservation and the Gospel of Efficiency,* p. 3; Wengert, *Natural Resources,* pp. 3–7.

85. Frederick Law Olmsted, "Public Parks and the Enlargement of Towns," in *Civilizing American Cities: A Selection of Frederick Law Olmsted's Writings on City Landscapes,* ed. S. B. Sutton (Cambridge: MIT Press, 1971), pp. 65, 69. Olmsted's remarks were intended here to emphasize some of the dehumanizing aspects of big-city life and thus the need for parks as opportunities "of relief from it" (p. 66).

86. *Vegelahn* v. *Guntner,* 167 Mass. 92, 108, 44 N.E. 1077 (1896), quoted in Sax, "Takings and the Police Power," p. 40.

87. Rodgers, "Bringing People Back," pp. 219–220: "The policy is one of peaceful coexistence, and the courts work hard to achieve this reconciliation."

88. Sax, "Takings and the Police Power," p. 40.

89. Ibid. Why, then, did Holmes's ruling in *Pennsylvania Coal* v. *Mahon* limit the police power as a check on destructive industry? Bosselman and his colleagues suggest that it was precisely Holmes's feeling that real property was more tangible than other forms of property that encouraged him to apply a more rigid "conception of property rights" in land cases than in other examples of police regulation. Thus Holmes was especially concerned that the state not avoid its obligations to landed property simply by pretending that control was not seizure. See Bosselman, Callies, and Banta, *The Taking Issue*, pp. 243–244.

90. Veblen, *Theory of the Leisure Class;* Toll, *Zoned American;* Babcock, *The Zoning Game,* chap. 1; Delafons, *Land-Use Controls;* and Constance Perin, *Everything in Its Place: Social Order and Land Use in America* (Princeton, N.J.: Princeton University Press, 1977).

91. Edward M. Bassett, *Zoning: The Laws, Administration and Court Decisions During the First Twenty Years* (New York: Russell Sage Foundation, 1936), p. 12.

92. Toll, *Zoned American.*

93. Ibid., pp. 193, 192.

94. Herbert Hoover, "Foreword," U.S. Department of Commerce, Advisory Committee on Zoning, *A Standard State Zoning Enabling Act* (Washington, D.C.: GPO, 1924), p. iv, quoted in Scott, *American City Planning,* p. 194; Toll, *Zoned American,* pp. 200–202.

95. *Village of Euclid* v. *Ambler Realty Co.,* 272 U.S. 365 (1926), reprinted in Haar, *Land-Use Planning,* pp. 194–204.

96. Ibid., p. 201.

97. *Ambler Realty Co.* v. *Village of Euclid,* 297 F. 307, 313, 316, quoted in ibid., p. 203.

98. *Village of Euclid et al.* v. *Ambler Realty Company,* brief, Amici Curiae, in the Supreme Court of the United States, reprinted in Bettman, *City and Regional Planning Papers,* pp. 157–193.

99. Ibid., p. 173.

100. Ibid., pp. 162, 159–160.

101. Ibid., p. 171.

102. Ibid., p. 181.

103. Ibid., pp. 177–178.

104. Ibid., pp. 169–170. For an elaborate theoretical statement of this point, see Olson, *Logic of Collective Action.*

105. Bettman, *City and Regional Planning Papers,* pp. 178, 165.

106. *Village of Euclid* v. *Ambler Realty Co.,* 272 U.S. 365, 47 S. Ct. 114 (1926), in Haar, *Land-Use Planning,* p. 199.

107. Ibid., p. 200.

108. Ibid., p. 201.

109. Ibid., p. 202.

110. Ibid., p. 201.

111. Alfred Bettman, "The Decision of the Supreme Court of the United States in the Euclid Village Zoning Case," in *City and Regional Planning Papers,* pp. 55–56.

Part Two

Introduction: The Restructured Metropolis

1. Richard F. Babcock, "The Spatial Impact of Land-Use Controls and Environmental Controls," in Solomon, *The Prospective City,* p. 265. Babcock dates the Supreme Court's earliest recent foray into zoning as 1974, overlooking *James* v. *Valtierra,* 402 U.S. 137 (1971), which dealt with local referendums that might be used to exclude low-income housing.

2. Popper, *Politics of Land-Use Reform,* p. 9.

3. Ibid.

4. Other examples of the environmental interpretation of land use reform include Healy and Rosenberg, *Land Use,* p. 1; Reilly, *The Use of Land;* Noreen Lyday, *The Law of the Land: Debating National Land Use Legislation, 1970–1975* (Washington, D.C.: Urban Institute, 1976); Bosselman and Callies, *Quiet Revolution;* Walter A. Rosenbaum, *The Politics of Environmental Concern* (New York: Praeger, 1973).

5. Robert Caro, *The Power Broker: Robert Moses and the Fall of New York* (New York: Random House, 1975), esp. chaps. 37 and 38; Casper and Wellstone, *Powerline;* Hartman, *Yerba Buena;* Edel, "Urban Renewal"; Nicholas Freudenberg, *Not in Our Backyards! Community Action for Health and the Environment* (New York: Monthly Review Press, 1984); Peter Hall, *Great Planning Disasters* (Berkeley and Los Angeles: University of California Press, 1982); Meyerson and Banfield, *Politics, Planning, and the Public Interest;* K. Ross Toole, *The Rape of the Great Plains* (Boston: Atlantic Monthly–Little, Brown, 1976); Worthy, *Rape of Our Neighborhoods;* Young, *Power over People;* Schwartz, *We Are Talking About Homes.*

6. Brian Anson, *I'll Fight You for It,* p. 5.

7. Although James O'Connor does not specifically develop the notion of urban restructuring, the idea suggested here owes much to the analysis he developed ten years ago in *The Fiscal Crisis of the State.* For more contemporary views, see Mollenkopf, *The Contested City,* esp. chap. 1; and Susan S. Fainstein and Norman I. Fainstein, "Economic Change, National Policy, and the System of Cities," in Susan S. Fainstein et al., *Restructuring the City: The Political Economy of Urban Redevelopment* (New York: Longman, 1983), pp. 1–26. David Harvey, in *Limits to Capital,* offers a comprehensive theoretical rationale for the logic of the spatial restructuring of capital. And Neil Smith (*Uneven Development: Nature, Capital and the Production of Space* [Oxford: Basil Blackwell, 1984]) argues persuasively that, for capital, "space is on the agenda as never before" (p. 89). Harvey and Smith are especially articulate in stressing the global dimension of this restructuring process.

8. Freudenberg, *Not in Our Backyards!* p. 21.

9. Barry Commoner, *The Poverty of Power: Energy and the Economic Crisis* (New York: Bantam, 1977), pp. 208–209.

10. Engler, *Politics of Oil;* Engler, *Brotherhood of Oil.*

11. Freudenberg, *Not in Our Backyards!* pp. 21–22.

Chapter 4

1. Erickson, *Everything in Its Path,* p. 82.

2. An observer early in the twentieth century made the point well: "For a number

of years some Texas towns have stood still, while others have greatly advanced. San Antonio, one of the oldest cities of the United States, has gone along in a 50–50 fashion for many years" (Howart Evarts Weed, "Civic Development in Oklahoma and Texas Cities," *American City* 2 [April 1910]: 159). The comment applied until well into the 1960s.

3. San Antonio Economic Development Foundation (EDF), "San Antonio: Good for Growing Things, Like Profits and People," pamphlet, n.d. The EDF is a private group established by the city to promote San Antonio in the race for municipal jobs and business locations. Composed of some of the city's leading entrepreneurs, EDF in 1974 contracted with the Fantus Corporation, a New York consulting firm that handles a sizable portion of the national corporate relocation market, to study San Antonio's commercial situation. Fantus replied that the city leaders would be wise to "attract industries that would not upset the existing wage ladder." It also noted that the city's average hourly earnings rates in manufacturing were lower in 1975 than those for every other major Texas city except El Paso. But then, San Antonio is not a manufacturing town. Slightly more than a third (35.4 percent) of all wages were paid by government, 23.7 percent by the federal government. See Fantus Company, "Economic Development Program, Industry Location Appraisal," Exhibit 17, p. 53; *San Antonio Express,* 25 November 1979.

4. City of San Antonio, City Planning Commission, "The San Antonio Master Plan," draft, "Foreword," San Antonio, 16 January 1980, p. 1.

5. "Henry Cisneros Talks to San Antonio," *San Antonio Express,* 3 April 1981.

6. Cited in William Lilley III, "The Homebuilders' Lobby," in *Housing Urban America,* 2d ed., ed. Jon Pynoos, Robert Shafer, and Chester W. Hartman (Hawthorne, N.Y.: Aldine, 1980), p. 36.

7. For one of the few efforts by a political scientist to explore the implications of spatial, historical, economic, and political intersections, see Daniel J. Elezar, *Cities of the Prairie: The Metropolitan Frontier and American Politics* (New York: Basic Books, 1970). See also, for the Texas case, D. W. Meinig, *Imperial Texas: An Interpretive Essay in Cultural Geography* (Austin: University of Texas Press, 1969).

8. James W. Ingram and Chia Shun Shih, *Utility Analysis for the Urban Growth Inside the Recharge Zones of the Groundwater Resources of San Antonio, Texas* (San Antonio: Division of Environmental Studies, University of Texas at San Antonio, 1977), pp. 1–2.

9. V. O. Key, Jr., *Southern Politics in State and Nation* (New York: Random House, 1949), p. 254; Jack Bass and Walter DeVries, *The Transformation of Southern Politics* (New York: Basic Books, 1976), p. 305; Kirkpatrick Sale, *Power Shift: The Rise of the Southern Rim and Its Challenge to the Eastern Establishment* (New York: Random House, 1975). Although they do not discuss Texas, Peter Wiley and Robert Gottlieb (*Empires in the Sun: The Rise of the New American West* [New York: Putnam, 1982]) apply the Texas model to analysis of the far western states and their major cities.

10. Ingram and Shih, *Utility Analysis,* p. 52; Richard C. Bath, "Texas Groundwater Policy," a paper prepared for presentation at the meeting of the Southwestern Political Science Association, Houston, Texas, 1978.

11. Ingram and Shih, *Utility Analysis,* p. 53.

12. Thomas A. Baylis, "Leadership Change in Contemporary San Antonio," in *The Politics of San Antonio: Community, Progress, and Power,* ed. David R. John-

son, John A. Booth, and Richard J. Harris (Lincoln: University of Nebraska Press, 1983), p. 99.

13. During this period, only five of the city council members lived on the west or southwest sides. At-large elections under GGL control ensured that, in the words of Edward Banfield and James Q. Wilson, the "underdogs" were kept "in their places" and out of city government. See Robert Lineberry, *Equality and Urban Policy: The Distribution of Municipal Public Services* (Beverly Hills, Calif.: Sage, 1977), pp. 56–57; Charles L. Cottrell and R. Michael Stevens, "The 1975 Voting Rights Act and San Antonio, Texas: Toward a Federal Guarantee of a Republican Form of Local Government," *Publius* 8 (Winter 1978): 84–85; John A. Booth and David R. Johnson, "Elites and Urban Development in San Antonio: Charter Change as a Means of Elite Control," a paper prepared for presentation at the meeting of the Southwestern Political Science Association, Houston, Texas, 1978, p. 35; Luther Lee Sanders, *How to Win Elections in San Antonio the Good Government Way, 1955–1971* (San Antonio: Urban Studies Department, St. Mary's University, 1975); Edward Banfield and James Q. Wilson, *City Politics* (Cambridge: Harvard University Press, 1965), p. 171.

14. John A. Booth and David R. Johnson, "Community, Progress, and Power in San Antonio," in Johnson, Booth, and Harris, *Politics of San Antonio*, p. 24.

15. Ibid.; see also Richard A. Jones, "San Antonio's Spatial Economic Structure," in Johnson, Booth, and Harris, *Politics of San Antonio*, pp. 28–52.

16. Jones, "San Antonio's Spatial Economic Structure," p. 33. The city grew from 65.5 to 184 square miles in total land area. Another 80 square miles were gobbled up between 1970 and 1978. Thus, altogether, San Antonio grew 400 percent in area during the postwar period. The basis of this impressive growth was the state's 1963 Municipal Annexation Law. As befits its expansionist traditions, Texas has one of the most liberal annexation laws in the nation. Cities may control an extraterritorial jurisdiction extending five miles from their municipal boundary. Any unincorporated subdivisions in the extraterritorial jurisdiction are subject to central-city land use controls and may be annexed without their consent. Indeed, cities are authorized to annex up to 10 percent of their territory each year without referendum. Houston expanded from 160 to 521 square miles between 1970 and 1978, Dallas from 112 to 336, and Fort Worth from 94 to 234 square miles. See Arnold Fleischmann, "Sunbelt Boosterism: The Politics of Postwar Growth in San Antonio," in *The Rise of the Sunbelt Cities*, ed. David C. Perry and Alfred J. Watkins, vol. 14, Urban Affairs Annual Reviews (Beverly Hills, Calif.: Sage, 1977), pp. 151–168; John J. Harrigan, *Political Change in the Metropolis*, 2d ed. (Boston: Little, Brown, 1981), p. 290; Bollens and Schmandt, *The Metropolis*, table 11.1, p. 307.

17. "The Edwards Aquifer Story," a pamphlet produced by the Edwards Underground Water District, 1977, p. 4.

18. Col. McDonald D. Weinert, general manager, Edwards Underground Water District, interview, conducted by Joan Hanlon, 2 May 1978. All future mentions of Weinert's views, unless otherwise noted, are taken from this source.

19. *San Antonio Express*, 26 July 1959.

20. The Edwards Underground Water District is an example of what the Advisory Commission on Intergovernmental Relations (ACIR) calls "far and away the most rapidly growing" of the various types of local government in the United States, the "special district." By 1977, according to the ACIR, there were no fewer than 25,962

special-purpose governments in the United States. Texas, with 1,425, is fourth among all the states in the number of its special governments. Typically established by local action under the authority of state law, special districts usually perform a single function, such as fire protection, water supply, soil conservation, irrigation, or energy supply, which for budgetary or political reasons the local general-purpose city or county government may refuse to perform, and which local power elites, especially suburban boosters, find it useful to screen out of the public view. Thus lack of accountability is one of the most typical features of the special-district form. As John J. Harrigan has noted, "The major reason for the popularity of special districts undoubtedly lies in the fact that they can raise money for needed services at the same time that they maintain a low political and fiscal visibility" (*Political Change in the Metropolis,* p. 242). See also U.S. Advisory Commission on Intergovernmental Relations, *State and Local Roles in the Federal System* (Washington, D.C.: GPO, 1981), p. 253.

21. Texas, *Revised Civil Statutes,* chap. 12, Water Districts, Article 8280-219, pp. 480, 486.

22. "Edwards Aquifer Story." As Weinert put it, "We have no authority to tell a person they cannot draw a well or how much water they can remove." Bexar County's early representatives on the board were not ones to dissent from the dominant conservatism. They included a professional engineer, who also served as vice-president and member of the board in the construction firm owned by H. B. Zachary, the "most influential man" in the city, according to one San Antonio newspaper poll. Another was a geologist and petroleum engineer with ties to the oil industry. A third was a major landowner and farmer who served on the boards of a prominent local bank and an insurance company. In an editorial urging support for these men, the *San Antonio Express* proclaimed: "These men have helped the South Texas Chamber of Commerce in its four-year effort to set up the Edwards Underground Water District and are the logical ones to get its work underway" (*San Antonio Express,* 26 July 1959); Jan Jarboe, "Who Pulls the Strings in San Antonio?" *S.A. Magazine,* March 1977, p. 79.

23. *San Antonio Express,* 8 April 1961.

24. Ibid., 13 January 1965.

25. City of San Antonio, Office of the Planning Engineer, *San Antonio Bexar County Urban Transportation Study, 1964–1985, Report No. 2 (Part A),* May 1966, p. 14.

26. *San Antonio Express,* 24 June 1964.

27. "The Big Trouble at San Antonio Ranch," *Business Week,* 3 November 1977, p. 78.

28. Glen Hartman, "No Rush for Water," *San Antonio Express-News,* 20 August 1978, p. 3-H.

29. See Congressional Quarterly, *Man's Control of the Environment* (Washington, D.C.: Congressional Quarterly, 1970), p. 19.

30. Research and Planning Consultants, *Texas Land Use, Report No. Two: Existing Mechanisms* (Austin: Division of Planning Coordination, Office of the Governor, 1973), p. 72.

31. And, as E. E. Schattschneider observed, "the audience determines the outcome" of most political conflicts (*Semisovereign People,* p. 2).

32. *San Antonio Express-News,* 15 February 1970.

33. Briscoe and his family owned 414,000 acres in Uvalde County and southwest Texas lands. For data on Texas landownership, see Chiles, "Who Owns Texas?" pp. 122ff.

34. "Big Trouble at San Antonio Ranch," *Business Week*, p. 78.

35. Head was the driving force behind the project. Christian's Austin public relations firm, Christian, Miller and Honts (CMH), was invited along to help secure the necessary political clearances and subsidies. His contacts in Austin and Washington were top-notch. Head was especially anxious for two public props. First, he wanted a HUD subsidy for the New Town. Next, Head used allies on the Texas Board of Regents in an effort to locate the new branch of the state university on his site. The effort failed, and the new college at San Antonio was placed about six miles east of Ranchtown. But Head did somewhat better than the city itself, for UTSA was located almost twenty miles from downtown, far from the west side's young. For a detailed look at the Ranchtown case, see Wayt T. Watterson and Roberta S. Watterson, *The Politics of New Communities: A Case Study of San Antonio Ranch* (New York: Praeger, 1975). On the UTSA site-selection process and much else of interest on the political economics of higher education in Texas, see Ronnie Dugger, *Our Invaded Universities* (New York: W. W. Norton, 1974), pp. 212–288.

36. Watterson and Watterson, *Politics of New Communities*, p. 79.

37. Robert Sohn, "Citizens for a Better Environment," cited in *San Antonio Light*, 2 May 1973.

38. Cited in Ingram and Shih, *Utility Analysis*, p. 65.

39. Watterson and Watterson, in *Politics of New Communities*, detail the tactics of Head and his friends (pp. 18–26, 60–70). Also see Martha Derthic, *New Towns In-Town: Why a Federal Program Failed* (Washington, D.C.: Urban Institute, 1972), chap. 3, for a look at San Antonio's earlier experience with a proposed federal project that was killed after the military expressed hostility to public housing adjacent to Fort Sam Houston.

40. Watterson and Watterson, *Politics of New Communities*, pp. 29–30.

41. Ranchtown's sponsors had a point. There was in fact an anti-outsider dimension to the Ranchtown opposition. Fred Pfeiffer, for example, head of the San Antonio River Authority, told *Business Week*, "Either this project was politically wired or it has a lot more merit than the local people can see in it" ("Big Trouble at San Antonio Ranch," p. 78). In several interviews local builders scoffed at the prospect of inexperienced outsiders coming into the city with hopes of building a new town from scratch.

42. District Judge Adrian Spears later observed that the environmentalists "lost the case . . . but they won the war to protect and save the Edwards Aquifer." By forcing the application of tougher standards and alerting the public to the dangers of development, Spears suggested that the land would not be subject to the prevailing style of cut-and-run growth. He even ruled that the plaintiffs' legal fees should be paid in part by the SAR sponsors, although this decision was later overturned on appeal (Watterson and Watterson, *Politics of New Communities*, pp. 46–47).

43. The Alamo Area Council of Governments is an example of the closest approximation to regional government in U.S. federalism. AACOG, like the other 292 metropolitan regional councils, is, in the words of John J. Harrigan, "a voluntary association

of local municipalities and counties that join forces for the purpose of coordinating their activities on regional problems." Strongly encouraged by federal legislation, these councils serve as screening and coordination devices for many federal development programs, as well as for studying and formulating policy. However, they have no formal authority or power, save that of their review functions in respect to the national programs. As Harrigan observes, "COGs can do little to make local governments follow their decisions" (*Political Change in the Metropolis,* pp. 331–332); U.S. Advisory Commission on Intergovernmental Relations, *State and Local Roles,* table 107, p. 268. Nonetheless, as this case study will suggest, COGs can have some importance in developing a regional political consciousness and strategy on pressing issues.

44. Letter sent by Al J. Notzen III to officials of various local governments, 25 May 1973, in "Edwards Task Force—1973 and Before," in files of the Alamo Area Council of Governments, San Antonio, Texas (hereafter cited as AACOG File).

45. Al J. Notzen III, interview, March 1978.

46. Memorandum from Col. McDonald D. Weinert to the board of directors, EUWD, 28 June 1972, AACOG File. Weinert felt that the politics of water was getting out of hand: too many interest groups were involved. A letter sent in 1973 by William Spice, Jr., chairman of the board of directors of the EUWD, to San Antonio Mayor Charles Becker, suggests the staff's opinion that it was time for the experts to take over. Spice urged the mayor not to hold a city council meeting at which construction standards were to be discussed. He recommended instead reconvening the old Bexar County Edwards Aquifer Protection Committee. The existing authorities, he said, such as the San Antonio City Council, San Antonio River Authority, AACOG, and the EUWD, "know what regulations need to be imposed on construction in the Recharge Zone . . . without any lengthy study or expenditure of funds." He concluded by recommending a return to the rule of experts: "The working people of the agencies I have designated can provide the political entities which must make a decision with the necessary legal and technical information on which policy decisions can be made" (Letter from William Spice, Jr., Chairman of the Board, EUWD to Hon. Charles Becker, Mayor, San Antonio, Texas, 29 May 1973, AACOG File). From this point on, the EUWD opposed continuance of the AACOG Task Force.

47. *San Antonio Express,* 22 June 1973.

48. The chairman of the local Sierra Club chapter informed the TWQB that "while some improvement over previous proposals is evident, we again find there is no evidence of real commitment to protection of this vital public resource. . . . It is obvious to us that the current proposal is simply another in a long series of attempts to give the appearance of concern while withholding the substance of protection" (Letter from Anthony A. Athens, Jr., to James Showers, director, Hearings and Enforcement Division, TWQB, 18 October 1973, AACOG File).

49. "Suggested Modifications to Proposed Aquifer Protection Order, June 11, 1973," AACOG File.

50. Glen Hartman, city council member, San Antonio, Texas, interview, March 1978.

51. Jarboe, "Who Pulls the Strings in San Antonio?" pp. 46–48.

52. G. E. Harrington, interviews, March 1978 and July 1983. Harrington was a prominent local builder, president of the San Antonio Home Builders Association, and chairman of the city planning commission. After leaving politics to earn his bachelor's

degree, he returned in 1981 to win a seat on the city council. In addition to supplying his views, Mr. Harrington generously made available to the author his personal files on the aquifer issue. Materials from this source will hereafter be cited as Harrington File.

53. Cipriano F. Guerra, Jr., director of Planning and Community Development, San Antonio, Texas, memorandum to directors of Public Works, Building and Planning, Traffic and Transportation, and the city attorney, 7 November 1975, pp. 2–3, Harrington File.

54. Frank Vega, "Activity Report for Edwards Aquifer Protection Office," City of San Antonio, October 1975, Harrington File.

55. Paul Burka, "The Second Battle of the Alamo," *Texas Monthly*, December 1977, p. 221.

56. Sylvan Rodriguez, "The Aquifer Controversy: Is It Really About Clean Water?" *S.A. Magazine*, September 1977, p. 23.

57. Ibid.

58. *San Antonio Express*, 4 December 1974. Local builders were also quite concerned about an even greater federal "intrusion," the national land use policy legislation under discussion in Congress. See chapters 5 and 6 below.

59. Hartman interview.

60. Guerra memorandum, p. 2 (see n. 53).

61. *San Antonio Express*, 3 January 1976.

62. See *James* v. *Valtierra*, 402 U.S. 137 (1971); and *City of Eastlake* v. *Forest City Enterprises, Inc.*, 426 U.S. 668 (1976).

63. Father Albert Benevides, cited in Rodriguez, "The Aquifer Controversy," p. 24. Benevides adds, though, that the "moratorium [was] simply a clean water issue."

64. Haar, *Land-Use Planning*, p. 124.

65. *San Antonio Express*, 2 February 1976.

66. Ibid., 9 March 1976.

67. Ibid., 28 April 1976.

68. Ibid., 26 October 1976.

69. Hill noted that the board's announcement was made without "data, technical evidence or reasonable rationale," hence the policy was "arbitrary, capricious and unreasonable." Moreover, given that the WQB's statutory responsibility was to protect the entire Edwards aquifer, its decision to exempt low-density counties from the order effectively relinquished the state's environmental protection authority to the counties, because it now would require affirmative action by the county governments to resume the controls. This was unlikely, given the rural hostility to growth management. Thus, for Hill, the order was illegal. See *San Antonio Express*, 26 October 1976.

70. *San Antonio Light*, 14 December 1976. Yantis declared that the new approach would assure the "safety, independence and autonomy" of the rural counties.

71. *San Antonio Express*, 16 November 1978.

72. The 1975 amendments to the Voting Rights Act were designed to extend the law's coverage to include violations of the voting guarantees in the Fourteenth Amendment. The earlier 1964 law protected Fifteenth Amendment rights against discrimination "on account of race, color or previous condition of servitude." The new amendments allowed federal protection for ethnic minorities such as San Antonio's Mexican-Americans. For an excellent discussion of the law's application to San Antonio, see Cottrell and Stevens, "The 1975 Voting Rights Act."

73. *San Antonio Express*, 26 May 1977.

74. Charles E. Lindblom, "The Market as Prison," *Journal of Politics* 44 (May 1982): 328.

75. *San Antonio Express*, 4 June 1977.

76. Hartman interview; *San Antonio Light*, 10 June 1977.

77. *San Antonio Light*, 10 June 1977; *San Antonio Express*, 11 June 1977; *San Antonio News*, 10 June 1977.

78. Labor unions, not a strong force in San Antonio's affairs, also voiced criticism. The leader of the plumbers' and pipefitters' union threatened to join the developers in their suit "if a single worker loses his job as a result of the moratorium." He suggested that the other construction trades were ready to file suit as well (*San Antonio News*, 16 June 1977).

79. Interview, Barnardo Eureste, city council member, San Antonio, Texas, March 1978. At the time of the vote Eureste summarized the builders' attitude this way: "They think that once they own the land, the city owes them plats, it owes them permits and [utility] connections." Eureste, of course, saw obligations the other way: landed property owed duties to the collective landowner. Council member Helen Dutmer expressed this view somewhat more colorfully: "I had rather die with a drink of water in my hand than a fistful of money." See Don Politico, "Council Plays Russian Roulette," *San Antonio Light*, 12 June 1977.

80. *San Antonio Light*, 22–23 June 1977. The Chicago firm was also an influential voice in deliberations on national land use policy.

81. *San Antonio News*, 2 August 1977; *San Antonio Light*, 2, 5, 23 August 1977. Attorney Richard F. Babcock told the council that the ordinance "in effect, does with certain exceptions, provide for a moratorium."

82. *San Antonio Express*, 9 September 1977.

83. Ibid., 26 January 1978.

84. Ibid., 21 October 1979; 31 January 1981. The newspaper rhapsodized about a "war of the shopping malls," one whose bullets would doubtless be fired in the advertising pages of the *San Antonio Express*.

85. "Proposed Development Controls for the Edwards Aquifer" (Boston: Metcalf and Eddy Engineering Consultants, 1979), p. S–15, and chap. 4, "Institutional Arrangements," p. 1-4-10. Thus the technicians turned the issue back to the officials: "The decision to proceed and timing of this action . . . must be a political decision." The election of Republican William P. Clements as governor of Texas in 1978 ensured that little momentum came from the state to make such moves. Clements, owner of the largest independent oil-drilling corporation in the world, Sedco, was not a friend of environmental protection.

86. Sidney Plotkin, "The Abating of Pluralism in San Antonio," a paper prepared for presentation at the annual meeting of the Southwest Political Science Association, Houston, Texas, April 1980.

87. The proposal was made by a subcommittee of the city's Edwards Aquifer Advisory Committee (*San Antonio Express*, 16 August 1979). For the limits of private government on land, see n. 69, chapter 3.

88. The statement was made by lawyer Stanley Rosenberg to the San Antonio Bar Association (*San Antonio Express*, 30 January 1979).

89. Rochelle L. Stanfield, "A Serious Drinking Problem," *National Journal*, 3 November 1984, p. 2093.

90. Sam Guzman et al., *Public Policy for Chemicals: National and International Issues* (Washington, D.C.: Conservation Foundation, 1980), p. 1; Mark Reisch, *Hazardous Wastes, Issue Brief* (Washington, D.C.: Congressional Research Service, Library of Congress, 1980).

91. U.S. Environmental Protection Agency, Draft Environmental Impact Statement for Subtitle C, at V-36 (January 1979), cited in Bacow and Milkey, "Overcoming Opposition," p. 265, n. 1; see also Brown, *Laying Waste*.

92. The U.S. Environmental Protection Agency (EPA) is making efforts to adopt analytical approaches allowing it to focus on pollutants, not through their media of transportation, i.e., air, water, or land, but in terms of their overall geographic or industrial impact in specific regions. The technique, known as "integrated environmental management," is designed ostensibly "to achieve more efficiency at no loss to human health," according to William Drayton, EPA's assistant administrator in the Carter administration. But critics, such as Drayton, wonder whether the technique is designed to reduce corporate costs more than pollution. See Lawrence Mosher, "Distrust of Gorsuch May Stymie EPA Attempt to Integrate Pollution Wars," *National Journal*, 12 February 1983, p. 322.

93. Nelson, *Zoning and Private Property Rights*, pp. 144, 128, 145.

94. Popper, *Politics of Land-Use Reform*, pp. 155f. Also see Healy and Rosenberg, *Land Use*, p. 225; and Jackson, *Land Use*, p. 83.

95. City of San Antonio, City Planning Commission, "The San Antonio Master Plan," Economic Benefit Section of Chapter IV, San Antonio, Texas, 5 January 1979, pp. 9–10. A later draft made this observation, conceding defeat to unnamed elements of public opinion: "The Master Plan initially conceived by the Planning Commission envisioned a dominant, prescriptive role for city government which would employ the police power and fiscal policy to manage the growth and development of the city in a way that would achieve a pre-determined spatial distribution of the population by the year 2000. This concept was ultimately rejected by the City Council after . . . public debate" ("The San Antonio Master Plan," draft, "Foreword," 16 January 1980, p. 1). The plan remains in the draft stage, held up by strong business resistance since 1975.

Chapter 5

1. Lyday, *Law of the Land*.

2. Ibid.; and see n. 4, Introduction to Part Two, above.

3. G. William Domhoff, *Who Rules America Now? A View for the Eighties* (Englewood Cliffs, N.J.: Prentice-Hall, 1983), p. 82; Domhoff, *The Powers That Be: Processes of Ruling Class Domination in America* (New York: Random House, 1978), pp. 61–127.

4. Domhoff, *Who Rules America Now?* p. 84; and Domhoff, *The Powers That Be*, p. 122. As Domhoff notes, this perspective is at odds with those theorists of the capitalist state, such as Claus Offe, who insist that the governmental apparatus formulates general class policies more or less autonomously, independently of private voices. See Claus Offe, "Political Authority and Class Structures," in *Critical Sociology: Selected*

Readings, ed. Paul Connerton (New York: Penguin, 1976), pp. 388–421; and Fred Block, "The Ruling Class Does Not Rule: Notes on the Marxist Theory of the State," in *The Political Economy: Readings in the Politics and Economics of American Public Policy,* ed. Thomas Ferguson and Joel Rogers (Armonk, N.Y.: M. E. Sharpe, 1984), pp. 32–46.

5. It should, perhaps, be stressed that nothing in Domhoff's thesis, or in Gramsci's for that matter, implies that it is possible in some objective sense for the policy planners to "really" know the big needs of capitalism. Even less do these ideas imply that the policy planners represent an elite conspiracy to dominate the masses with secret plots. First, there is enough evidence of disagreement among planners to suggest that even thinkers who accept ruling-class assumptions can disagree sharply about how best to make capitalism work. Second, most of the significant policy research is publicly available; indeed, a major purpose of such documents is to persuade the public to support their findings. Rather, Gramsci and Domhoff are arguing that in the capitalist system, business people and even government officials are much too challenged just to keep things going on a daily basis to spend time pondering the general needs of their class or blueprinting the future against all contingencies. This is where the policy experts, foundations, institutes, university centers, and law firms come in.

6. Popper, *Politics of Land-Use Reform,* pp. 11, 13; Bosselman and Callies, *Quiet Revolution,* p. 1.

7. Walker and Heiman, "Quiet Revolution for Whom?" pp. 78–79.

8. Babcock, *The Zoning Game;* Reilly, *The Use of Land.*

9. John H. Mollenkopf, "The Postwar Politics of Urban Development," in Tabb and Sawers, *Marxism and the Metropolis,* pp. 117–152; Charles Abrams, *The City Is the Frontier* (New York: Harper & Row, 1965).

10. Mollenkopf, *The Contested City,* p. 15.

11. John Friedmann and Clyde Weaver, *Territory and Function: The Evolution of Regional Planning* (Berkeley and Los Angeles: University of California Press, 1979), chap. 4.

12. Jane Jacobs, *The Death and Life of Great American Cities* (New York: Random House, 1961), p. 9.

13. The logic here parallels James O'Connor's thesis that rationalization of urban development implied a political alliance between large corporations and the weaker, unorganized segments of the working class, especially black and brown people. This alliance would come to fruition in the form of what O'Connor called a "social industrial complex" (*Fiscal Crisis of the State,* pp. 51–57). For a critical discussion of O'Connor's thesis in light of the proposal for a national land use policy, see Sidney Plotkin, "Policy Fragmentation."

From the standpoint of capitalist economic geography, too, it is possible to see why controls on the land interest are crucial to its continued role as coordinator of the spatial needs of business. As David Harvey argues, the anarchic nature of real estate competition and land speculation frequently leads to "individual landholders acting in their own immediate self-interest and seeking to maximize the ground-rent they can appropriate." This can generate "allocations of capital to land in ways that make no sense from the standpoint of the overall requirements of accumulation." Short of outright monopolization of real estate by capital, "the final line of defense is the state, which can take on a variety of powers of land use regulation, land expropriation, land use planning, and, finally, actual investment, to counter the incoherency and periodic speculative fevers land markets are periodically heir to" (Harvey, *Limits to Capital*, p. 371). See also Massey and Catalano, *Capital and Land*, chap. 8.

14. Committee for Economic Development, *Guiding Metropolitan Growth* (New York: Committee for Economic Development, 1960), p. 5.

15. Marx, *Economic and Philosophic Manuscripts*, p. 102.

16. Abrams, *The City Is the Frontier*, pp. 156–157; Mollenkopf, *The Contested City*, p. 15.

17. Allison Dunham, "A Legal and Economic Basis for City Planning (Making Room for Robert Moses, William Zeckendorf, and a City Planner in the Same Community)," *Columbia Law Review* 58 (May 1958): 659.

18. National Commission on Urban Problems, *Building the American City*, pp. 152–156; Jewel Bellush and Murray Hausknecht, eds., *Urban Renewal: People, Politics and Planning* (New York: Doubleday, 1967); Scott, *American City Planning*, chap. 7.

19. Henry E. Hoagland and Leo D. Stone, *Real Estate Finance*, 3d ed. (Homewood, Ill.: Irwin, 1965), pp. 5–6; National Commission on Urban Problems, *Building the American City*, pp. 158–159.

20. National Commission on Urban Problems, *Building the American City*, pp. 153, 162–163.

21. *Berman* v. *Parker*, 348 U.S. 26, in Williams, *American Land Planning Law*, 2:1688–1694.

22. Ibid., pp. 1691–1692.

23. In re Opinion of the Justices, 322 Mass. 769 (1955), reprinted in Haar, *Land-Use Planning*, pp. 642–648.

24. National Commission on Urban Problems, *Building the American City*, pp. 160–167.

25. *Village of Belle Terre* v. *Boraas*, 416 U.S. 1 (1974), in Williams, *American Land Planning Law*, 2:974–986.

26. Ibid., p. 919.

27. Bollens and Schmandt, *The Metropolis*, table 4.1, p. 89, based on data from U.S. Bureau of the Census, "Governmental Organization," *Census of Governments: 1977*, vol. 1, no. 1 (Washington, D.C.: GPO, 1978), p. 11.

28. Committee for Economic Development, *Modernizing Local Government*, Statement on National Policy by the Research and Policy Committee of the Committee for Economic Development (New York, July 1966), excerpt reprinted, in section entitled "Local Governments," in *National Urban Problems*, ed. Harry B. Yoshpe and F. R. Burdette (Washington, D.C.: Industrial College of the Armed Forces, 1970), p. 126.

29. Ibid., p. 125; in *Building the American City*, the National Commission on Urban Problems made the point this way: "If the coercive powers of government for regulation and taxation are to be responsibly exercised, they must be subject to control by the affected area or community" (p. 327).

30. President John F. Kennedy, "1961 Housing Message," *Congressional Quarterly, Almanac, 1961* (Washington, D.C.: Congressional Quarterly, 1962), p. 883; Congressional Quarterly, *The U.S. Economy* (Washington, D.C.: Congressional Quarterly, 1972), p. 5 (table 2); Lilley, "The Homebuilders' Lobby," p. 33.

31. Carl M. Brauer, *John F. Kennedy and the Second Reconstruction* (New York: Columbia University Press, 1977), pp. 127–131, 205–211; Arthur M. Schlesinger, Jr., *A Thousand Days: John F. Kennedy in the White House* (Boston: Houghton Mifflin, 1965), chap. 35; Scott, *American City Planning*, pp. 565–570, 587–588; Theodore Sorensen, *Kennedy* (New York: Bantam, 1966), pp. 540–542; William H. Whyte, *The Last Landscape* (New York: Doubleday, 1970).

32. Babcock, *The Zoning Game*, p. 12.

33. Ibid., pp. 153–185; and two articles by Charles Haar: "Wayne Township: Zoning for Whom? In Brief Reply," *Harvard Law Review* 67 (April 1954): 986–993; "Zoning for Minimum Standards: The Wayne Township Case," *Harvard Law Review* 66 (April 1953): 1051. In these articles, Haar criticized a New Jersey Supreme Court decision upholding Wayne Township's rules for minimum dwelling size as a means of protecting the value of vacation homes against what the court called "the next onward wave of suburban development" (*Lionshead Lake, Inc.* v. *Township of Wayne*, 10 N.J. 165, 89 A.2d 693 [1952]). See also Wright, "Constitutional Rights," pp. 852–853, and nn. 50–53.

34. Kennedy, "1961 Housing Message," p. 883.

35. Ibid. The president also proposed new credit incentives to be "used selectively" to encourage construction of moderate- and low-income housing, for these price ranges promised "the largest and the most immediate potential housing market."

36. Ibid., p. 886.

37. Bosselman and Callies, *Quiet Revolution*, p. 1.

38. Committee for Economic Development, *Modernizing Local Government*, p. 123.

39. President Lyndon B. Johnson, "The Great Society: The Goals," Public Papers of the Presidents of the United States, Lyndon B. Johnson, 1963–1964, 1:704–707, reprinted in *The Great Society Reader: The Failure of American Liberalism*, ed. Marvin E. Gettleman and David Mermelstein (New York: Random House, 1967), pp. 16–17. Also see Scott, *American City Planning*, pp. 610–635; Otis L. Graham, Jr., *Toward a Planned Society: From Roosevelt to Nixon* (New York: Oxford University Press, 1976), pp. 159–166; Bernard J. Frieden and Marshall Kaplan, *The Politics of Neglect: Urban Aid from Model Cities to Revenue Sharing* (Cambridge: MIT Press, 1975); Kenneth W. Tolo, ed., *The American City: Realities and Possibilities, A Symposium* (Austin, Texas: Lyndon B. Johnson School of Public Affairs, 1974).

40. President Lyndon B. Johnson, "Message on Housing and Urban Development," *Congressional Quarterly, Almanac, 1965* (Washington, D.C.: Congressional Quarterly, 1966), p. 1407.

41. For an account of the urban riots, see Jerome H. Skolnick, *The Politics of Protest* (New York: Ballantine, 1969). This was a report by the Task Force on Violent Aspects of Protest and Confrontation of the National Commission on the Causes and Prevention of Violence. Also see Richard E. Rubenstein, *Rebels in Eden: Mass Political Violence in the United States* (Boston: Little, Brown, 1970), pp. 117–140. Rubenstein was a staff member of the task force.

42. *Report of the National Commission on Civil Disorders*, pp. 473, 475.

43. Cited in Alexander Polikoff, *Housing the Poor* (Cambridge: Ballinger, 1977), p. 29. For Kaiser's interests in housing, see U.S. Advisory Commission on Intergovernmental Relations, *Urban and Rural America: Policies for Future Growth*

(Washington, D.C.: GPO, 1968), pp. 80–81. The views of HUD officials were identical. Cf. Scott, *American City Planning,* p. 631; Tolo, *The American City.*

44. National Commission on Urban Problems, *Building the American City,* pp. 241–243, 235–236.

45. Michael Lipsky and David J. Olson, "The Processing of Racial Crisis in America," *Politics and Society* 6, no. 1 (1976): 94. Indeed, at the very moment the many presidential commissions were issuing scathing attacks on suburban selfishness and racism, the Johnson administration used the siting of a nuclear accelerator to assist one of America's wealthiest suburbs in ridding itself of a working-class village located within its boundaries; see Theodore J. Lowi and Benjamin Ginsberg et al., *Poliscide* (New York: Macmillan, 1976). Moreover, the strategy of suburban housing integration did not go uncriticized by black activists, some of whom saw it as a device to limit their control of big city governments. See Richard A. Cloward and Frances Fox Piven, *The Politics of Turmoil: Poverty, Race and the Urban Crisis* (New York: Random House, 1975), pt. 3.

46. Domhoff, *The Powers That Be,* pp. 88–90; O'Connor, *Fiscal Crisis of the State,* pp. 68–69.

47. U.S. Advisory Commission on Intergovernmental Relations, *Urban and Rural America,* pp. 129, 135. The commission stressed that needs for more centralized land clearance mechanisms were rooted in diseconomies of urban congestion, the locational mismatch of jobs and people, the linkage of urban and rural problems, and urban sprawl (p. 129).

48. Lilley, "Homebuilders' Lobby," p. 33.

49. U.S. Advisory Commission on Intergovernmental Relations, *Urban and Rural America,* pp. 80–81. But see the larger discussion of "New Communities in America and Their Objectives," in ibid., chap. 4, pp. 62–106. See also Leo Grebler, *Large-Scale Housing and Real Estate Firms: Analysis of a New Business Enterprise* (New York: Praeger, 1973); Edward P. Eichler and Marshall Kaplan, *The Community Builders* (Berkeley and Los Angeles: University of California Press, 1967); Robert C. Fellmeth, *Politics of Land: Ralph Nader's Study Group Report on Land Use in California* (New York: Grossman, 1973); Barry Checkoway, "Large Builders, Federal Housing Programs, and Postwar Suburbanization," in Tabb and Sawers, *Marxism and the Metropolis* (2d ed., 1984), pp. 152–170; Robert Sigafoos, *Corporate Real Estate Development* (Lexington, Mass.: Lexington Books, 1976); Feagin, *The Urban Real Estate Game,* chap. 3; and Tom Schlesinger and Mark Erlich, "Housing: The Industry Capitalism Didn't Forget," in Bratt, Hartman, and Meyerson, *Critical Perspectives on Housing,* pp. 139–164.

50. O'Connor, *Fiscal Crisis of the State,* pp. 13–15. Despite the large number of producers (the National Association of Home Builders counts one hundred thousand members), patterns of concentration and centralization of capital in construction have been evident since the 1930s. As early as 1939 the 4 percent of all contractors whose output equaled or surpassed $100,000 annually accounted for half of all construction, whereas 27 percent of the work was completed by the 0.5 percent who did $500,000 or more in business (Miles Colean and Robinson Newcomb, *Stabilizing Construction: The Record and Potential* [New York: McGraw-Hill, 1952], p. 85). Nevertheless, as the Temporary National Economic Committee concluded in its study of construction, "there is no other general industry group which shows as little concentration in large

enterprises as the construction industry" (U.S. Congress, Department of Commerce, Temporary National Economic Committee, Testimony of Dr. Willard Thorpe, *Investigation of Concentration of Economic Power, Construction Industry,* 75th Cong., 1st sess., 1939, pt. 2:5184). Thorpe added, however, and his views are no less apt today, that the "disorderly and bitter competition" engendered by such a great dispersal of producers is tempered by "agreements, collusions, price controls, the use of building codes, union restrictions" and other policies that help insulate and protect builders. Oligopolistic traits thus appear within the competitive sector (ibid., p. 5189).

51. Quoted in Martin Mayer, *The Builders: Houses, People, Neighborhoods, Governments, Money* (New York: W. W. Norton, 1978), p. 257.

52. Ibid., pp. 258, 264. There was much optimism about the prospects of "a high-technology housing industry" and "space-age" efficiency. See Christopher A. Sims, "Efficiency in the Construction Industry," in Pynoos, Shafer, and Hartman, *Housing Urban America,* pp. 358–371.

53. Grebler, *Large-Scale Housing and Real Estate Firms,* pp. 7–9.

54. Quoted in "Ryan Homes: Stellar Performer in the Housing Slump," *Business Week,* 25 August 1975, p. 49. Profit-making opportunities were also noted in connection with housing rehabilitation. According to one stock analyst writing in 1967, "The potential market for private enterprise to rehabilitate slum housing in our cities . . . is several trillions of dollars" (J. Wilson Newman, "Does Business Have a Future?" in *Business and the Cities,* ed. Neil W. Chamberlin [New York: Basic Books, 1970]), p. 385. See also U.S. Gypsum Company, "The Opportunity in Rehabilitation," in the same work, pp. 388–391, 393–394.

55. National Commission on Urban Problems, *Building the American City,* p. 445.

56. Sharon M. Oster and John M. Quigley, "Regulatory Barriers to the Diffusion of Innovation: Some Evidence from Building Codes," in Pynoos, Shafer, and Hartman, *Housing Urban America,* p. 373. Their study also noted that "wealthier jurisdictions, presumably more exclusive suburbs, are also more likely to prohibit these cost saving techniques" (p. 382).

57. *Developing New Communities: Application of Technological Innovations,* prepared by David A. Krane, architect, and Keyes, Lethbridge and Condon, architects, Associated Architects and Planners for Fort Lincoln New Town for Edward J. Logue, Principal Development Consultant, District of Columbia Redevelopment Land Agency, National Capitol Planning Commission, and District of Columbia Government (Washington, D.C.: U.S. Department of Housing and Urban Development, 1968), pp. 3, 9. "The management and production techniques of the construction industry in the United States," said the report, "are anachronistic and fragmented when compared with those of large corporations or government agencies such as NASA."

58. Richard F. Babcock, "The Courts Enter the Land Development Marketplace," *City* 5 (January–February 1971): 58–64.

59. Walker and Heiman, "Quiet Revolution for Whom?" p. 71. In their words, the Urban Land Institute "took the lead in pressing for zoning reform." A comprehensive example of the ULI perspective is found in Randall W. Scott, ed., *Management and Control of Growth,* 3 vols. (Washington, D.C.: Urban Land Institute, 1975).

60. Schlesinger and Erlich, "Housing," p. 141; "Builders Assault the No-Growth Laws," *Business Week,* 9 June 1973, p. 26; "Builders See a Bleaker Future," *Business Week,* 9 June 1973, p. 86; "Packaging Land for Profit," *Business Week,* 18 August

1973, p. 89. The National Association of Realtors ad may be found in *Business Week,* 30 July 1979, p. 49. For more scholarly analyses of the effects of exclusion on housing, see Richard F. Babcock and Fred P. Bosselman, *Exclusionary Zoning: Land Use Regulation and Housing in the 1970s* (New York: Praeger, 1973); Michael N. Danielson, *The Politics of Exclusion* (New York: Columbia University Press, 1976); Scott, *Management and Control of Growth,* esp. vol. 1, chap. 6; Don K. Allensworth and Robert Linowes, *The Politics of Land Use: Planning, Zoning, and the Private Developer* (New York: Praeger, 1973).

61. Walker and Heiman, "Quiet Revolution for Whom?" p. 72, n. 34.

62. Marion Clawson, *Suburban Land Conversion in the United States* (Baltimore: Johns Hopkins University Press, 1971), p. 165; Cox, "Capitalism and Conflict," pp. 439–440.

63. *James v. Valtierra,* 402 U.S. 137 (1971), in Williams, *American Land Planning Law,* 2:968–974.

64. See chapter 4, n. 62, above.

65. *James v. Valtierra,* pp. 971, 973.

66. Senator Henry Jackson, "Introduction of the National Land Use Policy of 1970, S. 3354," *Cong. Rec.,* 91st Cong., 2d sess., 29 January 1970, pt. 116, p. 1758; Lyday, *Law of the Land,* pp. 8–12.

67. Jackson, "Introduction of National Land Use Policy," pp. 1758–1759, 1757.

68. William E. Schands and Robert G. Healy, *The Lands Nobody Wanted: Policy for National Forests in the Eastern United States* (Washington, D.C.: Conservation Foundation, 1977). But cf. Ralph Nader Congress Project, *The Environment Committees: A Study of the House and Senate Interior and Agriculture Committees* (New York: Grossman, 1975), p. 15; and Culhane, *Public Lands Politics.*

69. Quoted in Lyday, *Law of the Land,* p. 15.

70. Jackson, "Introduction of National Land Use Policy," p. 1758. A bit later, however, the senator suggested a sensitivity to deeper social strains. "In the past," he told the Senate during its debate on reform of land use policy, "many land-use decisions were the exclusive province of those whose interests were selfish, short-term and private." See *Cong. Rec.,* 92d Cong., 2d sess., 18 September 1972, pt. 118:31069.

71. No cues were taken from the committee's bitter experience with wilderness-preservation legislation. With that issue, conservationists tried to introduce the zoning model into public-land management by prohibiting all development in specially designated areas. However, they slammed into "the economic development [model] there and . . . its core . . . notions of flexibility and multiple use." The result was a nine-year struggle that drew plenty of national attention before a Wilderness Act was passed in 1965. So shaken were the traditional public-land interests that they demanded a new policy to legitimize the doctrines of "multiple use" and "flexible administration." See Allin, *Politics of Wilderness Preservation,* p. 115.

72. National Environmental Policy Act, 83 Stat. 853 (1970), sec. 102(B).

73. Senator Mike Gravel, in Senate Committee on Public Works and Committee on Interior and Insular Affairs, *The Operation of the National Environmental Policy Act of 1969,* 92d Cong., 2d sess., 1973, p. 25.

74. Lyday, *Law of the Land,* pp. 10–11.

75. Jackson wanted state planners "to collect and analyze . . . data" in connection with "population . . . trends; economic trends, location patterns, and projections; di-

rections and extent of urban and rural growth; public works . . . and economic development programs . . . ; ecological, environmental, geological and physical conditions
which are of relevance to decisions concerning the location of new communities, commercial development, heavy industries, transportation and utility corridors . . . ;
[and] the projected land use requirements of the State for recreation, urban growth,
commerce, transportation, the generation of energy, and other important uses for at
least the next fifty years" (Senate, *A Bill to Establish a National Land Use Policy,*
S. 3354, 91st Cong., 2d sess., 1970, sec. 403; hereafter cited as S. 3354).

76. It would include the secretaries of the interior, agriculture, the army, transportation, housing and urban development, and health, education, and welfare, as well as
the chairman of the Federal Power Commission. The council chairman would be designated by the president. The Interior Department was viewed as the "lead agency" for
land use policy. Ibid., sec. 3.

77. Lyday, *Law of the Land,* quoting William Van Ness, pp. 7, 11. In Hearings on
S. 3354, Jackson put it this way: "The thing that has disturbed me and which led to the
introduction of this legislation is the fact that in all 50 States . . . we do not have an
adequate forum to adjudicate these conflicts" (Senate Committee on Interior and Insular Affairs, *National Land Use Policy. Hearings Before the Subcommittee on Environment and Land Resources on S. 3354,* 91st Cong., 2d sess., pt. 1, 1970, p. 16;
hereafter cited as Senate, *Land Use, Hearings,* 1970).

78. Senate, *Land Use, Hearings,* 1970, pt. 1, pp. 147, 2.

79. Ibid., testimony of Governor Winthrop Sargent. Governor Love, fresh from
efforts to pass a Colorado land use law, pointed to towns such as Colorado Springs and
said, "There is no way . . . they voluntarily are going to limit the size of that particular
city." He added that "the transfer" from the old English common law of property "to
the present zoning was difficult enough, but this will be far more difficult" (pt. 1,
p. 143). This position was in line with the views of the National Governors Conference, which was on record in support of a National Community Development Policy,
including national guidance "as to what lands are appropriate for urban development,
agricultural production, conservation, and open space and recreation." It also sought a
"reassertion of state authority in zoning where local land practices constitute unreasonable barriers to land development and capital investment policies." See the *Report
of the National Governors Conference Committee on Rural and Urban Development,*
cited in ibid., pt. 2, pp. 490, 497.

80. Ibid., pt. 1, p. 341.

81. Letter of W. Donald Crawford, managing director, Edison Electric Institute, to
Senator Henry M. Jackson, 21 May 1970, reprinted in ibid., pt. 2, pp. 411–412. Cf.
the testimony of Harry G. Woodbury, senior vice-president, Consolidated Edison Co.
of New York, in ibid., pt. 2, pp. 416, 415, 420. To allay Crawford's fears, John N.
Nassikas, chairman of the Federal Power Commission, urged an amendment to facilitate close cooperation between public and private planners, including collaborations
aimed at "the maximum joint use of existing properties and other desirable points of
environmental management." In addition, state planners should "consult with the principal . . . electric and gas pipeline industries in their respective areas with regard to
the interrelationship of utilities' needs and State and regional plans for future siting
and right-of-way, together with related environmental factors" (ibid., pt. 1, pp. 160–
161). Similar collaboration with environmental and consumer groups was not advised,

however. For later experiments in power-plant siting policy, see chapter 7 of this volume. As Lyday points out, environmentalists were suspicious that "the bill was designed primarily to help the power industry in its battle with local government over plant locations." Strangely, though, she quotes Crawford's concerns about the environmental impact of a state land-planning agency but not his belief in centralized power-plant-siting authority in the hands of public utilities; see *Law of the Land*, pp. 7, 13.

82. Testimony of Peter Borrelli, Sierra Club, Senate, *Land Use, Hearings*, 1970, pt. 2, p. 466.

83. Testimony of James R. Turnbull, executive vice-president, National Forest Products Association, in ibid., pt. 2, pp. 443–449. But timber executives did not oppose national land use policy; indeed, from their perspective, inadequate access to land "lies at the root of many of the problems in our industry" as well as others such as "mining, power, and grazing." In the past, national land policy had been unnecessary, but nowadays "land decisions tend to reflect the confusion brought about by conflicting purposes among large and local elements of our national society" (ibid., pt. 2, p. 442). But cf. statements of the National Association of Home Builders and the National Association of Manufacturers, ibid., pt. 2, pp. 512, 514–516. The builders were concerned at the lack of mention of housing in the bill and suggested that Jackson contact the Subcommittee on Housing and Urban Affairs of the Banking and Currency Committee, which "has exercised for many years a significant role in the field of land use planning" (Letter of Joseph McGrath, Legislative Council, NAHB, to Senator Jackson, 27 July 1970, p. 512).

84. Ibid., testimony of Herman D. Ruth, American Society of Planning Consultants, pt. 1, pp. 350–351; testimony of Rex Allen, president, American Institute of Architects, pt. 1, p. 41; testimony of Thomas H. Haga, president, National Association of County Planners, pt. 2, p. 453.

85. Ibid., testimony of Russell Train, chairman, Council on Environmental Quality, pt. 1, pp. 101, 97.

86. Babcock, "Courts Enter the Land Development Marketplace," p. 59.

87. Schattschneider, *Semisovereign People*, pp. 39, 71; Lyday, *Law of the Land*, p. 7.

Chapter 6

1. O'Connor, *Fiscal Crisis of the State*, pp. 68–69.

2. Quoted in Dick Kirschten, "Environmentalists Tell Carter Thanks but No Thanks," *National Journal*, 23 June 1979, p. 1038. See also John Quarles, *Cleaning Up America: An Insider's View of the Environmental Protection Agency* (Boston: Houghton Mifflin, 1976), p. 12.

3. Domhoff, *The Powers That Be*, pp. 61–62.

4. Some of these linkages are spelled out in Lyday, *Law of the Land*, pp. 18–23. But a much more thorough job of tracing interconnections within "the reform network" is done by Walker and Heiman, "Quiet Revolution for Whom?" pp. 77–79.

5. Lyday, *Law of the Land*, pp. 21–22.

6. Ibid., pp. 22–25. John Ehrlichman was by no means the only high-echelon Nixon administration official with sympathies for corporate land use reform, though he was by far the most important. Vice-President Spiro T. Agnew, forced to resign after

prosecutors discovered that he had, as a Maryland official, accepted bribes from local construction interests, was another exponent of large-scale development. See National Committee on Urban Growth, *The New City* (New York: Praeger, 1969); Wirt et al., *On The City's Rim,* p. 187; Jonathan Barnett, "Beginning the Debate on a National Growth Policy," *Architectural Record* 149 (May 1971): 117–118.

7. House, "Report of the Council on Environmental Quality—Message from the President of the United States," *Cong. Rec.,* 91st Cong., 2d sess., 10 August 1970, p. 28040. Nixon added that "the solution" to our land use difficulties "does not lie in seeking escape from urban life" (p. 28039).

8. Lyday, *Law of the Land,* p. 22. The staff of the Office of Management and Budget saw through the environmental aspect and opposed reform of land use policy as a contradiction to the administration's "new federalism" program, its dedication to the individualistic theory of property, and its belief that formation of a national growth policy was beyond Washington's grasp. John Ehrlichman disagreed and helped the CEQ staff overcome the OMB objections. In Lyday's words, Gibbons and Reilly saw Ehrlichman as "the hero in the internal debate over . . . land use policy," to such an extent, in fact, that "administration support for the land use bill is more accurately described as Ehrlichman's support" (p. 25).

9. Congressional Quarterly, *Inflation and Unemployment* (Washington, D.C.: Congressional Quarterly, 1975), pp. 35–36.

10. Lilley, "Homebuilders' Lobby," p. 34.

11. Danielson, *Politics of Exclusion,* p. 216; Mayer, *The Builders,* p. 264. For similar experiences in the Johnson administration, see Derthic, *New Towns In-Town.*

12. Danielson, *Politics of Exclusion,* pp. 216–222.

13. The fullest account of the Warren case is in William Lilley III, "Housing Report/Administration and Congress Follow Courts in Promoting Residential Integration," *National Journal,* 11 December 1971, pp. 2431–2448. But see also Danielson, *Politics of Exclusion,* pp. 222–236, for a good discussion of the Nixon administration's queasiness in the politics of opening the suburbs from Washington; and Wirt et al., *On the City's Rim,* pp. 184–188.

14. Quoted in Danielson, *Politics of Exclusion,* p. 223.

15. Hugh McDonald, "U.S. Picks Warren as Prime Target in Move to Integrate All Suburbs," *Detroit News,* 21 July 1970, quoted in ibid., p. 224.

16. Danielson, *Politics of Exclusion,* pp. 228–229. Danielson cites a "Statement of Equal Housing Opportunity" offered by the president that reveals how sensitive the administration was to the suburban outrage over having to "accept" neighbors who did not pay to get in. The president pleaded that "the kind of land use questions involved in housing site selection are essentially local in nature: They represent the kind of basic choices about the future shape of a community, or of a metropolitan area, that should be chiefly for the people of that community or that area to determine. The challenge of how to provide fair, open, and adequate housing is one that they must meet; and they must live with their success or failure" (p. 229).

17. Testimony of Allison Dunham and Fred P. Bosselman, Senate, *Land Use, Hearings,* 1970, pt. 1, p. 341; Bosselman and Callies, *Quiet Revolution,* p. 320.

18. Babcock, "Spatial Impact," p. 281. The analogy of land use regulation with the more traditional objects of state regulation is developed in Richard F. Babcock and Diane A. Feurer, "Land as a Commodity 'Affected with a Public Interest,'" *Washing-*

ton Law Review 52, no. 2 (1977), a portion of which is reprinted in *Urban Land*, November 1977, pp. 7–11.

19. Bosselman and Callies, *Quiet Revolution*, pp. 318–319; letter to the editor from Russell Train, chairman, Council on Environmental Quality, *Washington Post*, 15 December 1971, reprinted, along with an exchange of letters between Jackson and Rogers Morton, secretary of the interior, in Senate Committee on Interior and Insular Affairs, *National Land Use Policy: Background Papers on Past and Pending Legislation and the Roles of the Executive Branch, Congress, and the States in Land Use Planning*, 92d Cong., 2d sess., 1972, p. 26 (hereafter cited as Senate, *Papers*, 1972). Cf. the similar views of Richard Babcock, *The Zoning Game*, chap. 10; and President Nixon's Commission on Population Growth and the American Future, chaired by John D. Rockefeller III, *Population and the American Future* (New York: New American Library, 1972), p. 215.

20. The American Law Institute, *A Model Land Development Code, Proposed Official Draft No. 1; Tentative Draft No. 6* (Philadelphia: American Law Institute, 1974), pp. 293 and passim. Also see the testimony of Professor Allison Dunham of the American Law Institute, in Senate, *Land Use, Hearings*, 1970, pt. 1, pp. 340ff.

21. Senate, *A Bill to Establish a National Land Use Policy*, S. 992, 92d Cong., 1st sess., 1971, sec. 102(a) (hereafter cited as S. 992), reprinted in Bosselman and Callies, *Quiet Revolution*, appendix, pp. 1–13; Lyday, *Law of the Land*, pp. 21–22.

22. S. 992, sec. 102(b)(c).

23. Rogers Morton, in Senate, *Papers*, 1972, p. 26. Interestingly, both Rogers Morton and Russell Train owned estates on Maryland's exclusive Eastern Shore. In 1974 the area was selected as the site for a large upper-middle-income residential project by the Rouse Company, builder of the planned community at Columbia, Maryland, and numerous large shopping centers, including the large North Star mall in San Antonio. According to Boyd Gibbons, who later wrote an account of Rouse's failure to gain clearance for the Wye Island project, area residents appealed to Train and Morton to help them keep it out. Morton "liked Rouse's concept of deep setbacks from the water and no private docks around the shore. But Rogers Morton thought Rouse was planning to put too many people on Wye Island" (*Wye Island*, p. 102). Unfortunately, Gibbons does not indicate what efforts, if any, were made by Train or Morton to resist their erstwhile ally. James Rouse was, at the time, a member of the Rockefeller Task Force on Land Use, whose executive director was William K. Reilly.

24. S. 992, secs. 102(c), 104(a).

25. Ibid., sec. 105(a): Enacting clause. This provision was added specifically to entice support from the National Association of Home Builders, for whom the Department of Housing and Urban Development was the preferred agency to oversee land use policy. The Interior Department was selected as lead agency because the White House deemed it important to locate its administration in a line agency with "recognized expertise" in land management—and with "extensive program contact with government officials at the state and local level," especially given that the focus of the bill was on regulation rather than planning. Moreover, Nixon wanted to consolidate all national-resource programs—exclusion as well as expansion programs—in a new Department of Natural Resources, with the old Interior Department at its core. Thus, the president opposed the desire of Congress to place authority over the coastal-zone policy in the Commerce Department's National Oceanic and Atmospheric Administration for the

same reason. Indeed, even after Congress stuck by its guns, the Nixon administration refused to fund the coastal-zone program pending establishment of the new department.

For expressions of support for centralized resource authority, see Senate Committee on Interior and Insular Affairs, *National Land Use Policy. Hearings Before the Committee on Interior and Insular Affairs on S. 632 and S. 992*, 92d Cong., 1st sess., pt. 1, 1971 (hereafter cited as Senate, *Land Use, Hearings,* 1971), testimony of secretary of the interior, Rogers Morton, p. 85; and testimony of the chairman of the Council of Environmental Quality, Russell Train, p. 91. See also Train's testimony in Senate Committee on Interior and Insular Affairs, *Land Use Policy and Planning Assistance Act of 1973. Hearings Before the Subcommittee on Environment and Land Resources on S. 268*, 93d Cong., 1st sess., 1973, pt. 1, p. 190 (hereafter cited as Senate, *Land Use, Hearings,* 1973).

26. Babcock, *The Zoning Game*, p. 173; Walker and Heiman, "Quiet Revolution for Whom?"

27. Senator Henry Jackson, in Senate, *Papers,* 1972, pp. 24–25. But the call for standards put Jackson himself in contradiction with his declared commitment to a "policy neutral" bill. That is, on the one hand, he wanted merely a rational forum for the adjudication of multijurisdictional conflicts, a Lockean umpire to settle by "standing rules, indifferent and the same to all parties . . . all the differences that may happen between any members of society" (Locke, *Two Treatises,* p. 367). But on the other hand, he felt that national policy should push the states "to consider . . . the real concerns of national, state and local land use" as against the existing pattern based on "expediency, tradition, archaic legal principles" and "selfish, short-term and private" interests. This implied concern for values, for definite standpoints with regard to the appropriate types of expansion and exclusion. Jackson never confronted the contradiction between his implicit, and often explicit, commitments to large-scale expansion and his Lockean conception that adjudication "should not be viewed as mission-oriented, either in the narrow sense of fostering a specific set of activities or in the larger sense of pursuing exclusively the goal of environmental protection or the goal of improving social services." Appeals to technocratic balancing acts were frequently made to avoid clear signals. The problem lay, of course, not in Jackson's mind but in his working ideological apparatus and its inability to identify the contradictions of exclusion and expansion. It was inconceivable, within his liberal, pragmatic outlook, to believe that internal system conflicts could be resolved only through the imposition of one set of interests at the expense of another; rather, all conflicts could be "managed" without serious harm to any of the contending forces. See Jackson, "Introduction of National Land Use Policy," p. 1759; *Cong. Rec.,* 92d Cong., 2d sess., 18 September 1972, pt. 118, p. 31069. "The Land Use Battle That Business Faces," *Business Week,* 26 August 1972. Also see the debate over procedure and substance in the case of the Energy Mobilization Board, chapter 7 below.

28. Quoted in Senate Committee on Interior and Insular Affairs, *Land Use Policy and Planning Assistance Act of 1973,* S. Rept. 197 to accompany S. 268, 93d Cong., 1st sess., 1973 (hereafter cited as Senate, *Interior Report,* 1973), p. 48. In his formal testimony Loftis noted that in "instances" where "the activities of State or interstate land use agencies . . . impinge on . . . the welfare of the nation as a whole . . . Federal policy must dominate and thereby affect State and Local government decisions and private initiative." See testimony of John L. Loftis, vice-president, Exxon U.S.A.,

in Senate, *Land Use, Hearings,* 1973, pt. 2, p. 87. See also Statement of the American Petroleum Institute, ibid., pt. 1, appendix, pp. 361–362.

29. Testimony of W. Lloyd Tupling in Senate, *Land Use, Hearings,* 1973, pt. 2, pp. 92–93; testimony of William J. Duddleson, Conservation Foundation, in House Committee on Interior and Insular Affairs, *Land Use Planning Act of 1973. Hearings Before the Subcommittee on the Environment on H.R. 4682 and Related Bills,* 93d Cong., 1st sess., 1973, p. 376 (hereafter cited as House, *Land Use, Hearings,* 1973); testimony of Bernard Siegan in House Committee on Interior and Insular Affairs, *Land Use and Resource Conservation. Hearings Before the Subcommittee on Energy and the Environment on H.R. 3510 and Related Bills,* 94th Cong., 1st sess., 1975, pp. 292, 294, 305 (hereafter cited as House, *Land Use, Hearings,* 1975). Also cf. the testimony of John R. Quarles, Jr., general counsel, Environmental Protection Agency, in Senate, *Land Use, Hearings,* 1973, pp. 301–302; and see the letter of Thomas Jorling, former minority counsel of the Senate Committee on Public Works, to the *New York Times,* cited by Senator Edmund Muskie, *Cong. Rec.,* 92d Cong., 2d sess., 19 September 1972, pt. 118, p. 31201.

30. Senator Edmund Muskie, *Cong. Rec.,* 18 September 1972, pt. 118, pp. 31072, 31203. Muskie added, "There is no way of setting up a process of land use policy administered by a Federal bureaucracy that does not get that bureaucracy involved in making judgments about what the policy will be" (p. 31203).

31. Testimony of Rogers Morton, secretary of the interior, in Senate, *Land Use, Hearings,* 1973, pt. 1, p. 294; testimony of Richard H. Slavin, director, Planning and Community Affairs Agency, State of Washington, and president, Council of State Planning Agencies, National Governors Conference, in Senate, *Land Use, Hearings,* 1971, pt. 2, pp. 326–327. Besides, Morton noted during the 1971 hearings, clear standards in a national planning bill would contradict "the American way of doing business" (p. 133). These were affirmative statements of what Theodore J. Lowi calls "interest group liberalism," that is, the default of the liberal capitalist state in the face of competing pressure-group demands. Frank J. Popper's analysis of state land use legislation largely confirms the predictions of observers such as Duddleson, Siegan, and Muskie that organized economic power would set the terms of control at higher levels, much as the Lowi model explains. None of these analyses, however, goes deeper than the manifest group interests to explore the contradictory socioeconomic structure that is their foundation. See Theodore J. Lowi, *The End of Liberalism: The Second Republic of the United States,* 2d ed. (New York: W. W. Norton, 1979). Popper observes: "Under extreme pressure and without real alternatives," state reformers "succeeded in operating primarily through bargains" (*Politics of Land-Use Reform,* p. 207).

32. Senate Committee on Interior and Insular Affairs, *Land Use Policy and Planning Assistance Act of 1972,* S. Rept. 869 to accompany S. 632, 92d Cong., 2d sess., 1972 (hereafter cited as Senate, *Interior Report,* 1972). The committee noted that after thorough consultations with interested and expert parties, it concluded that "most states now lack and probably could not develop in less than five to ten years, the capacity to undertake and implement a comprehensive planning effort for their total land resource base" (p. 20). Yet planners were calling precisely for national development plans; see, e.g., testimony of James G. Martin, vice-president, National Service to Regional Councils, in Senate, *Land Use, Hearings,* 1971, pt. 2, p. 310. Jackson now joined Fred Bosselman and David Callies in arguing that "those who cry for compre-

hensive regulation of all development have not thought through the problem" (*Quiet Revolution*, p. 320).

33. *Cong. Rec.*, 19 September 1972, pt. 118, p. 31202. Lyday (*Law of the Land*, pp. 28–30) argues that before joining the administration Jackson had "different objectives" and was "operating on different assumptions." Whereas he "was looking for a way to help resolve controversies over the use of land," the White House "aimed at more limited development and preservation objectives," seeing "local land use regulation" as "the problem." But what was the problem of "local" control if not its tendency to exclude conflicting needs and interests? Indeed, the whole legal tradition out of which the ALI's recommendations came presupposed conflict avoidance as the basic function of land use policy. Lyday tends to stress relatively insignificant distinctions at the expense of larger ones that really signify alternative interventionist strategies by capitalist states. What distinguished Jackson's approach from the CEQ-ALI model was not a different goal but a conception of regulation that was organically linked to planning, instead of seeing regulation as a distinct function of government. The former conception was an attempt to come to terms with twentieth-century realities through technocracy, the latter through an essentially Lockean strategy of legal domination.

34. See Senate, *Interior Report*, 1972, p. 19; Senate, *Land Use, Hearings*, 1971, pt. 1, p. 92; Lyday, *Law of the Land*, p. 25. The sanctions would be applied on a percentage-reduction basis over three years—ranging from 7 percent the first year to a maximum of 21 percent—for failure to submit regulatory plans acceptable to the secretary of the interior. Safeguards abounded in the proposed sanctions process, however. Consultation with HUD and EPA was required as a condition of the Interior Department's recommendation to the president to apply sanctions. And threatened states could appeal to a special ad hoc review board appointed by the president and empowered to overturn "unreasonable" deprivations. The board would be composed of a governor "from a state with no particular interest in the question," an "impartial Federal official," and a private citizen selected by the first two. Since it would be the president's appointee who might be overridden, Senator George Aiken (R-Vt.) wondered whether presidents are "always neutral." See *Cong. Rec.*, 18 September 1972, pt. 118, p. 31091.

35. *Cong. Rec.*, 18 September 1972, pt. 118, p. 31078; testimony of Russell Train, Senate, *Land Use, Hearings*, 1971, p. 93; Lyday, *Law of the Land*, p. 30. For a detailed summary of the different forms of sanctions that land use reformers attempted to incorporate in the bill, see *Cong. Rec.*, 93d Cong., 1st sess., 18 June 1973, pt. 119, pp. 11312–11313.

36. One amendment, for example, established "an advisory body to each state planning agency composed of chief elected officers of local government" and assured mayors of an equal role with states in advising federal agencies about coordination of inter-governmental relations. The rights of individuals and localities to appeal state decisions were also affirmed. Big cities joined with the National Association of Home Builders to strengthen HUD's influence in the review of state plans and to assure that housing was a top regulatory priority. The Interior Department's role was limited to administration of the grant program, but formation of guidelines was shifted to the Executive Office of the President. Another amendment declared that nothing in S. 632 should be construed to give Washington any constitutional authority, i.e., police power, to zone nonfederal lands. The only major defeat suffered by the local govern-

ments was the Senate's rejection of pleas for federal compensation of property-tax revenues lost as a result of state-imposed growth restrictions. Suburban interests did not celebrate some of the big-city victories, especially the prominence given housing, but comfort was taken from a measure that ensured community autonomy in land use decision making. Most of these changes were worked out in consultation with the Banking and Currency Committee in order, as Jackson put it, to "strengthen the role of local governments in . . . land use decision making." See *Cong. Rec.*, 19 September 1972, pt. 118, p. 31193; *Congressional Quarterly 1972, Almanac* (Washington, D.C.: Congressional Quarterly, 1973), p. 827; testimony of Robert Knecht, mayor of Boulder, Colorado, chairman of National League of Cities' Committee on the Environment, in Senate, *Land Use, Hearings*, 1971, pt. 1, p. 164; William K. Gernhauser, commissioner, Lucas County, Toledo, Ohio, National Association of Counties, in ibid., pt. 2, pp. 271–275.

37. *Cong. Rec.*, 18 September 1972, pt. 118, p. 31083.

38. *New York Times*, 26 June 1972. The *Times* was a consistent supporter of land use policy reform, as were *Business Week*, the *Wall Street Journal*, *Time*, and the *Washington Post*. Major stories and editorials were run by all these journals on the need for centralized controls. See, e.g., "The New American Land Rush," *Time*, 1 October 1973; "New Land Ethic: Its Spread Raises Political and Legal Issues to Be Resolved by Public," *New York Times*, 4 September 1973; "The Land Use Battle That Business Faces," *Business Week*, 26 August 1972; "Coping with the Hassles," *Wall Street Journal*, 15 August 1972; "Planning the Second America," *Washington Post*, 24 November 1971.

39. *Cong. Rec.*, 18 September 1972, pt. 118, p. 31091. For the strong doubts of an environmental advocate, see Thomas Jorling's letter to the editor of the *New York Times* (reprinted in *Cong. Rec.*, 19 September 1972, pt. 118, p. 31201). Even the EPA's general counsel, John R. Quarles, Jr., could do no more than promise conservationists that state regulation "will be tilted to some extent perhaps toward greater environmental protection" (Senate, *Land Use, Hearings*, 1973, pp. 301–302). The San Antonio quotation is from G. E. Harrington, Builders, Inc., personal communication, February 1977.

40. See n. 8 above.

41. *Cong. Rec.*, 18 September 1972, pt. 118, p. 31087.

42. See the section "Police Powers" in chapter 2, above.

43. *Cong. Rec.*, 18 September 1972, pt. 118, pp. 31089–31090.

44. Testimony of Russell Train, in House Committee on Interior and Insular Affairs, *National Land Use Planning. Hearings Before the Subcommittee on the Environment on H.R. 4332 and Related Bills*, 92d Cong., 1st sess., 1971, p. 112 (hereafter cited as House, *Land Use, Hearings*, 1971); testimony of Rep. Richard Lamm, Colorado, in Senate, *Land Use, Hearings*, 1973, pt. 2, p. 261; see also testimony of William H. Rodgers, visiting professor of law, Georgetown University Law School, in House, *Land Use, Hearings*, 1973, pp. 573–574. Bosselman and his associates concluded their review with the comment that "a dramatic overruling of the *Pennsylvania Coal* case would help deflate the myth that now makes the taking clause so powerful," although courts should "still evaluate regulations against their own standards of reasonableness" (Bosselman, Callies, and Banta, *The Taking Issue*, pp. 326–327).

45. *Cong. Rec.*, 18 September 1972, pt. 118, p. 31087.

46. Ibid., p. 31088.

47. Ibid., p. 31089.

48. One environmentalist complained, "At each step in the process, we have re-treated from the proposals as initially produced and we have been moving more and more towards the status quo." See testimony of William J. Duddleson, Conservation Foundation, in House, *Land Use, Hearings,* 1973, p. 378. The four liberal opponents were Muskie, William Proxmire (D-Wis.), Thomas Eagleton (D-Mo.), and Fred Harris (D-Okla.).

49. Lyday, *Law of the Land,* pp. 35–37. Nelson's amendment prohibited builders of projects exceeding fifty lots from expanding beyond the capacity of existing public utilities without approval by the state. Restrictions were also placed on flood-plain construction: see Senate, *A Bill to Establish a National Land Use Policy,* S. 268, 93d Cong., 1st sess., 1973, secs. 202(d), 601(k)(l). Buckley's amendment may be found in sec. 612(h). But cf. sec. 203(d), which specified that "any method . . . employed by the State shall include . . . authority to prevent arbitrary and capricious restriction or prohibition of development of public facilities or development of regional benefit." Of course, the "arbitrary and capricious" test was the standard police-power limit and remained to be defined by the courts. Jackson's celebration of the bill may be found in *Cong. Rec.,* 15 June 1973, pt. 119, p. 11273.

50. Senate, *Interior Report,* 1973, "Minority Views of Senators Paul Fannin (Arizona), Clifford P. Hansen (Wyoming) and Dewey Bartlett (Oklahoma)" (p. 154).

51. Testimony of Russell Train, Senate, *Land Use, Hearings,* 1973, pt. 1, p. 186; testimony of John Whitaker, House, *Land Use, Hearings,* 1973, pp. 228–229; Gladwin Hill, "New Land Ethic," *New York Times,* 4 September 1973, pp. 1, 23 (see n. 38, above); Reilly, *The Use of Land.* Among the Task Force members were Laurance S. Rockefeller; Walter E. Hoadley, executive vice-president and chief economist, Bank of America; John R. Price, Jr., vice-president, Manufacturers Hanover Trust; James W. Rouse, chairman of the board and chief executive officer, The Rouse Company. Several academics and state regulators were also on the panel, in addition to one representative from the League of Women Voters, Mayor Pete Wilson of San Diego, and Vernon E. Jordan, Jr., executive director of the National Urban League.

52. Reilly, *The Use of Land,* pp. 22–23, 27–29. The ALI's model code was expected "to furnish invaluable aid in the modernization of out-of-date state enabling acts" (p. 25), while the national land use bill was "urgently recommended" (p. 21). Reilly's role in authoring the bill was not indicated in the report.

53. Senate, *Interior Report,* 1973, pp. 55, 57, 156. For the chamber's role, see Lyday, *Law of the Land,* p. 47.

54. "Coping with the Hassles," *Wall Street Journal,* 15 August 1972; Lyday, *Law of the Land,* pp. 33, 7.

55. Wayne Aspinall, "Turns and Curves on a Well-Traveled Road: The Vicissitudes of Establishing Land Use Planning Policy," in *National Land Use Policy,* Proceedings of a special conference sponsored by the Soil Conservation Society of America, 27–29 November 1972 (Ankeny, Iowa: Soil Conservation Society, 1973), pp. 1–16. Aspinall fought for creation of a Public Land Law Review Commission to arouse corporate and political backing for multiple-use doctrine and to assist in his longstanding battle against executive withdrawal of public lands from entry. The com-

mission was established by President Johnson in 1965 and published its findings in 1970; Aspinall was its chairman. Needless to say, its main theme was to encourage "use of all public lands in a manner that will result in the maximum net public benefit." Environmentalists were enraged at its revival of the private-disposal option, a theme more recently given prominence by James Watt. See House Committee on Interior and Insular Affairs, *Establishment of Public Land Law Review Commission*, H. Rept. 1008, 88th Cong., 1st sess., 1964; U.S. Public Land Law Review Commission, *One Third of the Nation's Land* (Washington, D.C.: GPO, 1970), p. 42; House Committee on Interior and Insular Affairs, *Public Land Policy Act of 1971. Hearings Before the Subcommittee on the Environment on H.R. 7211*, 92d Cong., 1st sess., 1971, passim (hereafter cited as House, *Public Lands, Hearings,* 1971); see also chapter 3 above.

56. Arthur J. Magida, "The House and Senate Interior and Insular Affairs Committees," in Nader Congress Project, *Environment Committees*, p. 21; "It Isn't Who's for You That Matters in '72, It's Who Hates You," *Wall Street Journal*, 28 September 1972; "The Land Use Battle That Business Faces," *Business Week*, 20 August 1972; testimony of Charles Stoddard, Friends of the Earth, and other environmental spokesmen in House, *Public Lands, Hearings*, 1971, pp. 265, 388, 387. As the *Wall Street Journal* suggests, Aspinall's defeat heralded the onset of today's single-issue election campaigns organized by interest groups against undesirable incumbents. It should be added that the environmentalists' success was abetted by reapportionment: Aspinall found himself the new representative of Boulder, Colorado, home of the University of Colorado and one of the nation's most environmentally sensitive constituencies. This area said "No!" to the Olympics in 1970.

57. Magida, "House and Senate Interior and Insular Affairs Committees," p. 36. Udall's brother Stewart was secretary of the interior in the Kennedy administration and was one of the more even-handed occupants of that post in the twentieth century.

58. Statement of Morris Udall in House, *Land Use, Hearings*, 1971, pp. 84–85.

59. Bertram Gross, *The Legislative Struggle: A Study in Social Combat* (New York: McGraw-Hill, 1953), pp. 193–194.

60. House, *A Bill to Establish National Land Use Planning*, H.R. 10294, 93d Cong., 2d sess., sec. 301(a) (hereafter cited as H.R. 10294).

61. Testimony of Dan Denning, U.S. Chamber of Commerce, House, *Land Use, Hearings*, 1973, pp. 561–564. Similarly, see the testimony of Gene C. Brewer, National Association of Manufacturers, ibid., pp. 446–447. But the classic expression of the business view was left to Joseph McGrath of the National Forest Products Association: "If this planning process is to succeed, it must be supported by those who are regulated or those whose lands are being planned for. . . . This involvement, we believe, should be on a more formal basis than that afforded the general public" (ibid., pp. 514–515).

62. Quoted in "Land Use Legislation: A Precarious Future," *Congressional Quarterly Weekly Report*, 1 March 1975, p. 430. This is an excellent summary of the lobbying effort that defeated the land use bill, and I draw on it heavily in the discussion below.

63. Quoted in Lyday, *Law of the Land*, p. 46.

64. Schattschneider, *Semisovereign People*, p. 2.

65. Lyday, *Law of the Land*, p. 34.

66. For overviews of the situation, compare "The End of the Cowboy Economy," *Business Week,* 24 November 1973, with "Keynesian Chickens Come Home to Roost," *Monthly Review* 25 (April 1974): 1–12.

67. For the dismal litany, see *Business Week,* issues of 16 February 1974, 20 April 1974, 3 August 1974, 31 March 1975, and 12 April 1976.

68. Congressional Quarterly, *Inflation and Unemployment,* pp. 35–36; "Nixon's Push to End Subsidies," *Business Week,* 25 August 1973, pp. 44–45; *Golden* v. *Ramapo,* 30 N.Y. 2d 359 (1972). Cf. Bernard J. Frieden, *The Environmental Protection Hustle* (Cambridge: MIT Press, 1979).

69. It included, in addition to the Chamber of Commerce itself, the American Land Development Association, the National Crushed Stone Association, the National Sand and Gravel Association, the Associated General Contractors of America, the National Association of Home Builders, the American Mining Congress, the National Forest Products Association, the National Association of Electric Companies, the National Cattlemen's Association, and the American Farm Bureau (Congressional Quarterly, "Land Use Legislation," p. 430).

70. Interview with member of Representative Morris Udall's staff, December 1976 (anonymity requested); Congressional Quarterly, "Land Use Legislation," p. 430; testimony of John Hart, vice-president and treasurer, National Association of Home Builders, in House Committee on Interior and Insular Affairs, *Land Use Planning. Hearings Before the Subcommittee on the Environment on H.R. 10294,* 93d Cong., 2d sess., 1974, pp. 138–148 (hereafter cited as House, *Land Use, Hearings,* 1974).

71. Congressional Quarterly, "Land Use Legislation," p. 430; Lyday, *Law of the Land,* pp. 45–48; Norman J. Ornstein and Shirley Elder, *Interest Groups, Lobbying and Policymaking* (Washington, D.C.: Congressional Quarterly Press, 1978), p. 37; "U.S. Chamber: It Speaks Through Members," *Congressional Quarterly Weekly Report,* 15 November 1975, pp. 2457–2463.

72. "National Land Use Bill Threatens Rights of Property, States," *Vermont Watchman,* January 1974, p. 13. The article added that planning "would, worst of all, turn loose upon the hapless citizens of the various states a horde of planners and lawyers, paid by the taxpayers, whose advancement requires success in preventing those citizens from making normal use of their own property."

73. H.R. 10294, secs. 101–102, 104; and House Committee on Interior and Insular Affairs, *Land Use Planning Act of 1974,* H. Rept. 798 to accompany H.R. 10294, 93d Cong., 2d sess., 1974, pp. 43–44 (hereafter cited as House, *Interior Report,* 1974).

74. House, *Interior Report,* 1974, "Dissenting Views," p. 77.

75. The vote was 9 to 4. Most members who voted against the bill "grumbled that environmentalists had delayed construction of the Trans-Alaskan pipelines, refineries, power plants and reclamation projects . . . [while] Sam Steiger told them H.R. 10294 would give environmentalists even more ground for litigation" ("House Rules Committee Sets Back Land Use Bill," *Congressional Quarterly Weekly Report,* 2 March 1974, p. 559). It is unclear who besides Steiger and Rhodes attended the White House meeting, or even whether they actually spoke to the president. Most observers questioned whether they met with Nixon himself. More likely, they discussed the issue with an assistant such as Kenneth Cole, Ehrlichman's replacement as chief domestic adviser. A copy of the Steiger substitute, H.R. 11325, 93d Cong., 1st sess., may be found in

House, *Interior Report*, 1974, pp. 82–96. With regard to implementation of the land use plans, it says simply, "States are *encouraged* to utilize general purpose local governments, including regional units, for planning, review, and coordination purposes as to the regional implications of local plans and implementation programs." (emphasis added)

76. *Congressional Quarterly Weekly Report*, 2 March 1974, p. 559, and 1 March 1975, pp. 429–430; "Land Use Bill Knifed," *New York Times*, 28 February 1974, p. 36; Lyday, *Law of the Land*, pp. 2, 51.

77. Testimony of L. L. "Moon" Mullins, Mississippi; R. C. Longmire, Oklahoma Conservation Commission; and Daniel Witts, Southwestern Cattle-raisers Association, in House, *Land Use, Hearings*, 1974, pp. 85, 228, 212. Udall's statement is at p. 62. Not all witnesses spoke against the bill, however. Cf. the statement from Walter E. Hoadley, chief economist with the Bank of America, who noted that in H.R. 10294 the "emphasis on process, rather than on plans, is practical and realistic" (pp. 420–421). Hoadley, it should be noted, was a member of the Rockefeller Task Force on Land Use. Also see the testimony of Mark H. Freeman representing the League of New Community Developers (pp. 91ff.); and Maxwell E. Rich of the National Rifle Association (p. 157).

78. The Rules Committee reversed itself by an 8 to 7 vote (*New York Times*, 15 May 1974). Also see the exchange between Steiger and Marston in House, *Land Use, Hearings*, 1975, p. 68. After badgering Marston about the time he spent lobbying for the bill in 1974, Steiger was told by Secretary Rogers Morton, "A whole lot of my time was spent trying to pass it, Sam. I am sorry I did not get it done" (p. 68).

79. "Home Builders Moan That Nobody Cares," *Business Week*, 25 May 1974. The article notes that the association's new president, Lewis Cenker, "is making no-growth his special concern during his year in office. Under the slogan 'sensible growth,' he is urging builders to form 'coalitions' with groups that favor more housing to try to persuade local officials that growth can be good." Also see "Trouble in Housing for Years Ahead," *Business Week*, 13 July 1974, pp. 56–60. With land values rising at a rate of 15 percent annually, and growth restrictions mounting, "properly zoned land carrying all the necessary permits is at a premium."

80. Testimony of David Calfee, Environmental Policy Center, in House, *Land Use, Hearings*, 1973, pp. 380–381; "Udall Accuses Nixon of Sacrificing the Environment to Politics," *New York Times*, 31 March 1974, p. 47. Udall added the complaint that "conservationists have no central policy institutions, no actual conventions, no place where they produce unified policy. . . . In my opinion, this the conservation movement must do or perish as an effective agent of political change"; "Cultivated Grass Roots," *New York Times*, 15 March 1974; Lyday, *Law of the Land*, pp. 43–45.

81. Letter, 10 June 1974, Office of Representative Morris K. Udall, co-signed by ten other Representatives, four Democrats and six Republicans. It included a "summary of prepared amendments to H.R. 10294."

82. Ibid.

83. *Cong. Rec.*, 92d Cong., 1st sess., 11 June 1974, pt. 129, pp. 18801, 18804, 18805, 18808.

84. "House Kills Land Use Bill on Procedural Vote," *Congressional Quarterly Weekly Report*, 15 June 1974, p. 1570. According to *CQ*, one key urban delegation split because of the personal bickering of top state political leaders. In Illinois, fear

that Governor Daniel Walker would use a state land use agency against the interests of Chicago led Mayor Richard Daly to persuade several of the city's representatives to switch their votes against the bill. In *CQ*'s words, "If the Chicago delegation had been united in its support, the bill would have been approved for consideration—by one vote." Instead it broke 4 to 3 (*Congressional Quarterly Weekly Report*, 1 March 1975, p. 432); also see "House Vote Kills Bill on Land Use," *New York Times*, 12 June 1974, pp. 1, 16. It is testimony to the numerous concessions made to local government forces over the four years of the bill's consideration that over half of the 46 Republican votes for debate came from predominantly suburban districts.

85. House Majority Leader Thomas P. "Tip" O'Neill joined Udall in blaming the White House for the defeat. O'Neill insisted that "the Administration pulled the rug out from under the bill," and Udall damned "the shabby hypocrisy of the White House" ("House Vote Kills Bill on Land Use," *New York Times*, 12 June 1974). In 1975 Udall sought in vain to pass the bill once again but failed even to extract it from his own Interior Committee. See "Land Use Bill Killed," *Congressional Quarterly Weekly Report*, 19 July 1975, p. 1520.

86. Popper, *Politics of Land-Use Reform*, p. 14.

Chapter 7

1. See Introduction to Part Two, n. 10. For other confirmation of oil's political might, see Harvey O'Connor, *The Empire of Oil* (New York: Monthly Review Press, 1962); John M. Blair, *The Control of Oil* (New York: Random House, 1978); David Howard Davis, *Energy Politics*, 3d ed. (New York: St. Martin's, 1982); Anthony Sampson, *The Seven Sisters: The Great Oil Companies and the World They Shaped* (New York: Viking, 1975); James Ridgeway, ed., *Powering Civilization: The Complete Energy Reader* (New York: Pantheon, 1982).

2. Oil imports as a percentage of U.S. consumption rose from 8.5 percent in 1954 to 20 percent in 1965 and then up to 35.5 percent in 1973, as the industry's carefully guarded import quotas were loosened to keep up with the rate of economic growth and the need to absorb Middle East surpluses. Domestic producers, naturally, were unhappy with this tendency, but then, as Robert Engler points out, "the issue of imports periodically threatens to destroy the heavily financed image of oildom as one big happy family." See Joel Darmstadter and Hans H. Landsberg, "The Economic Background," in *The Oil Crisis*, ed. Raymond Vernon (New York: W. W. Norton, 1976), table 8, p. 31; Engler, *Politics of Oil*, p. 230.

3. John Hanrahan and Peter Gruenstein, *Lost Frontier: The Marketing of Alaska* (New York: W. W. Norton, 1977), pp. 121–125.

4. Clawson, *Federal Lands Revisited*, table 3–1, p. 91.

5. Ibid., p. 93; Arrandale, *The Battle for Natural Resources*, p. 83.

6. Gerald R. Ford, State of the Union Address, 1975, *Congressional Quarterly Almanac*, 1976, pp. 9A–9B; Popper, *Politics of Land-Use Reform*, pp. 37–41; "Huge Investment, But Still a Hurdle to Growth," *Business Week*, 1 June 1981, pp. 68–69; Commoner, *The Poverty of Power*, chap. 9.

7. Engler, *Politics of Oil*, p. 80.

8. Ibid., p. 429, and chap. 15 passim.

9. "Energy Scare's Impact on the Stock Market Fades into History," *Wall Street Journal*, 4 May 1976; *New York Times*, 1 September 1977, and 18 January 1978.

10. Davis, *Energy Politics*, pp. 85–87.

11. Hanrahan and Gruenstein, *Lost Frontier;* Arrandale, *The Battle for Natural Resources*, p. 41; "The Great Alaskan Oil Freeze," *Business Week*, 26 February 1979; Engler, *Brotherhood of Oil*, p. 23.

12. See "Continental Shelf Leasing Bill Cleared," *Congressional Quarterly Almanac*, 1978, pp. 668–673. The bill reflected strong pressure from industry to minimize the potential for local resistance, although "any person having an interest which is or may be adversely affected" by Washington's leasing program was permitted to file suit against it. Cf. "Judge Voids the Sale of U.S. Leases for Oil off Northeast Coast," *New York Times*, 18 February 1977; Davis, *Energy Politics*, pp. 87–88; Arrandale, *The Battle for Natural Resources*, p. 111. Engler nicely captures the spirit of federal impatience with local exclusion: "When, in 1974, at a special dinner (resplendent with the presence of President Ford and Secretary of State Kissinger) designed to 'sell' offshore drilling to recalcitrant coastal state governors, the newly elected chief executive of Maine asked about state participation in such federal planning, [Interior Secretary Rogers] Morton told him to sit down and await the question period" (*Brotherhood of Oil*, pp. 198–199; see also pp. 150–151).

13. Testimony of A. F. Kaulakis, vice-president, Energy Development, The Pittston Co., in House Committee on Interior and Insular Affairs, *Priority Energy Project Act. Hearings Before the Subcommittee on Energy and the Environment on H.R. 4573*, 96th Cong., 1st sess., 11 July 1979, pp. 43–46, 131–163 (hereafter cited as House, *Interior, EMB Hearings*, 1979); Claudia Copeland, "A Case Study of the SOHIO Oil Pipeline Project (PACTEX), 1975–1979," in U.S. Senate, *Energy Development Project Delays: Six Case Studies. A Report Prepared by the Congressional Research Service of the Library of Congress for the Committee on Environment and Public Works*, 96th Cong., 1st sess., October 1979, pp. 105–132 (hereafter cited as *Project Delays*); "Company Vows to Overcome Decision to Block Pipeline Under Puget Sound," *New York Times*, 5 May 1982.

14. Amelia Armitage, "A Case Study of the Kaiparowitz Coal Project, 1962–1976," in *Project Delays*, pp. 9, 11–24; Toole, *Rape of the Great Plains;* "The Mountain States: Cooling the Boom from Energy Resources," *Business Week*, 27 January 1975, pp. 108–113; Rosenbaum, *Politics of Environmental Concern*, chap. 8; Davis, *Energy Politics*, pp. 36–40; Arrandale, *The Battle for Natural Resources*, pp. 86–93; Clawson, *Federal Lands Revisited*, pp. 92–95. Clawson writes that "until about 1970, [coal] leasing was largely neglected at policymaking levels within the department [of Interior]. The requirements of the leases were not strictly enforced, and the potential values of western coal were apparently unappreciated." For example, from 1970 to 1974, existing leases covered 7,507,000 acres of coal lands. They were valued by the Interior Department at approximately $307 million, from which the U.S. taxpayer extracted royalty payments of $3.2 million, or about $0.15 per ton, a return on investment substantially less than 1 percent on the dollar. See table A-10 in Clawson, p. 290.

15. Casper and Wellstone, *Powerline;* Young, *Power over People;* House Committee on Interior and Insular Affairs, *Report to Accompany H.R. 4230, Facilitating the Transportation of Coal by Pipeline Across Federal and Non-Federal Lands*, 97th

Cong., 2d sess., pt. 1; "Preserving Western Water Rights—A Key to Coal Slurry Pipeline Bill," *National Journal,* 8 May 1982, pp. 820–821.

16. *Cong. Rec.,* 2 October 1979, S.13865.

17. Testimony of John G. McMillian, chairman and chief executive officer, Northwest Energy Company, in House, *Interior, EMB Hearings,* 1979, p. 47; the Schlesinger statement is cited in "Controversy Abounds over Authority of the Proposed Energy Mobilization Board," *Congressional Quarterly,* 26 September 1979, p. 2134.

18. Senate Committee on Interior and Insular Affairs, *State Land Use Programs; Summaries of Land Use Regulation in Eight States Prepared by the Environmental Quality Committee of the Young Lawyers Section, the American Bar Association, and a 50-State Survey of State Land Use Controls Prepared by "Land Use Planning Reports,"* 93d Cong., 2d sess., 1974; Natural Resources Defense Council, *Land Use Controls in the United States: A Handbook on the Legal Rights of Citizens,* ed. Elaine Moss (New York: Dial, 1977), pp. 271–272; Casper and Wellstone, *Powerline;* Popper, *Politics of Land-Use Reform;* Joan B. Aron, "Intergovernmental Politics of Energy," *Policy Analysis* 5, no. 4 (1979): 451–471; Theodore J. Maher and Tom Hauger, "The Energy Crisis," *The Book of the States, 1976–1977,* vol. 21 (Lexington, Ky.: Council of State Governments, 1976), pp. 505–514.

19. For the complete text of the bill, see Senate Committee on Interior and Insular Affairs, *Land Resource Planning Assistance Act and the Energy Facilities Planning and Development Act. Hearings Before the Subcommittee on Environment and Land Resources on S. 984 and S. 619,* 94th Cong., 1st sess., 1975, pp. 4–29 (hereafter cited as Senate, *Land Use, Hearings,* 1975). The bill's "findings" noted that "facilities adequate to meet the Nation's current and future energy needs be sited and constructed in a timely and rational fashion without undue delay and with early opportunity for thorough public review" (p. 5).

20. Ibid., p. 8. "Information in the report shall be organized to provide an adequate forecast on a national, regional and marketing area basis, of the demand for energy and various types of facilities, and the supply of sites available for the construction of such facilities." In effect, the FEA was being authorized to write a national land plan for energy that came close to being a national energy plan.

21. Federal intervention was also triggered when states failed to resubmit a program rejected by the FEA within sixty days of its disapproval (ibid., p. 14).

22. Testimony of Eric Zauzner, acting deputy administrator, Federal Energy Administration, ibid., p. 95.

23. Ibid., p. 96.

24. Testimony of James Wright, director, Environmental Systems Development, Westinghouse Electric Corporation; and F. W. Mielke, Jr., chairman, Power Plant Siting and Land Use Committee, Edison Electric Institute, ibid., pp. 888, 912. Wright, whose employer regularly reminds Americans that "Westinghouse is a powerful part of your life," called for a softer approach. The company had learned, apparently, from years of battling communities opposed to nuclear and electric power plants, that siting was a "social problem," not a technical one. It urged an eager administration and a frustrated senator to exercise restraint. "If the law went through . . . the reaction . . . would be quite great." Instead, Wright suggested that, like Westinghouse, the government should recognize that resistance to the new technologies was based on a strongly felt desire for "protection of indigenous values . . . things people want to hold and

want to have . . . things not protected by law or regulation." Such corporate sensitivity to deep-seated human values is admirable, except that the corporate perspective saw these values as elements of a problem to which "a solution" was sought. Thus the people who hold these values become objects of industrial manipulation. For, as Westinghouse explained, "in order to . . . get some handle on that we have added several professional sociologists to our staff and currently we are making value-judgments of society as a whole." The metaphor is illuminating: handles are for things, not people. Public relations experts call this approach "issue management" or "issue analysis." It became extremely popular in corporate circles during the mid-1970s. *Business Week* called it "a determination to identify budding political and social pressures before they get out of hand and to prepare a defensive corporate strategy in advance." Other business journalists said this was especially important in the oil industry, whose managers were engineers "not born with silver spoons in their mouths." One might suspect that the empty-mouth experience would help such men understand "the values" of the underlying population. But drilling for oil filled the mind with discipline, the belly with nourishment, and the pockets with profit, and naturally, these fogged the memory. A scholar of business administration warned executives to reacquaint themselves with the climate down below: "After limiting their thinking to engineering and financial variables for so long . . . business leaders now must get used to the human climate of political behavior, which is often the result of irrational acts"; see "The Corporate Image: PR to the Rescue," *Business Week,* 22 January 1979, for the quotation from Otto Herbinger of Boston University, as well as a fascinating account of the corporate perspective on public opinion. Also see "Oil Managers Scorned on Facing New Challenges," *New York Times,* 10 June 1974. On the financial troubles facing utilities, see Carol J. Loomis, "For the Utilities It's a Fight for Survival," *Fortune,* March 1975, pp. 97ff.

25. See the testimony of John W. Sampson, chairman, Atomic Industrial Forum, Inc., Senate, *Land Use, Hearings,* 1975. He added that a "vigorous and persuasive" administration "could prove rewarding" (p. 96). An executive from Florida Power and Light suggested a different approach. He recommended splitting the approval process for "hardware" and location and establishing a single national licensing process for each of the basic reactor models, designating their characteristics for state siters. "We should not be required to answer any of the questions more than once." Students, those arrested by the police, presidential candidates, and patrons of singles bars may appreciate his point; but whether corporate executives selling nuclear reactors deserve the privilege above other interrogated citizens is questionable. See the testimony of Don Dunlop, vice president, Environmental Affairs, Florida Power and Light, ibid., pp. 864, 867.

26. Testimony of F. W. Mielke, Jr., ibid., p. 911. He emphasized that this was an emergency action necessary to get things moving right away. The long-range task was to deal directly with "the root causes of delay" by amending "the several single-purpose acts that in the aggregate now tie up the building of new power facilities." Basic environmental policy reform was the real key to expedited energy-plant construction. Contrast this argument for removal of roadblocks with the opinion of Donald Cook, chairman of the board of American Electric Power Company: "You get a liberal who has an idea he wants to push, that he believes is in the public interest, and he will stop at nothing, absolutely nothing, in order to push it. He believes the end justifies the

means, period. I'm talking about the people at the Environment Protection Agency"; see "Donald Cook Takes on the Environmentalists," *Business Week,* 26 October 1974.

27. Davis, *Energy Politics,* p. 116.

28. Ibid., p. 117.

29. The supply data are culled from the following sources: Newsday Service, "Energy Crisis: Policies Remain Same Despite Public Outcry," *San Antonio Express,* 6 September 1979; Fred Cook, "How Big Oil Turned Off the Gas," *The Nation,* 28 July–4 August 1979; Richard Corrigan, "The Gasoline Shortage—It's Real, but Is It Necessary?" *National Journal,* 23 June 1979, pp. 1028–1031. Immediately before the shortage reached its depth in late spring, *Business Week* published several articles suggesting a less than active search for oil in the United States. "Despite the rising cost and the uncertainty of foreign crude supplies," it reported, "the search for additional oil and gas has started to slip badly." The number of drilling rigs in operation dropped 16 percent between November 1978 and early spring 1979. As one executive explained, "Oilmen are now keeping their hands in their pockets." Similarly, refinery operations lagged, falling to 85 percent of capacity in June, about 10 percent less than normal during the peak driving season. Secretary James Schlesinger announced in early May that unless refinery rates moved upward, he would have oil executives in for "polite conversations." After two months of jawboning, the refineries remained underutilized, as the industry proclaimed that its "inventories are not swollen"—this despite the fact that although imports increased 10 percent in mid-June, refinery runs dropped 2 percent! The growth in industry profits was somewhat healthier, however. For the first quarter of 1979, the average increase equaled 300 percent. See "A Big Dip in Drilling for U.S. Oil and Gas," *Business Week,* 26 March 1979; "A Priority That Could Make Gasoline Scarcer," *Business Week,* 2 July 1979.

30. "Memorandum for the President," Stuart Eisenstat, reprinted in *Washington Post,* 7 July 1979, p. A10 (hereafter cited as Eisenstat memorandum).

31. Public opinion survey by NBC News and the Associated Press, cited in Corrigan, "The Gasoline Shortage," p. 1028.

32. "Carter Would Sign Oil Control Extension," *Washington Post,* 5 May 1979; SOCAL, Standard Oiler "Commentary," August 1979; "A Premature Gasoline Drought," *Business Week,* 21 May 1979. The magazine also quotes an Atlantic-Richfield executive for whom the crisis "points up what bad shape we're in. It shows that all the controls of the last five years just haven't worked."

33. Eisenstat memorandum.

34. For a listing of Carter's visitors from oildom, see "Capping Third World Gushers," *The Nation,* 28 July–4 August 1979, pp. 68–69.

35. "Carter Television Address Text," *Congressional Quarterly Weekly Report,* 21 July 1979, pp. 1469–1472.

36. Ibid.

37. "Carter Kansas City Address Text," in ibid., pp. 1472–1475.

38. "Specifications for Establishment of Operation of an Energy Mobilization Board," in House Committee on Interstate and Foreign Commerce, *Priority Energy Project Act of 1979. Hearings Before the Subcommittee on Energy and Power on H.R. 4499, H.R. 4573, and H.R. 4862,* 96th Cong., 1st sess., 1979, pp. 144–146 (hereafter cited as House, *Commerce, EMB Hearings,* 1979). All citations from the specifications are from this source and will not be individually noted.

39. Ibid.

40. House, *Interior, EMB Hearings,* 1979: testimony of Louise C. Dunlap, executive vice-president, Environmental Policy Center, p. 62; testimony of Jonathan Gibson, Sierra Club, p. 65; statement of Cong. James Weaver (D-Ore.), p. 36. See also Charlene Sturbitts, Senate Environment and Public Works Subcommittee on Environmental Pollution, cited in "Controversy Abounds over Authority of the Proposed Energy Mobilization Board," *Congressional Quarterly Weekly Report,* 29 September 1979, p. 2137.

41. Dunlap testimony in House, *Interior, EMB Hearings,* 1979, p. 63; and statement of Roy N. Gamse, deputy assistant administrator for planning and evaluation, U.S. Environmental Protection Agency, ibid., pp. 101–104. Also, for the EPA response to charges that environmental decision processes were holding up key energy facilities, see the statement of Gus Speth, acting chairman, Council on Environmental Quality, in House, *Commerce, EMB Hearings,* 1979, pp. 178–184. Speth informed the committee that of the 938 NEPA court suits brought during the first eight years of the law's existence, 94 involved energy projects, and 26 of these, or 28 percent, involved nuclear plants, which would be unaffected by EMB. Moreover, Speth added, "About 50 percent of these cases involved energy projects where the federal agency with lead responsibility failed to prepare an EIS [environmental impact statement]." Finally, of all the energy cases, only 15 resulted in the application of temporary or preliminary injuctions (p. 182). Compare this figure with the industry's conclusion that twenty major energy projects were recently canceled because of regulatory delay. At the same time, however, to the extent that Speth was effectively taking Washington off the hook as the prime cause of delays, the responsibility of state and local excluders would seem to loom even larger. Not for nothing did corporate lobbyists insist on waivers of state and local as well as national protectionist policies.

42. Gibson testimony in House, *Interior, EMB Hearings,* 1979, p. 65. Insofar as environmentalists might be compelled to accept an Energy Mobilization Board, they stressed that its organic legislation must include carefully drawn standards of action, especially with respect to designation of priority projects, abbreviation of decision schedules and procedures, and judicial review.

43. Testimony of Edward A. Helme, associate director of the National Governors Association Energy Resources Program, House, *Commerce, EMB Hearings,* 1979, p. 188. Also see the letter sent by Governor Scott M. Matheson of Utah on behalf of the governors of Montana, North Dakota, Colorado, and New Mexico to Senator Henry M. Jackson, chairman, Energy and Natural Resources Committee, reprinted on pp. 189–190; Neal R. Pierce and Jerry Hagstrom, "Western Governors Seek Stronger Voice over Energy Policy for Their Region," *National Journal,* 13 October 1979, pp. 1692–1693; "Western Governors Are Skeptical on Effects of Carter's Energy Plan," *New York Times,* 21 July 1979, p. 17; and Price, *Regional Conflict and National Policy.*

44. Statement of Rep. Steven D. Symmes (R-Ida.) in House, *Interior, EMB Hearings,* 1979, p. 21.

45. V. O. Key, Jr., *Politics, Parties, and Pressure Groups,* 5th ed. (New York: Thomas Y. Crowell, 1964), p. 85.

46. "Business Wary on Carter Plan," *New York Times,* 17 July 1979, pp. D1, 12; "Start at Square One," editorial, *Business Week,* 23 July 1979; John M. Berry, "Car-

ter's Energy Policy: The Vital Ingredient Is Still Missing," *Fortune,* 13 August 1979, pp. 106–109. It is suggestive of the prevailing corporate uncertainty about the Carter plan that *Business Week* criticized the president for failing to decide "whether to relax environmental standards to encourage the burning of coal . . . and if so, by how much," whereas *Fortune* applauded that "it is to the President's credit . . . that he is risking the wrath of environmentalists by pushing the importance of coal and setting up a high-powered Energy Mobilization Board."

47. Testimony of John G. McMillian, chairman and chief executive officer, Northwest Energy Co., Salt Lake City, Utah, Senate Committee on Energy and Natural Resources, *Energy Supply Act (Title II). Synthetic Fuels Production Act (Title VI). Hearings Before the Committee on Energy and Natural Resources,* 96th Cong., 1st sess., on S. 1308 and S. 1377, 20 June and 9, 13 July 1979, p. 9 (hereafter cited as Senate, *Energy, EMB Hearings,* 1979); testimony of Carleton B. Scott, director, Environmental Sciences Department, Union Oil Co. of California, on behalf of the American Petroleum Institute, House, *Commerce, EMB Hearings,* 1979, p. 79.

48. Testimony of Chris Farrand, director, Corporate Planning, Peabody Coal Co., on behalf of the National Coal Association, House, *Commerce, EMB Hearings,* 1979, p. 86.

49. Testimony of Hon. Charles B. Curtis, chairman, Federal Energy Regulatory Commission, House, *Commerce, EMB Hearings,* 1979, p. 150.

50. "Carter Environmental Message Text," *Congressional Quarterly Weekly Report,* 11 August 1979, p. 1670. Conservation groups were unimpressed. "It was kind of underwhelming," said one in response to the message (p. 1667). See also "Environmentalists Fear a Retrenching by Carter," *New York Times,* 17 July 1979, p. D12. A shrewd observer, Brock Evans of the Sierra Club, summed up the political realities this way: "We are certainly up against a mood of panic, but in Washington things are never as bad as they seem" (ibid.). It was a sound judgment.

51. In effect, this lineup of excluders framed a Rocky Mountain–New England coalition deeply suspicious of forced energy development. A variety of petty capitalists—ranchers, farmers, fishing interests, and the tourist industry—had solid material incentives to ally with environmentalists in defense of exclusionary political rights. Moreover, the protectionists were well situated institutionally. Besides Udall, who was now chairman of House Interior, Muskie led the Environment and Public Works Subcommittee on Environmental Pollution, while Ribicoff chaired the Government Operations Committee. Protectionists were weakest in the House Commerce Committee, where Wirth served as unofficial leader of the exclusion interest. The other principal legislative outpost for Energy Mobilization Board policy, the Senate Energy and Natural Resources Committee, favored an agency quite close to the president's original outline. Although sentiment existed there for a stronger bill, the chairman, Henry B. Jackson of Washington, kept the committee from moving noticeably beyond the Carter draft specifications.

52. Statement of Rep. Morris Udall, House, *Interior, EMB Hearings,* 1979, p. 18; see also Senate, Statement of Sen. Abraham Ribicoff on Amendment #308 to S. 1308, *Cong. Rec.,* 96th Cong., 1st sess., 2 October 1979, pt. 125, p. 13863 (hereafter cited as Senate, *EMB Debate,* 1979).

53. Statement of Senator Henry Jackson, Senate, *Energy, EMB Hearings,* 1979, p. 187. Statement of Rep. Jim Wright, House, *Interior, EMB Hearings,* 1979, p. 25.

A moment later Wright used a different image: "We are nibbled to death by the minnows and the piranha fish."

54. For this argument see Senate, *Energy, EMB Hearings,* 1979, pp. 189–191.

55. House, Statement of Rep. Morris Udall on H.R. 5660, *Cong. Rec.,* 96th Cong., 1st sess., 30 October 1979, pt. 150, p. 9940 (hereafter cited as House, *EMB Debate,* 1979); House, *Interior, EMB Hearings,* 1979, p. 18.

56. House Committee on Interior and Insular Affairs, *Priority Energy Project Act of 1979,* H. Rpt. 96–410 to Accompany H.R. 4985, 96th Cong., 1st sess., 1979, pt. 1, p. 4. The committee provided that federal agency schedules may be modified by the board where established timetables "are unreasonable and present a substantial impediment to decisionmaking." Proposed waivers would be submitted by the board to the president. Upon the latter's recommendation, such waivers would take effect unless disapproved by either house of Congress (ibid.). EMB might also recommend waivers to governors in connection with state or local timetables. But states could not be ordered to speed up decision making.

57. Senate Committee on Energy and Natural Resources, *Priority Energy Project Act of 1979,* S. Rpt. 96–33 to Accompany S. 1308, 96th Cong., 1st sess., 1979, p. 39. The key vote came on September 19, when, by an 8 to 1 tally, the committee chose to limit the waiver to procedural rules—but with the understanding that the committee refused to accept the distinction between procedural and substantive changes: "Senate Energy Unit Says Fast Track Board Can Waive Only Procedural Law," *Congressional Quarterly Weekly Report,* 22 September 1979, p. 2054.

58. For background on Dingell's changing regulatory views, see Irwin B. Arieff, "Dingell: Stubborn, Abrasive and at Center of Energy Issue," *Congressional Quarterly Weekly Report,* 10 November 1979, pp. 2517–2520; also Richard E. Cohen, "House May Get an Energy Committee, and Dingell May Be Left Out in the Cold," *National Journal,* 2 February 1980, pp. 188–191. Dingell's increased sympathies for industry complaints about overzealous environmental control were strongly influenced by his representation of northwest Detroit, an area with obvious ties to auto-industrial interests.

59. House Committee on Interstate and Foreign Commerce, *Priority Energy Project Act of 1979,* H. Rpt. 96–410 to Accompany H.R. 4985, 96th Cong., 1st sess., 1979, pt. 2, p. 24.

60. House, *Commerce, EMB Hearings,* 1979, p. 242.

61. The Commerce Committee voted 16 to 26 against deletion of the full waiver. After the decision, three top environmental officials—Gus Speth, chairman of the White House Council on Environmental Quality; Cecil Andrus, secretary of the Department of the Interior; and Douglas Costle, administrator of the Environmental Protection Agency—sent a letter of protest to the president (which was soon leaked to the press) complaining that opposition to Wirth's amendment "undermines our credibility" ("Curb Panel in Energy, Aides Ask," *New York Times,* 13 September 1979, p. 27). Carter replied to his official critics, according to an account by John Osborne, by insisting that the matter of how much authority was necessary to override environmental laws was up to the president, and he warned them to "stop confusing Congressmen with their views" ("White House Watch—A Touch of Oil," *New Republic,* 6 October 1979, p. 11). Also see Stephen Chapman, "Energy Muddlization," *New Republic,* 29 September 1979, pp. 9–13. Congressman Dingell observed about the affair, "I find

it difficult to ascertain the administration's position on anything. . . . The administration has the capacity to surprise its friends and please its enemies" (cited in Chapman, "Energy Muddlization," p. 10).

62. See the statement of Senator Abraham D. Ribicoff, Senate, *EMB Debate,* 1979, pp. 13863–13865.

63. Among the local and state groups backing the substitutes were the National Governors Association, the National Association of Counties, the National Conference of State Legislators, the U.S. Conference of Mayors, and the National League of Cities. They were joined by environmental organizations: the National Wildlife Federation, the Sierra Club, the Wilderness Society, Environmental Action, the Environmental Defense Fund, Friends of the Earth, and the Environmental Policy Center.

64. An assorted ideological grouping of eighteen Republicans joined twenty-one mostly liberal Democrats in supporting the substitute. Among the Republican backers were senators as ideologically diverse as Jacob Javits (N.Y.), Lowell Weicker (Conn.), Orrin Hatch (Utah), and Jesse Helms (N.C.). Interestingly, senators representing coastal states, where oil drilling was a proximate danger to local fishing and tourism, voted 12 to 5 in favor of the substitute, whereas those representing the four mountain states (Montana, Wyoming, Colorado, Utah) slated for large-scale coal and syn-fuel development, split their votes 4 to 4. The Colorado, Montana, and Alaska delegations all split their votes, reflecting uncertainty about the implications of EMB more than party loyalty (e.g., Democratic votes from Montana and Alaska went against the president's bill) (Senate, *EMB Debate,* 1979, p. 13940).

65. Among the 25 votes against EMB, conservative Republicans were prominent. They included Helms (N.C.), Garn and Hatch (Utah), Lugar (Ind.), Roth (Del.), Schmitt (N.Mex.), and Armstrong (Colo.). Western Democrats also tended to dissent; they included Baucus (Mont.), Burdick (N.Dak.), Gravel (Alaska), and McGovern (S.Dak.) (Senate, *EMB Debate,* 1979, p. 14054).

66. Cited in "House Endorses 'Fast Track' Energy Board," *Congressional Quarterly Weekly Report,* 3 November 1979, p. 2448.

67. For a recent review of this crisscrossing maze of responsibilities, see David B. Walker, *Toward a Functional Federalism* (Cambridge: Winthrop, 1981).

68. For a list of many of the state laws indirectly subject to waiver under Santini-Lujan, see House, Statement of Rep. Henry Waxman, *Cong. Rec.,* 96th Cong., 2d sess., 27 June 1980, pt. 126, pp. 5726–5727 (hereafter cited as House, *EMB Conference Report,* 1979).

69. House, *EMB Debate,* 1979, p. 10005. Walker, in *Toward a Functional Federalism,* concludes that "the basic dilemma confronting any administration that now relies primarily on improved and uniform procedures and processes to strengthen intergovernmental management is that such efforts cannot be separated from the drastically expanded size, scope, and substantive concerns of today's intergovernmental programs and of their recipients" (p. 118). Walker's views derive from his perspective as assistant director of the Advisory Commission on Intergovernmental Relations.

70. House, *EMB Debate,* 1979, pp. 10014, 9948–9949.

71. The voting pattern on these decisions—the Udall substitute, the Eckhardt amendment, and the final vote—was dominated by the traditional Southern Democrat–Republican coalition prevailing against a fragmented Democratic party. This was a kind of "business-as-usual" vote reflecting conservative corporate power in American politics. The pattern was most evident and significant on the extremely close Udall-

Wirth-Clausen (U-W-C) amendment. Democrats as a group favored the amendment by a tiny eight-vote margin, 134 to 126. Republicans rejected it 43 to 107, and Southern Democrats, 4 to 76. Traditional bastions of petroleum industry influence, Texas and Louisiana, opposed Udall 4 to 26. By contrast, delegations from states most exposed to new energy pressures overwhelmingly favored the substitute. The coastal states approved by a vote of 80 to 33, and the mountain states, including Alaska, voted yes, 8 to 3. This pattern continued on the subsequent votes, although defeat of U-W-C, reinforced by the reassurance of the Santini-Lujan amendment, persuaded large numbers of Democrats to join the president's backers in favor of the Commerce Committee bill. Thus, on the Eckhardt amendment, Democrats voted no by a narrow margin, 126 to 129, whereas on the final vote, the party regrouped, massively voting to support the president, EMB, and the energy industry, 192 to 64. Northern Democrats voted two to one for EMB.

72. The Conference Committee included all eighteen members of the Senate Energy Committee, twelve members of the House Commerce Committee, and six from the House Interior Committee. See "Mobilization Board Conferees Face Off Soon," *Congressional Quarterly Weekly Report,* 1 December 1979, p. 2712.

73. House Conference Report on S. 1308, H. Rpt. No. 96–1119, *Priority Energy Project Act of 1980,* Title II, Sec. 317, *Cong. Rec.,* 96th Cong., 2d sess., 21 June 1980, pt. 126, pp. 5486–5487.

74. Douglas C. Bauer, senior vice-president, Edison Electric Institute, cited in Christopher Madison, "New Board to Cut Red Tape May Cause Some Problems of Its Own," *National Journal,* 10 May 1980, p. 763. Cf. "Why the EPA Still Has Clout," *Business Week,* 10 September 1979, where the journal concluded early in the struggle over the EMB that the price of a strong board would be the subjection of its decisions "to Congressional approval, throwing the issue back into the political arena, where environmentalists would stand a good chance of thwarting the board" (p. 131).

75. Opponents of the board appeared on the House floor sporting lapel buttons emblazoned with the words "Even More Bureaucracy," with the first letter of each word given special emphasis.

76. House, *EMB Conference Report,* 1980, p. 5790.

77. "House Shelves Energy Mobilization Board," *Congressional Quarterly Weekly Report,* 28 June 1980, pp. 1790–1792. A good deal of heat was generated during the debate over the Conference Committee's intent that the waiver of federal law also applied to state policies derived from national law. This point had been made quite clearly during the earlier discussions, and many Republicans were now feigning innocence to justify partisan votes.

78. Harrison Brown, *The Challenge of Man's Future* (New York: Viking, 1954), p. 51.

79. John M. Deutch, cited in "Synthetic Fuels Appeal Fades," *New York Times,* 6 May 1983, p. D14.

80. "Summary of Proposed DOE Budget," *Power Line,* 8 February 1983, p. 2; Congressional Budget Office, *An Analysis of the President's Budgetary Proposals for Fiscal Year 1984* (Washington, D.C.: GPO, 1983), pp. 124–127.

81. Lawrence Mosher, "Synfuels Subsidies—What Some Call 'Insurance,' Others Call a Giveaway," *National Journal,* 7 May 1983, pp. 965–968; "Synthetic Fuels Appeal Fades," *New York Times,* 6 May 1983, p. D14.

82. Daniel Yergin and Martin Hillenbrand, eds., *Global Insecurity: A Strategy for*

Energy and Economic Renewal (New York: Penguin, 1983), p. 27; Charles K. Ebinger, ed., *The Critical Link: Energy and National Security in the 1980s*, rev. ed. (Cambridge: Ballinger, 1982), pp. xxiii, xxx.

Chapter 8

1. Fredy Perlman, "Introduction: Commodity Fetishism," in *Essays on Marx's Theory of Value*, ed. Isaak Illich Rubin, trans. Miloš Samardžija and Fredy Perlman (Detroit: Black and Red, 1972), p. xi.

2. Milton Friedman, *Capitalism and Freedom* (Chicago: University of Chicago Press, 1962), p. 26; Poulantzas, *State, Power, Socialism*, p. 72.

3. Thomas Hobbes, *Leviathan* (Baltimore: Penguin, 1968), p. 297.

4. Habermas, *Legitimation Crisis*, p. 23.

5. Marcuse, *One-Dimensional Man*, p. 245.

6. Clawson, *Federal Lands Revisited*, p. 256.

7. Block, "The Ruling Class Does Not Rule," p. 34.

8. Irving S. Shapiro, "Business and the Public Policy Process," in *Business and Public Policy*, ed. John T. Dunlop (Cambridge: Harvard University Press, 1980), p. 25.

9. See, e.g., Ralph Miliband, *The State in Capitalist Society* (New York: Basic Books, 1969).

10. Nicos Poulantzas, *Classes in Contemporary Capitalism*, trans. David Fernbach (London: Verso / New Left Books, 1978), p. 293; Greer, *Big Steel*, p. 205.

11. In *Village of Arlington Heights* v. *Metropolitan Housing Development Corp.*, 429 U.S. 252 (1976), the failure of the plaintiffs to show that local officials acted with a racially motivated intent persuaded the Court to sustain the exclusionary zoning ordinance. And the case of *Warth* v. *Seldin*, 422 U.S. 490 (1974), found the Court unwilling to uphold the right of nonresidents to sue a locality on the basis of its exclusionary land use and housing policies. As noted in chapter 1, the Court has also so far refrained from adopting the Brennan doctrine, which supports the payment of compensation to landowners whose ownership rights have been temporarily enjoined by an illegal ordinance.

12. Weaver and Babcock, *City Zoning*, pp. 248, 253; Charles M. Haar and Daniel W. Fessler, *The Wrong Side of the Tracks* (New York: Simon & Schuster, 1986).

13. *Associated Homebuilders of the Greater Eastbay, Inc.* v. *City of Livermore*, 135 Cal. Rptr. 41, 557 P. 2d 473 (1976), cited in Babcock, "Spatial Impact," p. 268; Michelman, "Property, Utility, and Fairness," p. 1204.

14. Berchin, "Regulation of Land Use," p. 905.

15. Peter E. Millspaugh, "Eminent Domain: Is It Getting Out of Hand?" *Real Estate Law Journal* 11 (1982): 115.

16. "Developments in the Law, Zoning," p. 1478.

17. Habermas, *Legitimation Crisis*, p. 62; Poulantzas, *State, Power, Socialism*, p. 191.

18. Miliband, *Marxism and Politics*, p. 74.

19. Polanyi, *The Great Transformation*, pp. 36–37.

20. "Brooklyn Sets Landfill Fight to Keep Out Stratford," *New York Times*, Connecticut Weekly Section, 22 June 1986.

21. Popper, *Politics of Land-Use Reform*, p. 228.

22. Berchin, "Regulation of Land Use," p. 935.

23. Garrett Hardin, "The Tragedy of the Commons," in Hardin and Baden, *Managing the Commons*, p. 20. For Hardin, however, private property is itself a reasonable, if not necessarily "just," institution for the conservation of resources, because it gives each owner a vested interest in saving. What he fails to note is that for private property to function in market systems, owners create a "commons" by dumping costs outside their fences.

24. Lynd, "Power in American Society," p. 26.

25. Draper, *Marx's Theory of Revolution*, 2:414.

26. Poulantzas, *State, Power, Socialism*, pp. 55–56.

27. Despite, or rather because of, these long-entrenched patterns, housing remains in short supply for millions of Americans, and in deplorably poor condition for many others. According to one Wall Street observer of the industry, nearly 70 percent of all households are unable to purchase an 80 percent mortgage on a median-price home. At the same time, however, many housing and finance experts see the growth of investment in housing—a process driven in no small part by speculative lust for unearned increment—as a force sapping the industrial base. In 1982, for example, approximately $1.1 trillion was outstanding on mortgage loans for one-to-four–family units, an amount equal to fully 20 percent of all private credit outstanding. In the words of the Congressional Budget Office, this trend, coupled with "the recent decline in productivity growth has raised concerns that the United States may be allocating too much capital to housing at the expense of other sectors of the economy." Adding sociological respectability to this view, George Sternlieb of Rutgers University argues that American development has reached a "postshelter" stage, characterized by consumers' penchant to "overinvest" in more shelter than they need. Recent efforts to deregulate the banking system, thus forcing savings and loan associations to charge higher interest rates on mortgage loans, become understandable as part of a larger business-government strategy to reduce aid for what *Business Week* calls "an industry that has been coddled for half a century." The housing plan suggested here should be seen, therefore, as part of an effort to protect housing opportunities as much as to change the commercial treatment of shelter. See "Housing's Storm," *Business Week*, 7 September 1981, pp. 60–66; "Homebuilding's New Outlook," *Business Week*, 7 November 1983, pp. 92–99; Congressional Budget Office, *The Housing Finance System and Federal Policy: Recent Changes and Options for the Future* (Washington, D.C.: GPO, 1983), pp. xiii–xiv; 1; also see chapter 1, n. 56, above.

28. Emily Paradise Achtenberg and Peter Marcuse, "Toward the Decommodification of Housing," in Bratt, Hartman, and Meyerson, *Critical Perspectives on Housing*, pp. 474–483; and Chester Hartman and Michael E. Stone, "A Socialist Housing Alternative for the United States," in ibid., pp. 484–513. These articles, especially the latter, include more specific and detailed discussion along the general lines suggested here.

29. In fact, much of the existing private housing stock, including that in the preferred suburban locales, is profoundly indebted to the state. According to the Congressional Budget Office, federal "tax expenditures" for housing—e.g., income foregone by Washington due to housing-related exemptions in the tax code—equaled nearly $40 billion in 1983 and will rise to $63.3 billion in 1988. These include the deductibility of mortgage interest and property tax payments (worth $25 and $8.8 bil-

lion respectively in 1984), the deferral of capital gains taxes on the sale of homes (worth $3.8 billion in 1984), and the exclusion from taxation of $125,000 in capital gains income for house sales by persons 55 years or older (worth $1.3 billion in 1984). See Congressional Budget Office, *Tax Expenditures: Current Issues and Five-Year Budget Projections for Fiscal Years 1984–1988* (Washington, D.C.: GPO, 1983), table A-1, Appendix A; and Congressional Budget Office, *Housing Finance System and Federal Policy,* p. 24. As the CBO notes in its study of housing finance, "Middle and upper-income households receive most of the benefits from these tax provisions" (p. 24). In addition, federally underwritten mortgage-backed securities, that part of the secondary mortgage market underpinned by federal loan guarantees, equaled nearly $190 billion in 1982, no less than 15 percent of outstanding mortgage debt in the nation (p. 45; table 4, p. 46). At the same time, however, total federal expenditures for all facets of the public housing program came to only $2.6 billion, a tiny fraction of the sums indirectly allocated through tax breaks and loan guarantees for the purchase of homes in the "private sector," homes often doubly guaranteed by local land-use protection ordinances (Congressional Budget Office, *Federal Subsidies for Public Housing: Issues and Options* [Washington, D.C.: GPO, 1983], p. xi).

30. A major component in the effort to control new housing prices should be a vast expansion of public housing construction. Progressives should encourage the abolition of tax breaks and guarantees for private home construction as a concealed form of state subsidy. Public contributions to the satisfaction of basic human needs should not be shrouded in budget tables but should explicitly be made a lever for the mass production of housing for all income strata. Such expenditures should be funneled to regional and local planning bodies, which can either invest in their own housing enterprises or subcontract to private builders. The important thing is that the myth of private housing deserves to be shattered once and for all. With the federally backed long-term mortgage, shelter has been a substantially public good since the 1930s (between 1930 and 1970, for example, the percentage of homeownership in the U.S. rose from 48 to nearly 65 percent), although its concealment by financial devices has helped to perpetuate beliefs in exclusion while "officially" public "projects" have had to carry the stigma of the "handout" (Congressional Budget Office, *Housing Finance System and Federal Policy,* p. ix).

31. For an overview of these moves and a sampling of various legislative approaches to plant shut-down controls, see *Plant Closings: Issues, Politics, and Legislation,* ed. William Schweke (Washington, D.C.: Conference on Alternative State and Local Policies, 1980). Moreover, in *City of Oakland* v. *Oakland Raiders,* a case involving Oakland's effort to block the Raiders football team's proposed move to Los Angeles, the principle was upheld that a local government may use its powers of eminent domain to condemn the property of a departing corporation. And in the Poletown case, the Michigan Supreme Court supported Detroit's use of eminent domain to alleviate unemployment and retain essential industry (*City of Oakland* v. *Oakland Raiders,* 31 Cal. 3d 656; 183 Cal. Rptr. 673, 646 P. 2d 835 [1982]; and *Poletown Neighborhood Council* v. *City of Detroit,* 410 Mich. 616 [304 N.W. 2d 455 (1981)]). Workers and progressive lawyers in Pittsburgh are currently testing such possibilities in connection with abandoned steel plants; see Tri-State Conference on Steel, *Steel Valley Authority: A Community Plan to Save Pittsburgh's Steel Industry,* 2d ed. (Pittsburgh: Tri-State Conference on Steel, n.d.).

32. It might well be argued that in line with the logic of this argument, public subsidies should be treated as the legal equivalent of equity ownership in the plant. In fact, given the vital role of organized community life as the indispensable setting for industry, the municipality's stake might well be treated as the functional equivalent of bondholding: the city should be a creditor of first standing.

33. Aaron Wildavsky, "Birthday Cake Federalism," in *American Federalism: A New Partnership for the Republic,* ed. Robert B. Hawkins, Jr. (San Francisco: Institute for Contemporary Studies, 1982), p. 187.

34. George Gilder, "A Supply-Side Economics of the Left," *The Public Interest* 72 (Summer 1983): 41.

35. Casper and Wellstone, *Powerline,* p. 17.

36. Joyce Maynard, "The Story of a Town," *New York Times Magazine,* 11 May 1986, p. 41.

37. Joshua Cohen and Joel Rogers, *On Democracy: Toward a Transformation of American Society* (New York: Penguin, 1983), p. 161; Goodman, *The Last Entrepreneurs,* p. 101.

38. Noble, "Present Tense Technology," p. 9.

39. Samuel Bowles, David M. Gordon, and Thomas E. Weisskopf, *Beyond the Wasteland: A Democratic Alternative to Economic Decline* (New York: Doubleday, 1983); Bluestone and Harrison, *Deindustrialization of America;* Maurice Zeitlin, "The People's Bank," *Democracy* 2 (April 1982): 69–80; Gar Alperovitz and Jeff Faux, *Rebuilding America* (New York: Pantheon, 1984); Martin Carnoy and Derek Shearer, *Economic Democracy: The Challenge of the 1980s* (Armonk, N.Y.: M. E. Sharpe, 1980).

40. Bowles, Gordon, and Weisskopf, *Beyond the Wasteland,* p. 331; Zeitlin, "People's Bank," p. 75.

41. Mike Cooley, *Architect or Bee?* comp. and ed. Shirley Cooley (Boston: South End Press, 1980), p. 107.

42. Bowles and his colleagues suggest that on difficult siting questions, communities should engage in joint decision making, with compensation paid "where no locality would otherwise welcome a socially needed project" (*Beyond the Wasteland,* pp. 344–346). As much of the foregoing analysis suggests, such approaches tend to beg the question of the exclusion-minded community. Indeed, as part of their own "environmental bill of rights," these authors call for absolute local rights to bar the siting of dangerous facilities. Outright bans may be a good short-range strategy when corporations are demanding centralized land-clearance programs, but they do not represent a socially responsible way of dealing with the larger issues of particular versus general interests in siting questions. Communities do have social responsibilities to larger constituencies; the liberal land use reformers were not wrong in making this point. Nor were they incorrect in recognizing that in some cases force must be applied in the overall social interest. The point is to encourage public participation at earlier stages of the planning process so that the most perplexing locational issues can be eased. But conflict and coercion are inevitable.

43. David Montgomery, "Comment: Making History But Not Under Circumstances Chosen by Ourselves," *Monthly Review,* March 1984, p. 23. This essay is in response to an article in the same issue by Jeremy Brecher, "Crisis Economy: Born Again Labor Movement?" pp. 1–18.

44. Bluestone and Harrison, *Deindustrialization of America*, p. 19.

45. As William Kapp noted at the end of his study *The Social Costs of Private Enterprise*, "Instead of concealing the possibility of conflicts . . . it is more realistic to recognize the reality of the conflict and accept it, with the Federalists and Karl Marx, as the essential characteristic of the political process" (p. 261).

Selected Bibliography

The bibliography is divided into six sections, the first of which includes general and theoretical works that were of special value in formulating the framework of this study. The next two sections designate texts and articles in the areas of land, public policy, and historical studies. The fourth and fifth sections list key legal works and cases cited in the book, and the last includes the main government reports and documents.

Although not specifically noted below, several magazines, journals, and newspapers were essential to the analysis of business trends and land policy: the *New York Times*, the *Wall Street Journal*, the *Christian Science Monitor*, the *Congressional Quarterly*, *Business Week*, the *National Journal*, and the *Congressional Record*.

Theoretical Works

Ackelsberg, Martha A. "Women's Collaborative Activities and City Life: Politics and Policy." In *Political Women: Current Roles in State and Local Government*, edited by Janet A. Flammang, pp. 242–259. Sage Yearbooks in Women's Policy Studies, vol. 8. Beverly Hills, Calif.: Sage, 1984.

Agnew, J. Q. "Homeownership and the Capitalist Social Order." In *Urbanization and Urban Planning in Capitalist Society*, edited by Michael Dear and Allen J. Scott, pp. 457–480. New York: Methuen, 1981.

Althusser, Louis. *For Marx*. Translated by Ben Brewster. London: New Left Books, 1977.

———. *Lenin and Philosophy, and Other Essays*. Translated by Ben Brewster. New York: Monthly Review Press, 1971.

Bachrach, Peter, and Morton Baratz. *Power and Poverty: Theory and Practice*. New York: Oxford University Press, 1970.

Barker, Charles Albro. *Henry George*. New York: Oxford University Press, 1955.

Bell, Daniel. *The Cultural Contradictions of Capitalism*. New York: Basic Books, 1978.

Benevolo, Leonardo. *The Origins of Modern Town Planning*. Cambridge: MIT Press, 1971.

Bentham, Jeremy. *An Introduction to the Principles of Morals and Legislation*. Introduction by Lawrence J. Lafleur. New York: Hafner, 1948.

Berle, Adolf A., Jr., and Gardiner C. Means. *The Modern Corporation and Private Property*. Rev. ed. New York: Harcourt, Brace & World, 1967.

Block, Fred. "The Ruling Class Does Not Rule: Notes on the Marxist Theory of the State." In *The Political Economy: Readings in the Politics and Economics of American Public Policy,* edited by Thomas Ferguson and Joel Rogers, pp. 32–46. Armonk, N.Y.: M. E. Sharpe, 1984.

Bowles, Samuel, and Herbert Gintis. *Democracy and Capitalism: Property, Community, and the Contradictions of Modern Social Thought*. New York: Basic Books, 1986.

Braverman, Harry. *Labor and Monopoly Capital: The Degradation of Work in the Twentieth Century*. New York: Monthly Review Press, 1974.

Brown, Harrison. *The Challenge of Man's Future*. New York: Viking, 1954.

Carnoy, Martin. *The State and Political Theory*. Princeton, N.J.: Princeton University Press, 1984.

Castells, Manuel. *The City and the Grassroots: A Cross-Cultural Theory of Urban Social Movements*. Berkeley and Los Angeles: University of California Press, 1983.
————. *The Urban Question: A Marxist Approach*. Translated by Alan Sheridan. Cambridge: MIT Press, 1979.

Chandler, Alfred D. *The Visible Hand: The Managerial Revolution in American Business*. Cambridge: Harvard University Press, 1977.

Cockburn, Cynthia. *The Local State*. London: Pluto, 1977.

Cohen, Joshua, and Joel Rogers. *On Democracy: Toward a Transformation of American Society*. New York: Penguin, 1983.

Commons, John R. *Legal Foundations of Capitalism*. Madison: University of Wisconsin Press, 1968.

Connerton, Paul, ed. *Critical Sociology: Selected Readings*. New York: Penguin, 1976.

Cox, Kevin R. "Capitalism and Conflict Around the Communal Living Space." In *Urbanization and Urban Planning in Capitalist Society,* edited by Michael Dear and Allen J. Scott, pp. 431–455. New York: Methuen, 1981.

Crozier, Michael J., Samuel P. Huntington, and Joji Watanuki. *The Crisis of Democracy: Report on the Governability of Democracies to the Trilateral Commission*. New York: New York University Press, 1975.

Dear, Michael, and Allen J. Scott, eds. *Urbanization and Urban Planning in Capitalist Society*. New York: Methuen, 1981.

Dewey, John. *The Public and Its Problems*. Chicago: Holt, 1927.

Dobb, Maurice. *Studies in the Development of Capitalism*. New York: International Publishers, 1947.

Dolbeare, Kenneth M. *Democracy at Risk: The Politics of Economic Renewal*. Chatham, N.J.: Chatham House, 1984.

Domhoff, G. William. *The Powers That Be: Processes of Ruling Class Domination in America.* New York: Random House, 1978.

———. *Who Rules America Now? A View for the Eighties.* Englewood Cliffs, N.J.: Prentice-Hall, 1983.

Dowd, Douglas F. *The Twisted Dream: Capitalist Development in the United States Since 1776.* 2d ed. Cambridge, Mass.: Winthrop, 1977.

Draper, Hal. *Karl Marx's Theory of Revolution.* 2 vols. New York: Monthly Review Press, 1978.

Edel, Matthew. "Homeownership and Working Class Unity." *International Journal of Urban and Regional Research* 6 (June 1982): 205–221.

Engels, Friedrich. *The Condition of the Working Class in England.* Translated by W. O. Henderson and W. H. Chaloner. Stanford: Stanford University Press, 1968.

———. *The Housing Question.* Moscow: Progress Publishers, 1979.

Friedman, Milton. *Capitalism and Freedom.* Chicago: University of Chicago Press, 1962.

Galbraith, John Kenneth. *The New Industrial State.* Boston: Houghton Mifflin, 1967.

Gaventa, John. *Power and Powerlessness: Quiescence and Rebellion in an Appalachian Valley.* Urbana: University of Illinois Press, 1980.

George, Henry. *Progress and Poverty.* New York: Robert Schalkenbach Foundation, 1948.

Giddens, Anthony, and David Held, eds. *Classes, Power, and Conflict: Classical and Contemporary Debates.* Berkeley and Los Angeles: University of California Press, 1982.

Gilder, George. *Wealth and Poverty.* New York: Bantam, 1981.

Gordon, David M., Richard Edwards, and Michael Reich. *Segmented Work, Divided Workers: The Historical Transformation of Labor in the United States.* Cambridge: Cambridge University Press, 1982.

Gramsci, Antonio. *Selections from the Prison Notebooks.* Edited and translated by Quintin Hoare and Geoffrey Nowell Smith. New York: International Publishers, 1971.

Greenstone, J. David. *Labor in American Politics.* 2d ed. Chicago: University of Chicago Press, 1969.

Greer, Edward. *Big Steel: Black Politics and Corporate Power in Gary, Indiana.* New York: Monthly Review Press, 1979.

Habermas, Jürgen. *Legitimation Crisis.* Translated by Thomas McCarthy. Boston: Beacon, 1975.

Halévy, Elie. *The Growth of Philosophic Radicalism.* Translated by Mary Morris. Preface by A. D. Lindsay. Boston: Beacon, 1955.

Harvey, David. "Labor, Capital, and Class Struggle Around the Built Environment in Advanced Capitalist Societies." *Politics and Society* 6, no. 3 (1976): 265–295.

———. *The Limits to Capital.* Chicago: University of Chicago Press, 1982.

———. *Social Justice and the City.* Baltimore: Johns Hopkins University Press, 1973.

———. "The Urban Process Under Capitalism: A Framework for Analysis." In *Urbanization and Urban Planning in Capitalist Society,* edited by Michael Dear and Allen J. Scott, pp. 91–121. New York: Methuen, 1981.

Hayek, Friedrich A. *The Road to Serfdom.* Chicago: University of Chicago Press, 1967.

Hobbes, Thomas. *Leviathan.* Edited with an Introduction by C. B. Macpherson. Baltimore: Penguin, 1968.

Holloway, John, and Sol Picciotto, eds. *State and Capital: A Marxist Debate.* London: Edward Arnold, 1978.

Huntington, Samuel P. *Political Order in Changing Societies.* New Haven: Yale University Press, 1968.

Jefferson, Thomas. *The Portable Thomas Jefferson.* Edited with an Introduction by Merrill D. Peterson. New York: Viking, 1975.

Jessop, Bob. *The Capitalist State: Marxist Theories and Methods.* New York: New York University Press, 1982.

Kameny, Jim. "A Critique of Homeownership." In *Critical Perspectives on Housing,* edited by Rachel G. Bratt, Chester Hartman, and Ann Meyerson, pp. 12–40. Philadelphia: Temple University Press, 1986.

Kapp, K. William. *The Social Costs of Private Enterprise.* New York: Schocken, 1971.

Katznelson, Ira. *City Trenches: Urban Politics and the Patterning of Class in the United States.* Chicago: University of Chicago Press, 1981.

Lee, Everett S. "The Turner Thesis Re-Examined." *American Quarterly* 13 (Spring 1961): 77–87.

Leiss, William. *The Domination of Nature.* Boston: Beacon, 1974.

Levi, Margaret. "The Predatory Theory of Rule." *Politics and Society* 10, no. 4 (1981): 431–466.

Levi, Margaret, and Douglass C. North. "Towards a Property Rights Theory of Exploitation." *Politics and Society* 11, no. 3 (1982): 315–320.

Lindblom, Charles E. "The Market as Prison." *Journal of Politics* 44 (May 1982): 324–336.

Locke, John. *Two Treatises of Government.* Introduction and notes by Peter Laslett. New York: New American Library, 1960.

Lowi, Theodore J. "Decision Making vs. Policy Making: Toward an Antidote for Technocracy." *Public Administration Review* 30 (May–June 1970): 314–325.

———. *The End of Liberalism: The Second Republic of the United States.* 2d ed. New York: W. W. Norton, 1979.

———. *Incomplete Conquest: Governing America.* 2d ed. New York: Holt, Rinehart & Winston, 1981.

Lukács, Georg. *History and Class Consciousness.* Translated by Rodney Livingstone. Cambridge: MIT Press, 1971.

Lynd, Robert S. *Knowledge for What? The Place of Social Science in American Culture.* Princeton, N.J.: Princeton University Press, 1967.

———. "Power in American Society as Resource and Problem." In *Problems of Power in American Democracy,* edited by Arthur Kornhauser, pp. 1–45. Detroit: Wayne State University Press, 1957.

Lynd, Robert S., and Helen Merrell Lynd. *Middletown: A Study in Modern American Culture.* New York: Harcourt, Brace & World, 1956.

McConnell, Grant. *Private Power and American Democracy.* New York: Random House, 1966.

McWilliams, Wilson Carey. *The Idea of Fraternity in America.* Berkeley and Los Angeles: University of California Press, 1973.

Marcuse, Herbert. *One-Dimensional Man: Studies in the Ideology of Advanced Industrial Society.* Boston: Beacon, 1964.

Marcusen, Ann. "Class and Urban Social Expenditure: A Marxist Theory of Metropolitan Government." In *Marxism and the Metropolis: New Perspectives in Urban Political Economy,* edited by William K. Tabb and Larry Sawers, pp. 90–111. New York: Oxford University Press, 1978.

Marx, Karl. *Capital.* 3 vols. Edited by Friedrich Engels. Translated by Samuel Moore and Edward Aveling. New York: International Publishers, 1967.

——. *The Economic and Philosophic Manuscripts of 1844.* Edited with an Introduction by Dirk J. Struik. Translated by Martin Milligan. New York: International Publishers, 1964.

——. *Selected Writings in Sociology and Social Philosophy.* Translated by T. B. Bottomore. Edited with an Introduction and notes by T. B. Bottomore and Maximilien Rubel; Foreword by Erich Fromm. New York: McGraw-Hill, 1956.

Marx, Karl, and Friedrich Engels. *The Communist Manifesto.* New York: International Publishers, 1948.

——. *The German Ideology.* Edited with an Introduction by R. Pascal. New York: International Publishers, 1947.

——. *The Marx-Engels Reader.* Edited by Robert Tucker. New York: W. W. Norton, 1972.

Massey, Doreen, and Alexandrina Catalano. *Capital and Land: Landownership by Capital in Great Britain.* London: Edward Arnold, 1978.

Miliband, Ralph. *Marxism and Politics.* New York: Oxford University Press, 1977.

——. *The State in Capitalist Society.* New York: Basic Books, 1969.

Mill, John Stuart. *Principles of Political Economy.* Vol. 1. New York: Appleton, 1864.

Mills, C. Wright. *The Power Elite.* New York: Oxford University Press, 1956.

——. *The Sociological Imagination.* New York: Oxford University Press, 1959.

——. *White Collar: The American Middle Classes.* New York: Oxford University Press, 1951.

Mingione, Enzo. *Social Conflict and the City.* New York: St. Martin's, 1981.

Moore, Barrington, Jr. *Social Origins of Dictatorship and Democracy: Lord and Peasant in the Making of the Modern World.* Boston: Beacon, 1967.

Neumann, Franz. "The Change in the Function of Law in Modern Society." In *The Democratic and the Authoritarian State: Essays in Political and Legal Theory,* edited with a Preface by Herbert Marcuse, pp. 22–68. New York: Free Press, 1957.

Noble, David. "Present Tense Technology." *Democracy* 3 (Spring 1983): 8–24.

O'Connor, James. *The Fiscal Crisis of the State.* New York: St. Martin's, 1973.

Offe, Claus. "Political Authority and Class Structures." In *Critical Sociology: Selected Readings,* edited by Paul Connerton, pp. 388–421. New York: Penguin, 1976.

——. "Structural Problems of the Capitalist State." In *German Political Studies,* vol. 1, edited by Klaus Von Beyme, pp. 31–57. Beverly Hills, Calif.: Sage, 1974.

——. "The Theory of the Capitalist State and the Problem of Policy Formation." In *Stress and Contradiction in Modern Capitalism,* edited by Leon N. Lindberg, Robert Alford, Colin Crouch, and Claus Offe, pp. 125–145. Lexington, Mass.: D. C. Heath, 1974.

Olson, Mancur, Jr. *The Logic of Collective Action: Public Goods and the Theory of Groups.* Rev. ed. New York: Schocken, 1968.

Oppenheimer, Martin. *White Collar Politics.* New York: Monthly Review Press, 1985.

Ossowski, Stanislaw. *Class Structure in the Social Consciousness.* Translated by Sheila Patterson. London: Routledge & Kegan Paul, 1963.

Pahl, Roy. *Whose City? And Further Essays on Urban Society.* 2d ed. Harmondsworth: Penguin, 1975.

Parenti, Michael. *Power and the Powerless.* New York: St. Martin's, 1978.

Perlman, Fredy. "Introduction: Commodity Fetishism." In Isaak Illich Rubin, *Essays on Marx's Theory of Value,* translated by Miloš Samardźija and Fredy Perlman. Detroit: Black and Red, 1972.

Pierson, George W. "The M-Factor in American History." *American Quarterly* 14 (Summer 1962): 275–289.

Piven, Francis Fox, and Richard A. Cloward. *The New Class War: Reagan's Attack on the Welfare State and Its Consequences.* New York: Pantheon, 1982.

———. *Poor People's Movements: Why They Succeed, How They Fail.* New York: Random House, 1979.

Polanyi, Karl. *The Great Transformation.* Introduction by R. M. MacIver. Boston: Beacon, 1971.

Poulantzas, Nicos. *Classes in Contemporary Capitalism.* Translated by David Fernbach. London: Verso / New Left Books, 1978.

———. *Political Power and Social Classes.* Translated and edited by Timothy O'Hagan. London: Verso / New Left Books, 1978.

———. *State, Power, Socialism.* Translated by Patrick Camiller. London: Verso / New Left Books, 1980.

Pratt, Geraldine. "Class Analysis and Urban Domestic Property: A Critical Reexamination." *International Journal of Urban and Regional Research* 6 (December 1982): 481–501.

Rex, John, and Robert Moore. *Race, Community, and Conflict.* London: Oxford University Press, 1967.

Ricardo, David. *The Works of David Ricardo, with a Notice of the Life and Writings of the Author by J. R. McCulloch.* London: John Murray, 1852.

Said, Edward. *The Question of Palestine.* New York: Times Books, 1979.

Saunders, Peter. "Domestic Property and Social Class." *International Journal of Urban and Regional Research* 2 (June 1978): 233–251.

———. *Social Theory and the Urban Question.* New York: Holmes & Meier, 1981.

Schattschneider, E. E. *The Semisovereign People: A Realist's View of Democracy in America.* New York: Holt, Rinehart & Winston, 1960.

Schlatter, Richard. *Private Property: The History of an Idea.* New Brunswick, N.J.: Rutgers University Press, 1951.

Schumpeter, Joseph A. *Capitalism, Socialism, and Democracy.* 3d ed. New York: Harper & Row, 1962.

Slater, Philip. *The Pursuit of Loneliness: American Culture at the Breaking Point.* Boston: Beacon, 1970.

Smith, Adam. *An Inquiry into the Nature and Causes of the Wealth of Nations.* 2 vols. Introduction by M. Blaug. Homewood, Ill.: Irwin, 1963.

Smith, Neil. *Uneven Development: Nature, Capital and the Production of Space*. Oxford: Basil Blackwell, 1984.

Tabb, William K., and Larry Sawers, eds. *Marxism and the Metropolis: New Perspectives in Urban Political Economy*. New York: Oxford University Press, 1978.

Tocqueville, Alexis de. *Democracy in America*. 2 vols. Edited by Philips Bradley. New York: Random House, 1945.

Truman, David. *The Governmental Process*. New York: Knopf, 1951.

Turner, Frederick Jackson. "The Significance of the Frontier in American History." In *The Frontier in American History*, Foreword by Ray Allen Billington, pp. 1–38. New York: Holt, Rinehart & Winston, 1962.

Turner, John Roscoe. *The Ricardian Rent Theory in Early American Economics*. New York: New York University Press, 1921.

Veblen, Thorstein. *Absentee Ownership: The Case of America*. Introduction by Robert Lekachman. Boston: Beacon, 1967.

———. *The Theory of Business Enterprise*. Introduction by Douglas Dowd. New Brunswick, N.J.: Transaction Books, 1978.

———. *The Theory of the Leisure Class*. Introduction by C. Wright Mills. New York: New American Library, 1953.

Walker, Richard A. "A Theory of Suburbanization: Capitalism and the Construction of Urban Space in the United States." In *Urbanization and Urban Planning in Capitalist Society*, edited by Michael Dear and Allen J. Scott, pp. 383–429. New York: Methuen, 1981.

Weber, Max. *From Max Weber: Essays in Sociology*. Edited by Hans Gerth and C. Wright Mills. New York: Oxford University Press, 1958.

Welter, Rush. *The Mind of America, 1820–1860*. New York: Columbia University Press, 1975.

Westergaard, John, and Henrietta Resler. *Class in a Capitalist Society: A Study of Contemporary Britain*. New York: Basic Books, 1975.

Williams, William Appleton. "Is the Idea and Reality of America Possible Without Empire?" *The Nation*, 2–9 August 1980, pp. 99–119.

Wolfe, Alan. *The Limits of Legitimacy: Political Contradictions of Contemporary Capitalism*. New York: Free Press, 1977.

Wright, Erik Olin. *Class, Crisis and the State*. London: New Left Books, 1978.

Land, Public Policy, and Historical Sources

Abernethy, Thomas P. *The Western Lands and the American Revolution*. New York: Appleton-Century, 1937.

Abrams, Charles. *The City Is the Frontier*. New York: Harper & Row, 1965.

———. *Revolution in Land*. New York: Harper, 1939.

Agar, Herbert, and Allen Tate. *Who Owns America? A New Declaration of Independence*. Boston: Houghton Mifflin, 1936. Reprint, Washington, D.C.: University Press of America, n.d.

Allensworth, Don K., and Robert Linowes. *The Politics of Land Use: Planning, Zoning, and the Private Developer*. New York: Praeger, 1973.

Allin, Craig W. *The Politics of Wilderness Preservation*. Westport, Conn.: Greenwood, 1982.

Alperovitz, Gar, and Jeff Faux. *Rebuilding America*. New York: Pantheon, 1984.

American Law Institute. *A Model Land Development Code, Proposed Official Draft No. 1; Tentative Draft No. 6*. Philadelphia: American Law Institute, 1974.

Anson, Brian. *I'll Fight You for It: Behind the Struggle for Covent Garden*. London: Jonathan Cape, 1981.

Arrandale, Tom. *The Battle for Natural Resources*. Washington, D.C.: Congressional Quarterly, 1983.

Babcock, Richard F. *The Zoning Game: Municipal Practices and Policies*. Madison: University of Wisconsin Press, 1966.

Babcock, Richard F., and Fred P. Bosselman. *Exclusionary Zoning: Land Use Regulation and Housing in the 1970s*. New York: Praeger, 1973.

Banfield, Edward C. *The Unheavenly City Revisted*. Boston: Little, Brown, 1974.

Banfield, Edward, and James Q. Wilson. *City Politics*. Cambridge: Harvard University Press, 1965.

Barnes, Peter, ed. *The People's Land: A Reader on Land Reform in the United States*. Emmaus, Pa.: Rodale, 1975.

Bass, Jack, and Walter DeVries. *The Transformation of Southern Politics*. New York: Basic Books, 1976.

Bassett, Edward M. *Zoning: The Laws, Administration, and Court Decisions During the First Twenty Years*. New York: Russell Sage Foundation, 1936.

Beard, Charles A. *Economic Origins of Jeffersonian Democracy*. New York: Macmillan, 1915.

Bellush, Jewel, and Murray Hausknecht, eds. *Urban Renewal: People, Politics and Planning*. New York: Doubleday, 1967.

Bettman, Alfred. *City and Regional Planning Papers*. Edited by Arthur C. Comely. Foreword by John Lord O'Brian. Cambridge: Harvard University Press, 1946.

Billington, Ray Allen, with James Blaine Hedges. *Westward Expansion: A History of the American Frontier*. 4th ed. New York: Macmillan, 1974.

Blair, John M. *The Control of Oil*. New York: Random House, 1978.

Bluestone, Barry, and Bennett Harrison. *The Deindustrialization of America: Plant Closings, Community Abandonment, and the Dismantling of Basic Industry*. New York: Basic Books, 1982.

Bollens, John C., and Henry J. Schmandt. *The Metropolis: Its People, Politics, and Economic Life*. New York: Harper & Row, 1982.

Bookchin, Murray. *The Limits of the City*. New York: Harper & Row, 1974.

Bosselman, Fred, and David Callies. *The Quiet Revolution in Land Use Control*. Washington, D.C.: U.S. Government Printing Office, 1971.

Bowles, Samuel, David M. Gordon, and Thomas E. Weisskopf. *Beyond the Wasteland: A Democratic Alternative to Economic Decline*. New York: Doubleday, 1983.

Boyte, Harry C. *The Backyard Revolution: Understanding the New Citizen Movement*. Philadelphia: Temple University Press, 1980.

Bratt, Rachel G., Chester Hartman, and Ann Myerson, eds. *Critical Perspectives on Housing*. Philadelphia: Temple University Press, 1986.

Brown, Dee. *Bury My Heart at Wounded Knee*. New York: Random House, 1971.

Brown, Michael. *Laying Waste: The Poisoning of America by Toxic Chemicals*. New York: Washington Square Press, 1981.

Calef, Wesley. *Private Grazing and Public Lands: Studies of the Local Management of the Taylor Grazing Act.* Chicago: University of Chicago Press, 1960.

Carnoy, Martin, and Derek Shearer. *Economic Democracy: The Challenge of the 1980s.* Armonk, N.Y.: M. E. Sharpe, 1980.

Caro, Robert. *The Power Broker: Robert Moses and the Fall of New York.* New York: Random House, 1975.

Casper, Barry M., and Paul David Wellstone. *Powerline: The First Battle of America's Energy War.* Amherst: University of Massachusetts Press, 1981.

Caudill, Harry. *Night Comes to the Cumberlands: A Biography of a Depressed Area.* Boston: Atlantic Monthly–Little, Brown, 1963.

———. *The Watches of the Night.* Boston: Atlantic Monthly–Little, Brown, 1976.

Chamberlin, Neil W., ed. *Business and the Cities.* New York: Basic Books, 1970.

Choate, Pat, and Susan Walter. *America in Ruins: The Decaying Infrastructure.* Durham, N.C.: Duke University Press, 1981.

Clawson, Marion. *The Federal Lands Revisited.* Baltimore: Resources for the Future series, Johns Hopkins University Press, 1983.

———. *Suburban Land Conversion in the United States: An Economic and Governmental Process.* Baltimore: Resources for the Future series, Johns Hopkins University Press, 1971.

Clawson, Marion, and Burnell Held. *The Federal Lands: Their Use and Management.* Baltimore: Resources for the Future series, Johns Hopkins University Press, 1957.

Cloward, Richard A., and Frances Fox Piven. *The Politics of Turmoil: Poverty, Race and the Urban Crisis.* New York: Random House, 1975.

Colean, Miles, and Robinson Newcomb. *Stabilizing Construction: The Record and Potential.* New York: McGraw-Hill, 1952.

Colglazier, William, Jr., ed. *The Politics of Nuclear Waste.* New York: Pergamon, 1982.

Committee for Economic Development. *Guiding Metropolitan Growth.* New York: Committee for Economic Development, 1960.

———. *Modernizing Local Government.* Statement on National Policy by the Research and Policy Committee of the Committee for Economic Development. New York, July 1966. Reprinted in part in *National Urban Problems,* edited by Harry B. Yoshpe and F. R. Burdette, pp. 119–129. Washington, D.C.: Industrial College of the Armed Forces, 1970.

Commoner, Barry. *The Closing Circle: Nature, Man and Technology.* New York: Knopf, 1971.

———. *The Poverty of Power: Energy and the Economic Crisis.* New York: Bantam, 1977.

Congressional Quarterly. *Man's Control of the Environment.* Washington, D.C.: Congressional Quarterly, 1970.

Culhane, Paul J. *Public Lands Politics: Interest Group Influence on the Forest Service and the Bureau of Land Management.* Baltimore: Resources for the Future series, Johns Hopkins University Press, 1981.

Danielson, Michael N. *The Politics of Exclusion.* New York: Columbia University Press, 1976.

Danielson, Michael N., and Jameson W. Doig. *New York: The Politics of Urban Re-*

gional Development. Berkeley and Los Angeles: University of California Press, 1982.

Davis, David Howard. *Energy Politics*. 3d ed. New York: St. Martin's, 1982.

Delafons, John. *Land-Use Controls in the United States*. Cambridge: Joint Center for Urban Studies of the Massachusetts Institute of Technology and Harvard University, 1962.

Derthic, Martha. *New Towns In-Town: Why a Federal Program Failed*. Foreword by Joseph L. Califano, Jr. Washington, D.C.: Urban Institute, 1972.

Downie, Leonard, Jr. *Mortgage on America: The Real Cost of Real Estate Speculation*. New York: Praeger, 1974.

Downs, Anthony. *Neighborhoods and Urban Development*. Washington, D.C.: Brookings Institution, 1981.

———. *Opening Up the Suburbs: An Urban Strategy for America*. New Haven: Yale University Press, 1973.

Edel, Matthew, Elliot D. Sclar, and Daniel Luria. *Shaky Palaces: Homeownership and Social Mobility in Boston's Suburbanization*. New York: Columbia University Press, 1984.

Eichler, Edward P., and Marshall Kaplan. *The Community Builders*. Berkeley and Los Angeles: University of California Press, 1967.

Elezar, Daniel J. *Cities of the Prairie: The Metropolitan Frontier and American Politics*. New York: Basic Books, 1970.

Engler, Robert. *The Brotherhood of Oil*. Chicago: University of Chicago Press, 1977.

———. *The Politics of Oil*. Chicago: University of Chicago Press, 1967.

Erikson, Kai T. *Everything in Its Path: Destruction of Community in the Buffalo Creek Flood*. New York: Simon & Schuster, 1976.

Fainstein, Susan S., Norman I. Fainstein, Richard Child Hill, Dennis Judd, and Michael Peter Smith. *Restructuring the City: The Political Economy of Urban Redevelopment*. New York: Longman, 1983.

Feagin, Joe. *The Urban Real Estate Game: Playing Monopoly with Real Money*. New York: Prentice-Hall, 1983.

Fellmeth, Robert C. *Politics of Land: Ralph Nader's Study Group Report on Land Use in California*. Introduction by Ralph Nader. New York: Grossman, 1973.

Foner, Eric. *Free Soil, Free Labor, Free Men: The Ideology of the Republican Party Before the Civil War*. New York: Oxford University Press, 1970.

———. *Politics and Ideology in the Age of the Civil War*. New York: Oxford University Press, 1980.

Foss, Philip O. *Politics and Grass: The Administration of Grazing on the Public Domain*. Seattle: University of Washington Press, 1960.

Freudenberg, Nicolas. *Not in Our Backyards! Community Action for Health and the Environment*. Foreword by Lois Marie Gibbs. New York: Monthly Review Press, 1984.

Frieden, Bernard J. *The Environmental Protection Hustle*. Cambridge: MIT Press, 1979.

Frieden, Bernard J., and Marshall Kaplan. *The Politics of Neglect: Urban Aid from Model Cities to Revenue Sharing*. Cambridge: MIT Press, 1975.

Friedmann, John, and Clyde Weaver. *Territory and Function: The Evolution of Regional Planning*. Berkeley and Los Angeles: University of California Press, 1979.

Gates, Paul Wallace. *The Farmer's Age, 1815–1860*. New York: Holt, Rinehart & Winston, 1960.

———. *The History of Public Land Law Development*. Written for the U.S. Public Land Law Review Commission, with a chapter by Robert W. Swenson. New York: Arno, 1979.

Gettleman, Marvin E., and David Mermelstein, eds. *The Great Society Reader: The Failure of American Liberalism*. New York: Random House, 1967.

Gibbons, Boyd. *Wye Island: The True Story of an American Community's Struggle to Preserve Its Way of Life*. New York: Penguin, 1979.

Goodman, Robert. *The Last Entrepreneurs: America's Regional Wars for Jobs and Dollars*. New York: Simon & Schuster, 1979.

Graham, Otis L., Jr. *Toward a Planned Society: From Roosevelt to Nixon*. New York: Oxford University Press, 1976.

Grebler, Leo. *Large-Scale Housing and Real Estate Firms: Analysis of a New Business Enterprise*. New York: Praeger, 1973.

Guzman, Sam, Konrad Von Moltke, Francis Irwin, and Cynthia Whitehead. *Public Policy for Chemicals: National and International Issues*. Washington, D.C.: Conservation Foundation, 1980.

Hacker, Louis M. *The Triumph of American Capitalism*. New York: Simon & Schuster, 1940.

Hall, Peter. *Great Planning Disasters*. Berkeley and Los Angeles: University of California Press, 1982.

Hanrahan, John, and Peter Gruenstein. *Lost Frontier: The Marketing of Alaska*. Introduction by Ralph Nader. New York: W. W. Norton, 1977.

Harrigan, John J. *Political Change in the Metropolis*. 2d ed. Boston: Little, Brown, 1981.

Hartman, Chester. *Yerba Buena: Land Grab and Community Resistance*. San Francisco: Glide Publications, 1974.

Hays, Samuel P. *Conservation and the Gospel of Efficiency: The Progressive Conservation Movement, 1890–1920*. New York: Atheneum, 1969.

Healy, Robert, and John S. Rosenberg. *Land Use and the States*. 2d ed. Baltimore: Johns Hopkins University Press, 1979.

Hibbard, Benjamin Horace. *A History of the Public Land Policies*. Foreword by Paul Wallace Gates. Madison: University of Wisconsin Press, 1965.

Hicks, John D. *The Populist Revolt: A History of the Farmers' Alliance and the People's Party*. Lincoln: University of Nebraska Press, 1961.

Hite, James C. *Room and Situation: The Political Economy of Land Use Policy*. Chicago: Nelson-Hall, 1979.

Hoagland, Henry E., and Leo D. Stone. *Real Estate Finance*. 3d ed. Homewood, Ill.: Irwin, 1965.

Ingram, James W., and Chia Shun Shih. *Utility Analysis for the Urban Growth Inside the Recharge Zones of the Groundwater Resources of San Antonio, Texas*. San Antonio: Division of Environmental Studies, University of Texas at San Antonio, 1977.

Ise, John. *The United States Forest Policy*. New Haven: Yale University Press, 1920.

———. *The United States Oil Policy*. New Haven: Yale University Press, 1926.

Jackson, Kenneth T., and Stanley K. Schultz, eds. *Cities in American History.* New York: Knopf, 1972.

Jackson, Richard H. *Land Use in America.* New York: Wiley, 1981.

Jacobs, Jane. *The Death and Life of Great American Cities.* New York: Random House, 1961.

Johnson, David R., John A. Booth, and Richard J. Harris, eds. *The Politics of San Antonio: Community, Progress and Power.* Lincoln: University of Nebraska Press, 1983.

Jones, Bryan D., and Lynn W. Batchelor, with Carter Wilson. *The Sustaining Hand: Community Leadership and Corporate Power.* Lawrence: University of Kansas Press, 1986.

Key, V. O., Jr. *Southern Politics in State and Nation.* New York: Random House, 1949.

Lineberry, Robert. *Equality and Urban Policy: The Distribution of Municipal Public Services.* Beverly Hills, Calif.: Sage, 1977.

Livermore, Shaw. *Early American Land Companies: Their Influence on Corporate Development.* New York: Commonwealth Fund, 1939.

Lorimer, James. *The Developers.* Toronto: Lorimer, 1978.

Lowi, Theodore, and Benjamin Ginsberg et al. *Poliscide.* New York: Macmillan, 1976.

Lyday, Noreen. *The Law of the Land: Debating National Land Use Legislation, 1970–1975.* Washington, D.C.: Urban Institute, 1976.

Maass, Arthur. *Muddy Waters: The Army Engineers and the Nation's Rivers.* Cambridge: Harvard University Press, 1951.

McKelvey, Blake. *The Urbanization of America, 1860–1915.* New Brunswick, N.J.: Rutgers University Press, 1963.

Magaziner, Ira C., and Robert B. Reich. *Minding America's Business: The Decline and Rise of the American Economy.* New York: Random House, 1983.

Main, Jackson Turner. *The Antifederalists, Critics of the Constitution, 1781–1788.* Chapel Hill: University of North Carolina Press, 1961.

Marsh, George Perkins. *The Earth as Modified by Human Action: A New Edition of Man and Nature.* New York: Scribner, Armstrong, 1874.

Mayer, Martin. *The Builders: Houses, People, Neighborhoods, Governments, Money.* New York: W. W. Norton, 1978.

Meinig, D. W. *Imperial Texas: An Interpretive Essay in Cultural Geography.* Introduction by Lorrin Kannamer. Austin: University of Texas Press, 1969.

Meyerson, Martin, and Edward Banfield. *Politics, Planning and the Public Interest: The Case of Public Housing in Chicago.* New York: Free Press, 1955.

Milne, Lynne, M. Kavanaugh, J. Russell Boulding, and Bernard Shanks. *The Great Giveaway: Public Oil, Gas and Coal and the Reagan Administration.* Sierra Club, National Heritage Report no. 1. San Francisco: Sierra Club, 1982.

Mingay, G. E. *The Gentry: The Rise and Fall of a Ruling Class.* London: Longmans, 1976.

Mollenkopf, John H. *The Contested City.* Princeton, N.J.: Princeton University Press, 1983.

Müller, Ronald E. *Revitalizing America: Politics for Prosperity.* New York: Simon & Schuster, 1980.

Mumford, Lewis. *The City in History: Its Origins, Its Transformations, and Its Prospects.* New York: Harcourt, Brace & World, 1961.

————. *The Culture of Cities*. New York: Harcourt, Brace, Jovanovich, 1970.

Ralph Nader Congress Project. *The Environment Committees: A Study of the House and Senate Interior and Agriculture Committees*. New York: Grossman, 1975.

National Committee on Urban Growth. *The New City*. Introduction by Vice-President Spiro T. Agnew. New York: Praeger, 1969.

Natural Resources Defense Council. *Land Use Controls in the United States: A Handbook on the Legal Rights of Citizens*. Edited by Elaine Moss. New York: Dial, 1977.

Nelson, Robert H. *Zoning and Private Property Rights: An Analysis of the American System of Land-Use Regulation*. Cambridge: MIT Press, 1980.

Nettles, Curtis P. *The Roots of American Culture: A History of American Colonial Life*. New York: Appleton-Century-Crofts, 1963.

The New American State Papers: The Public Lands. 8 vols. Introduction by Margaret Beatty Bogue. Wilmington, Del.: Scholarly Resources, 1973. Vol. 3: *Land Prices and Preemption Rights*. Vol. 4: *Bounty Lands, Revenues*.

O'Connor, Harvey. *The Empire of Oil*. New York: Monthly Review Press, 1962.

Olmsted, Frederick Law. *Civilizing American Cities: A Selection of Frederick Law Olmsted's Writings on City Landscapes*. Edited by S. B. Sutton. Cambridge: MIT Press, 1971.

Peffer, Louise E. *The Closing of the Public Domain*. Stanford: Stanford University Press, 1951.

Perin, Constance. *Everything in Its Place: Social Order and Land Use in America*. Princeton, N.J.: Princeton University Press, 1977.

Peterson, Paul E. *City Limits*. Chicago: University of Chicago Press, 1981.

Pinchot, Gifford. *Breaking New Ground*. New York: Harcourt, Brace, 1947.

Pirenne, Henri. *Medieval Cities*. Princeton, N.J.: Princeton University Press, 1948.

Polikoff, Alexander. *Housing the Poor*. Cambridge, Mass.: Ballinger, 1977.

Popper, Frank J. *The Politics of Land-Use Reform*. Madison: University of Wisconsin Press, 1981.

Price, Kent A., ed. *Regional Conflict and National Policy*. Baltimore: Resources for the Future series, Johns Hopkins University Press, 1982.

Pynoos, Jon, Robert Shafer, and Chester W. Hartman, eds. *Housing Urban America*. 2d ed. Hawthorne, N.Y.: Aldine, 1980.

Quarles, John. *Cleaning Up America: An Insider's View of the Environmental Protection Agency*. Boston: Houghton Mifflin, 1976.

Reich, Robert B. *The Next American Frontier*. New York: Times Books, 1983.

Reilly, William K., ed. *The Use of Land: A Citizens' Policy Guide to Urban Growth*. New York: Thomas Y. Crowell, 1973.

Reisch, Mark. *Hazardous Wastes, Issue Brief*. Washington, D.C.: Congressional Research Service, Library of Congress, 1980.

Ridgeway, James, ed. *Powering Civilization: The Complete Energy Reader*. New York: Pantheon, 1982.

Robbins, Roy. *Our Landed Heritage: The Public Domain, 1776–1936*. Lincoln: University of Nebraska Press, 1962.

Rohrbough, Malcolm J. *The Land Office Business: The Settlement and Administration of American Public Lands, 1789–1837*. New York: Oxford University Press, 1968.

Rosenbaum, Walter A. *The Politics of Environmental Concern*. New York: Praeger, 1973.

Sale, Kirkpatrick. *Power Shift: The Rise of the Southern Rim and Its Challenge to the Eastern Establishment.* New York: Random House, 1975.

Sampson, Anthony. *The Seven Sisters: The Great Oil Companies and the World They Shaped.* New York: Viking, 1975.

Sanders, Luther Lee. *How to Win Elections in San Antonio the Good Government Way, 1955–1971.* San Antonio: Urban Studies Department, St. Mary's University, 1975.

Sawers, Larry, and William K. Tabb, eds. *Sunbelt / Snowbelt: Urban Development and Regional Restructuring.* New York: Oxford University Press, 1984.

Schands, William E., and Robert G. Healy. *The Lands Nobody Wanted: Policy for National Forests in the Eastern United States.* Washington, D.C.: Conservation Foundation, 1977.

Schlesinger, Arthur M., Jr. *The Age of Jackson.* Boston: Little, Brown, 1945.

Schwartz, Lynne Sharon. *We Are Talking About Homes: A Great University Against Its Neighbors.* New York: Harper & Row, 1985.

Schweke, William, ed. *Plant Closings: Issues, Politics, and Legislation.* Washington, D.C.: Conference on Alternative State and Local Policies, 1980.

Scott, Mel. *American City Planning Since 1890.* Berkeley and Los Angeles: University of California Press, 1969.

Scott, Randall W., ed. *Management and Control of Growth.* 3 vols. Washington, D.C.: Urban Land Institute, 1975.

Sigafoos, Robert. *Corporate Real Estate Development.* Lexington, Mass.: Lexington Books, 1976.

Smith, Frank E. *The Politics of Conservation.* New York: Harper & Row, 1966.

Smith, Henry Nash. *Virgin Land: The American West as Symbol and Myth.* New York: Random House, 1950.

Solomon, Arthur P., ed. *The Prospective City: Economic, Population, Energy, and Environmental Developments.* Cambridge: MIT Press, 1980.

Stephenson, George. *Political History of the Public Lands, 1840–1862.* New York: Russell & Russell, 1917.

Sutton, Imre. *Indian Land Tenure: Bibliographical Essays and a Guide to the Literature.* New York: Clearwater, 1975.

Thomas, Dana L. *Lords of the Land.* New York: Putnam, 1977.

Thompson, E. P. *Whigs and Hunters: The Origin of the Black Act.* New York: Pantheon, 1975.

Thurow, Lester. *The Zero-Sum Society: Distribution and the Possibilities for Economic Change.* New York: Penguin, 1981.

Toll, Seymour. *Zoned American.* New York: Grossman, 1969.

Tolo, Kenneth W., ed. *The American City: Realities and Possibilities, A Symposium.* Austin, Texas: Lyndon B. Johnson School of Public Affairs, 1974.

Toole, K. Ross. *The Rape of the Great Plains.* Boston: Atlantic Monthly–Little, Brown, 1976.

Tri-State Conference on Steel. *Steel Valley Authority: A Community Plan to Save Pittsburgh's Steel Industry.* 2d ed. Pittsburgh: Tri-State Conference on Steel, n.d.

Watterson, Wayt T., and Roberta S. Watterson. *The Politics of New Communities: A Case Study of San Antonio Ranch.* New York: Praeger, 1975.

Weaver, Clifford L., and Richard F. Babcock. *City Zoning: The Once and Future Frontier.* Chicago: American Planning Association, Planners Press, 1979.

Webb, Walter Prescott. *The Great Frontier.* Austin: University of Texas Press, 1951.

Weinberg, Albert K. *Manifest Destiny: A Study of Nationalist Expansionism in American History.* Chicago: Quadrangle, 1963.

Wengert, Norman I. *Natural Resources and the Political Struggle.* New York: Doubleday, 1955.

Whyte, William H. *The Last Landscape.* New York: Doubleday, 1970.

Wiley, Peter, and Robert Gottlieb. *Empires in the Sun: The Rise of the New American West.* New York: Putnam, 1982.

Williams, Oliver P. *Metropolitan Political Analysis: A Social Access Approach.* New York: Free Press, 1971.

Wirt, Frederick M., Benjamin Walter, Francine F. Rabinovitz, and Deborah R. Hensler. *On the City's Rim: Politics and Policy in Suburbia.* Lexington, Mass.: D. C. Heath, 1972.

Wolfe, Peter. *Land in America: Its Value, Use, and Control.* New York: Pantheon, 1981.

Wood, Robert. *Suburbia: Its People and Their Politics.* Boston: Houghton Mifflin, 1958.

Worthy, William. *The Rape of Our Neighborhoods—And How Communities Are Resisting Take-overs by Colleges, Hospitals, Churches, Businesses, and Public Agencies.* New York: Morrow, 1976.

Young, Arthur Nicholas. *The Single Tax Movement in the United States.* Princeton, N.J.: Princeton University Press, 1916.

Young, Louise B. *Power over People.* New York: Oxford University Press, 1973.

Zahler, Helen. *Eastern Workingmen and National Land Policy.* New York: Columbia University Press, 1942.

Land and Policy Articles

Achtenberg, Emily Paradise, and Peter Marcuse. "Toward the Decommodification of Housing." In *Critical Perspectives on Housing,* edited by Rachel G. Bratt, Chester Hartman, and Ann Meyerson, pp. 474–483. Philadelphia: Temple University Press, 1986.

Anderson, Terry L., and P. J. Hill. "From Free Grass to Fences: Transforming the Commons of the American West." In *Managing the Commons,* edited by Garrett Hardin and John Baden, pp. 200–216. San Francisco: Freeman, 1977.

Ashton, Patrick T. "The Political Economy of Suburban Development." In *Marxism and the Metropolis: New Perspectives in Urban Political Economy,* edited by William K. Tabb and Larry Sawers, pp. 64–89. New York: Oxford University Press, 1978.

Aspinall, Wayne. "Turns and Curves on a Well-Traveled Road: The Vicissitudes of Establishing Land Use Planning Policy." In *National Land Use Policy,* Proceedings of a special conference sponsored by the Soil Conservation Society of America, November 27–29, 1972, pp. 1–16. Ankeny, Iowa: Soil Conservation Society, 1973.

Babcock, Richard F. "The Courts Enter the Land Development Marketplace." *City* 5 (January–February 1971): 58–64.

———. "The Spatial Impact of Land-Use and Environmental Controls." In *The Prospective City,* edited by Arthur P. Solomon, pp. 264–287. Cambridge: MIT Press, 1980.

Babcock, Richard F., and Diane A. Feurer. "Land as a Commodity 'Affected with a Public Interest.'" *Urban Land,* November 1977, pp. 7–12.

Barnett, Jonathan. "Beginning the Debate on a National Growth Policy." *Architectural Record* 149 (May 1971): 117–118.

Baylis, Thomas A. "Leadership Change in Contemporary San Antonio." In *The Politics of San Antonio: Community, Progress and Power,* edited by David R. Johnson, John A. Booth, and Richard J. Harris, pp. 95–113. Lincoln: University of Nebraska Press, 1983.

Burka, Paul. "The Second Battle of the Alamo." *Texas Monthly,* December 1977, pp. 139–143, 218–238.

Cottrell, Charles L., and R. Michael Stevens. "The 1975 Voting Rights Act and San Antonio, Texas: Toward a Federal Guarantee of a Republican Form of Local Government." *Publius* 8 (Winter 1978): 79–100.

Edel, Matthew. "Urban Renewal and Land Use Conflicts." In *Problems in Political Economy: An Urban Perspective,* edited by David M. Gordon, pp. 519–527. 2d ed. Lexington, Mass.: D. C. Heath, 1977.

Fainstein, Susan S., and Norman I. Fainstein. "Economic Change, National Policy, and the System of Cities." In *Restructuring the City: The Political Economy of Urban Redevelopment,* by Susan S. Fainstein, Norman I. Fainstein, Richard Child Hill, Dennis Judd, and Michael Peter Smith, pp. 1–26. New York: Longman, 1983.

Fleischmann, Arnold. "Sunbelt Boosterism: The Politics of Postwar Growth in San Antonio." In *The Rise of the Sunbelt Cities,* edited by David C. Perry and Alfred J. Watkins, vol. 14, Urban Affairs Annual Reviews, pp. 151–168. Beverly Hills, Calif.: Sage, 1977.

Foner, Eric. "Class, Ethnicity, and Radicalism in the Gilded Age: The Land League and Irish America." In *Politics and Ideology in the Age of the Civil War,* pp. 150–200. New York: Oxford University Press, 1980.

Freilich, Robert H., and Davis T. Greis. "Timing and Sequencing Development: Controlling Growth." In *Future Land Use: Energy, Environmental, and Legal Constraints,* edited by Robert W. Burchell and David Listokin, pp. 59–106. New Brunswick, N.J.: Center for Urban Policy Research, Rutgers University, 1975.

Frieden, Bernard J. "The Environmental Attack on Home-Building." In *The Prospective City: Economic, Population, Energy, and Environmental Developments,* edited by Arthur P. Solomon, pp. 288–308. Cambridge: MIT Press, 1980.

Gilder, George. "A Supply-Side Economics of the Left." *The Public Interest* 72 (Summer 1983): 29–43.

Goldsmith, William W. "Bringing the Third World Home: Enterprise Zones for America?" In *Sunbelt / Snowbelt: Urban Development and Regional Restructuring,* edited by Larry Sawers and William K. Tabb, pp. 339–350. New York: Oxford University Press, 1984.

Gordon, David. "Capitalist Development and the History of American Cities." In *Marxism and the Metropolis: New Perspectives in Urban Political Economy,* edited by William K. Tabb and Larry Sawers, pp. 25–63. New York: Oxford University Press, 1978.

Green, Harold P., and Marc Zeil. "Federal-State Conflict in Nuclear Waste Management: The Legal Bases." In *The Politics of Nuclear Waste,* edited by E. William Colglazier, Jr., pp. 110–137. New York: Pergamon, 1982.

Hardin, Garrett. "The Tragedy of the Commons." In *Managing the Commons*, edited by Garrett Hardin and John Baden, pp. 16–30. San Francisco: Freeman, 1977.

Hartman, Chester, and Michael E. Stone. "A Socialist Housing Alternative for the United States." In *Critical Perspectives on Housing*, edited by Rachel G. Bratt, Chester Hartman, and Ann Meyerson, pp. 484–513. Philadelphia: Temple University Press, 1986.

Hopper, Kim, and Jill Hamberg. "The Making of America's Homeless: From Skid Row to New Poor, 1945–1984." In *Critical Perspectives on Housing*, edited by Rachel G. Bratt, Chester Hartman, and Ann Meyerson, pp. 12–40. Philadelphia: Temple University Press, 1986.

Jackson, Kenneth T. "Metropolitan Government Versus Suburban Autonomy: Politics on the Crabgrass Frontier." In *Cities in American History*, edited by Kenneth T. Jackson and Stanley K. Schultz, pp. 442–462. New York: Knopf, 1972.

Meyer, Peter. "Land Rush: A Survey of America's Land." *Harper's*, January 1979, pp. 45–60.

Mollenkopf, John H. "The Postwar Politics of Urban Development." In *Marxism and the Metropolis: New Perspectives in Urban Political Economy*, edited by William K. Tabb and Larry Sawers, pp. 117–152. New York: Oxford University Press, 1978.

Newman, J. Wilson. "Does Business Have a Future?" In *Business and the Cities*, edited by Neil W. Chamberlin, pp. 384–386. New York: Basic Books, 1970.

Oster, Sharon M., and John M. Quigley. "Regulatory Barriers to the Diffusion of Innovation: Some Evidence from Building Codes." In *Housing Urban America*, edited by Jon Pynoos, Robert Shafer, and Chester W. Hartman, pp. 372–383. 2d ed. Hawthorne, N.Y.: Aldine, 1976.

Plotkin, Sidney. "Policy Fragmentation and Capitalist Reform: The Defeat of National Land-Use Policy." *Politics and Society* 9, no. 4 (1980): 409–445.

Rakoff, Robert M. "Ideology in Everyday Life: The Meaning of the House." *Politics and Society* 7, no. 1 (1977): 85–104.

Reich, Robert B. "Industrial Evolution." *Democracy* 3 (Summer 1983): 10–20.

Rohatyn, Felix. "The Coming Emergency and What Can be Done About It." *New York Review of Books* 4 (December 1980): 20–26.

Ross, Steven J. "Political Economy for the Masses: Henry George." *Democracy* 2 (July 1982): 125–134.

Schlesinger, Tom, and Mark Erlich. "Housing: The Industry Capitalism Didn't Forget." In *Critical Perspectives on Housing*, edited by Rachel G. Bratt, Chester Hartman, and Ann Meyerson, pp. 139–164. Philadelphia: Temple University Press, 1986.

Shapiro, Irving S. "Business and the Public Policy Process." In *Business and Public Policy*, edited by John T. Dunlop, pp. 23–33. Cambridge: Harvard University Press, 1980.

Tate, Allen. "Notes on Liberty and Property." In *Who Owns America? A New Declaration of Independence*, edited by Herbert Agar and Allen Tate, pp. 80–93. Boston: Houghton Mifflin, 1936. Reprint, Washington, D.C.: University Press of America, n.d.

Walker, Richard A., and Michael K. Heiman. "Quiet Revolution for Whom?" *Annals of the Association of American Geographers* 71, no. 1 (1981): 67–83.

White, Michelle J. "Self-Interest in the Suburbs: The Trend Toward No-Growth Zoning." *Policy Analysis* 4, no. 2 (1978): 185–203.

Zeitlin, Maurice. "The People's Bank." *Democracy* 2 (April 1982): 69–80.

Legal Texts and Law Review Articles

Bacow, Lawrence S., and James R. Milkey. "Overcoming Opposition to Hazardous Waste Facilities: The Massachusetts Approach." *Harvard Environmental Law Review* 6, no. 2 (1982): 265–301.

Bennett, Barry. "Eminent Domain and Redevelopment: The Return of Engine Charlie." *DePaul Law Review* 31 (1981): 115–151.

Berchin, Sondra E. "Regulation of Land Use: From Magna Carta to a *Just* Formulation." *UCLA Law Review* 23 (June 1976): 904–933.

Berger, Lawrence. "The Public Use Requirement in Eminent Domain." *Oregon Law Review* 57 (1978): 203–246.

Blackstone, Sir William. *Blackstone's Commentaries, with Notes of References to the Constitution and Laws of the Federal Government of the United States and of the Commonwealth of Virginia.* Edited by St. George Tucker. 5 vols. New York: Augustus M. Kelly, 1969.

Bosselman, Fred, David Callies, and John Banta. *The Taking Issue.* Written for the Council on Environmental Quality. Washington, D.C.: U.S. Government Printing Office, 1973.

Callies, David L., and Gail M. Tamashiro. "Enterprise Zones: The Redevelopment Sweepstakes Begin." *Urban Lawyer* 15 (Winter 1983): 231–289.

Cormack, Joseph M. "Legal Concepts in Cases of Eminent Domain." *Yale Law Journal* 41 (December 1931): 221–261.

"Developments in the Law, Zoning." *Harvard Law Review* 91 (May 1978): 1407–1728.

Dunham, Allison. "A Legal and Economic Basis for City Planning (Making Room for Robert Moses, William Zeckendorf, and a City Planner in the Same Community)." *Columbia Law Review* 58 (May 1958): 650–671.

Ellickson, Robert C. "Suburban Growth Controls: An Economic and Legal Analysis." *Yale Law Journal* 86 (January 1977): 385–511.

Freilich, Robert N. "Solving the 'Taking' Equation: Making the Whole Equal the Sum of the Parts." *Urban Lawyer* 15 (September 1983): 447–485.

Freund, Ernst. *The Police Power: Public Policy and Constitutional Rights.* Chicago: Callaghan, 1904.

Haar, Charles M., ed. *Land-Use Planning: A Casebook on the Use, Misuse, and Reuse of Urban Land.* 3d ed. Boston: Little, Brown, 1976.

―――. "Wayne Township: Zoning for Whom? In Brief Reply." *Harvard Law Review* 67 (April 1954): 986–993.

―――. "Zoning for Minimum Standards: The Wayne Township Case." *Harvard Law Review* 66 (April 1953): 1051–1063.

Haar, Charles M., and Daniel W. Fessler. *The Wrong Side of the Tracks.* New York: Simon & Schuster, 1986.

Horwitz, Morton J. *The Transformation of American Law, 1780–1860.* Cambridge: Harvard University Press, 1977.

Hurst, James Willard. *Law and the Conditions of Freedom in the Nineteenth-Century United States.* Madison: University of Wisconsin Press, 1956.

Kent, James. *Commentaries on American Law.* 4 vols. 2d ed. New York: O. Halstead, 1832.

Lenhoff, Arthur. "Development of the Concept of Eminent Domain." *Columbia Law Review* 42 (April 1942): 596–638.

Lewis, Emily J. "Comment: Corporate Prerogative, 'Public Use' and a People's Plight: *Poletown Neighborhood Council* v. *City of Detroit.*" *Detroit College of Law Review* 4 (Winter 1982): 907–929.

Mansnerus, Laura. "Public Use, Private Use, and Judicial Review in Eminent Domain." *New York University Law Review* 58 (May 1983): 409–456.

Meidinger, Errol E. "The 'Public Uses' of Eminent Domain: History and Policy." *Environmental Law* 11 (1980): 1–66.

Michelman, Frank I. "Property, Utility, and Fairness: Comments on the Ethical Foundations of 'Just Compensation' Law." *Harvard Law Review* 80 (April 1967): 1165–1258.

Millspaugh, Peter E. "Eminent Domain: Is It Getting out of Hand?" *Real Estate Law Journal* 11 (1982): 99–115.

Rodgers, William H., Jr. "Bringing People Back: Toward a Comprehensive Theory of Taking in Natural Resources Law." *Ecology Law Quarterly* 10 (1982): 205–252.

Sager, Lawrence Gene. "Insular Majorities Unabated: *Warth* v. *Seldin* and *City of Eastlake* v. *Forest City Enterprises, Inc.*" *Harvard Law Review* 91 (May 1978): 1373–1425.

Sax, Joseph L. "Takings and the Police Power." *Yale Law Journal* 74 (November 1964): 36–76.

————. "Takings, Private Property and Public Rights." *Yale Law Journal* 81 (December 1971): 149–186.

Schreiber, Harry N. "Property Law, Expropriation and Resource Allocation by Government, 1789–1910." *Journal of Economic History* 33 (March 1973): 232–251.

Stoebuck, William B. "A General Theory of Eminent Domain." *Washington Law Review* 47 (August 1972): 553–608.

Tigar, Michael E., with Madeleine R. Levy. *Law and the Rise of Capitalism.* New York: Monthly Review Press, 1977.

Williams, Norman, Jr., ed. *American Land Planning Law: Cases and Materials.* 2 vols. New Brunswick, N.J.: Rutgers University, Center for Urban Policy Research, 1978.

Wright, Robert R. "Constitutional Rights and Land Use Planning: The New Era and the Old Reality." *Duke Law Journal*, no. 4 (October 1977): 841–867.

"Zoning for the Regional Welfare." *Yale Law Journal* 89 (March 1980): 748–768.

Cases

Agins v. *City of Tiburon*, 447 U.S. 255, 100 S. Ct. 2138 (1980).

Barbier v. *Connolly*, 113 U.S. 27 (1885).

Berman v. *Parker*, 348 U.S. 26 (1954).

City of Oakland v. *Oakland Raiders*, 31 Cal. 3d 656; 183 Cal. Rptr. 673, 646 P. 2d 835 (1982).

City of Eastlake v. *Forest City Enterprises, Inc.*, 426 U.S. 668 (1976).

Construction Industry Association of Sonoma County v. *Petaluma*, 375 F. Supp. 574 (1974), Revd., 522 F. 2d 897 (1975), cert. den. 96 S. Ct. 1148 (1976).

Euclid v. *Ambler Realty Co.*, 272 U.S. 365 (1926).

Golden v. *Ramapo*, 30 N.Y. 2d 359 (1972).

Hadacheck v. *Sebastian*, 239 U.S. 394 (1915).

In Re Seattle, 96 Wn. 2d 616 (1981).

James v. *Valtierra*, 402 U.S. 137 (1971).

Just v. *Marinette County*, 56 Wis. 2d 7, 201 N.W. 2d 761 (1972).

Lionshead Lake, Inc. v. *Township of Wayne*, 10 N.J. 165, 89 A. 2d 693 (1952).

Metropolitan Housing Development Corp. v. *Village of Arlington Heights*, 434 U.S. 1025 (1978).

Morris County Land Improvement Company v. *Parsippany Troy Hills*, 40 N.J. 539, 193 A. 2d 232 (1963).

Nectow v. *City of Cambridge*, 277 U.S. 183, 48 S. Ct. 447, 72 L. ED. 842 (1928).

Pennsylvania Coal Co. v. *Mahon*, 260 U.S. 393 (1922).

Poletown Neighborhood Council v. *City of Detroit*, 410 Mich. 616, 304 N.W. 2d 455 (1981).

Pumpelly v. *Green Bay Company*, 13 Wall. 166 (1871).

Reinman v. *Little Rock*, 237 U.S. 171 (1915).

San Diego Gas & Electric Co. v. *City of San Diego*, 450 U.S. 621, 101 S. Ct. 1287 (1981).

Shelley v. *Kraemer*, 334 U.S. 1 (1947).

Soon Hing v. *Crowley*, 113 U.S. 703 (1885).

Southern Burlington County N.A.A.C.P. v. *Township of Mount Laurel*, 67 N.J. 151, 336 A2d. 713 (1975); appeal dismissed and cert. denied, 423 U.S. 808 (1976).

St. Louis Poster Advertising Co. v. *City of St. Louis*, 249 U.S. 269 (1919).

Village of Belle Terre v. *Boraas*, 416 U.S. 1 (1974).

Warth v. *Seldin*, 422 U.S. 490 (1974).

Welch v. *Swazey*, 214 U.S. 91 (1909).

Government Reports, Hearings, Documents

City of San Antonio. City Planning Commission. "The San Antonio Master Plan." Economic Benefit Section of Chapter IV, San Antonio, Texas, 5 January 1979.

City of San Antonio. Office of the Planning Engineer. *San Antonio Bexar County Urban Transportation Study, 1964–1985. Report No. 2 (Part A)*, May 1966.

National Commission on Urban Problems. *Building the American City.* Washington, D.C.: U.S. Government Printing Office, 1968.

President's Commission for a National Agenda for the Eighties. *A National Agenda for the Eighties.* Introduction by John Herbers. New York: New American Library, 1981.

President's Task Force on Suburban Problems. *Final Report.* Edited by Charles Haar. Cambridge, Mass.: Ballinger, 1968.

Public Land Law Review Commission. *One Third of the Nation's Land.* Washington, D.C.: U.S. Government Printing Office, 1970.

Report of the National Commission on Civil Disorders. Introduction by Tom Wicker. New York: Bantam, 1968.

Report of the President's Commission on Housing. Washington, D.C.: U.S. Government Printing Office, 1982. Excerpts reprinted in *1983 Zoning and Planning Law*

Handbook, edited by Fredrick A. Stom, pp. 329–401. New York: Clark Boardman, 1983.

Research and Planning Consultants. *Texas Land Use, Report No. Two: Existing Mechanisms*. Austin: Division of Planning Coordination, Office of the Governor, 1973.

U.S. Advisory Commission on Intergovernmental Relations. *State and Local Roles in the Federal System*. Washington, D.C.: U.S. Government Printing Office, 1981.

——— *Urban and Rural America: Policies for Future Growth*. Washington, D.C.: U.S. Government Printing Office, 1968.

U.S. Congress. Congressional Budget Office. *An Analysis of the President's Budgetary Proposals for Fiscal Year 1984*. Washington, D.C.: U.S. Government Printing Office, 1983.

———. *Federal Subsidies for Public Housing: Issues and Options*. Washington, D.C.: U.S. Government Printing Office, 1983.

———. *The Housing Finance System and Federal Policy*. Washington, D.C.: U.S. Government Printing Office, 1983.

———. *Tax Expenditures: Current Issues and Five-Year Budget Projections for Fiscal Years 1984–1988*. Washington, D.C.: U.S. Government Printing Office, 1983.

U.S. Congress. House. Committee on Interior and Insular Affairs. *Establishment of Public Land Law Review Commission*. H. Rept. 1008. 88th Cong., 1st sess., 1964.

———. *National Land Use Planning. Hearings Before the Subcommittee on the Environment on H.R. 4332 and Related Bills*. 92d Cong., 1st sess., 1971.

———. *Public Land Policy Act of 1971. Hearings Before the Subcommittee on the Environment on H.R. 7211*. 92d Cong., 1st sess., 1971.

———. *Land Use Planning Act of 1973. Hearings Before the Subcommittee on the Environment on H.R. 4682 and Related Bills*. 93d Cong., 1st sess., 1973.

———. *Land Use Planning. Hearings Before the Subcommittee on the Environment on H.R. 10294*. 93d Cong., 2d sess., 1974.

———. *Land Use and Resource Conservation. Hearings Before the Subcommittee on Energy and the Environment on H.R. 3510 and Related Bills*. 94th Cong., 1st sess., 1975.

———. *Nuclear Waste Facility Siting. Hearings Before the Subcommittee on Energy and the Environment*. 96th Cong., 2d sess., pt. 5, 1979.

———. *Priority Energy Project Act. Hearings Before the Subcommittee on Energy and the Environment on H.R. 4573*. 96th Cong., 1st sess., 1979.

———. *Priority Energy Project Act of 1979*. H. Rept. 96–410 to Accompany H.R. 4985. 96th Cong., 1st sess., pt. 1, 1979.

———. *Facilitating the Transportation of Coal by Pipeline Across Federal and Non-Federal Lands*. H. Rept. 97–423 to Accompany H.R. 4230. 97th Cong., 2d sess., 1982.

U.S. Congress. House. Committee on Interstate and Foreign Commerce. *Priority Energy Project Act of 1979. Hearings Before the Subcommittee on Energy and Power on H.R. 4499, H.R. 4573, and H.R. 4862*. 96th Cong., 1st sess., 1979.

———. *Priority Energy Project Act of 1979*. H. Rept. 96–410 to Accompany H.R. 4985. 96th Cong., 1st sess., pt. 2, 1979.

U.S. Congress. House. Conference Report on S. 1308. H. Rept. No. 96–1119, *Priority Energy Project Act of 1980*. Title 11, Sec. 317. 96th Cong., 2d sess., 21 June 1980. *Congressional Record*, 126:H5492–5495.

U.S. Congress. House. "Report of the Council on Environmental Quality—Message from the President of the United States." 91st Cong., 2d sess., 10 August 1970. *Congressional Record,* 116:28040.

U.S. Congress. Senate. *Energy Development Project Delays: Six Case Studies. A Report Prepared by the Congressional Research Service of the Library of Congress for the Committee on Environment and Public Works.* 96th Cong., 1st sess., 1979.

U.S. Congress. Senate. Committee on Energy and Natural Resources. *Energy Supply Act (Title II). Synthetic Fuels Production Act (Title VI). Hearings Before the Committee on Energy and Natural Resources.* 96th Cong., 1st sess., on S. 1308 and S. 1377, 1979.

U.S. Congress. Senate. Committee on Interior and Insular Affairs. *National Land Use Policy. Hearings Before the Subcommittee on Environment and Land Resources on S. 3354.* 91st Cong., 2d sess., 1970.

————. *National Land Use Policy Act.* S. Rept. 1435 to Accompany S. 3354. 91st Cong., 2d sess., 1970.

————. *National Land Use Policy. Hearings Before the Subcommittee on Environment and Land Resources on S. 632 and S. 992.* 92d Cong., 1st sess., 1971.

————. *Papers on Land Use Policy.* 92d Cong., 1st sess., 1971.

————. *Land Use Policy and Planning Assistance Act of 1972.* S. Rept. 869 to Accompany S. 632. 92d Cong., 2d sess., 1972.

————. *National Land Use Policy: Background Papers on Past and Pending Legislation and the Roles of Executive Branch, Congress, and the States in Land Use Planning.* 92d Cong., 2d sess., 1972.

————. *National Land Use Policy Legislation, 93d Congress. An Analysis of Legislative Proposals and State Laws.* Prepared by James W. Curlin and Robert K. Lane, Environmental Policy Division, Congressional Research Service, Library of Congress. 93d Cong., 1st sess., 1973.

————. *Land Use Policy and Planning Assistance Act of 1973. Hearings Before the Subcommittee on Environment and Land Resources on S. 268.* 93d Cong., 1st sess., 1973.

————. *Land Use Policy and Planning Assistance Act.* S. Rept. 197 to Accompany S. 268. 93d Cong., 1st sess., 1973.

————. *State Land Use Programs; Summaries of Land Use Regulation in Eight States Prepared by the Environmental Quality Committee of the Young Lawyers Section, the American Bar Association, and a 50-State Survey of State Land Use Controls Prepared by "Land Use Planning Reports."* 93d Cong., 2d sess., 1974.

————. *Readings on Land Use Policy Prepared by the Environmental Policy Division, Congressional Research Service, Library of Congress.* 94th Cong., 1st sess., 1975.

————. *Land Resource Planning Assistance Act and the Energy Facilities Planning and Development Act. Hearings Before the Subcommittee on Environment and Land Resources on S. 984 and S. 619.* 94th Cong., 1st sess., 1975.

U.S. Congress. Senate. Committee on Public Works and Committee on Interior and Insular Affairs. *The Operation of the National Environmental Policy Act of 1969.* 92d Cong., 2d sess., 1973.

Index

345

Compositor: G & S Typesetters, Inc.
Printer: Braun-Brumfield, Inc.
Binder: Braun-Brumfield, Inc.
Text: 10/12 Times Roman
Display: Helvetica Bold